They took out coal, coke, cement and general cargo and returned with nitrate, a valuable fertiliser. France also had a large sailing fleet in this trade, but in the final years their ships were happy to load whatever was on offer.

The route taken by sailing ships from one port to another was dictated by the prevailing winds. When sailing from Europe towards Australia they always went around the world from west to east to take advantage of the strong westerly winds that encircle the Earth in the Southern Ocean. However, [...] West Coast ports of Chile a[...] rounding of Cape Horn had [...] west. When leaving Spencer Gulf it was customary to head well to the south to take advantage of 'Great Circle' navigation. Once past Cape Horn the sailer went over towards the east to pick up the South-East Trade Winds. After the doldrums she utilised the North-East Trades to get to the north, when the westerlies of the North Atlantic pushed her towards the English Channel.

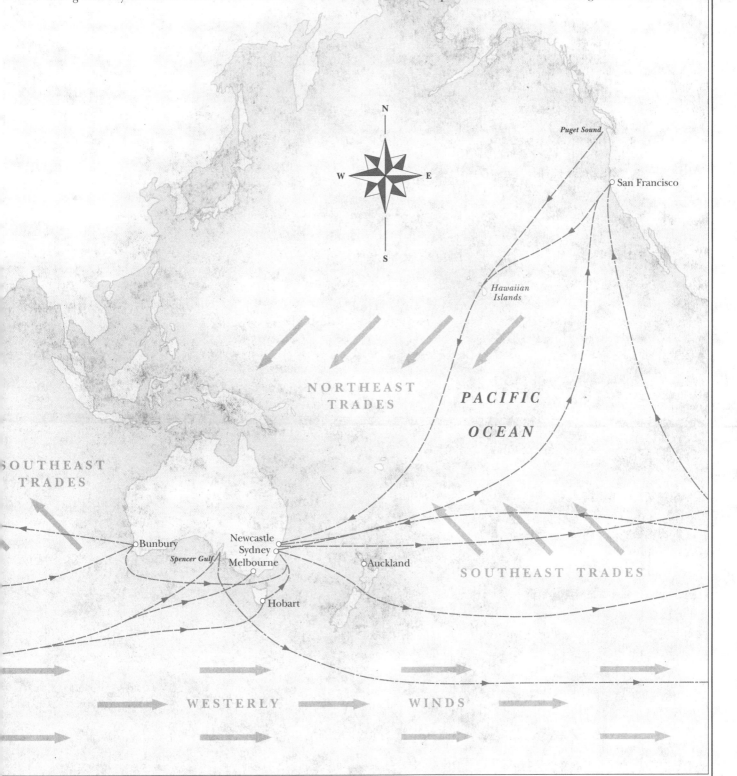

WINDJAMMERS
The Final Story

I am the albatross that awaits you
At the end of the world.
I am the forgotten soul of the dead seamen
Who sailed across Cape Horn
From all the seas of Earth.
But, they have not died
In the fury of the waves.
Today, they fly on my wings
Towards Eternity,
In the last crevice
Of the Antarctic winds.

Sara Vial
Chile, December 1992

This poem, in Spanish, is inscribed on a tablet near the monument which the International Association of Cape Horners (AICH), in collaboration with the Government of Chile, has erected on the peak of Cape Horn, in memory of the thousands of sailing ship mariners who in the pursuit of their calling have made this rounding and of those who lost their lives in the attempt. Admiral Benavente was responsible, through the Chilean AICH, for raising the funds. The Navy of Chile made the stainless steel plates and transported them to the island. Commander-in-Chief of the Navy, Admiral Jorge Martinez Busch, presided over the unveiling.

WINDJAMMERS

The Final Story

A collection of memoirs, poems and paintings depicting life in the last commercial sailing ships

Robert Carter

Caring
for Life

ROSENBERG

First published in Australia in 2004
by Rosenberg Publishing Pty Ltd
PO Box 6125, Dural Delivery Centre NSW 2158
Phone: 612 9654 1502 Fax: 612 9654 1338
Email: rosenbergpub@smartchat.net.au
Web: www.rosenbergpub.com.au

National Library of Australia Cataloguing-in-Publication data:

Carter, Robert, 1931 Aug. 27- .

Windjammers, the final story : a collection of paintings,
stories, poems describing the life in the last commercial
sailing ships, 1905-1957.

Bibliography.
Includes index.
ISBN 1 877058 04 1.

1. Windjammers (Sailing ships). 2. Sailing ships.
3. Seafaring life. I. Title.

387.220904

Cover design: Highway 51 Design Works
Illustrator: Robert Walsh
Endpaper maps: Lamond Art & Design

Set in 11 on 14 point New Baskerville
Printed in China through Colorcraft Ltd., Hong Kong

10 9 8 7 6 5 4 3 2 1

CONTENTS

Olivebank

LIST OF MAPS AND PLATES

Lawhill

Front Endpaper: The Routes of the Last Windjammers Around the World
Back Endpaper: *Left:* The Baltic and the Åland Islands
              Right: Spencer Gulf

Plates

(Plates I to XVI are between pages 32 and 33; Plates XVII to XXXII are between pages 128 and 129; Plates XXXIII to XLVIII are between pages 192 and 193.)

ACKNOWLEDGMENTS

Skansen

It is difficult to individually thank the many hundreds of 'Cape Horners' and other sailing ship mariners who have given me their stories without the possibility of omitting someone. My first thanks go to those whom I have identified in the text, whose stories were provided via the loan of diaries, handwritten letters, long-distance phone calls and lengthy interviews. There could be a hundred more who have sent letters, given me photographs, newspaper clippings or answered a specific question, whose names are not mentioned. Also there are those I have met at various Cape Horner gatherings whose names were never known or not remembered—like the roomful of German Cape Horners I met when I was invited to a *Stammtisch* at Blankenese on the Elbe, and others on similar occasions at the Nautical Club in Mariehamn, their anecdotes sometimes written down on table napkins.

With the passage of time, most who have told me of their experiences are no longer with us. And there are those who were not mariners who indirectly inspired me to keep working away at this book and the paintings it contains. Such a person was the late Solveig Erikson who, in 1979 at the International Association of Cape Horners (AICH) Congress in Adelaide, listened to my plans to write this book. She said, 'Yes, you must do it and show the world your beautiful paintings of our ships!' Twenty years later she graciously entertained me at her home in Norra Esplanade Gatan, Mariehamn, the ancestral home of her father-in-law, Gustaf Erikson. She said, 'You must get your book published soon as there are not many of us left.'

Then there is Captain Henrik Karlsson, director of the Åland Maritime Museum, who has been a great friend in the last home of the sailing ship. He has given much of his time in reading my manuscript and organising two exhibitions of my paintings in Mariehamn. And Anita Pensar, curator at the museum, who also read my manuscript and corrected not only inaccuracies but also spelling and grammatical errors, even though her native tongue is Swedish!

Right in the beginning there were Marie Ryan and Margaret and Mary Tancred, who managed to decipher my scribbled notes and typed and retyped the first manuscript without the benefit of a computer. There was no cut and paste in those days.

Most of those who have informed me have done so in English, even though they were from Scandinavia, France and Germany. There were, however, some letters and diaries in French which a long-time friend, Gay Fletcher, translated for me. While the term 'Cape Horner' specifically refers to a mariner in a commercial sailing ship who has rounded Cape Horn, there were many others who led a similar life under sail who never went anywhere near that Cape. Some of my informants were in this category; their experience of shipboard life was identical and their stories no less interesting.

I would like to thank Jason Hopton (*Passat*, 1948), past secretary of the Australian Cape Horners Association and editor of their journal, for the help he has given me over 25 years in confirming pieces of information and putting me in touch with many who have informed me.

The following have also contributed information, photographs and data or else headed me in the right direction: Warwick Andrews; Admiral Benevente, Navy of Chile; Neil Cormack, Editor *Cape Horners Journal*; Robert Hopping; Axel Stenross, Maritime Museum Port Lincoln; Alan Palmer, Mariehamn; Jenetta Russell; Sara Vial; Anne Spencer; Stan Squire, Port Victoria Maritime Museum; Audrey Walker, Treasurer Australian Cape Horners Association.

And finally I would like to thank Elizabeth, my wife, who has endured my preoccupation with sailing ships for over 50 years.

Robert Carter

To Elizabeth

FOREWORD

Abraham Rydberg

Many books have been written about the last windjammers and I hope that we can look forward to reading many more. Here we have a good one.

It is a unique book in the sense that Robert Carter has had the rare opportunity to acquire first-hand information about the last of the wind-driven ships from the final generation of sailing ship sailors. There are still a few of them left in the world but most of them have crossed the bar a long time ago. Eben Anderson was Robert Carter's mentor. Aptly chosen as a mentor, I think you will agree, when you read about his long career in sailing vessels. His friendship with Captain Anderson led on to other contacts in the world of square rig and to worldwide connections through the Finnish grain ships.

As a youth, Robert Carter even corresponded with the famous sailing ship owner, Gustaf Erikson of Mariehamn in the northern Baltic Sea. As an associate member and past office bearer of the Australian section of the International Association of Cape Horners, many of his friends there have told him stories of their voyages under sail. Through his research and a great interest in the last sailing ships and the people who manned them, there are few persons in the world with a greater knowledge of this particular issue. The book is an interesting blend of interviews, diary extracts and stories, all illustrated with Robert Carter's beautiful and detailed paintings. These paintings are not just illustrations of ships: each, with its own description, reveals yet another story or happening from the days of sail. We are also given a good insight into the various reasons why commercial sail lost the battle against powered vessels, how it was able to exist until halfway through the twentieth century and also some very colourful accounts of the harsh life in the last of the windjammers.

The beauty of sail *and* the romance are also there. Maybe we even get the answer as to why some men chose to sail in these ships instead of in more comfortable and better-paid jobs in steamers.

This book I can recommend to anybody who is interested in the last days of the windjammers. It is also an important historic account of a time that seems very distant, until you discover that some of it actually happened after World War II. As an Ålander I am amazed by the knowledge that Robert Carter has of ships and people from a place a world apart.

In *Windjammers: The Final Story*, he also draws a picture of how the sea is a bridge connecting people and countries. In this role the great windjammer was a wonderful participant!

Henrik Karlsson
Director, Åland Maritime Museum
Mariehamn, Finland

INTRODUCTION

Falmouth Pilot

This book is intended to reveal to the generation now living at the dawn of the twenty-first century the events, happenings and real life stories from the final 50 years in the life of the last commercial sailing ships. This era ended in 1959.

In the last decade there has been a proliferation of restorations and the building of new traditional sailing vessels for the purposes of sail training and adventure-type excursions in so-called 'tall ships'. Every major maritime nation now possesses at least one sail-training ship along with a plethora of other vessels engaged in charter work, together with stationary museum ships.

My study, worldwide, of sail-driven ships reveals there are now thousands of people, of many nationalities, who have experienced a voyage under contemporary square rig, while those who have gone to sea in smaller traditional fore and aft rigged vessels are too numerous to evaluate.

Recently I made a voyage in the Russian full-rigged training ship *Nadezhda* out of Vladivostok. Along with me were 24 other passengers, male and female, generally under the age of 30, who felt a passion for sailing ships. Thrown together in this environment we spent many hours talking about ships and the sea. We discussed why we each should take such a trip and want to join with the crew in the working of the ship, in spite of the many inconveniences and some element of danger when working aloft. We came to the conclusion that the ship driven by sails has some mystical, indescribable spell over certain individuals and that this influence, which attracted boys (in past days) to sea, when the trade routes of the world were opening up, was still at work. All of my shipmates from that voyage were highly enthusiastic but lamentably there was a lack of any real knowledge of the age of commercial sail, how life in those ships compared with what they were seeking to emulate and how there were men and women still living who experienced life in the last cargo-carrying sailing ships. While this book had been in the making for many years, I determined that it must be completed to tell the untold stories from times long gone to all those who would now voyage under sail.

The fact that this book has emerged 50 years after the last commercial voyages by sailing ships is a result of my research into the commercial sailing ship during this time, coupled with a love of marine art and painting. The magnificence of Sydney Harbour, and the sound of the Tasman Sea, which have been within sight and hearing for all the years I have lived, also had something to do with it. These influences under which I came at an early age have had a great effect on this book and on the paintings it contains. Not only did my meeting up with several of the last commercial sailing ships in commission fire my imagination and interest, but my frequenting of the waterfront of this great port and sailing on its waters steeped me in maritime lore that had to be expressed in some way.

My later involvement with the Cape Horners Association of Australia put me in touch with the diverse group of seafarers from around the world who made up its membership, and who shared the brotherhood of having rounded Cape Horn in a commercial sailing ship. This latter experience has allowed me to enter into the realm of the Cape Horn sailor through the use of the spoken word and the 'spinning of yarns', giving me an understanding which would never have been possible through reading alone. This has heightened my perception of the era to a point where I almost feel that I was a participant.

Sydney Harbour, or Port Jackson as it is correctly named, was a magical place in which a boy of my interests could grow up. There was always something going on around the foreshores or out in the stream, particularly at the end of World War II. A constant procession of ships arrived from every maritime nation in the world so that, together with the harbour-bound craft that were necessary to maintain its function, there was always something to see. Shipping losses from enemy action meant that ships of all types and vintages were in use; significantly for me, these still included a handful of sailing ships. The four-masted barques *Lawhill* and *Pamir*, the five-masted schooner *City of Alberni*, the barque *Kaiulani*, all made visits during this time, along with the intercolonial schooner *Huia*, a regular trader to Sydney. Living in the harbourside suburb of Manly gave me many opportunities to study shipping. I grew up with two other boys, Warwick Andrews and Geoff McKeown, who shared this love of ships and the sea. Inseparable then, we have been lifelong mates. Our youth was spent surfing, sailing and messing around in boats. We took a great interest in everything that went on around the foreshores of the harbour and the craft that used it, and could identify just about every ship that visited Sydney more than once.

It was a simple matter to board a ferry at Manly and travel to Circular Quay. If one did not disembark, it was possible to make the return journey without paying the fare. This provided 14 miles' worth of viewing of the ships at anchor and those leaving and entering port. If I had the fare I would go ashore and start a trek around the wharves to Darling Harbour and Cockle Bay, where the apple and potato steamers unloaded their cargoes from Tasmania. Along the way were dozens of finger wharves, now demolished, and on shore the hubbub of activity generated by the movement of the great mass of cargo heading to and arriving from the world's markets.

This was the mercantile heart of Sydney. Nearby, the city's fruit and vegetable markets disposed of the endless crates of produce brought by the coastal fleet, together with that which arrived at the rail terminal at the end of the bay. This rail terminal also brought thousands of bales of wool from all over New South Wales to temporary residence in the huge wool stores at nearby Pyrmont and Circular Quay. They bore the time-honoured names of the pastoral merchants: Australian Mercantile Land & Finance, Farmers and Graziers, Pitt Son and Badgery, Goldsborough Mort and Dalgety, to name but a few. After the wool sales, which were a ritual in themselves, the wool was moved to the wharves where the bales were compressed further and loaded into the ships that took it to the United Kingdom, Japan, the United States and Europe. Walking along the streets outside these wool stores gave one the reward of sniffing the wholesome aroma of greasy wool, which mingled further on with the nutty odours of bagged grain at the wheat wharves.

The ships of those postwar years were colourful, and characteristic of the trade in which they were engaged. At east Circular Quay the China Navigation Co. steamers *Taiping* and *Changte* tied up, easily recognisable by their counter sterns and the iron bars separating the well decks from the bridge and passenger accommodation amidships, protection from China Sea pirates. My old friend Captain Eric Beeham, later a Sydney harbour pilot, who served in these ships, had many stories from them.

Over at west Circular Quay the handsome postwar freighters of the Swedish Australian Line berthed. They were painted pale grey with green boot topping, and bore the Aboriginal names of several Australian country towns, such as *Wangaratta* and *Coolangatta*. If they were not in port, their place would be taken by ships of the Wilhelm Wilhelmsen line of Norway. In Campbells Cove I always looked for Messageries Maritimes' white-painted island trader, *Polynesian*, from Noumea. And then at Walsh Bay there were always the Burns Philp ships that serviced their Pacific interests, recognisable anywhere by the black and white chequered band on their funnels. Around into Darling Harbour and Pyrmont my steps would take me, past trucks, hand-pushed barrows and even horse-drawn wagons, all lined up waiting their turn to deliver or load a variety of boxes, crates, bags and bales. There were no such things as containers in those days.

It was here that representatives of the world's, but mainly Britain's, mercantile fleets could be seen. Important looking Port Line, British India and Clan Line cargo liners competed with Blue Star, Ellerman and Blue Funnel ships for sheer good looks and clean lines. Across the bay at Pyrmont there were the big white passenger ships of the P&O line and the buff-painted Orient liners, and at Woolloomooloo, Matson liners from the west coast of the United States. As world shipping reconstructed itself after the war there was an abundance of the once grey-painted liberty and victory ships, now in peacetime colours.

Amongst all this was the coastal fleet, whose ships were so familiar as to almost go unnoticed. This was particularly so of the colliers that brought coal from Newcastle to the Australian Gas Light Co.'s works at Mortlake up the Parramatta River. Even the residential suburb of Manly, where I lived, had its own gasworks on the foreshore, to which the little collier *Caldare* brought coal once a week.

Much larger were the ships of the Adelaide Steamship Co., Huddart Parker, Howard Smith, McIlraith & McEacharn, Australian United Steam Navigation Co. and James Patrick, and the ubiquitous Union Steamship Company of New Zealand, whose ships handled the trade between Australia and New Zealand and beyond. The Colonial Sugar Refinery had several ships, including *Fiona* and *Rona*, which supplied their Pyrmont refinery with raw sugar and molasses from their Queensland and Fiji mills.

The streets around the wharves were no less interesting. For one thing they were mostly constructed from hardwood blocks, which gave them a quaint cobbled appearance, although much smoother than stones. This tended to muffle the clip-clop of the horse-drawn wagons, with their steel-tyred, spoked wheels, that were still in use because of wartime petrol rationing. From the western side of the Harbour Bridge, Hickson Road, Sussex Street and Day Street traversed a labyrinth of smaller lanes and driveways, with other streets now obliterated by the western freeway and Darling Harbour re-development. There were shipping agents, merchants, wool brokers, banks, ship chandlers, ship providores, plumbers, foundries, marine surveyors and engineers. On every corner there seemed to be a pub, with names like Wool Brokers Arms, Mercantile, Glasgow Arms, Hunter River, First and Last, which seemed crowded at all times even though they closed each day at 6 pm. As I walked past these pubs, often termed blood-houses, I would peep inside, attracted by the noise, not realising that much of the shipping business of the port was conducted in places such as these. Outside in the street, where horse manure was still to be seen and smelt, the rattle of the ships' steam winches as slings of cargo were raised or lowered was almost continuous, and I was fascinated by the different types of people to be seen. Women were rarely seen in these areas, apart from the odd barmaid from one of the pubs.

The men were easy to place into a category. Stevedores, or wharfies as they are called on the Australian waterfront, were in abundance. Those not working on a wharf would sit around outside in the hope that a job would become available. They all looked the same, and wore the same dark grey working trousers and sweat-stained felt hat, and smoked hand-rolled cigarettes. Some even wore a waistcoat from some long-discarded Sunday suit. Ships' crews wore blue dungarees, and looked different from their labouring counterparts ashore. Lascar (east Indian) seamen wore a short blue tunic and when in pairs walked hand in hand.

The pleasure I derived from this maritime pageant was initiated in 1942, when the American barque *Kaiulani* dropped anchor almost at the foot of the street where I lived. This was the first sailing ship I had ever seen. Although I did not know it, I was about to become a witness to and observer of what would be the last years of commercial sail. How this sailing ship came to Sydney is described in detail in Chapter 6, but it was the end of a voyage that commenced on the US west coast in September 1941. It was a most unlikely encounter, almost halfway through the twentieth century. Sydney had been experiencing one of the usual southerly storms when *Kaiulani* arrived at the harbour entrance. She was under tow and, because of the anti-submarine boom nets closing off the main stream, anchored in North Harbour. I have no doubt that most of the thousands of residents who lived nearby gave this ship no more than a curious glance, and even those who walked down to view her more closely in a very short time had forgotten she existed.

For me it was quite different. I was completely fascinated by this apparition almost from another age. Before she was moved farther up the harbour, I would go to the end of my street at every available opportunity and gaze at her, wanting her to stay there forever. The day before she was moved I rowed out to her anchorage and looked up at her rusty sides and tall masts. Several of the crew called out in the accents of those American servicemen who were soon to invade wartime Sydney. She was an enchanting addition to the playground that North Harbour was to me. In no way was she another *Cutty Sark*, resplendent in black hull paint, gingerbread scrollwork and fine clipper lines, or another mighty white-painted *Herzogin Cecilie*, capturing the imagination of youth along the docks of the Thames or Elbe. She was scarred, rusty and had electric welding in areas where the steel rivets placed by her builders, Arthur Sewell & Co., in 1899, were growing tired. But she showed her kind to me, and in so doing laid down the keel blocks for this book.

My meeting up with one of the last sailing ships in commission prompted me to find out as much as I could about this type of vessel. When *Kaiulani* went, I longed for another sailing ship to appear, although I had no way of knowing how few were still sailing the seas, or where they were. Incredibly, another did appear, two years later. In the meantime I searched the local library and second-hand bookshops for anything about sailing ships. I found myself drawing what must have been ungainly sailing ships in unlikely situations. It appears I had some skill with a paintbrush at that stage, for I entered and won a competition for a war loan poster. I remember the prize was five pounds and was presented by a soldier, a young lieutenant, who had recently been awarded the Victoria Cross. His name was Cutler and he later became Governor of New South Wales.

In wartime Sydney, drawing materials were hard to come by, and I used the backs of old blueprints that my father had discarded. He had been a naval architect in England's Devonport dockyard before coming to Australia and I unwittingly learned much about ship construction from these drawings. Steamer hulls were not dissimilar from the latter-day steel sailing ships, especially in the method of plating, the construction of deck fittings, and the use of traditional shipbuilding crafts. The graceful counter stern was common to both steam and sailing ships for many years.

My dreams of meeting up with another sailing ship materialised in 1944, and again just over a year later, when the four-masted barque *Lawhill* made two visits to Sydney. I could not wait to pay her a visit, as I knew my readings had given me only a superficial knowledge of sailing ships, and I was intent on learning as much as I could while there was still the chance. I can vividly recall my impressions as I stood on the wharf, looking at one of the last big commercial sailing ships left in commission. So different was she from *Kaiulani*, so much bigger it was difficult to take in everything at once. Berthed at No.1 Walsh Bay, right beside the Harbour Bridge, she looked more than out of place amongst the other ships in port. Quite apart from the four raked masts towering above the wharf sheds was the fact that she was still painted in her pre-war colours of black hull, white trim and boot topping. All other ships in port were painted wartime grey. I suppose there was little point in trying to subdue her hull colours when a cloud of canvas would reveal her presence even over the horizon.

I walked along the wharf and looked up at her bowsprit, the tip of which hovered 10 metres (35 feet) above the water, and at her figurehead of the usual female form, gazing silently ahead. Further along the wharf I walked, to the massive anchors, still hanging at the hawse after being broken out of the bed of the harbour a few days earlier. The huge links in her anchor cable were as long as my forearm and just as thick. I stood under the foreyard reaching 15 metres (50 feet) out over the wharf, and craned my neck to look up to the tops of the masts, more than 50 metres (165 feet) above me. All those ropes, wires and chains!

I had been looking up for some time, my eyes sweeping the network of her rigging, when I noticed several seamen working high on one of the masts. I felt the urge to climb up too! Further towards the stern I walked, and came to where her cargo of cocoa beans was being unloaded from an after hatch. A hundred metres (330 feet) from where I had stood looking at the figurehead, I now stood looking at the poop, with its varnished charthouse and white whaleback wheelhouse. A boy not much older than I was scraping the teak railing around the poop, obviously quite at home. I envied this boy who could sail the southern oceans in a ship such as this instead of studying for a school certificate. I wondered where he came from, and how he came to be in the crew. Thirty years later I was to meet up with many of the crew from those wartime voyages, and I have often wondered if he was one of them. Another thing I noticed was the smell. No hot, oily steamship smells here. Instead, a delightful mixture of Stockholm tar, food, paint, rope and canvas, against a backdrop of traces of cargoes of pungent guano, aromatic Baltic timber and sweet Australian grain. I walked up the gangway.

Skirting her after hold, I climbed a ladder to a raised deck amidships that I learned later was called the Liverpool house. Set into the deck were box-like ventilators with hinged lids which also acted as skylights. Looking down it was possible to see into the crews' quarters and the galley. A black funnel from the galley stove was smoking away. It was here that the mainmast thrust itself skywards, with strong steel stays leading down to outside the steel bulwarks. I became aware of another sensation. Unlike the steamers I was used to, this ship seemed alive. It must have been the effect of the wind on her masts and yards. Further adding to the illusion were the subtle noises from aloft—the creaking of wooden blocks and the constant sighing of the wind in the rigging.

I walked further to where the for'ard well deck ended at the foremast and the break of the fo'c'sle. This raised deck housed the crews' lavatories as well as a cage containing two pigs. The smells from both overcame all the romantic aromas from the rest of the ship. Up on the fo'c'sle head I looked back to where I had just been, aware that the sail-driven ship was tightening its hold over me. It was only natural that I should consider trying to sign on, but she had a full crew and my father bluntly said no! From North Head I watched her depart from Sydney under sail and was rewarded by the sight of the British battleship *King George V* entering the harbour at the same time, although my eyes remained firmly focused on *Lawhill* until I could see her no more.

In those days, commercial shipping was an important part of everyday life in a seaport like Sydney. The war now over, the arrival and departure of shipping was reported in the daily press. I used to scan these columns in the hope that another sailing ship would come to Sydney. I knew that there was one operating in New Zealand. Then one day there was a small announcement that the four-masted barque *Pamir* was loading a cargo of timber for Sydney. I could not believe my luck. When she was due, I sat on the cliffs on the northern headland of the harbour with my two mates, Warwick and Geoff, searching the horizon for her white sails, but nothing appeared. We knew little about engineless ships then, and didn't realise that they never arrived when expected. It was another week before *Pamir* anchored, in spectacular circumstances, in Watson's Bay. I remember catching a ferry which passed close to her anchorage. She was riding fairly high out of the water due to her light cargo, and a light rain glistened on her steel hull, masts and yards.

She was moved to Circular Quay later that day, and for the next three months I tried to visit her every day. My aim was to sign on, but if that were not possible I intended to learn everything I could about the square-rigged sailing ship, first hand. Captain Collier, her master, was a very patient man, and he put up with my constant presence. He even said that he would sign me on if a vacancy occurred. I watched the crew unbending sail, or shaking out furled sails that had become wet with rain, and tending this great ship that needed constant attention. I watched while they painted, seized, spliced, oiled, tarred and polished, offering to help and probably getting in the way.

With Harold Underhill's book *Masting and Rigging* in one hand, and a sketchpad in the other, I traced out line after line, squinting into the sky and tripping over ringbolts in the deck. I ventured into the rigging, gingerly at first, not out of fear, but not wanting a shout from below to end the glorious adventure I was having aloft. On reaching the deck after an unsuccessful attempt to get over the main crosstrees, third mate Alan Jenkins said, 'Aren't you game to go all the way up?' I knew then that I had his approval. With my Brownie box camera dangling from my neck, I climbed about the rigging looking for hand and foot holds that would enable me to sketch the details that were obscured from deck. By the time *Pamir* was ready to leave, I could name every stay, line and fitting, and describe its function or use.

No vacancy occurred in the crew, and I watched her make ready for sea with a heavy heart. I sat on the wharf and wondered if I could stow away without being seen, but there were too many officials hovering around. She slipped out into the stream under tow and started setting sail to help the tug along. I caught a Manly ferry which trailed her out to the heads, by which time she had almost all sail set. In contrast to her stormy arrival, it was a sunny autumn afternoon that *Pamir* moved out to sea, before a light south-westerly breeze, closing for all time the era of commercial sail for Port Jackson and the Tasman Sea.

I was now at an age that I had to start thinking of a career, and all I could think about was going to sea, even in a steamship. In 1949 *Pamir* and the similar *Passat* loaded grain at Port Victoria, South Australia, for what were to be the last deepwater voyages by commercial sailing ships. Along with many other boys and a few girls I tried to get a place in one of the crews, without success. They sailed off to Falmouth around Cape Horn and into mercantile history. The sailing ship, as a commercial entity, was no more. I was accepted for a cadetship with the Australian National Line, but with the passing of sail I found the sea as a career less impelling. Even though I enjoyed it, three years in the Naval Reserve convinced me of that. At the prompting of my father I embarked on an engineering career, thinking that maybe marine engineering would keep me involved with ships. As the years rolled by, however, marriage and a family directed my course firmly away from the sea.

I continued my study of sailing ships and painting them, however, and enrolled at the Royal Art Society, as I was aware that I needed some guidance. Having endured several years of drawing nude bodies, fruit and plaster statues, I ventured to tell my art master that I really wanted to paint sailing ships. He laughed and said it was impossible as they no longer existed; there was only one way to paint, and that was from life. This deflated me somewhat, but I quietly disagreed with him. I really felt that this was all I wanted to paint, and I struck a compromise. I wandered the waterfront as I had as a boy, and looked at the ships, now piled high with containers. I studied and painted the light on their hulls, the formation of the rust and the curves of their waterlines. As I sketched and painted, I imagined them as sailing ships, their derricks becoming masts and yards.

I travelled overseas frequently, and at every opportunity I visited maritime museums. Their ships became targets for my sketchbook, so I felt that I was complying to some extent with my art master's directions—except that as I sketched their silent forms tethered to a quayside, I relied on my imagination and what I observed out at sea to provide the background of wind and wave.

I devoured everything that I could on sailing ships. My library of books on sail grew. One day I added to it *Mate in Sail*, written by Captain Jim Gaby. He described his life at sea in sailing ships in much the same way that many of the authors of my other books described theirs. This book differed, however, in that it had a largely Australasian theme and was illustrated by Dennis Adams, an Australian marine artist whose work I admired. Captain Gaby, it turned out, lived not far from me and I made his acquaintance. We were soon to become firm friends. I was thirsty for first-hand information on sailing ships and he welcomed the opportunity to discuss a subject he loved. Jim was at the time patron of the Australian Cape Horners Association. To qualify for membership one had to have rounded Cape Horn in a commercial sailing ship. Jim had a close friend, Captain Eben Anderson, a master mariner who had rounded Cape Horn four times in the second decade of the twentieth century. They both took a close interest in my paintings, and were an invaluable source of information, advice and criticism. It was Jim who gave me a copy of the poem 'Pictures', by C. Fox Smith, saying that if I took notice of 'Bill's' pronouncements I couldn't go far wrong.

Jim and Eb had a bond other than that of the sea. Jim was a writer and Eb was a poet. We would often meet and they each would read his latest poem or story and suggest to the other subtle changes to metre or wording. Then would come the scrutiny of my latest painting and I would go away a little depressed, but wiser in the way of a ship. They could never fault the accuracy of the ship or the rigging, but there were always comments like, 'I don't think I would be carrying royals with those clouds building up' or 'Your mizzen yards are not braced around enough'. I learned at an early stage to always overhaul the buntlines on my ships, as this omission was what riled them about most of the marine paintings they saw.

Through these two grand old sailor men, I was introduced to dozens, then hundreds, of other sailing ship mariners who were members of the Cape Horners Association. They all had stories to tell; as many different nationalities were involved, I wrote to those I could not visit. I now found that I could not paint a picture unless it portrayed a ship, situation or incident that had been described to me. In fact, I had collected so much data it was often difficult to decide how to best use it.

It was Captain Anderson who first suggested that I write a book containing the memoirs of those who had contributed to my research, or a book featuring a collection of my paintings. He said, 'I have been looking at your paintings for about ten years now, and I wish I could see them all together. You should put them into a book and you should write about them, for you know more about sailing ships than anyone I know.'

Captain Anderson died at the age of 96. I have tried to create the type of book he visualised.

1 THE LAST DAYS OF SAIL

Favell

The sailing ship has been described by many as man's most beautiful creation, and those who have been privileged to see a large square rigger under sail would certainly agree. The beauty of the sailing ship has inspired men and women for centuries—so too has it inspired this book and the paintings it contains. It is not so much a book about ships as about the people who sailed in them and the effects their experiences had on their lives; people who, 50 years later and more, wanted to relive and recount those experiences.

The great wealth of information I collected necessitated its categorisation in some way. I have chosen to arrange the stories by country of ship ownership rather than chronologically, although there is a chronological element beginning early in the twentieth century.

I have avoided statistics about the ships, their tonnages, dimensions, lengths of voyages and so on, except where it is relevant to a particular story or theme. All this information is available many times over in other books. Nor is it my intention to delve deeply into the development of the sailing ship, as this has been done by others, although all seem to ignore the period covered by this book.

Rather, my aim is to paint a picture in words as well as on canvas of the last years of the commercial sailing ship, as experienced and witnessed by a generation still living, at least while this book was being researched. Perhaps there are some dates that do not tally with published records, but I have chosen to use the dates that appeared in my informants' chronicles, for I believe them to be source documents, and my paintings are intended to be illustrations of 'happenings' rather than portraits of particular ships.

While the main content of this book is derived from American, British, Finnish, French, German, New Zealand, Swedish and Australian sources, this does not mean there was not a level of maritime activity in many other nations, rather that the aforementioned countries had high levels of sailing ship ownership in the period covered compared with others.

Most of the content has been recorded from personal interviews and contact with the last living men and women who experienced life first-hand in the last commercial sailing ships, as opposed to the pure sail-training ships of the day. Wherever possible I have kept much of the text in the first person, just as it was told to me, and in the storytellers'own words. This means that in some cases I have allowed grammatical errors and imperfect sentence construction from diaries to prevail.

I have selected a broad range of experiences from a variety of sources over a wide span of years. Those who have contributed range from masters to seamen, passengers and apprentices. There are women as well as men, from the Åland Islands, Denmark, Finland, France, Germany, New Zealand, Norway, South Africa, Sweden, the United Kingdom, the United States and Australia. So much was offered, and not everything could be used. Many experiences were almost identical. A number of informants feature prominently, others only briefly, but each was important in revealing the true mosaic of sailing ship life. Some diaries covered an entire voyage without much attention to detail. I have included a few of these to give a broad picture of a 'round the world' windjammer voyage. Of no less importance are those from which I have extracted detailed items that illustrate the life, culture and happenings.

The earliest story came from Perce Golding, who sailed in the four-masted barque *Port Jackson* in 1906, the most recent from those who sailed in the four-masted barques *Passat* and *Pamir* in 1949. A story from Carl-Otto Dummer, a survivor of the *Pamir* tragedy in 1957, has also been included, even though she had been fitted out with an auxiliary engine at that stage. My oldest informant was Captain Eben Anderson, who died at the age of 96 in 1992. The youngest is Brian 'Pinocchio' Peters, who as a youth twice rounded Cape Horn under sail in *Passat*, in the 1948 and 1949 voyages.

Inevitably many of my informants will not see their words in print, but all endorsed my endeavours to record what they saw and felt. This book will probably be the last factual record of the last years of commercial sail to be written.

Chapter 2 is a composite derived from the hundreds of stories that resulted from a brief interview, perhaps by phone, or else as a half-page reply to one of my letters. I have tried to illustrate the common activities that all experienced and most took for granted.

Most people, at least those born since World War II, are quite surprised when they hear me speak of the number of sailing ship mariners with whom I have become acquainted. They have no perception of the transition from sail to powered vessels, of the fact that sailing ships were used in various trades well into the twentieth century even while being replaced by steam, that many sailing ships were built in the 1890s and on into the twentieth century. The year the *Titanic* was launched, 1911, also saw the four-masted barque *Passat* slide down the ways of Blohm & Voss in Hamburg. Five similar steel four-masted barques were built in Germany thereafter, the last in 1926. The construction of these last sailing ships might have seemed an anachronism, but there were still about 20 involved in useful work at the outbreak of World War II. Most were large steel ships capable of lifting 3000 tons of cargo or more.

That commercial sailing ships were still sailing in the fifth decade of the twentieth century is the result of a variety of factors. The ships portrayed in this book were all built during the period when the large square-rigged sailing ship was reaching the peak of its development—the last decade of the nineteenth century and the first decade of the twentieth century. This was not a stubborn stand by those who refused to believe that the steamship was here to stay. Steam replaced sail only slowly; it took over 80 years for the transition to take place and even then, economic, geographic and political factors prolonged the lives of many working sailers beyond World War I.

In North America and in particular the United States, in both east and west coast shipyards, sailing ships in the form of large wooden schooners and barquentines with four, five and six masts were being built in relatively large numbers up to 1920. These are covered more fully in Chapter 6, on North American sail.

Those who ran sailing ships did so because there were many niches in world trade not being serviced by steamships, for various reasons. In the second half of the nineteenth century, for example, most of the production from the Pennsylvania oil fields was transported by sailing ships, both in bulk and as case oil. One reason was the natural reluctance to carry this flammable material in steam-driven vessels. The Anglo American Oil Company built eight large sailing ship tankers after 1900, two of them, the four-masted barques *Brilliant* and *Daylight*, being over 3700 tons. A story from the latter appears in Chapter 6.

Speed was not as much a factor at that point as predictable passage times; the quest for speed which produced the clipper ships of the mid nineteenth century was replaced by the less spectacular demand of reducing overheads and delivering as much cargo as possible. Steamships, when run at economical speeds, were slower than sailing ships with a good fair wind, but travelled in straight lines and at a constant speed. However, they had expensive engines, used expensive fuel, required specialist, higher paid crews, and could only travel to places where fuel was available for the return voyage. In addition, one-third of their hull space was taken up by the engines, boilers and fuel bunkers. Sailing ships had hulls open from one end to the other and thus could carry a larger amount of cargo. While sails and rigging were expensive, running costs were lower than for steamships of the period. So the stage was set for the final development of the wind ship.

This development was logical and undramatic. The sailing ship was at her best on long distance hauls, as her fuel, the wind, was free—and while the wind might be absent on many occasions it allowed her to trade almost anywhere. The aim became to have larger, fuller hulls and smaller crews. Most of the clippers that were built in the mid nineteenth century were less than 1000 tons; they were first constructed from wood and later were of composite construction (wood on iron frames). Britain's well-established iron and steel industry resulted in all large sailing ships built there after about 1860 being constructed from iron and, later in the century, from steel. While steel lacked the corrosion resistance of iron, it was stronger and allowed hulls to be built larger; this benefited the steamship but also allowed the size of sailing ships to be increased.

The favoured rig up to this time was the ship, technically a three-masted vessel, square-rigged on each mast. It was necessary to add another mast to drive the longer hull through the water; this also required more crew. It was found that reducing the fourth mast to fore and aft rig had no appreciable effect on speed, and so the four-masted barque became the rig that most of the last steel sailing ships adopted. It was ideal for long distance hauls, and the increased water-line length allowed a good turn of speed. Steel was used for the lower masts and yards and all standing rigging.

In all, 447 four-masted, square-rigged steel vessels were built in Britain, Germany and France, the last in 1926. Of these, 130 were four-masted ships but only 11 of this rig were built after 1890. Six five-masted steel barques were also built, and one five-masted, full-rigged steel ship. This was the mighty *Preussen*, built in 1902. She had a net tonnage of 4765 and was 124 metres (407 feet) long. Of less capital cost, and smaller, was the barque (three-masted); these were built by the thousands, although few were constructed after the turn of the century, at least from steel.

While Britain built most of the world's shipping during this period, France and Germany brought the large steel sailing ship to the peak of its development. The French believed, as did the Germans and Scandinavians, that the sailing ship was an essential factor in the training of seamen. The French government paid subsidies to shipowners for new sailing ships to be built, and an operational subsidy for each mile voyaged. Under this system the French built, or had built, 300 large steel three- and four-masted sailing ships after 1880, and the two five-masted barques *France I* and *France II*. The latter, built in 1911, was short of *Preussen* in net tonnage but longer by 3 metres (10 feet). These French ships were known as the Bounty Ships; the removal of some of the uncertainty from sailing ship operation allowed the use of the latest innovations, and the provision of quality gear and accommodation. The Germans had no subsidies but used the sailing ship as a foundation for building up their mercantile and naval fleets by requiring all officers to have four years' experience under sail before being eligible to sit for their master's certificate. Their crew numbers, including cadets, consequently were up to three times that in equivalent British ships. It is extraordinary that Britain had no such requirement, despite having the world's largest merchant sailing ship fleet. Nevertheless, while young aspiring mercantile officers could go straight into steam, many sought out sailing ship apprenticeships well into the twentieth century.

The last British sailing ship owners were John Stewart, Sir William Garthwaite, Thomas Law and J. Hardie, whose names are repeated many times over in this book. The last large commercial sailing ship registered in Great Britain was the full-rigged ship *William Mitchell*, which was broken up in 1928.

World War I, which saw enemy action eliminate hundreds of ships, gave sail a reprieve due to the need to transport large amounts of materials by any means possible, and many laid-up sailing ships were put back into service. Eventually, however, a worldwide recession in the early 1920s caused a shipping slump that laid up most of the survivors. By 1929 there were no large sailing ships under the

Red Ensign, and it was finally conceded that British sail was finished. In other European countries the odd owner or consortium was endeavouring to run a sailing ship or two, with the unique exception of Gustaf Erikson of Mariehamn, Finland.

Erikson, a sailing ship master and then ship owner, had a firm commitment to sailing ships, believing in his own ability to run them profitably and in their worth in training seamen. Fortunately for him, most maritime nations of Europe shared his belief in the latter and this provided him with a plentiful source of cheap labour to crew his ships. As the bottom fell out of the shipping market in the early 1920s he bought up sailing ships almost at scrap prices as others were discarding them, and thus acquired many fine vessels. Many in the Hardy and Laeisz fleets ended up under his flag. With little capital he built up a fleet which from 1913 numbered 46 ships, 34 of them over 1000 tons. Erikson still had 11 large steel sailing ships operational at the outbreak of World War II. After the war, though by then an old man, he was very much involved in getting his remaining ships fitted out again. Three of them, *Passat, Pamir* and *Viking*, made voyages in their old trade to Australia. Sadly, he did not live to see them return to Mariehamn, as he died in August 1947.

The last commercial voyages of the Erikson ships took place in 1946–47, when the four-masted barques *Viking* and *Passat* took cargoes of sawn timber to South Africa. *Passat* sailed on to Bunbury in Western Australia and loaded a cargo of sleepers for Port Swettenham in Malaya, then sailed on to Port Victoria in ballast to load grain for the United Kingdom. *Viking* loaded a cargo of coke for Santos and then went on to Port Victoria to load grain, finding herself in port with *Passat* and *Lawhill*. Three four-masted barques together in the one port, in the year 1948! The following year *Passat* again made the voyage to Port Victoria and was joined by *Pamir*, just returned to Finnish ownership by New Zealand. This was the last voyage with Australian grain for either of them.

Maybe it was just as well that Gustaf Erikson did not witness the end or have to decide in 1950 that he would not send his ships to sea again. In one of his letters to me just after the war, he wrote that it would be a sad day when there were no more sailing ships. He said that his one wish was to see his ships at sea again after being laid up during the war. His name and the names of his ships will go down in maritime history. His fleet stretched the age of sail into the atomic era. Names like *Lawhill, Olivebank, Archibald Russell, Killoran* and *Hougomont*, ex-limejuicers that would otherwise have faded away in the twenties, are still written about and discussed where lovers of sail gather. And his once-famous 'P' Liners, *Passat* and *Pommern*, survivors still, are there for future generations to gaze at in wonder and awe.

What type of person manned the last sailing ships? The answer to this question is complex, almost as complex as why the sailing ship survived in trade as long as she did. At least in the period covered by this book, there were three very broad categories: ordinary seamen, who early in the twentieth century spent most of their lives at sea, often moving between sail and steam depending on where their last voyage took them; the aspiring cadet or apprentice officer, who considered a sail apprenticeship an advantage or a prerequisite for a coveted sail endorsement to his 'ticket'; and those seeking the adventure of just one voyage or maybe two. This latter category did not emerge until the twenties and thirties, when it was obvious that there soon would be no more sailing ships. The harshness of sailing ship life eliminated most of those seeking adventure, although some went on to a career at sea, helped by a level of education that allowed their maritime studies to continue.

Most of those who remained seamen knew no other life; because there was little work ashore in the years following World War I, signing on a nomadic sailing ship at least provided accommodation, food and a wage that, although low, did accumulate by voyage end, albeit somewhat depleted by purchases from the slop chest. Steamships offered better conditions, but many seamen stuck to sail, in large part because there were so many aspects of their calling they had become proficient in that they looked almost condescendingly upon 'steamboat sailors'. Those who 'went into the fo'c'sle' (signed on as seamen) could, after the necessary sea time, sit for Board of Trade examinations for second mate, and even higher, if they had the education and funds to attend navigation classes. However, most were itinerant, going from one ship to the next, resigned to never knowing where the next year of their lives would be spent.

The latter-day sailing ship was a nomad—having no set trade route, she was sent wherever there was a cargo. So too were most of the fo'c'sle hands, having no home ashore except the Sailors' Home or some doss house. The crew could be signed on for a round trip, being discharged on returning to the home port, or for a set destination. The articles they signed acknowledged that the seaman would be paid the going rate, would not be required to serve beyond 60° North or South, and would receive rations described as being 'full and plenty'. Many of my informants would question the 'full and plenty', as well as the 60° condition, for a west about rounding of Cape Horn could take a ship much further south than 60° when on a long leg trying to make westing against a westerly gale.

Repatriation to the port of signing on was rare. It was common for a round trip to take several years, as cargoes were frequently loaded along the way for other destinations. It was an acknowledged practice for crews to jump ship at outlying ports to savour the shore attractions and to sign on to another ship when their money ran out. Such sprees only lasted a few days, as shipmasters kept to a minimum any money advanced out of a seaman's accrued wages. When a ship lost hands through desertion, it was common to pick up replacements at waterfront boarding houses or 'off the beach'. Individuals known as 'crimps' acted as brokers, offering shipmasters 'good hands' for a fee. The same hands had probably been enticed to jump another ship several days previously on the promise of a better ship and conditions and under the influence of a large amount of cheap alcohol. The master would pay up the seaman's boarding house bill and the crimp's fee, later to be deducted from his wages on signing off. The practice of 'shanghaiing' was still in existence in many ports of the world in the first two decades of the century. Newcastle in New South Wales, one of the world's great sailing ship ports, was notorious for this, and many a seaman was hoisted aboard a soon-to-depart sailing ship lying at the 'farewell buoys', at the entrance to the Hunter River, while still in a drunken sleep. This aspect of the seaman's life is described superbly in Stan Hugill's book

Sailortown, in which he describes the areas in each of the world's great ports where seamen headed after a long voyage.

The British mercantile marine of the period was the world's largest, and many nationalities were thrown together in the fo'c'sle. The working of a sailing ship was universal so language was never a problem. Even though all orders were in English, experienced seamen could predict an order and go straight to the correct lines, at night, in any conditions.

Most of the 'foremast hands' (seamen, as opposed to apprentices) who have advised me speak of the 'fo'c'sle boss'. He could be of any nationality and assumed this position on joining the ship. It started when he walked into the fo'c'sle. If the bunk he preferred was taken he merely threw his seabag into it. The occupier either moved out or fought. The boss had to be a first-class seaman as well as fighter. When working on deck or aloft he automatically took the most difficult tasks. When hauling on the braces or halyards he took up a position at the front of those tailing on, and aloft he was always first into the rigging as his place was always on the extreme end of the yardarm. If someone beat him to it, even 40 metres (130 feet) up, then fists would be used over the territory. This developed from the intense pride in workmanship or, to be more correct, seamanship, that rivalled that of established crafts ashore. Pride in this ability, often referred to as having 'every finger a fish hook and every hair a rope yarn', helped the seaman of the early twentieth century to endure some of the harshest conditions that would ever be experienced by working man.

The sailing ship was a complex, powerful, savage and at times helpless mistress, who demanded a unique collection of skill, guts and patience. Unforgiving and cold blooded, she was swift in her ability to kill and maim and ready to destroy the unworthy, who would woo her much like the mythical Lorelei of the Rhine.

In spite of this, almost all of those to whom I have spoken look back to their time in sail with pride, nostalgia and even pleasure. Some stayed at sea and went on to command. Others came ashore and never went back. I can recall only two out of hundreds who said they would not do it again. Even a one-legged Norwegian seaman I met several years ago, who lost his limb when it was caught between a set of bitts and a wire sheet, told me he 'would go back to sea in sail tomorrow if there was a chance!'

Many of the diaries lent to me contained brief comments that described graphically aspects of life in the last sailing ships. These diaries all have a similar ring, revealing over and over that the working of a large sailing ship on a globe-encircling voyage was pretty standard, and resulted in hundreds of those interviewed making the same statement: 'It was a fairly uneventful voyage'. Others, however, gave very close insights into the life and what was experienced and what was often forgotten. Verbal questioning rarely produced the same type of comment.

This vivid description came from the diary of Jack Horward. He was a seaman in the four-masted barque *Archibald Russell*, sailing from Port Germein towards

Falmouth in 1939*:

> The wind is impossible to sail against and is even worse than any storm previously encountered. At mid day (change of watch) all hands are called out to take in the upper topsails. We went up in a screaming squall, accompanied by hail, sleet and snow. The fore upper topsail has blown to shreds—does the sail maker curse! We 'sail' on under almost bare poles heading due east almost 180 miles from the coast of South America. The old ship is trembling and shaking when the seas crash over her from stem to stern. The rigging is straining and groaning above the roar of the wind. It is impossible to keep food on the table so we eat out of our hands.
>
> [Later:]
> Tonight at 11 pm when I was 'police', I was sent up to unfurl the main royal, about 180 feet up. It was my worst experience aloft. As soon as I had freed the lee side, the sail started to shake and flap furiously. Repeatedly my foothold on the footrope was lost and I was left suspended by my left hand frozen on the jackstay, until my feet had found the shaking footrope again. As well as the bucking and shaking caused by the sail the yard was jerking about six inches each way through the loose parral on the mast and there I was trying to unfasten some damn stupid complicated knot that some 'farmer' had used to make fast the sail. I looked for something to grab hold of, in case I lost my grip but being right at the top of the mast there was absolutely nothing. I shouted, cursed and screamed with rage and pain and threw all caution to the wind and went at it furiously using both hands on the knots. After what seamed an eternity I finished, shouted 'all clear' to the 2nd Mate and waited until the yard was hoisted, to overhaul the buntlines. This done, I descended to the deck, to start bracing. For some reason I felt good, as I felt that I had achieved something.
>
> [Next day:]
> Lookout late tonight was a revelation. I have heard of ships ghosting along but tonight I could really appreciate just what that implied. It was a perfect evening, a warm mellow breeze, and the ship moving silently through the water. Above, the massive spars,—yards, masts and rigging, thrown into dramatic relief against the starlit sky and those great billowing sails appearing in the moonlight, to be carved from marble.

One who was happy to leave sailing ships at the end of his four-year apprenticeship was Captain Tim Hehir, who freely admitted that it was his father's intention to 'make a man of him'. He joined the four-masted barque *Lauriston* in Sydney in 1912, and through his words one can visualise the impact of the introduction to sailing ship life on this 15-year-old boy:

> For at least thirty days on the run to the Horn we had continual bad weather, the gale changing between south west and north west. The ship was submerged in frothing, tumbling water from rail to rail, and all work on deck was in water, sometimes waist deep. Our fo'c'sle was awash with two feet of water that drenched all our possessions. Many times the galley was washed out and we subsisted on sea biscuits for days. It didn't matter if one had a top bunk as turning in in wet clothes resulted in one's donkey's breakfast [straw mattress] becoming sodden. Our clothes, apart from oilskins stayed on our backs for weeks. Ten men living in a space of about twelve feet by ten feet created a stench I can still smell. Some tried to dry their wet clothes by hanging them around the fo'c'sle. The salt water and perspiration soaked garments steamed and gave off nauseous fumes, which mingled with the ever-present bowel smells. The least offensive was the slumbering breaths of exhausted men, heavy with stale tobacco and rotten salt

* It was usual to state that a sailing ship was headed 'towards' a certain destination rather than 'to'.

meat. There was no heating or ventilation in the fo'c'sle as the skylight had to be kept closed to keep out the water. The only light was a smoky kerosene lamp which added to the other fumes.

Another quote from Jack is dated 16 May 1939. Sent aloft with another seaman to furl the mizzen royal in heavy wind in the middle of the night, Jack describes in vivid terms what was a commonplace event. This took place over 50 metres (165 feet) above the deck.

In the inky blackness the ratlines and shrouds we climb are not even visible so you feel your way up comparatively slowly. I could not see Stefan but could hear his curses. We reach the bucking yard and lay out along it, one each side. Knowing Stefan to be a fast worker I went at the sail madly and lost a couple of fingernails for my trouble. Twice I was thrown off the footrope but clawed back frantically, hanging on to the jackstay with one hand. When a man is up aloft and unable to make an impression on a ballooning sail despite all his efforts, a strength beyond that of his normal self seems to come to him and he becomes almost super-human. So it was for me on this occasion for I made record time. I discussed this with Hanlon some time later and he said the best thing to do is what the Finns do. 'Do your block' and go at it crazily. You do things, which later you realise were madness but 99 times out of 100 you get away with it. When the sail was fast I found my eyes had become more or less accustomed to the darkness so I stayed aloft for a moment to study the scene below. For'ard, the ship was churning great masses of spray and water, throwing it far into the air and to the side. The fo'c'sle head is rarely visible being covered by the seas. The outline of the ship could be seen by the phosphorescence on the foam along the bulwarks and very faintly the fo'c'sle lights glimmered through the portholes reflecting on the wet decks. Aloft, the sails and rigging groaning and the wind screaming. It was a magnificently exhilarating scene!

Brian Hay, a seaman in the 1949 voyage of the four-masted barque *Passat*, makes further reference to the noises in a sailing ship:

One would think that without engines a sailing ship would be a fairly quiet place. In fact it was not. In a gale, the wind screamed through the rigging so loud it was deafening and it was impossible to hear the orders. The sea pounded on to the hull and waves crashed on board. The wash ports, which were thick steel about 60 cm [24 inches] square clanged shut as the ship rolled. The blocks screeched and the parrels of the yards groaned as we braced them around. When a sail blew out the remnants tore to shreds with a noise like rifle shots. With a good fair wind when the sea was not excessively rough the hull slid through the water with a great hissing sound!

In contrast, the words of Dudley Turner, seaman in the last voyage of the British ship *Monkbarns* in 1925, come to mind. He describes, as did many, one of the more pleasant aspects of windjammer life—sailing in the trade winds:

On fine nights the watch used to gather on the main hatch and spin yarns or sing songs. There was always someone with a mouth organ or concertina. I remember one night in particular. We were in the tropics and it was a beautiful moonlit night, with the sky crammed with stars, and fleecy trade wind clouds low on the horizon. It was one of those still nights when there was nothing to be heard but the occasional creak of a block and the gentle tumbling of our bow wave. There was no need to speak above a whisper. Someone started up a song and soon everyone was singing. The result was very pleasing, even though the words were very sentimental, perhaps because the thoughts of the singers were far away, and no restraint on their innermost thoughts. Then eight bells were struck, echoed by the bell on the fo'c'sle head, and the lookout man's long drawn out, 'all's well, lights burning bright'. Then the voice of the watch officer, 'all hands muster in their respective watches at the break of the poop'! The wheel and the lookout was relieved and the ship settled down for the night.

Going to sea in a windjammer was an experience like nothing else!

Apprentice or cadet officers were in a slightly different category, and were exposed to a wider range of working conditions, depending on whose ships they were in. British ships employed apprentices, whose families paid a premium for the privilege of serving for four years and hopefully being in a position to sit for a second mate's certificate at the end of this period. They had to perform the same work as the seamen and additionally had to perform the unpleasant tasks that seamen would not usually be asked to do, such as cleaning out the pigpens and toilets. German and French ships employed cadets but tended to have a more structured training programme than the British, who in many cases used apprentices as cheap labour. Most of those interviewed who went to sea as cadets ended up as officers and ultimately master.

The remaining category, the adventure sailors or 'one trippers', as they were known by professional seamen, emerged when it was realised that sail was nearing its demise. The fleet of sailing ships owned by Gustaf Erikson provided the opportunity to experience a voyage under sail before it was too late.

The nature of sailing ship crews underwent a change from the old days. Boys from the Ålands, intent on a career at sea, and seasoned by earlier voyages around the Baltic, made up much of Erikson's crews, joined by those from other countries who would pay a premium of 50 pounds for a voyage as an apprentice. Even in the thirties, two years under sail was a prerequisite for those sitting for a second mate's certificate in many European countries. Stories about the Erikson windjammers and their main activity of lifting cargoes of Australian grain for Europe reached the Americas too, and there was usually the ubiquitous Yank in the fo'c'sle. In some way there was a synergistic influence at work, providing a source of cheap labour that helped prolong the life of sail.

The hot, dusty, primitive but friendly grain ports of Spencer Gulf cast their spell over some of these Nordic lads, often through the charms of the country girls they met at the local dances and the nurses from Port Augusta hospital who flocked to the ports when the grain ships came in. Others were attracted by the higher wages paid to seamen on the Australian coast, or the generally freer Australian life style. Whatever the reason, many jumped ship, and their places were taken by Australians when the deep-laden grain ships were ready for sea. Although worlds apart in culture, language and customs, these fledgling sailors fell into place in the tough wind ship crews.

The sailing ship was a supreme leveller, and an alliance began that still exists today. Australians are always welcome in Mariehamn, as I have found on several visits, and I have left laden with greetings and good wishes for old Australian shipmates from bygone years. In this distant northern land the talk always includes the place names of Spencer Gulf, Port Victoria, Port Lincoln, to name a few, and for an Australian traveller far from home this is music to the ears.

While the nature of crews underwent a change after World War I, the working of a sailing ship remained the same. Maritime unions, particularly those under the red ensigns of Britain, Australia and New Zealand, had forced higher standards of working conditions in powered vessels, but sailing ships by their very nature defied change and the unions ignored them—at least until the post-World War II years, when the four-masted barques *Pamir*, *Passat* and *Viking* resumed their grain-carrying voyages from Spencer Gulf. *Pamir*'s crew had increased from about 20 to 35 in the war years; as if insurance premiums, maintenance costs, high wages and maritime safety laws were not enough, the previously unheard-of union demand of crew repatriation struck the death blow to any chance of commercial sailing ship operation after these last Cape Horn voyages in 1949. *Pamir*, returned to Finnish ownership, still had a large proportion of New Zealand crewmen who were members of the Seaman's Union. The last words in the diary of Desmond Fisher (steward in *Pamir*'s last voyage) reveal the end:

> The A.B.s were flown home on a chartered plane and the provedore department was allowed to stay on in Britain without pay until we joined the *Orcades* as passengers on 16 December 1949. On this day our pay started again and stopped on our arrival in New Zealand on 16 January 1950.

Maybe it was just as well that Gustaf Erikson did not live to see his last windjammers return home.

Cape Horn

This place name is heard more than any other in the biographies and narratives of those who made the globe-encircling voyage from Europe to Australia and New Zealand and return, in sailing ships. It is the tip of an island, a Chilean possession and the southernmost part of the South American continent. It is at 56° 48' S, in the path of the extremely strong westerly winds that encircle the globe at this latitude. Sailors, especially those in sail, gave it the name Cape Stiff. Until the opening of the Panama Canal in 1914, ships travelling from one coast of the Americas to the other either had to round this point or go through the Strait of Magellan.

The Roaring Forties were advantageous to ships sailing on the Europe–Australia run, but those voyaging from Europe and the east coast of the Americas to the West Coast all had to round Cape Horn—against generally gale-force winds in huge seas. Its reputation was founded on this arduous west about rounding, in which many ships foundered or were dismasted trying to make headway. The remains of a number of those that survived are still to be seen in the Falkland Islands, where they headed after sustaining damage. Those that were able to carry out repairs could make another attempt, the others were destined to stay there until they rusted away.

Oil on canvas, 55 x 75 cm, in the collection of Viking Sundblom, Mariehamn

Plate I

Final Voyage

The year is 1920 as the newly rigged barque *James Craig* prepares to leave her anchorage in Johnson's Bay in Sydney Harbour for Newcastle, to load a cargo of coal for Hobart. Riding high out of the water, she carries only the ballast necessary to get her there. The crew is making final preparations for her departure. The tug has taken the towrope and the mate peers over the rail to see how much anchor cable has still to come in. It was customary for some sail to be loosened but not sheeted home until off the land and the tow dropped.

For the preceding eight years *James Craig* had been used as a coal hulk in Port Moresby. She was towed back to Sydney in 1919 where she was refitted by her new owners, Henry Jones & Company of Hobart, better known for their IXL jam. She remained in service until 1922, then, taken to Recherche Bay south of Hobart, she waited for a cargo that never came. In 1925 she was sold, again to take up duty as a coal hulk, bunkering steamers that came to Hobart. In the early 1930s this work ran out and she was returned to Recherche Bay. Run onto a sandbank, a hole was blown in her bottom to stop her breaking adrift and menacing other ships. In 1972 she was inspected by a group from Sydney Maritime Museum and temporary repairs were carried out in Hobart to enable her to be towed to Sydney in 1981, for the restoration that has now spanned 25 years.

Oil on canvas, 55 x 75 cm, in the collection of Charles Ellis, Sydney

Plate II

Durban Bound

This painting symbolises the period in the life of the four-masted barque *Lawhill* after she was seized as a war prize by the South African government on 21 August 1941. The firm of Sturrock & Co. became her managing agents. This period was significant in that it gave *Lawhill* a new career late in her life. Had she been in home waters she would have been laid up in Mariehamn with others of the Erikson fleet—*Pommern,* *Viking* and *Passat*—to await the more favourable times at the end of hostilities. In this case her age (built 1892) might have gone against her (*Passat* was built in 1911, *Pommern* in 1903, *Viking* in 1907). *Passat* and *Viking* went to sea again but *Pommern* did not. Not that the Ålanders would have forsaken *Lawhill,* for she was a far more interesting ship than *Pommern,* but economics would have dictated which ship would be enshrined as a national monument.

A visit I made to Cape Town, even though it was many years after *Lawhill* ceased to exist, has allowed me to visualise this scene. She sailed out of Table Bay on six voyages between 1943 and 1947, on this occasion in ballast. It was April 1946, a short voyage to Durban to load coal for Buenos Aires. A grey-painted liberty ship enters the bay and her tug moves off with toot from her whistle. A cargo liner of the Holland–South Africa line heads off to the west in her newly painted peacetime colours.

Oil on canvas, 55 x 75 cm, in the collection of Jörgen Lönn, Stockholm

Plate III

The Heaving Line

A ritual experienced by all those who went to sea in sailing ships was 'taking a tow' (it also applies to powered vessels). Taking a tow, in this case bringing the four-masted barque *Olivebank* into port, was accompanied by much activity on board. Prior to taking the towrope, sail would be reduced so that the speed of the sailing ship matched that of the tug. In this painting the upper sails—topgallants and royals— are furled and the courses are 'up in their gear', that is, hauled up to the yards but not yet furled. The topsails are always left to last in case it is necessary to abort the tow at the last moment, when the sailing ship must have the ability to get going again quickly. The breeze is setting in towards the land and the skipper must judge the right moment to take in the remaining sail. The anchors are already over the side, with the mate observing that all is ready for them to be dropped when needed.

A degree of licence has been taken with the tug in the foreground, for few of my informants named the tugs they used on entering port. Here I have chosen to portray the tug *Waratah*, which worked for much of her life out of the port of Newcastle, New South Wales. Rescued from almost derelict condition by a group within the Sydney Maritime Museum, thousands of hours went into her restoration and she is now is a working exhibit, familiar to all those who use the harbour of Sydney.

Oil on canvas, 60 x 90 cm, in the collection of Anthony Cox, Sydney

Plate IV

In London's River

The full-rigged ship *Monkbarns* is moved up to a buoy in the Thames in 1926, at the end of her last commercial voyage. Seamen commonly called the Thames 'London's river'. In Chapter 3, Dudley Turner describes the last hours of this voyage very vividly. *Monkbarns* was built in 1895 for David Corsar & Co. and was sold to John Stewart & Co. in 1911, under whose flag she remained until 1926.

Monkbarns had been away for three years, on a nomadic voyage that saw her load coal in Newcastle, New South Wales, for Chile three times, and guano or nitrates for the return trips. She led the tramping life of a typical limejuicer except that on one occasion she was embayed in floe-ice south of Cape Horn, which held her captive for three months. I have not heard of this happening to any other sailing ships trying to round the Horn—she must have sailed well to the south to get a good slant up to westward.

Monkbarns left Callao on 21 January 1926 for the United Kingdom with a full load of guano. After rounding Cape Horn her master, Captain Davies, became ill and the mate took over. He put into Rio de Janeiro and the captain was taken to hospital, where he died on 21 March 1926. The mate was given command and *Monkbarns* continued on to London.

Oil on canvas, 55 x 75 cm, in the collection of Phillip Fowler, Hobart

Plate V

Falmouth for Orders

Laden with grain, the four-masted barque *Garthpool* leaves Port Jackson on 1 March 1926, headed towards Falmouth for orders. She arrived there on 5 September 1926, after spending 45 days in Rio de Janeiro, repairing damage to her rudder caused by heavy weather. All those familiar with the entrance to Port Jackson (Sydney Harbour) will recognise this scene. In the background is the red-striped Hornby Light, situated on the southern headland at the entrance to the harbour. The pilot steamer *Captain Cook* follows her out to sea to pick up the pilot. An Alfred Holt Blue Funnel cargo liner in the background heads up the western channel to her berth in Darling Harbour.

The squat-looking 'bald-headed rig', a term that describes a sailing ship with no royal yards, is evident here. It was also known as the 'Jubilee rig', supposedly because this configuration emerged during Queen Victoria's Jubilee year. *Garthpool*'s likeness to her near sister, *Lawhill*, is also obvious. The main distinguishing features are *Garthpool*'s open railing around her Liverpool house, and that her topgallant masts are stepped conventionally. *Lawhill* was unique in that her topgallant masts were stepped abaft the topmasts. Built in 1891 for Charles Barrie's Dundee–Calcutta Line, *Garthpool* was first named *Juteopolis*, referring to Dundee's nickname 'City of Jute'. She and *Lawhill* were often called the 'Dundee Twins'. *Garthpool* was wrecked on Bonavista Island in the Cape Verde Islands in 1929.

Oil on canvas, 55 x 70 cm, in the collection of Andrew Carter, Sydney

Plate VI

Off the South Foreland

The full-rigged ship *Garthwray* reaches up the English Channel, off the South Foreland, passing a Thames barge heading off to Cornwall for a cargo of pipeclay. (This vessel's tanned sails are typical of the small coastal craft of the day; this was a method of preserving sailcloth.) The year is 1922. Built in 1889 as the *Wray Castle*, after three changes of ownership *Garthwray* was bought in 1917 by Sir William Garthwaite's Marine Navigation Co. of Canada and renamed.

She is on the last leg of a voyage that commenced four years earlier, in September 1917, at Newport in Wales. The latter-day sailing ship has been described in this book as a nomad, perhaps heading off on the first leg of a voyage with a charter, but nothing arranged beyond her first destination. Sometimes there was nothing in her hold but ballast, and her first charter would commence on the other side of the world. *Garthwray* had just spent four years on such a nomadic voyage, which took her from Newport, Wales to South Georgia in the South Atlantic, Melbourne, New York, Melbourne, Newcastle, New South Wales, Caleta Beuna, Chile, Cape Town, Sydney, Newcastle, Valparaiso, Taltal, and then Falmouth for orders. She was ordered to Leith in Scotland to discharge.

Not long after rounding the South Foreland, *Garthwray* sprang a leak, which resulted in her taking 30 days to reach Leith from Falmouth. She was wrecked in 1924 on the Santa Maria Islands north of Iquique.

Oil on canvas, 55 x 75 cm, in the collection of John Stanley, Sydney

Plate VII

Landfall at Sunset

The barque *White Pine* makes landfall off the Grey River, New Zealand, on her 76th crossing of the Tasman Sea and the end of her sailing career, in 1922. The last of the fleet of sailing ships that traded between Australia and New Zealand, she was a fast sailer and once made the crossing between Newcastle and Auckland in seven days. This iron-hulled vessel was built in 1879 for the Natal trade with Great Britain as *Quathlamba*, named after the mountain range in southern Africa now called the Drakensbergs. Auckland shipowner J. J. Craig bought her in 1899. She usually carried white pine to Australia, returning with coal and general cargo. In 1905 he renamed her *Hazel Craig* after his second daughter. In 1917 Craig sold her to Captain Proctor, who renamed her *White Pine* after the timber she usually transported.

The smaller vessel is a New Zealand scow, a unique craft used in New Zealand waters until the 1920s to transport timber and logs from inland forests to the coastal towns. They had a shallow draft to cross river bars and were able to stand upright when the tide went out. They were little more than a box with the corners cut off at the forward end. They sailed surprisingly well but needed the two and sometimes three centreboards, raised and lowered by a hand-turned winch, which reduced leeway and helped in steering. At the end of this voyage, *White Pine* was bought by James Patterson and rigged down for use as a coal hulk in Melbourne until 1947, when she was towed to sea and sunk off Barwon Heads.

Oil on canvas, 55 x 75 cm, in the collection of James Vale, Sydney

Plate VIII

Running the Easting Down

'Running the easting down' was the term used by sailors to describe the long haul from the Atlantic through the Roaring Forties towards Australia and then onwards to Cape Horn. This painting of the four-masted barque *Hougomont* was inspired by stories told by Captain Eben Anderson, an apprentice in this ship in 1912–14. He described the way her master, Captain McDonald, chose to run before a gale. 'All sails set upon the main except the mainsail' is not prescribed in *Tait's Seamanship* as the correct procedure, nor would a candidate for a second mate's certificate have been wise to explain to the examiner that it kept the ship balanced, but as Eben explained, 'Old Mac was an excellent seaman and had many ideas of his own how to get the best out of his ship.'

Hougomont, built in 1897, spent most of her life under the ownership of J. Hardie & Co. of Glasgow until Gustaf Erikson bought her in 1924. In 1932 she was dismasted in the Great Australian Bight. Superb seamanship allowed her to make Port Adelaide under jury rig. It was considered too costly to re-rig her so any fitting that was useable was stripped and taken back to Mariehamn aboard *Herzogin Cecilie.* Her figurehead and skylight now reside in the Ålands Sjofartsmuseum. She was then towed to Stenhouse Bay on the tip of Yorke Peninsula and sunk as a breakwater. In May 1999 I was in Port Victoria for the 50th anniversary of the last grain ship voyage out of Spencer Gulf. As Stenhouse Bay was only 100 kilometres away, I took Captain Eben Anderson's ashes with me. Although the bones of *Hougomont* had long since disappeared into the sands, I knew, as I sprinkled the ashes into the clear water, that his remains had found an appropriate resting place.

Oil on canvas, 55 x 70 cm, in the collection of Professor Jonathon Carter, Sydney

Plate IX

In Carrick Roads

A sunny afternoon in Carrick roads, the entrance to Falmouth Harbour, and Erikson's four-masted barque *Olivebank*, deep-laden with Australian grain, heaves to after a voyage from Port Victoria, South Australia. *Olivebank* called at this port five times for her orders in the thirties. The pilot cutter in the foreground is typical of the type of craft that was used for this purpose before engine-driven craft took over.

A certain amount of romantic licence has been taken here. Perhaps *Olivebank* never arrived at Carrick roads on a sunny afternoon; perhaps the pilot cutter met up with her further out to sea. Several craft in the distance are also significant—they are Falmouth Quay punts, usually cutter or yawl rigged, which were a feature of this port. They derived a living from the ocean-going ships that called in for their orders. Their stumpy masts allowed them to sail alongside the large sailer without becoming entangled in the lower yards. They purveyed vegetables, fruit, meat and fish, tobacco and newspapers to the crews who had subsisted on sailing ship fare for the previous three or four months.

Olivebank continued in trade until 1939. Sailing from Port Victoria on 20 March, she discharged her grain cargo in Barry Dock, sailing for Mariehamn on 29 August. On 8 September she ran through a North Sea minefield and struck a mine, sinking quickly. Captain Granith went down with his ship. The 14 survivors of her crew of 21 were picked up two days later by a Danish fishing boat.

Oil on canvas, 55 x 75 cm, in the collection of Goran Lif, Stockholm

Plate X

All Gone the Tow Rope, Skipper!

The four-masted barque *Archibald Russell* drops her tow outside the River Orwell on a grey afternoon, the following wind pushing up the flooding tide as she heads off for her home port of Mariehamn. In ballast, she rides high out of the water, responding eagerly to the fresh breeze. Her topsails have been set to help the tug along. The tug hand calls out to his skipper that the tow has been dropped and some crew in *Archibald Russell* go aloft to loose more sail, while others on the fo'c'sle head prepare to bring the anchors inboard.

Archibald Russell was the last large steel sailing ship built in the United Kingdom, launched in 1905 at Scott's Shipbuilding & Engineering Co. yard in Greenock for J. Hardie & Co. In spite of the late date she did not have a Liverpool house. She, *Olivebank* and *Pommern* were the last four masters in commission with open well decks. Like her sister *Hougomont* she lost many men overboard. Her final voyage commenced on 3 April 1939 from Port Germein, South Australia, reaching Falmouth on 2 August. From here she sailed to Hull to discharge her cargo in Alexandra Dock. During the war, rigged down so that her masts would not provide a navigation marker for the Luftwaffe, her hull became a store ship. In 1947 she was towed from Hull to Newcastle to be broken up in the yard of J. J. King & Co. of Gateshead on Tyne. Her last master, Captain Sommarlund, came out of retirement to take command for this final voyage of 30 hours.

Oil on canvas, 60 x 75 cm, in the collection of Birgitta Johansson, Mariehamn

Plate XI

On the Nickel Run

The four-masted barque *Wulfran Puget* eases along gently at about 5 knots with a fair wind. In her belly is a cargo of nickel ore loaded in New Caledonia. The large deposits of this ore on this island provided a regular cargo for French ships for many years. The 'nickel run' took French ships to New Caledonia around the Cape of Good Hope, through the westerlies of the Southern Ocean and around Tasmania up into the Pacific.

Some of the characteristics of the French-built windjammer are apparent here. The painted ports favoured by the A. D. Bordes Line differ slightly from those favoured by the British, who introduced them on ships trading east to China as they supposedly deterred Chinese pirates (who might think they had fallen in with a warship). The upper black band is quite narrow compared with the British style, which had the whole bulwark strake black. The ports tend to be smaller and had another black band below them. Below this was the traditional French grey down to the waterline. On the fo'c'sle head the hollow steel box-section cathead projects boldly as another identifying feature. Perhaps not so obvious are the lengthened poop and fo'c'sle. *Wulfran Puget* was built in 1895 and remained in service until 1926 when she was broken up.

Oil on canvas, 35 x 45 cm, in the collection of Roger Morgan, Brisbane

Plate XII

Au Revoir *Bretagne*

Leaving Hobart in 1923, the French bounty ship, the barque *Bretagne*, is pictured in Storm Bay, with Tasman Island on her port hand, heading off towards Astoria on the American North West coast for a grain cargo. A typical Tasmanian ketch crosses her bow in what many would say was a risky manoeuvre. However, the barque is still sheeting home her foresail and her speed would not be more than 2 or 3 knots. The mainsail is still 'up in its gear' so that it will not obscure the way ahead until the barque is well out to sea.

There was a strong connection between French commercial sailing ships and the port of Hobart, from 1881 when the French bounty scheme was introduced until the early 1930s. Large deposits of nickel ore in New Caledonia brought hundreds of French ships through the Roaring Forties of the Southern Ocean; instead of heading through Bass Strait the ships sailed around Tasmania, adding miles to the journey and thereby earning extra bounty. They often called at Hobart to replenish stores or to see if their orders had been changed. Even if their charter was to load nitrate on the West Coast of South America, the west winds of the Southern Ocean route gave them a good passage time which justified the extra miles sailed. *Bretagne* made many voyages via Hobart on her way to New Caledonia, the Pacific North West and Newcastle, New South Wales, for coal. Built in 1901, she was broken up in 1926.

Oil on canvas, 75 x 105 cm, in the collection of the artist

Plate XIII

Off the West Coast

Deep laden with saltpetre, the four-masted barque *Padua* heads south for Cape Horn and the voyage home to Hamburg. Along with *Priwall* and *Peking*, she was the last of the German nitrate fleet, a symbol of the trade that existed between Chile and Germany for over 50 years. The harsh coastline south of Caleta Buena stands out boldly, a backdrop familiar to most who served in square-rigged ships in the early twentieth century: hot, dusty and arid, a collection of huts and sheds, a small jetty, barges used to ferry nitrate out to the ships anchored offshore; an almost sheer wall of dry rock rising to heights of 1000 metres; a mountain plateau inland from this coastal escarpment, like foothills to the snow-clad peaks of the Andes and their coastal spur, the Cordilleras, rising to over 4000 metres and visible 50 miles out to sea. Even the waters that abut this coast are unfriendly and unforgiving, the seamanship learned off Cape Horn being of little use if a 'norther' struck while at anchor at the base of this great wall. This vicious gale builds up rapidly without warning and the sailer's crew could only hope that their anchors would hold until it passed. Many ships dragged ashore before this wind and the heavy, ever-present Pacific swell.

Padua was built in 1926, and went into the Australian grain trade when the nitrate trade declined until 1939. During World War II she was rigged down to become a store ship. Given to Russia as reparations, she became *Kruzenshtern*, one of the largest sail-training ships afloat today.

Oil on canvas, 55 x 75 cm, Deutsches Schiffahrtsmuseum, Bremerhaven

Plate XIV

Stretching a New Topsail

The magnificent *Preussen*, the pride of the Laeisz fleet, launched in 1902, was the only five-masted full-rigged ship ever built. This painting is a reconstruction of the Elbe waterfront with the host of smaller craft that plied the North Sea and beyond. The river barge in the foreground carries a load of coal, another bagged cement, both significant exports from this port. *Preussen* rides high out of the water, indicating that her homeward cargo of nitrate has been discharged.

In port, sails were usually unbent for various reasons. They needed repairs—patches, whole cloths, boltropes, cringles, etc. had to be renewed—and removing them made it easier for masts and yards to be painted. If not unbent it would be necessary to unfurl them (shake them out) to dry them after rain—if the wind were not too strong. Here a new topsail is being stretched, bent onto the yard to check if it sets to the sail maker's liking. The term 'stretching' meant only that the head was pulled out to the end of the yard as rovings were tied on.

In 1910, *Preussen* collided with the cross-channel steamer *Brighton* when the steamer misjudged *Preussen*'s speed and attempted to cross her bows. With her rigging damaged, *Preussen* became uncontrollable and despite the efforts of two tugs drifted ashore at Dover. She could not be floated off, remaining there until her bones sank into the sands.

Oil on canvas, 65 x 90 cm, in the collection of the artist

Plate XV

Fünf Tage und Vierzehn Stunden (Five Days and Fourteen Hours)

The fastest ever east to west rounding of Cape Horn by a commercial sailing ship was recorded in 1938 by the German four-masted barque *Priwall*, under the command of Captain A. Hauth. There was no official recognition, merely the ship's log and navigation charts showed this to have taken place. It was usual to take the time from when the ship crossed Lat. 50°S in the Atlantic to 50°S in the Pacific (Cape Horn is 56°S). The westerly winds usually encountered in the Southern Ocean and, more often than not, gales, pushing up huge seas, could result in the rounding time sometimes exceeding six weeks.

Built by Blohm & Voss in Hamburg for the Laeisz Flying P Line, *Priwall* was launched in 1920 for the nitrate trade with Chile. Apart from two voyages to Australia for grain in 1934 and 1935, she remained in this trade until her last voyage under the Laeisz flag, to Valparaiso, Chile, in 1939. *Priwall* remained in Valparaiso until Chile declared war on Germany in 1941. She was taken over, painted white, renamed *Lautaro* and run as a cargo-carrying training ship, making a voyage to San Francisco in 1943. In 1945, off the coast of Peru with a full cargo of nitrate, she caught fire and became a total loss. Some licence has been taken here, in that Cape Horn would have been out of sight and flags were never flown, as they were expensive and would have blown to shreds in these conditions.

Oil on canvas, 60 x 90 cm, in the collection of Roger Morgan, Brisbane

Plate XVI

2 LIFE IN A SAILER

Parma

How did life in the last sailing ships differ from that in powered vessels? What work had to be performed in order to take a 3000-ton steel sailing ship around the world with no other means of propulsion than her sails, and deliver her cargo in a sound condition? The answers to these questions are not all that dissimilar from country to country, period to period and person to person. The working of a big sailing ship remained similar wherever she was owned, and I treat this chapter fairly broadly, highlighting national differences as they occur.

Some of the activities experienced in the past days of sail were quite different from what is done in modern training ships. Modern training ships do not carry cargo and have permanent ballast. Trainees have little to do with anchors (no walking 'round the capstan or securing anchors on the fo'c'sle head) as modern anchors are of the stockless type, nor are they involved with the extensive maintenance work that was carried out by ABs in earlier days.

Securing hatches

Before a ship could sail and once the last of the cargo had been loaded the hatches had to be secured. The hatches were rectangular openings in the ship's deck. They had steel sides (coamings) about 3 feet high through which the cargo was loaded into the ship's hold. The for'ard and after ends were angled up in the centre like a shallow gable. There was provision for a strong beam or beams called a 'fore and after' to be fitted between these ends. This beam had a ledge along its sides to take strong planks of timber called hatch boards that could be laid at right angles to it, out to the sides of the hatch coaming. The hatch boards could be up to 4 inches (10 centimetres) thick and any gaps between them were caulked. The hull of a sailing ship had only two watertight bulkheads, one for'ard and one aft, and great pains were taken to seal these hatches as water getting into the hull could not only ruin the cargo but sink the ship! Canvas covers were then stretched over the hatch boards and coaming and clamped along the sides with wooden wedges. The corners were sewn with strong sail twine. Heavy planks were then placed over the covers and held in place with chains, which were tightened with rigging screws and wedges. They were always secured by ABs and the carpenter.

I have been told of hatches being broached by heavy seas breaking on board. Frantic efforts would be required to secure the hatch before the volume of water pouring below sank the ship.

Anchoring

One of the first major activities of any voyage was getting under weigh and getting the anchors on board. Anchors and anchoring form an important subject in any maritime syllabus, and in a sailing ship were responsible for an enormous amount of work and effort, and also danger.

Powered and sailing ships have one thing in common—complete dependence on their anchors as the ultimate means of control. The powered vessel, in addition to at least one main driving screw or propeller, may have bow thrusters that can be used to move her away from the quay or to manoeuvre her in confined waters. However, without fuel, or without a tug, the only way she can stay in one position is to drop anchor.

The sailing ship is even more vulnerable in that her fuel, the wind, is unpredictable, often too strong or absent altogether, and at other times coming from the wrong direction. At sea, a sailing ship was able to cope with any amount of wind and could square off and run before the gale if need be, or simply heave to. Heaving to was the process of reducing sail to a point where there was negligible forward thrust while still retaining control over the ship's heading. In light winds, rather than reducing sail, a proportion of the sails could be 'backed', that is, hauled around to oppose the forward movement of the hull. In each case a lot of leeway was produced, which had to be considered where this might place the ship in an undesirable position. This applied particularly when close inshore.

When approaching port, if a tug was not immediately available, the skipper had to decide whether to heave to or head out to sea again. With an offshore wind there was no immediate danger, but with an onshore wind the sailer could find herself pushed on to a lee shore and unable to tack off. Even with no wind, the swell and current could drive her ashore. This type of mishap accounted for the loss of more ships than any other.

If a sailing ship master found his ship on a lee shore, and unable to tack off, the only choice was to drop anchor. This was not necessarily going to save the ship, as the water might be too deep or the bottom incapable of holding the anchor. On the West Coast of South America the water is so deep close inshore that the whole cable can be out and the anchor still not be in the ground. The heavy chain cable provided much of the holding power of an anchor, and at least three times the depth of the water was the general rule for anchoring—'and then some', as my great informant Captain Eben Anderson once said.

Powered vessels that sailed the seas when these last sailing ships were trying to earn a living used stockless anchors that sat snugly in the hawse pipe, and could be dropped within minutes of being required. They could be taken in effortlessly using steam, electric or hydraulic winches in five or ten minutes, but were not as efficient at holding the ship as the bower anchor still in use by sailing ships. Bower anchors required many hours of hard work on the part of the crew to heave them up and get them on board. Even getting the anchor ready for dropping required much heavy and dangerous work. (The five-masted barque *France II*, built in 1911, had stockless anchors, as did most of the large American schooners built after the turn of the century, but this was an attempt to adapt to modern trends.)

The average large sailing ship had two main anchors, weighing several tonnes apiece. At sea they were lashed down on the fo'c'sle head deck, port and starboard, with only the stocks overside. To break the anchor out of the seabed and bring it into this position, the watch had to spend an hour tramping around the fo'c'sle head capstan, a vertical drum-type winch with a row of holes around the top into which wooden bars could be inserted. Pushing on these bars rotated the drum— called 'walking the capstan 'round'. While the capstan drum was used directly to haul on lines, for example the fore tack, the anchor cable went over a windlass on the main deck immediately below the capstan, connected to the capstan by a long shaft. The capstan usually had two rows of holes connected by different gearing to the windlass shaft, their choice depending on how heavy the load was. Other capstans along the main deck used the drum just to haul on lines.

These highly geared windlasses moved the cable very slowly, so that it took many revolutions of the capstan to move the chain cable even a metre or so. Some later sailing ships carried a steam boiler and donkey engine, usually situated in the forward deckhouse. If fuel was available and the mate chose to use this expensive commodity, it could be used to drive the windlass. From the windlass the anchor cable led down through the cable pipe into the chain locker, a compartment in the extreme bows of the ship below the forepeak and for'ard of the collision bulkhead. It was divided by a fore and aft bulkhead to separate the port and starboard cables. It was entered from the forepeak 'tween deck or a hatch under the fo'c'sle head.

A job given to first voyagers or apprentices was 'stowing the cable'. Captain Eric Macpherson, who sailed in the British four-masted barques *Vimiera* and *Garthsnaid*, described the process to me.

> On my first voyage, I was given this job without any instruction or training. The chain locker was pitch dark and the only light was a small oil lamp called a duckbill lamp. It was a round can with a spout like a teapot from which the wick protruded. It burnt no brighter than a candle. You stood on top of an uneven mass of chain armed with a 'chain hook', and wrestled with the huge links as they came down through the pipe. This hook was a steel bar about 1200 mm long with a two-pronged hook on one end and a tee handle on the other. It was used to flake the chain into an orderly pile so that it would run out freely when the anchor was dropped. Also if the chain wasn't flaked down correctly so that it took up a minimum of space, you found that space was running out and the last part of the job was on your hands and knees on top of an ever-increasing mountain of chain. The higher it got the harder it was to pull the heavy chain to one side. No point yelling out that space was running out. It was one of the worst jobs in the ship. The cable may have been out and lying on the bottom for months. It was covered with red rust,

green seaweed and black mud. Even sharp, barnacle-like marine growth formed during long periods at anchorage, causing many wounds and abrasions. We came out of the chain locker covered all over with this mixture, with only a bucket of salt water to wash it off. One of my greatest fears was that somehow the brake on the windlass would fail. A two tonne anchor would fall pretty fast, taking with it the chain cable on which one was standing. It does not take a lot of imagination to visualise what would happen to anyone in the locker.

This actually happened to Ålander Ingemar Palmer, who later became third mate in the four-masted barque *Viking* for her 1947 voyage to Australia. It was in a small steamer where Ingemar was learning his craft. Stowing the cable was a common practice in both sail and steam. Ingemar reckons that his survival resulted from several factors. He had stowed the cable properly in that it was flaked down neatly in a figure of eight pattern, and he was wearing strong boots with a hard sole. He relates:

> I was over to one corner of the chain locker when the brake slipped and the cable snaked out. Luckily it moved away from me until it reached the other side of the chain locker and then it began to move back towards me. My hard boots enabled me to push the edges of their soles on to a small ledge created by the overlap of the steel plating in the corner of the chain locker. The ledge was only about 12 mm [½ inch] wide and I could push back into the corner, at the same time lifting my body clear, as the cable on which I had been standing, roared out. I could only remain in this position for a few seconds and I had to keep repeating it as the cable came back towards me. Had I been standing on the cable I would have been taken out the cable pipe with it. The mate was terrified to take a look into the chain locker as he thought I would surely be dead.

Eventually the anchor broke the surface; when clear of the water it was described as being 'aweigh'. It should be pointed out that prior to this a tug would have taken the towline or some sail been set to get the ship moving. The tug would only be dispensed with if the anchorage were such that with a fair wind she could move directly out to sea. This was possible in Spencer Gulf, as the anchorages were in an open roadstead. At Port Lincoln there were haul-off buoys that allowed the sailer to haul herself away from the jetty if there was a fair wind of sufficient strength to overcome any tidal influence. There were several methods to get the anchor on board at this stage. A hand had to go over the side in a bowline to hook on the catfall or cat purchase, tackle used to take the weight of the anchor so that it could be brought on board. It was suspended from the cathead, a strong baulk of timber or steel projecting over the ship's side. Earlier ships used a fish tackle, a powerful sixfold tackle attached to the fore topmast head, or anchor davits. The more recent vessels used an anchor crane that could be swung out over either side and allowed the anchor to be lifted up over the side of the ship. Once on board the anchor was bedded down on deck on wood blocks and secured with chains, metal straps or rope strops.

This work took place as the ship stood out to sea after all sail was set. To bring the anchors inboard too soon was unwise in case the wind dropped or swung around. Thus the work of getting the anchor on board often had to be carried out on a bucking fo'c'sle head, sloping away to leeward. It was not an easy job, and the anchor had to be dragged, pushed, levered and manhandled into position, all without the fo'c'sle railing in place. It was a job for the ABs and always supervised by the mate.

Once the anchors were on board, the cables were unshackled, hauled up through the hawse pipe and dropped down into the chain locker. The cable pipes were sealed with a canvas bonnet to stop water getting into the hull and usually remained sealed until the next port of call, unless the mate decided to run the cable out along the deck and have the watch chip the rust off and paint it with red lead. The hawse pipes were sealed off with wooden plugs, which were caulked or sealed with cement. This stopped the spouts of water that drove up the pipes with considerable force when the ship ploughed into a sea. Before setting out on a long voyage the anchor cranes or davits were dismantled to prevent their being damaged by heavy seas.

Getting the anchor ready for dropping was just as difficult. Firstly the hawse pipe was opened, that is, the wooden blocks were removed and the cement chipped out. Then a line was lowered through into the chain locker and attached to the end link of the cable so it could be hauled up by the capstan. Prior to this the pawls on the capstan were reversed as the windlass had to be turned in the opposite direction. The cable was rove through the hawse pipe after being run over the windlass drum, brought up the outside of the hull and shackled onto the anchor, still lashed down on deck. The anchor crane was used to lower the anchor over the side. If there was no anchor crane a fish tackle was taken to the fore topmast head. The anchor was then slung under a device called the tumbler. This was a quick-release device attached to the cathead or, if no cathead was fitted, along the edge of the fo'c'sle deck that allowed the anchor to fall freely when a pin was knocked out. This method of handling anchors was universal in sailing ships, even those built in the twentieth century, apart from the exceptions with stockless anchors mentioned earlier.

In addition to the main anchors, a smaller anchor called the stream anchor was usually carried. Usually lashed down on deck at the break of the fo'c'sle or poop, it could be used as a stern anchor whenever it was necessary to align the ship in a particular direction. It was an even more difficult task to get this one into position. It was hoisted overside by a tackle from the masthead or a yard and suspended in the water under one of the ship's boats, rowed out to where it was needed and dropped. It usually had a wire rather than a chain cable, which was led up over a fairlead on the poop and made fast on the after mooring bitts.

An example of the helplessness of a sailing ship was given to me by Harry Meadows of South Australia, a seaman in the four-masted barque *Hougomont* on a short voyage between Coquimbo and Tocopilla on the West Coast. She had just delivered her coal cargo from Newcastle, New South Wales, and was heading in ballast towards Tocopilla to load nitrates. Caught in the powerful north-setting Peru Current, she found herself without wind and was carried almost 500 miles past her destination. This was not unusual on this coast; the same fate befell many sailing ships. The great depth of water even close inshore made it difficult to anchor and wait for a favourable wind. Standing high out of the water in ballast, *Hougomont* had no hope of working back. With an offshore wind, the procedure was to head several hundred miles out to sea to escape the current, head south and make another approach. In desperation after a month of frustrating calms, headwinds and current, her master Captain McMillan decided to head back to Australia, where she picked up another coal cargo at Newcastle, New South Wales—also destined for the West Coast.

Many other stories told of the frustration caused by adverse winds which could prevent, for many weeks, the sailer making headway towards her next port. Fred Chapman from New Zealand spoke of his voyage in the barque *Garthneill* in 1919. The ship was in Melbourne and received orders to go to Bunbury in Western Australia to load railway sleepers for Cape Town. Apparently most of the South African railway system is laid on sleepers cut from the jarrah forests inland from Bunbury. Fred related:

> We left Melbourne, high out of the water as we were in ballast and in Bass Strait ran into strong westerly winds. After almost two weeks we had made no westing and were down south of Tasmania. The skipper got fed up with this and decided to turn around and sail right around the world, taking advantage of the west winds and roaring forties. We arrived at Bunbury about three months later. The distance between Melbourne and Bunbury is about 1800 miles but we sailed over 14,000 miles.

Owen Williams from Birkenhead, South Australia, described a similar event when he was in the ship *Terpsichore* in 1919. His ship had delivered a cargo of cement from Rochester to Montevideo. Her master, Captain Morris Jones, received orders to proceed to Callao on the West Coast to load guano. Heading south towards Cape Horn, Captain Jones decided to turn east to avoid the gruelling west about rounding of the Horn and sail all the way around the world to reach his destination. However, while running her easting down in the southern Indian Ocean *Terpsichore* received damage, resulting in her master putting into Sydney for repairs. By the time the repairs were carried out, the guano charter was lost, so she loaded a wheat cargo in Sydney for the United Kingdom.

Taking a tow

An activity taken for granted by today's mariners, but often dispensed with if conditions and location allowed, is 'taking a tow'. When approaching port the master of a sailing ship had to weigh up the situation and decide whether it was safe to leave the tow until the last minute, thus saving money. As sailing ships rarely carried radio, even in the latter years, the shore signal station reporting a sailer offshore would be the first contact. The practice of calling at Falmouth or Queenstown (Cobh) for orders sending them to another port to unload resulted from the lack of radio. In the latter years these were all in the United Kingdom—Barry, Glasgow, London, Liverpool, Belfast, Hull, Sunderland. In earlier years continental ports such as Rotterdam, Antwerp, Le Havre and Hamburg were also likely. In places where there was a large volume of traffic, such as the approaches to the English Channel, tug masters waited around offering their services. There was quite a ritual involved. The tug master would range alongside the sailing ship and through a megaphone ask her skipper if he needed a tow. If the wind were fair and the weather fine the sailing ship master would refuse or ignore the offer until nearer port. Then came a period of haggling over the price before finally the towline was taken aboard. An example of this was given to me by Perce Golding, who sailed from London to Sydney in 1906 in the well-known four-masted barque *Port Jackson*, owned and operated by the famous shipowners of the clipper era, Devitt & Moore.

> We had just cleared the Thames and were heading off down channel when a thick fog came down. Even though we were cranking our 'Norwegian piano' [fog horn], a German steamer, *Pyrgis*, loomed up and collided with us, putting a gash in our starboard bow, luckily above the water line. We had no choice but to return to port and shortly afterwards the fog cleared. Off Dover a tug came up and the haggling commenced. Through a megaphone, 'Good day Captain, nasty fog, can I give you a line?'
> 'No, we'll carry on a little further.'
> 'You won't get better than forty pounds at this stage, Captain.'
> 'There are plenty of tugs where I'm going,' yelled the skipper.
> 'There's nasty weather coming up and it will be dark soon,' from the tug master.
> And so the conversation went on, with the result that we took the tow for twenty-five pounds but had to use our own line. All this time the tug had been on the port side and did not know of our gashed bow. When the line was made fast the tug veered over to starboard and he saw our damaged bow. He was quite irate as he reckoned he was entitled to salvage. He took us to Dover but only got his twenty-five pounds.

The towline was usually 6 inch (15 centimetre) manila and an important part of the sailing ship's gear. If it snapped it could mean disaster. Some ships had a towing hawse—a pipe adjacent to the hawse pipe through which the anchor cable was led. The towline was taken to bitts adjacent to the foremast. Otherwise the towline was led over a fairlead on the fo'c'sle head to bitts further aft. Tugs carried a variety of towlines but favoured longer lasting wire rope. In a tight spot the sailing ship master usually preferred to use the tug's line as it gave him control over when the tow was dropped.

I have been given numerous examples of ships making and leaving anchorage without a tug, one of the more daring being the arrival in Sydney in 1947 of the four-masted barque *Pamir*, then under the New Zealand flag. Captain Jim Gaby told me of this event as his shipmate in sail, Captain Collier, master of *Pamir*, had related it to him. (There is an account of it in Jim's book, *The Restless Waterfront*.) It is noteworthy enough to be repeated here, as to enter Sydney Harbour at night under sail with poor visibility was an extremely hazardous undertaking.

> *Pamir* made landfall off Broken Bay, 20 miles north of Sydney at 5 pm and radioed their position to the Company. They radioed back that they were sending a tug and it would leave the wharf at 6 pm. *Pamir* sailed down towards Sydney but there was no tug and the squally wind was jamming her against the land.
> 'I thought about heading for Botany Bay about 10 miles south of Sydney where there is a straight run in,' Collier said. 'But she wouldn't lay up to Botany so there was nothing else for it, Sydney or the rocks. We were carrying all sail except the royals and the six t'gallants were up there doing a good job. I hauled up all the courses so we could con her in and I told myself, 'Well Collier get her in or get your bags packed!' The pilot came out but we were squared away and I could not stop for him. She had to be travelling when she went through the Heads so that she'd have plenty of way on her when she rounded to. Any way, I have Sydney exemptions and there wasn't any point in the two of us worrying.'

Jim continues the story:

The big 3500 ton barque sailed in at 9.15 pm straight through the Sydney heads in a blinding south easterly rain squall. It could not have hit them at a worse time. Told about it the next morning, the lighthouse keeper wouldn't believe she didn't have engine power. No big ship, he reasoned, would have dared to come through the Heads on a squally night like that. With split second timing her helm was put hard down after she passed the Hornby light. Then her brace winches really came into their own; hand braces would never have rounded those yards fast enough. She rounded like a thoroughbred into the eastern channel, where she lost the wind in her square sails and only the speed of her drive through the heads and her fore and aft sails took her to windward of the hungry Sow and Pigs, a reef in Sydney Harbour. They were critical minutes, for the wind can be blowing from one direction at sea and from another direction in a land locked area. But she sailed up past the reef in pitch darkness with her square sails madly flapping in the veering wind and the burden still full on her fore and aft sails through the quarter of a mile before she could up helm and sail to anchorage.

It was often the practice for a sailing ship to be towed quite long distances from one port to another if it appeared uneconomical to sail. An example of this was the transfer of ships between Sydney and Newcastle, New South Wales, a distance of about 60 miles. Paying the towing fee might have been preferable to buying the ballast required or paying disposal fees when it was dug out. It certainly was not intended to save the labours of the crew. A tug would be needed anyway to leave and enter these ports and this distance could be covered in a day by any normal tug. The last sailing ship to be towed from Sydney to Newcastle was the four-masted barque *Lawhill* in 1944.

A graphic story was told by Captain Ted Wright from Stockton in the port of Newcastle. Ted was in the four-masted barque *Garthpool* (formerly *Juteopolis*, but now under the ownership of Sir William Garthwaite). It was 1922 and Ted had been in this ship since 1918, having joined her in New York. In those four years she took him to Newcastle, the West Coast of South America, Durban, Newcastle, West Coast, Cape Town, Western Australia, Mauritius and Port Lincoln, South Australia. Her skipper, Captain Aitkinson, according to Ted was a very old man and advised not to go to sea again when they reached Port Lincoln. He took no notice, saying there would be no funeral expenses if he died at sea. The apprentices took it in turns sitting with him and when at sea he had a stroke and died. The mate, Mr Collins, took *Garthpool* on to Falmouth and was then appointed master and ordered to Sunderland to unload. Ted told me of what happened as they left Falmouth.

There was very heavy weather at sea and the tug master advised us not to go out or we would 'cop it', but the new skipper was eager to please the owner and deliver the cargo.
    I was on lookout when we towed to sea. With the wind dead aft we had the fore and main lower topsail and fore upper topsail set, to help us along. It was dark with heavy rainsqualls when suddenly I caught sight of a green navigation light abeam and realised we had overtaken the tug. I rang the bell on the fo'c'sle head but through the screaming wind it could not be heard. I made my way aft along the catwalk as the deck was awash from rail to rail. I reported to the skipper but by this time the tug had cast off the towline as we could have dragged him over. The towline was dragging astern and at this point we heard a crash aloft. The chain sheet of the fore lower topsail had snapped and the sail

blew out. The flailing chain sheet severed the fore yard lift (20 mm wire) and the yard cockbilled [tilted upright]. This in turn broke the fore brace pendant and all sail on the foremast was shredded by the wind. The skipper did not want to send anyone aloft with all the chain and wire thrashing about and all we could do was to let her charge along. 'All hands' was called but there was not much anyone could do. We found there were no rockets on board and the only way we could signal our distress was to fly our ensign upside down. We were in shallow water now and in 20 minutes we would be on Start Point. Incredibly, a few minutes later the wind changed and we could alter course. At this point a Dutch tug came up and offered a tow but claimed salvage rights. We had no choice but to accept. The tug tried to fire rockets to us with a heaving line attached but the wind kept blowing them back. The tug was getting short of fuel and signalled that as we were out of immediate danger he would pick us up in the morning. Next day we rigged up a buoy with a small sail on it to sail a line over to the tug. He towed us to Weymouth. A court case followed over the salvage rights but the court ruled no salvage as the first towing attempt failed. The original tug thought we were lost as she had been into all the south coast ports looking for us. It had been a close call and the water was so shallow the cast off towline which had been trailing in the water had picked up sand and there were small crabs clinging to it when we got it on board.

It often happened that a sailing ship under tow ran down or capsized her tug. If the wind was fair it was usual to set some sail to help the tug along, and by the time the sailer was in a position to cast off she would have much of her canvas set. The most recent mishap of this nature was in 1946 when the four-masted barque *Passat*, setting off on her first postwar voyage to Australia, pulled over her tug, drowning eight men and one woman. (This incident is described in Chapter 8.)

Ballast

A factor more greatly influencing the economic viability of the sailing ship than is commonly realised was the ballast that she had to carry in order to remain upright if she had no cargo. From 1900 onwards, the freights offered to sailing ships began to be eroded more and more by the competition from powered vessels. Sailing ships had to make many voyages in ballast, without freight, to reach a destination where cargo might be available.

Ballast could be any dense material such as sand or building rubble. It came at a cost. It had to be purchased and it had to be loaded and unloaded. Very few of the latter-day sailing ships had water ballast tanks; those that did sacrificed cargo space, as the tanks took up the same space empty as when full. Not only that, water, being less dense than rock or sand, took up a greater space than the equivalent mass of solid ballast. The barque *Winterhude* had ballast tanks that could take 900 tons of sea water. In a vessel that could carry at the most 2500 tons of cargo this was a costly reduction in carrying capacity. It could, however, be pumped out in five or six hours using donkey-powered pumps. Some water ballast tanks had removable sections that allowed cargo to be loaded inside them.

Solid ballast was dumped into the hold by shore crane but the crew almost always had to dig it out, a process that could take weeks. This was prolonged by the fact that not all the ballast could be removed at the one time, as some cargo had to be loaded to maintain stability. This could mean that the ship had to be moved several times between the ballast grounds and the loading wharf. The type of ballast always interested the crew, as they knew what would give them a hard time when it had to be removed. Large pieces of brickwork or masonry defied being shovelled and had to be picked up by hand. Materials containing clay set hard after a three-month voyage and had to be chipped out with a pick. A cane basket holding about 400 kilograms (880 pounds) was used. A gantline went from the basket to a single block suspended in the rigging above the hold and down—if the crew was fortunate—to a steam winch. If a donkey was not carried or the skipper begrudged the use of coal, then a hand-turned dolly winch was the only mechanical aid.

Consider the process. The average large sailing ship of 3000 tons required up to 1200 tons of ballast. This required 3000 baskets to be filled and dumped. At some ports, as at many of the Spencer Gulf grain ports, ships were required to discharge their ballast at offshore ballast grounds, which might be several miles out to sea. The sailer could usually sail out to these if the wind was favourable. It might take two or three trips but it only cost the sweat of the crew. (See Alf Freestone's story about the ship *Grace Harwar* in Chapter 7.)

Off the West Coast the great depth of water close inshore allowed the ballast to be dumped overboard in the roadstead. At other destinations it was discharged onto the wharf and taken away in wagons to be used as landfill. This also cost money. Large areas of the western foreshore at Stockton, in the port of Newcastle, New South Wales, have been reclaimed from the river with ballast. In the Newcastle Chamber of Commerce report of 1899 it was stated that 'more ships come to Newcastle in ballast than the rest of Australia put together'. In 1907 about 2 million tonnes arrived there. This of course was because of the massive coal exports from this port, which attracted thousands of sailing ships and kept them in business until well into the twentieth century. The rubble from the San Francisco earthquake of 1906 provided the ballast for sailing ships unable to get a cargo out of that port. It was provided 'at no charge' and much of it ended up at Stockton. When the disposal of ballast in Sydney Harbour became a problem, Port Hacking became the dumping ground. Erkki Makkonen, a Finnish seaman in the four-masted barque *Pamir*, surprised me when he told me that when this ship loaded wheat in Sydney in 1934, they dumped the ballast into the harbour. *Pamir* had to 'strike' her t'gallant masts in order to pass under the newly completed Sydney Harbour Bridge to get to the wheat wharves and the great depth of the harbour in this vicinity upstream of the bridge (60 metres/200 feet) may have made dumping acceptable. It certainly would not be allowed today.

The stowing of ballast was of no less importance than stowing other bulk cargo. The same precautions had to be taken. Captain Jim Gaby told me of the problems associated with 'Callao shingle', which it appears was the only ballast available from the port of Callao. It consisted of smooth flat pebbles, dredged from the harbour bed directly into the ship. The British Board of Trade issued a notice to shipmasters recommending that great care be taken in securing this slippery cargo. Transverse as well as longitudinal shifting boards to prevent movement were required and the shingle had to be covered and tommed down. Jim said that a notice board at the Consul's office in Callao carried a list of ships that left loaded with this ballast and were never seen again. He recalled that the well-known full-rigged ship *Dalgonar* was lost in this way. One of the Craig barques of New Zealand actually carried a cargo free out of Callao rather than load Callao shingle as ballast.

It was claimed by Sam Hort of Sydney, who had considerable experience in the large wooden American schooners, that some could sail without ballast while others had permanent ballast, floored over. This was possible because they were not as lofty as square riggers, nor did they carry the press of sail that square riggers did. They also had a hard bilge. Albert Wargren, a Danish apprentice in the four-masted barque *Abraham Rydberg*, claimed that this ship, because her masts were not as high as many others, could be sailed in from the ballast grounds empty if the wind was light and fair.

A final story about ballast comes from Fred Maerz, who sailed in several of the Laeisz ships. He was seaman in the four-masted barque *Lisbeth* on a voyage from Santos in Brazil to Port Victoria, South Australia, in 1927. He relates:

> We could not get a cargo in Santos and decided to head for Port Victoria where we were certain to get a grain charter for the UK. For some reason the cost of ballast was high but we were offered coffee beans in sacks, obviously from a glut on the market. The master had to sign an undertaking that the coffee would be dumped at sea and not sold at our destination. We dumped a large proportion of our ballast but unofficial deals were struck with customs and port officials that resulted in everyone concerned having a supply of coffee for many years. The crew emptied the straw out of their mattresses and filled them with coffee beans which went with us back to Germany!

Maintenance

Not all jobs in a sailing ship consisted of work on deck or aloft with rope or canvas, 'working the ship'. This work, also known as 'sailorising', was what usually attracted boys to sea, and is still the attraction for those who make voyages in contemporary sailing ships. It was not the only ingredient needed in the making of a sailor, however.

Along with sailorising there were jobs that took place out of sight and sound of sea and sky, devoid of glamour and usually detested—cleaning the bilges was one. Usually performed in port between discharging a cargo and loading, it required a strong constitution. At some stage water would get into the hull, usually from the deck or perhaps from a slight leak in one of the hull plates. Above the bottom plating on the topside of the frames forming the main skeleton of the ship was a removable flooring called the ceiling. Remnants of bagged or bulk cargo found its way into this space. Coal dust was usually present, although one of the least offensive elements. Guano was bad but grain, when in contact with stale bilge water, fermented and generated putrid fumes that even blistered paintwork. And there were always the rotting remains of dead rats.

Temperatures in the airless dungeon-like hold could reach well in excess of 40°C (105°F) in places like the Gulf of Mexico, the West Coast or Spencer Gulf as the crew ladled the swill into buckets and hoisted them out one by one to be tipped over the side. Clean sea water was hauled back again to wash out the dregs before the next part of the process took place. The hull plating now exposed was inspected and chipped clean of rust with a chipping hammer. This tool, known to seamen the world over since the introduction of steel in shipbuilding, had two peins at right angles to each other. The user repeatedly hit the affected area with one side of the hammer and then the other, causing the flakes of rust to be dislodged—and causing a din far in excess of what is regarded in industry today as an acceptable noise level. The immense area of a ship's hull made chipping rust, both inside and outside, a never-ending job. The exposed steel plating was painted with red lead paint, mixed by the carpenter from red lead oxide and linseed oil.

Another material found in the paint locker was white lead. Mixed with melted-down tallow, its highly poisonous nature made it an effective anti-fouling agent. Along with red lead, this more or less determined the colour that ships were painted below the water line. Known as 'boot topping', it also extended a metre or so above the water line. Made into a thick paint with linseed oil, it was used to treat steel standing rigging against rust—very effectively. I was in Mariehamn several years ago on board the four-masted barque *Pommern*, now owned by the Mariehamn Municipality, when the rigging screws were being inspected for signs of deterioration. The threads had last been coated with white lead in the summer of 1945. They were in perfect condition.

On deck and on the hull, paintwork deteriorated rapidly and rust stains were always present. The constant pounding of the sea removed the paint that was applied when the ship was in port, and rust formed quickly in the salty environment. Paintwork was cleaned by washing or scrubbing it down with 'soda'. I have had conflicting definitions of this substance—some said it was caustic soda, others said it was washing soda. Whatever it was, it was highly effective on paintwork and skin alike. As seamen's hands were usually covered with cuts, blisters and abrasions from handling the rope, wires and chains of a sailer's working gear, this simple job was painful and detested. In British ships the word 'soogeeing' (from the Indian term *sugee moogee*) was used to describe the task.

Timber was stripped of paint, varnish or built-up coats of linseed oil by the sand and canvas method. It used three inexpensive ingredients—sand, old scraps of sail canvas formed into a pad, and a great deal of effort. The detested soda was included at times. The sand was used wet and the process was surprisingly effective. When a nitrate cargo was carried, a few bags were always purloined to be used in place of soda. An extract from Jack Horward's diary of his voyage in *Archibald Russell* in 1939 describes the process.

> *Friday, May 19, 1939* The whole of the port watch have been put to scrubbing the teak railings and fife rails this morning—cruel work in such cold weather. We have to dip pieces of sailcloth into strong caustic soda and rub it on to the varnish, then rub with sand and canvas and finally wash with icy salt water. Everyone's hands are already raw and blistered from handling wet ropes, so that the soda causes great pain. Then having to plunge them continually into sea water a few degrees above freezing makes it so much worse. We all hate it and curse constantly.

Desmond Fisher, steward in *Pamir* on her last voyage from Australia in 1949, stated that the second mate was a 'horror':

He had a deck boy and an ordinary seaman 'soogeeing' the main mast down in the Southern Ocean with salt water. It was so cold the water froze on the mast. When the matter was reported to the Captain he ordered the ridiculous practise to be stopped immediately.

Rightly or wrongly, in pre-war years this was an established practice; one must suspect that the militancy of some of the crew on this voyage had something to do with the captain's intervention.

The treatment of decks has often been misinterpreted by writers of sea stories. The merchant sailer had no use for the 'scrubbed decks' so often described. Before going to sea, many ships had their decks painted with a mixture of linseed oil and Stockholm tar. Both substances had a time-honoured place in a windjammer's paint locker, being universal preservatives. The life of rope was prolonged by Stockholm tar and seizings were always painted with it. One of the first aromas encountered when stepping onto the deck of a sailing ship arose from this substance. It was even used with a ribbon of old sailcloth to bind small wounds. The mixture of Stockholm tar and linseed oil protected the deck timbers from drying out, but gave them a dark oily appearance. The poop deck, the domain of master and mates, would receive better or more frequent treatment, and might be treated with linseed oil without the Stockholm tar.

In addition, the decks needed to be kept wet to keep their timbers swollen and watertight. So the daily task of washing down the decks was really one of wetting down the deck, and not necessarily done for the sake of cleanliness. The ships that feature in this book were steel-hulled but they had timber decks and sea water was always used, even in port, as salt is an excellent preservative and fresh water causes rot.

I have always been amazed at the ignorance of some owners of wooden boats, even those who purport to have knowledge of traditional craft. I was once associated with the small topsail schooner *New Endeavour*, which sailed out of Sydney Harbour in the seventies. She spent much of her time tethered to the quayside where one of the daily chores was to hose down her decks late in the day to make her attractive for the social groups that frequently chartered her. The water came from a wharf faucet and, added to the rain that fell on her decks over the years, was responsible for her eventual demise. The extremely good intentions of the working crew were offset by the fact that they had no knowledge of the fact that salt water should have been used, even though less convenient. Most wooden vessels of this type would have had 'salt stops', cavities under the deck scuppers that were filled with salt to dissolve in the rainwater that always crept through deck planking.

Likewise the practice of holystoning the decks was not a matter of scrubbing them to make them clean. The holystone, described in many books, was a large block of sandstone used as an abrasive device. It removed the built-up coats of linseed oil and tar and also the split and deteriorated surface of the deck planks. It was also used to remove the moss and algae that grew on decks which had been immersed in sea water for a long time. There are several explanations for the derivation of this word. That it resembled a large bible is least likely, as holystones came in all sizes and shapes. More likely the name comes from the fact that the stone was used by the sailor in a kneeling position, or that an old church being demolished originally provided a supply of sandstone blocks for this purpose.

Brass and copper fittings were polished with a material called 'bathbrick', a slab of compressed silicaceous silt, a very fine abrasive, which was also a domestic knife cleaner. It derived its name from the manufacturer, Bath & Co. A piece of old sailcloth was moistened with water, rubbed on the brick and then on to the fitting being polished.

Very few of the later sailing ships, even in the 1930s, had generators for electric light. Kerosene was used for lighting in later years, with a variety of other fuels used for various reasons. British sailing ships early in the century used Colza oil (of vegetable origin) or 'galley slush'. As the name implies the latter was old cooking fat, usually rancid and with many inclusions. The red and green navigation lights were fuelled with kerosene or a paraffin wax called Cero wax. The lamps were taken to the galley stove where the wax was heated up so that it could be poured into them. In large ships with a raised fo'c'sle deck the navigation lamps were mounted inside light houses, large cylindrical housings usually with a copper or brass domed top. They were accessible from the lamp room beneath and the seaman given the task of lamp trimmer was responsible for lighting them and making sure they remained lit. They were lit in the shelter of the lamp room and a hoisting device used to lift the lit lamp into position. The lamp burned no brighter than several candles but the light was magnified by the glass lens in the lantern. The heat of the lamp kept the wax in a molten state. Smaller ships carried removable brass lamps fitted to wooden housings that were secured to the for'ard shrouds or to a steel structure just for'ard of the shrouds. These were taken to a sheltered position where the lamp could be lit out of the wind. Navigation lights were not always lit, as the later sailing ships often traversed areas of ocean away from the main trade routes and kerosene and wax cost money.

The rigging of a sailing ship required constant maintenance and was the domain of ABs assisted by ordinary seamen and apprentices. It was supervised by the bosun or third mate. Heavy wire stays could be replaced at sea and masts could be struck to carry out repairs. Remember there was no electricity for power tools.

If a weakness was observed aloft it was repaired at once, even at night. Ratlines were every sailor's responsibility. They carried a length of marline or spun yarn in their pocket and if a siezing appeared to be frayed or worn it was fixed. No one had to tell them to do it for they knew that lives depended on it. A sheath knife was always worn on the belt in the middle of the back as it did not get caught on anything in this position. The watch on deck in daylight was not allowed to hang around waiting for something to happen. They painted, chipped rust, soogeed, and did whatever the mate found for them.

In addition to maintenance and working the ship, that is, trimming, setting and taking in sail, there were other routine procedures that all able members of the crew had to perform. They were 'lookout', 'wheel' and 'police'.

Lookout

Unlike the bridge on modern ships, the view for'ard from the poop and even from the midships bridge deck was largely obscured by the lower sails, masts and the maze of rigging leading down from aloft. It was from aft that a ship was conned. This evolved from the fact that the rudder and hence the steering position was at the rear of the ship. A seaman was stationed on the fo'c'sle head and was required to report anything of note such as other ships, land, lights, icebergs and so on. The person and the task were both termed 'lookout'. In modern ships, radar has given this role less importance, although the complete reliance on this navigation aid has resulted in many maritime disasters.

In heavy weather the fo'c'sle head was inundated by heavy seas and lookout was kept from the top of the for'ard deckhouse. The time on lookout was one or two hours, and at night it was tempting to take a nap, and easy to unintentionally fall asleep. The watch officer, mindful of this, often took a walk for'ard, especially if a landfall was imminent. In high southern latitudes it was essential for lookout to be kept night and day to report on icebergs. While on the topic of icebergs, it was usual to lower a thermometer overside to test the temperature of the water, for an iceberg could lower the temperature of the sea for many miles around. Experienced skippers claimed they could 'smell' ice. Every half hour the ship's time was struck on the bell on the poop by the 'policeman' or one of the apprentices on watch, taking the time from the charthouse clock which was adjusted each day when the day's run produced a new longitude. The lookout repeated this on the large bell that all ships carried at the break of the fo'c'sle. Accompanying this was his shouted response, 'All's well, and lights burning bright'. Bells were always 'struck' and never 'rung', except when at anchor in a fog.

'Police' or 'policeman'

All hands took turns at 'police' duties. They acted as messenger for the mate on deck, performed the duties of timekeeper and called the watch ten minutes before it was required on deck. The night watches were not required to carry out deck work if there was no sail handling to be done, as was the case during the day. In fine weather they would be required to hang around on the after deck within earshot of the mate and it was possible to catch some sleep on the main hatch or in the lee of a deckhouse. In heavy weather when the deck was awash they could remain in the fo'c'sle until called or under the fo'c'sle head. Of course this was an opportunity to hop into one's bunk and have a decent sleep. The main job of the 'policeman' was to get the watch out on deck without delay; if it took too long the privilege of staying in the fo'c'sle would be stopped for the remainder of the voyage and the 'policeman' would find himself in hot water.

Steering

Taking the helm, taking a trick, or just taking the wheel, was probably the job that had the most responsibility attached to it. In heavy weather, indifferent steering could cause the ship to broach to, which almost always caused dismasting or even worse. Most of the last large sailing ships built in the twentieth century had double wheels amidships, as well as an emergency steering station aft, apart from most of the last great four-masted barques built in Great Britain, which still had a single wheel right aft on the poop. A few were fitted with wheelhouses, a steel shell enclosing the steering position on all sides except for'ard, but most were open to the elements. This wheelhouse was to protect the wheel and steering gear, as much as the helmsman, from the following seas that could mount up in a gale and crash onto the poop. With this type of steering, the impact of seas on the rudder could cause a kick that could throw the helmsman over the top of the wheel. Rope lanyards were improvised to hold the helmsman in place and a second hand would help out in the position known as 'lee wheel'. The main helmsman always stood on the weather side of the wheel. The helmsman received his orders from the watch officer and talking on duty was not permitted unless it was to repeat an order to show that it was understood.

Captain J. Murray Lindsay of Perth, Western Australia, author of four books about his time at sea, gave me this description of his first time at the wheel in his first ship, the four-masted barque *Bengairn*, in 1915.

In the South-East Trades one afternoon in my watch on deck and with a chipping hammer in my hand, I was cleaning rust off a bulwark stanchion when 'Taffy' the Welsh second mate called me aft to the poop. 'Indeed now, Lindsay, if you want to learn to steer, go and take the lee wheel for an hour.' I almost trembled with excitement as I took hold of the big wheel on the lee side, opposite Paddy Whelan who was steering on the weather side. To a beginner it was an awesome sight, yet a majestic one as I looked up at the four masts of white canvas in front of me, all straining at their sheets and tacks to drive the ship along at a speed of eight knots. Close in front of me was the binnacle and steering compass. Paddy gave me the course, 'SE by S'. Even though there was a man holding the weather side of the wheel I could feel the rush of water past the rudder and immediately in physical contact with the wind and sea. I had both of these elements in my hands plus control of a great ship. With the wind free on the port side she only required a few spokes of the wheel to keep her on course.

Paddy gave me a few words of advice. 'Always remember, sonny, when steering a ship, the less wheel you use the better, just give her enough to hold her.' Unknown to the second mate and after a few minutes to let me get the feel of the ship, he took his hands off the wheel and let me handle it myself,—until I let her come up into the wind, shaking the weather leeches! 'What the hell are you doing, Lindsay?' Taffy's black eyes flashed in disapproval as Paddy took over again and brought the ship back on course. Through time and experience I became a proficient helmsman and took my regular 'trick' with the rest of the crew. My two hours at the wheel became the most enjoyable time in my training as a seaman. There was always the element of challenge, depending on where you were, the weather and most of all the trim of the sails. A good officer can trim the sails so that the ship almost steers herself; it's a matter of balance. A mate not so good can give the helmsman a hell of a two hours. A ship is either running free with a fair wind and steering a compass course, close hauled with a leading wind and sailing 'full and by' by which is meant nearly a head wind and with the yards on the backstays, but keeping the sails full to give her speed through the water, or 'by the wind', when the helmsman keeps the weather leeches of the mizzen royals shaking and hopes the wind will veer enough to make a compass course. Running with the wind aft and with the yards squared is the greatest test of a good helmsman. If there is a big sea running the ship will surf on top of a big wave and try to come broadside to both wind and wave. This is called 'broaching to', a highly dangerous situation, running the risk of having her hatches stove in and her decks completely under water or being dismasted.

Later ships with a raised midships bridge had the main steering wheels in this position. It was necessary to face aft when steering 'by the wind' in order to see the mizzen royal leeches.

The poop deck was hallowed ground reserved for officers; seamen were only allowed on it when a duty had to be performed. In fact the area abaft the main mast in a three master or the mizzen in a four master was considered out of bounds for the crew. The poop itself was further segregated in that the weather side was the master's domain when he was on deck; not even another officer would trespass unless called up to windward by the master. The seaman heading to or leaving the wheel always used the lee ladder from the main deck. Captain Murray Lindsay stated that as smoking was forbidden on the poop many helmsmen chewed tobacco; a spittoon was provided beside the wheel and it was the job of the most junior apprentice to clean this out each morning. Just as the poop was sacred so too was the fo'c'sle, and no officer, not even the master, would enter without asking permission. I have been told of unpopular officers being thrown bodily out on the deck when this courtesy was breached.

The idlers

In every sailing ship and, indeed, every steamship, there were those in the crew who did not work the standard watches of four hours on and four hours off, or whatever hours were favoured by that ship's nationality. They were the cook, steward, carpenter, sail maker and bosun, if one were carried. Known as the 'idlers', they worked from six in the morning to six at night, or even longer when daylight hours extended beyond these limits.

In the doldrums and trade winds, when there was little chance of an emergency, some men from each watch were put on 'day work', meaning they worked all through the daylight hours and had all night in. They carried out maintenance work about the decks and aloft or assisted the sail maker or carpenter. Bob Ryan, a seaman in the 1948 voyage of *Passat* from Port Victoria, told me that the mate even had them over the side chipping rust and painting as the ship made 12 knots in the trade winds. This was, of course, on the weather side.

The carpenter

The tasks performed by the carpenter, universally known as 'Chippy', were many and varied. Wood was not the only material he worked with. He tended to be a general mechanic or handyman who could use the forge to shape metal fittings that required replacement, and carry out repairs on winches and the donkey engine, if one were carried. Replacing damaged deck planks, and making new spars (several rough baulks of timber were usually carried for this emergency), were tasks undertaken at sea. When there were no urgent repairs the chippy made or rebuilt the blocks used in the running rigging, and it was his job to oil all the sheaves and blocks aloft in the rigging. It was also his job to sound the fresh water tanks and bilges and report the level to the mate. In fact, for anything at all that needed fixing, the carpenter was called.

The extent of the resourcefulness that was a necessary part of sailing ship life is illustrated by an example shown to me in Åland Maritime Museum. It was a ship's wheel rebuilt by chippy (later Captain) Gunnar Ecklund in 1937 from scraps of wood and simple hand tools after it had been smashed by a rogue sea. It looked as if it had just come from the makers.

Another such carpenter was Ålander Axel Stenross. Gil Robertson from Port Lincoln, a close friend of Axel's, gave me the following anecdotes. Axel, like many Åland boys, went to sea in the small wooden schooners that carried goods around the Baltic. He then became apprenticed as a shipwright in his father's shipyard before going to sea in 1924 as ship's carpenter in Gustaf Erikson's *Olivebank*. Erikson had only just bought the ship and she was lying at Liverpool, at this stage carrying the name *Caledonia* given to her by her previous owners. Axel, along with the master and crew, went over to England to take her to sea, travelling by train from London to Liverpool and arriving there at 5 am. There were three other sailing ships in port at the time and they could not find their ship. Finally Axel went on board one of them and found the ship's bell with the name *Olivebank* cast into it. As it was Gustaf Erikson's custom to give his ships back their original name, the first thing the master wanted to do was restore her name. Axel found some brass letters which he attached to the bow plating port and starboard, and these she carried until her sinking in September 1939. The ship was fairly run down as on her previous voyage no carpenter had been in the crew. Most of her blocks were in need of replacement and Axel set about repairing damage and making new ones. The only timber on board was Baltic pine, far too soft for blocks, so Axel went ashore and searched the nearby woodland for suitable trees. Several were felled, and after milling Axel started on the 1008 blocks that he subsequently made.

Axel must have been a top tradesman, as he negotiated a special wage with Erikson, higher than normally paid to a ship's carpenter. He also got Erikson to insure his tools, something unheard of in any ship at that time. He also negotiated a two-year rather than a three-year signing on period. This enabled him to pay off in Port Lincoln after two voyages and start his own boatyard. This was March 1927. Another Finn, sail maker Frank Laakso, signed off with him. They worked together building boats for many years. Over the next 50 years Axel's name became legend around Port Lincoln as he built many fine yachts for the local inhabitants. Axel retained a good relationship with the other Erikson sailing ships that visited Port Lincoln. Some time after he left *Olivebank*, her 'tween deck planking, of pitch pine planks about 6 metres long, 30 cm wide and 6 cm thick (20 feet x 13 inches x 2¼ inches), had to be replaced. The best of the old planks were taken to Port Lincoln for Axel to use in his boat building. After *Herzogin Cecilie* had her boiler explosion in 1935, the steel remains of her boiler house were taken to Port Lincoln for Axel. He used this steel in many ways; more than one sailing boat he built had a centreplate made from it. Axel used to send his worn broad-axes back to the makers in Finland, on board visiting windjammers, to have new tool-steel cutting edges welded on. Gustaf Erikson always thought he could entice Axel back to Mariehamn. A standard instruction given to his masters setting out for Spencer Gulf was 'Bring Axel back!' Erikson even offered to pay Axel's fees for navigation school and offered him a job as master in one of his ships if he did return.

The high regard in which Axel was held by the town of Port Lincoln resulted in his boatyard being placed on a heritage list and ultimately becoming the Axel Stenross Maritime Museum.

Sail maker

The sail maker, or 'Sails', was naturally enough another essential position in a sailing ship. After a ship had been fitted out with sails at the time of building, the sail maker on board carried out all subsequent repairs as well as making replacements. New bolts of canvas were carried in the ship's stores and when weather permitted the main deck would become the loft, with not only the sail maker hard at work but others recruited into the task of hand sewing the many hundreds of metres of seams. In smaller ships the master often became the sail maker. He would mark and cut out the sails, with ABs or others with the ability doing the sewing. Many sail makers learnt their trade in this manner.

Reg Rudd, an apprentice in the four-masted barque *Lauriston* from 1915, made these comments on sail making:

> When the weather fined up the captain and sail maker set about making a new mizzen topsail. The sail was drawn out in chalk on the deck, and then the canvas cloths were cut to this pattern, which the sail maker started to sew together. Jimmy, one of the other apprentices and I, were given the job of helping him and he taught us how to use the palm and needle and waxed thread. We soon picked it up and soon were going great guns, 6 stitches to the inch, under the sail maker's watchful eye. Then we made grommets for the eyelets and sewed them in and helped to sew the boltrope around the sail. The sail maker did all the difficult jobs.
>
> He made himself a pair of white cotton duck trousers and he showed us how to make them. We each made a pair and then the carpenter showed us how to make sea boots out of the greasy leather that was used for chafing patches on the sails

Mary Lang, a passenger in the four-masted barque *L'Avenir* in the 1930s, makes further comments on the subject of sail making in Chapter 7.

Streaming the log

This was the term given to the procedure of obtaining the ship's speed and distance run. The 'log' was a wooden float connected to a long line, designed to remain where it was thrown into the sea while the ship ran on. A crew member, generally an apprentice, held over his head a reel on which this log line was wound, allowing the line to run out. Tied into the line was a series of knots at appropriate intervals which were counted by the mate or second mate as they ran over the rail. A third crew member with a 14-second sand glass called out when to start counting and when to stop. The number of knots counted gave the ship's speed in knots, or nautical miles per hour. This device was used well into the twentieth century, and eventually replaced by a 'patent log', which used a helical vaned spinner which rotated on the end of a long line; its revolutions were counted by a mechanical device mounted on the taffrail. The speed and distance run are indicated on a dial. The term knot is still used and means 'one nautical mile per hour'. In spite of the conveniences of the metric system the nautical mile is also still in use; it is the distance subtended by one minute of arc at the earth's surface.

Donkey man

A piece of equipment rarely described in the literature of sail was the donkey boiler or donkey engine. Used to provide auxiliary power to help the crew with heavy tasks such as hoisting yards, raising the anchor and working cargo or ballast, it was by no means universal. Even when carried it was not always used, as fuel was expensive and muscles were cheap. The donkey boiler was usually a vertical thimble tube type, generally installed in the for'ard deckhouse. The funnel or smokestack and even the top of the boiler is sometimes seen protruding through the roof of the deckhouse in photographs of ships in port, but at sea the stack was unshipped to prevent it fouling the main staysail sheets. Some ships had a portable boiler mounted on skids that could be moved around the decks when working cargo. If no boiler was carried, one could be hired in port or the shore gang brought their own. In this case it was left on the quayside next to the ship and its winch connected by blocks to a position over the hatch. In the latter years diesel and hot bulb engines began to appear, mainly for working cargo. The responsibility of lighting the boiler, raising and maintaining steam was generally that of the carpenter; otherwise an ordinary seaman with very little training would be assigned to the task and referred to as the 'donkey man'.

Such a seaman was Birger Lindeman, who sailed in the four-masted barque *Lawhill* during the early forties. He described the procedure to me.

In *Lawhill* we had a small donkey boiler, two old steam winches (museum pieces) and an old diesel winch, a type of engine called a hot bulb engine. To start this engine we had to put a fairly large blowlamp on a cast iron bulb or hollow ball fixed to the top of the cylinder head. When it was red hot you grabbed the starting handle and turned the engine over. It usually started first time, that is if you remembered to turn the fuel on. To start up the donkey boiler, the fire was first laid with wood and when well alight, coal shovelled on. When the steam had risen to the required pressure it was ready for use, and that's where the hard work came in. To keep the fire going so that the steam pressure did not drop, it was slicing, raking, more coal to shovel on, ashes to clean out and at the same time keep an eye on the feed water gauges to make sure the water level did not drop too far down. I can't remember the exact pressure we worked at but [it] was between 90–110 pounds to the square inch. The safety valve blew at 115 pounds per square inch. We sometimes used sea water in the boiler but wherever possible fresh water was used in port. Sea water is not recommended as salt scale builds up inside the boiler acting as a heat shield and it gets more difficult to keep up pressure. This means more work for the stoker and more coal is used. A boiler clean was very costly. As far as I know the boiler was only inspected when the ship had a survey, which was not often. *Lawhill's* boiler was not big enough, especially when heaving up the anchor. She had a complicated chain drive from the for'ard winch which would race full bore and the links kept jumping out of the wheels and by the time the chain got to the windlass it was barely moving it with the mate calling the donkey man and the donkey boiler all the names he could think of.

Birger's description would be typical of many I have heard about sailing ship donkey boilers. Eb Anderson spoke of a similar situation in *Hougomont.*

Four or five hands were kept busy hauling buckets of water from the sea to top up the feed water tank. Another four or five lined up along the deck adjacent to the chain drive from the drum protruding from the boiler house to where it went around the windlass under the fo'c'sle head. Armed with capstan bars or pieces of wood they wrestled with the moving chain to stop its two parts becoming entangled or jumping off the drive drum. They weren't much of a labour saving device!

Engineers would be appalled by the use of salt water in a boiler. Even fresh water needs treatment to remove dissolved impurities. The built-up salt caused a massive heat barrier and could lead to parts of the boiler becoming overheated. How there were not more boiler explosions recorded is difficult to explain. The rigid government regulations in force today seemed to be unheard of, or unheeded. The most recent explosion recorded in a sailing ship was in the four-masted barque *Herzogin Cecilie* in Belfast in 1935. Two men were killed and extensive damage caused to the ship and rigging.

Working cargo

The articles signed and agreed to by seamen in most ships did not preclude the handling of cargo and thus, wherever the local port regulations did not require labour to be provided by the shore authorities, the ship master could make big savings in running costs. While shore cranes always loaded coal, for example, it was often shovelled out by the crew into baskets and hoisted up on deck by dolly winch. Even if a donkey engine was carried there was no guarantee that the skipper would allow its use. Where regulations required a shore gang to be employed, the crew chipped, painted and worked on board as usual, except that watches were not worked. The working day started at 6 am or daybreak, whichever was earlier, and ended at 6 pm or dusk.

The most notable example of cargo handling by ship's crews was the coal taken to the West Coast of South America. Just as Australian grain kept the sailing ship in business during the twenties and thirties, so did Australian coal provide a living in the two or three decades beforehand. Along with coal mined in the United Kingdom, most of it ended up in South America, usually on the West Coast, where it fuelled the railways or the steamships that traded to those parts. Thousands of sailing ships with a bellyful of Welsh or European coal crossed the Atlantic in a south-westerly direction to deliver it to ports such as Buenos Aires and Montevideo, or make the arduous west about rounding of Cape Horn to reach one of the many ports from Valdivia in the south of Chile to Guayaquil in Ecuador. The coal cargoes from Australia all came from Newcastle, New South Wales, and attracted most of the world's remaining sailing ships. There could be hundreds in port at the one time, lying three abreast at the Stockton tie-up wharves awaiting their turn to go to the coal loading cranes across the river at the 'Dyke'.

The last sailing ship to load coal in Newcastle was the *Forest Friend* in 1928. Most of those to whom I have spoken have told me about their experience with this cargo and the following is a composite of their stories.

The coal was brought to the wharf in rail wagons with tapered sides, which were actually hoppers on wheels. The hopper was lifted over the ship's hold by shore crane, a gate on the underside was opened and the contents fell into the ship. The truck held seven to eight tonnes and it required up to 400 truckloads to fill a large sailing ship. Naturally, the ship was enveloped by a pall of coal dust which found its way into every corner. Bunks, galley and saloon would have a fine coating of dust over all. From the mound of coal that built up in the bottom of the ship iron chutes were rigged so that shore gangs, known as 'trimmers', could shovel it out to the wings. A heavy cargo such as coal would not fill the hull space before the marks were reached, that is, the ship was as deep in the water as the Plimsoll mark allowed. To raise the centre of gravity, so that the ship was not too stiff, the coal was heaped up in the centre.

To stop the coal moving as the ship rolled, various precautions, necessary with any bulk cargo, were taken. Along the centre line of the ship, above the keelson, were steel pillars or stanchions supporting the 'tween and main decks. Heavy planks, known as shifting boards, were placed on edge between these stanchions and lashed to them. This divided the cargo into port and starboard components. In addition, it was usual to cover the coal with tarpaulins or old sails, held in place with further planks and tommed to the deck head or ship's side. In spite of these precautions it was not uncommon for the cargo to shift in heavy seas and survival required the crew to get below and shovel it back again, all the time facing the possibility of the cargo shifting further and burying them. Both watches were required. They had to get below through the forepeak and shovel hundreds of tonnes of coal uphill while the ship pitched and rolled and lay over at a severe angle. This allowed the seas to roll aboard, preventing any normal working of the ship.

Another hazard with coal was spontaneous combustion, which sometimes occurred when the coal was loaded wet. To detect increasing temperatures, a length of pipe was suspended vertically in the hold from the hatch coaming, the coal surrounding the pipe. During the voyage a hatch board would be removed and a thermometer lowered down the pipe. The carpenter usually performed this task. If, over several days, a rise in temperature was detected, or the coal started to smoulder, the only remedy was to hose it down. There have been many cases recorded of fires in coal cargoes leading to the abandoning of the ship when it was found that the smouldering coal could not be extinguished, and the pumping in of more water would have succeeded only in sinking the ship. The last sailing ship with fire in a coal cargo was the four-masted barque *Lawhill* in 1946 on the way to Bahia Blanca. She reached port and very little damage occurred.

On a lighter note, Eb Anderson relates that during his first voyage in the four-masted barque *Hougomont*, carrying a cargo of Welsh coal to Iquique, the mate ordered the cargo to be hosed down, not far from their destination. Eb suspects that this was the old trick of wetting down the coal to make it weigh heavier, thus creating a surplus which was sold privately by the master.

There were other tricks practised by masters and mates to generate a variance from the pit certificate that stated how much coal was loaded. Even if the coal had not been wetted it was possible to gain extra weight as it was discharged. The coal was shovelled into cane baskets, which were hoisted out of the hold onto scales on the deck. By wetting the baskets after they were weighed, a few extra ounces could be added to the next load.

Another trick made use of the long Pacific swells that rolled in to the West Coast ports. These South American ports, especially those where nitrates were mined, were quite primitive, with no shore facilities. All loading and unloading was carried out offshore, at quite exposed anchorages. The second mate, assisted by an apprentice who called out the weight, usually carried out the weighing of the coal. The local agent kept a close eye on the proceedings, but the apprentice was instructed to call out the weight as the ship started her slow rise over the next swell. The inertia of the basket of coal caused the scales to register more than they should. Doubtless the shore agent had his own tricks to dupe the Chilean railways of a percentage. It is unlikely that the Latin American traders were ignorant of what was going on, however. When water and stores were purchased for the return voyage they were provided at highly inflated prices.

The coal, once weighed, was hoisted out over the ship's side into barges, using two lower yards as derricks. These barges were quite large and were usually rowed by one or two *lancheros* (bargemen) with two long sweeps. Coal was valued so highly in this region that wherever the depth of water made it possible, local boatmen dragged nets and buckets around to retrieve any lumps that had fallen into the sea.

Thrift and parsimony

Nothing was ever wasted in a sailing ship. A complete culture evolved around this principle. The galley produced very little throwaway waste. Every morsel was consumed, for what was inedible to humans was fed to the pigs. When pigs were slaughtered their hair was shaved off to make paintbrushes. The fat skimmed from the surface of the water in which salt meat was cooked was used in many ways. While still fresh, or comparatively so, it was used in cooking, otherwise it was used as a lamp fuel or lubricant. The carpenter had many uses for this fat. Portions of masts that carried a hoisting yard had to be greased down. This essential task involved going aloft with a bucket of galley slush, as it was called, and coating the mast or track so that the yard would hoist easily or, more importantly, come down readily. The masts coated in this manner were the top, topgallant and royal masts. Another use was in lamps known as 'slush lamps'.

Old sails were never discarded. They might perhaps be sold by the master and the money pocketed, but only after they had outlived their usefulness as light weather sails. A 1914 story relating to this practice was told to me by Eben Anderson, then an apprentice in *Hougomont.*

> At the outbreak of the First World War, *Hougomont*, still under the command of Captain McDonald, was ordered to Hong Kong where she was to be sold. It was planned to rig her down and use her hull as an oil barge, bringing oil from North America under tow, to fuel the Far East units of the Royal Navy. When she arrived in Hong Kong much of her gear was sold off including her sails. Then came the cable informing Captain McDonald that she would not be hulked but would continue in service and to return to the U.K. The story circulating at Hardies was that the waterfront had to be combed for all the sold gear and sails, which in the meantime had increased in price. It was laughed at for years that she sailed back as a schooner rather than a square rigger!

Pulled apart sails could be used in various ways. Larger pieces were used as awnings or dodgers and smaller pieces to patch other sails. Every wind ship had canvas funnels that could be rigged in the tropics to take advantage of the rainstorms that dumped thousands of gallons of water on deck. The funnels collected water that ran from the poop, fo'c'sle and tops of deckhouses to top up the fresh water tanks that invariably ran low on prolonged voyages. In return for a plug of tobacco the sail maker might provide a seaman with old canvas from which to make clothes or perhaps a kit bag or ditty bag. Sand and canvassing consumed otherwise unusable fragments.

Rope and wire, likewise expensive commodities, were used many times over in various ways. Standing rigging properly maintained lasted for years but running rigging was subject to constant wear. Braces and halyards were 'end for ended' before wear became excessive. When a wire rope became worn the good sections were used where shorter pieces were adequate, such as footrope stirrups or strops for blocks. This is perhaps the best place to explain that the word 'rope' was used to describe the raw material and not, apart from several exceptions, to describe parts of the rigging. The word 'line' was preferred here, or else the actual descriptive name—brace, halyard, sheet and so on.

Old unlaid rope in short lengths had an important ongoing use. It was used to make 'baggywrinkle' or 'sennit'. Baggywrinkle was an anti-chafing material wound around standing rigging to minimise wear on sails that came in contact with these lines. Sennit was a woven or plaited length of rope yarn. As a five-strand plaiting it was used to attach the head of a sail to the jackstay along the yard. In this form it was known as a roband or roving. Whenever the weather was too bad to allow normal maintenance work on deck the watch was deployed on various tasks such as making baggywrinkle and sennit, usually under the fo'c'sle head, a comparatively dry area. Eb Anderson describes how baggywrinkle was made.

> To make 'baggywrinkle', two lengths of marline [a thin tarred cord] were strung out side by side, not quite touching, into which strands of unlaid rope about 200 mm long were woven. The rope strand was held horizontally underneath and at right angles to the stretched out marline. The ends were brought upwards and together and then pushed down between the two lengths of marline. Each successive strand was pushed

hard up against the last and eventually a ribbon began to form much like the mane of a horse. Many fathoms were needed. It was wound around the stay like a serving, the result being a soft cylindrical cladding surrounding the line. It was used on the lifts of the lower fixed yards to protect the lower topsails when aback. It also encased the fore, main and mizzen stays and sometimes the topmast stays to protect the courses and topsails when the yards were braced hard around. It also protected the spanker against the mizzen or jigger backstays when the wind was abaft the beam.

In later years, the use of sennit for robands appears to have been discontinued. Those questioned recall that rope yarns or short pieces of unusable rope were unlaid and used to secure the sail to the jackstay. Some had never heard of sennit.

Food

Food is a topic that most wind ship mariners would prefer to forget. It is not easy to relate the excesses of modern society to what the British Board of Trade regulations of those times proclaimed as 'full and plenty', but to keep everything in perspective the food consumed ashore by working men and women was also, by today's standards, plain and unimaginative. All my storytellers mention food or the lack of it, along with the sailorising, gales and foreign ports, indicating it was a major part of their existence. Most of those interviewed considered the cook, or 'doctor' as he was dubbed, to be the most important person on board, for when a sailing ship could be out of sight of land for 150 days a bad cook could affect harmony on board considerably. The steward lived aft with the officers and the domestic duties he performed were probably the least important. However, he was responsible for purchasing and issuing stores within the confines of a very tight budget and along with the cook always bore the brunt of the crew's dissatisfaction when stores ran low or the wrath of the skipper if the food bill was too high. The crew considered the theft of food fair game, and even though the stores were kept locked in the lazarette under the poop or saloon, and the key kept by the steward, it was still possible for extras to appear in the fo'c'sle or half deck. Such booty was always shared evenly.

I have been told many stories of raiding parties breaking in and making off with condensed milk or canned fruit after traversing the length of the ship from the forepeak, over or through the cargo. Dennis Adams, a well-known Australian marine artist, made a voyage in the *Lawhill* under the command of Artur Söderlund. Söderlund told him that as an AB in the same ship he was involved in another sort of raiding party. *Lawhill* was in Bordeaux and on the opposite quay was a great stack of wine barrels, under guard. A boat from *Lawhill* was lowered and equipped with many buckets and an auger. At nightfall the boat was silently manoeuvred under the quay and of course the obvious took place.

The quality and quantity of food varied from ship to ship, company to company and country to country. It is a topic that is difficult to discuss or compare as each individual had different expectations. While there were a few who actually said they enjoyed shipboard food, the only conclusion to be drawn from hundreds of interviews was that it was generally poor. It should be realised, however, that the sailing ship had no electricity or refrigeration. Even the water taken on in some ports was well below modern standards and many tales are told of the entire crew being affected by its bacterial inclusions.

During the competitive years of the emigrant clippers, food was more or less equal to that consumed ashore, at least for the passengers. Advertisements for passages to Australia contained references to the live cows carried and the fresh milk that would be available to first class passengers with small children. However, this book deals with the latter days of sail when running costs were cut to the bone and the seaman (at least in British ships) was considered to be at the lower end of the social scale. While the Board of Trade of Great Britain set minimum levels of sustenance for seamen, it had little control over the way its requirements were administered or how long a voyage would take. There were always some ship masters who were willing to take a risk on the quantity of food and water taken on board, particularly in out-of-the-way ports where prices were high. The quality of provisions purchased could result in a surplus in the ship's operating account and it was on this factor that some shipowners judged their masters, rather than the standard of their seamanship.

Various comments are made by my storytellers about the cook and this extract from Eben Anderson's long poem 'East-Nor-East' gives a humorous but inverted view of the sailing ship cook's ability. This verse covers the wishful thinking that was impossible to achieve in reality.

Thanks my friend, that suits my book,
My yarn is of an old sea cook.
An abler hand I've yet to meet
On galley stove or at fore sheet.
The bread he baked, the best of rooti,
Had everything, aye, even beauty.
No maggots in the harness cask
Could divert him from his task;
And he could make the worst provender
Sweet to palates, even tender.
We never heard a grizzler grouse
About the flavour of his scouse;
And as for—ugh—preserved potatoes,
Nil desperandum, he could bake those
In such a way one felt one must
At least enjoy the golden crust.
He mastered every kind of gash,
And we admired his cracker hash.
The sailor smiling in his bunk
Was dreaming of his dandyfunk.
He had a trick with minestrone,
Dried vegies and a salt beef bone.
On Thursdays we had pork and beans

Food for Kings and fare for Queens.
The stockfish soaked in the wash deck tub
He'd pound next day with limejuice rub
'Til it tasted like a lemon sole.
On felt that one could eat it whole
And oh! his lovely Sunday duff!
We got our whack, that's fair enough.
The ample ration they allowed
Was feathery light as a cirrus cloud.
The crew, they all went cock-a-hoop
When they scoffed their plates of split pea soup,
Cream-like, flavoured with salt pork,
It almost called for knife and fork.

Eben Anderson

Regardless of the victualling philosophies, all ships relied on one basic ingredient, salt meat. Either pork, beef or, no doubt, horse, it fed the world's seamen for centuries and was still in use when the last stories in this book were acted out. It was delivered to the ship in wooden casks of about 30-gallon capacity and relied on a strong brine solution to maintain bacteria at acceptable levels. Once opened it was transferred to a 'ready use' receptacle on the main deck known as the harness cask. Sydney Hamilton, a wine maker whose products are well known to many Australians, sailed in the four-masted barque *Chiltonford* in 1914, joining her as a seaman at Wallaroo at the age of 15. He stated:

> On reaching our home port the casks of meat were inspected by the Board of Trade inspector, who bored a hole about an inch in diameter in the head of the cask and inspected a sample of the contents. The hole was plugged with a wooden bung, sealed with hot wax and stamped with the Board of Trade stamp. I noted that there were five bungs in some of the casks indicating that some of the meat had made 5 voyages. The odour on opening a cask was unbearable. The meat was boiled for several hours in sea water to reduce the salt to a point where it could then be boiled in fresh water.

Many other comments are made in this book on salt meat. Also known as salt junk or salt horse, it was closely followed by the ship's biscuit as the universal foodstuff at sea. The latter were rock hard, about 120 mm (5 inches) square and lasted indefinitely, in spite of the weevils that obviously relished them. Like salt meat they had other names—bread, hardtack, Liverpool pantiles—and, particularly in British ships, formed the basis for many concoctions. Apprentices had to save a portion of their whack of rations and prepare these dishes themselves. Biscuits crushed into small pieces and cooked with pieces of salt meat became cracker hash; soaked in water with sugar and a few raisins it became dogsbody. The favourite was dandyfunk. This was powdered sea biscuit, achieved by hammering the biscuit contained in a small canvas bag with an iron belaying pin on the mooring bitts, adding fat and molasses, and baking it in the galley stove. This was not usually done by the cook, so could only be achieved if a rapport with that worthy had been built up beforehand. Other nationalities had their own concoctions, the most noteworthy being the blood pancakes savoured in Finnish ships. Sea biscuits were not usually rationed and were relied upon to fill the empty corners in the seaman's stomach. Their hardness and durability were such that they could be made into ornaments, some seamen painting pictures on them to be sold for a few shillings in port. The after guard (master and mates) had better food, but how much better depended on the nature of the master and, to some extent, the steward and cook.

All ships carried live pigs to be killed along the way for fresh meat. They were kept in a cage at the break of the fo'c'sle and usually were given the run of the decks when the weather was fine. It was the custom for one to be killed when Christmas fell at sea, and just before the end of the voyage. It was suspected that the latter was to make the crew forget the quality of the food during the voyage. Ships leaving Australia often took live sheep but they had to be eaten early in the voyage, as it was difficult to provide enough suitable fodder. Pigs on the other hand lived quite happily on galley scraps. Some masters held off slaughtering the last pig in the hope that it could be sold privately at the next port.

British sailing ships in the latter years had the reputation for being hungry ships. While there was an unwritten law at sea that, if a ship ran short of food, other ships encountered would give what they could spare, many non-British ships tended to avoid the limejuicers, steering away before they could be asked for food.

Early in the voyage it was almost a tradition for a deputation from the fo'c'sle to be made to the master, complaining about the food. It always resulted in words, maybe the skipper tasting the food offered as an example and the crew being told there was nothing wrong with it and to get back to work before they were logged.

German and French ships appear to have provided a standard of food many times superior, but they were aided financially by their bounty and training schemes. Helmut Schwabe, who sailed in the German four-masted barques *Padua* and *Pamir* under the Laeisz flag, gave me this description of food in a 'P' Liner.

> The food in *Padua* was adequate. Each crew member was, by law, entitled to the listed minimum food items each week, such as sugar, cheese and sausage to name a few. What we did not receive directly we got as cooked meals. There was a cook and a baker plus one of the boys who was rostered on as galley assistant. We had fresh bread, baked twice a week. If the cook was good, the crew was well off. Ours was okay. We took a large quantity of long lasting potatoes on board and the galley boy had to sort out the bad ones to keep the remainder good. When they ran out we had dried potatoes out of large cans. For breakfast we had peas and lentils with bacon sauce, porridge with well watered down condensed milk and a quarter of a loaf per man per day with margarine and plum jam with stones still in it.
>
> For lunch we had salt or corned beef, potatoes and beans, peas or cabbage. In the evenings we had soup, bread, cheese and met wurst. On Sundays we had a slice of cake, hard and sweet. We called it *Panzer Platte*—armour plate! Our favourite was corned beef with plum and dumpling soup—quite palatable. F. Laeisz motto was—A healthy well fed crew would work well.

The Laeisz philosophy on food was not shared by all German shipowners or masters, as is revealed by Otto Neumann. Otto was typical of the German boys who, like their counterparts from many nations, felt the drive to go to sea in sail. Starting off in the small schooners that serviced the smaller Baltic ports, his story has been told to me many times over by a multitude of other northern European boy seamen who graduated from these smaller craft. He chose to get under sail in one of the last big deepwater sailing ships, and rose to command in powered ships. Many of the German boy sailors ended up in the German Navy in World War II, some in the Luftwaffe, and a few have told me of their exploits in the U-boat fleets that created havoc with the Atlantic convoys. Otto relates:

> On my first small sailing ship, *Johanne*, a ketch of 130 tons, I had to take care of the cooking. After weighing anchor and setting sail I had to light the fire and cook the coffee, made from roasted barley from our former cargo. With that was a slice of black bread 9 x 9 x 1 cm, spread with a kind of margarine. You couldn't eat any more because the captain himself ate no more. For lunch we had between three of us 150 grams of peas or beans or canned carrots, cooked with 60 grams of bacon and one potato each and I cooked 6 dumplings in the potato water. We could also have another slice of bread with our barley coffee.

The food provided in the Erikson fleet was plain but acceptable, according to Brian Peters who sailed in the postwar voyages of the four-masted barque *Passat* in 1948 and 1949. He described it as *Husmanskost*, which is Swedish for 'country fare'. The time-honoured salt meat was still in use at this time as well as salted herrings. Australian canned fruit, purchased in Port Victoria in large quantities due to its quality and low price, was served on Sundays and of course pigs were carried to provide fresh meat. He revealed that the crew fed coal to the pigs to harden up their droppings to make it easier to clean up after them. All pigs were nicknamed 'Dennis' and suffered the indignity of being decorated at various times with paint, red lead and Stockholm tar as they wandered about the decks. In Finnish ships, a delicacy was made from pig's blood. Prior to slaughtering an incision was made in the pig's neck or heart and the blood collected in a basin. Immediately whisked with an eggbeater to prevent it congealing, it was mixed with flour, salt and eggs if they were available, otherwise egg powder. It produced blood pancakes, a great favourite.

Bengt Söderlund, an Ålander who sailed in the four-masted barque *Pommern*, told me of the loss of two of their pigs in a storm, revealing the importance of pigs in the eyes of the crew.

> On the run from Australia in the vicinity of the Falkland Islands it started to blow very hard, pressing the rail deep under water. Heavy seas rolled over the bow, smashing the pigsty to pieces. The pigs were then free on deck floating about like corks and started to go over the lee rail. We managed to save three out of the five, getting them under the fo'c'sle head. The carpenter got hold of one by the hind leg but his shoulder was pulled out of joint and he had to let go. We all cried to see our fresh meat going to the sharks. Their weight was then about 80 kg each.

Colin Pelham of Adelaide sailed in *Killoran* in 1927 as an ordinary seaman, from Port Lincoln to Falmouth for orders and Rotterdam to discharge. She was now under Gustaf Erikson, having been acquired from J. Hardie in 1924. He added this story regarding pigs.

We left Port Lincoln with three piglets in a sty under the fo'c'sle head. These of course grew to full size pigs and were to eventually supplement the meagre rations of the ship. A few weeks out and one was killed and prepared for the cook. Later in the voyage the second was killed and prepared similarly. The third grew into a very large pig and the crew became progressively more hungry. We were getting close to the 'Channel' but the cook was not allowed to kill it, so one dark and stormy night, able seaman Casperson,—a hard hitting Finn, put a wheat sack over its head and strangled it. The next morning, it happened to be Sunday, Casperson went aft and reported the death of the pig to the First Mate, and asked permission to prepare it for the cook. The request was relayed below to the Captain, a very old man, whom we saw on deck only twice during the voyage. The answer came back that as the pig had died it was obviously ill and Casperson was instructed to throw it over the side. So the crew went hungry after all. I suspect that the third pig was really destined for Finland and the Captain's own home as a sort of bonus for the trip.

Alcohol

Alcohol was forbidden in the fo'c'sle and half deck, although at the beginning of the voyage the odd bottle was secreted on board. The crew invariably arrived on board drunk but when the alcohol brought aboard ran out, no more was available. Perhaps a protracted or dangerous task on deck or aloft in a gale could earn the watch a tot of rum or whisky, and Christmas or a crossing the line ceremony might result in the call, 'splice the mainbrace'. In the early twentieth century the crew was often prevented from going ashore in certain ports, especially if it was likely that they would clear out when under the influence of alcohol. I have been told of cases of almost a year passing without the crew leaving the ship. The notable exception to the ban on alcohol was in French ships (as described in Chapter 4).

The master, unlike the crew, could take any amount of liquor on a voyage and Eb Anderson told me that one of his skippers, when refused permission to take his wife with him, took 12 cases of whisky instead.

Bengt Söderlund gave me this recipe for ship-brewed liquor.

We used a very simple method. We pooled our small ration of sugar and mixed it with water in a bucket, plus wheat from the cargo. In the warm trade wind weather it got very hot in the hold under the deck. It soon started to ferment and produced alcohol in two weeks. We used a piece of sackcloth over a bucket to strain the alcohol from the mash. The officers did not know about this, otherwise it would have been stopped immediately.

An interesting exception to the no alcohol rule was told to me by John Kaalund, who sailed from Sydney towards Liverpool in 1927, in the Swedish four-masted barque *C. B. Pedersen*. Lime juice has been discussed by many writers of sea stories and its use described by all those whose reminiscences appear in this book. In *C. B. Pedersen*, instead of lime juice, gin was issued daily to the crew. Supposedly the juniper berry that gives gin its distinctive flavour is rich in vitamin C. Others whom I have questioned say that this practice was not universal in Swedish ships.

In Chapter 8, Jason Hopton speaks of his time in the 1948 voyage of *Passat*; in his story there are many references to the consumption of alcohol at sea and in particular of a quantity that had been stolen from the ship's stores. I have discussed this with other wind ship mariners and it was considered the exception to the rule. It was known that this was likely to be the last ever voyage by a sailing ship, and alcohol consumption was high and not prevented. Most of my storytellers reveal that as the last years of the sailing ship approached it was easier for the crew to maintain at least a small stock of their own alcohol. On *Passat*'s last voyage in 1949, Captain Hägerstrand actually sold alcohol to crew members he considered 'responsible'.

Water and cleanliness

Along with the restriction on alcohol were restrictions on the use of water. Water was doled out to the crew in a measured quantity, half of which went to the cook. Ablutions were done only in salt water, as was the washing of clothes. Reg Rudd, who sailed in the four-masted barque *Lauriston* in 1915, has told me much of windjammer food and customs. Their water ration was kept in a 12-gallon tank at the foot of the port bunks.

> There was a three cornered shelf in the half deck with a hole in it to take half a keg. This was our washbasin. When at sea, with our water being rationed, the water in this was only changed once a week, on Sunday. After four people had washed in it for a week it was just slime but before throwing it away we washed our plates in it. During the week we only wiped them around with a piece of rope yarn.

Twenty-four years later, things hadn't changed much. Jack Horward, who sailed in the four-masted barque *Archibald Russell* from Port Germein towards Falmouth for orders in 1939, told me that one of the first jobs he was given was that of *backstörn*, a Swedish term meaning dishwasher and toilet cleaner, a job taken in turn for two weeks by first voyagers. The equivalent term in British ships was 'peggy'. He wrote in his diary:

> I was given two dirty brown cloths, thick with grease, a kerosene tin and told to wash up. I wondered where they kept the soap—ah here's Ayliffe. 'Hey, Peter, where's the wash up soap?'
> 'What wash up soap?'
> 'You know, the wash up soap!' indicating the dishes and the cloths.
> 'What wash up soap?'
> 'The bloody wash up soap,' I yelled.
> 'Well for Gawd's sake you can't use soap like that man! Ekonomie! Ekonomie!'

Asked about personal cleanliness, most of my informants say they would rather not think about their disregard for this. Baths were unheard of. A bucket of cold salt water and a scrub down was all that could be expected, carried out in one's watch below. In tropical downpours, all hands were given the opportunity to get out on deck naked to take a fresh water shower. Shaving and cleaning one's teeth were usually dispensed with. Turning in fully dressed was usual in the cold, stormy regions of the world. Working clothes were covered all over with paint, Stockholm tar and grease from various parts of the ship and rigging. The number of stories I heard about salt water boils, which erupted around the wrists and neck, led me to investigate this phenomenon. Medical opinion is that the chafing of wet, dirty garments was the cause rather than the salt water. All my informants describe the effect of handling wet ropes. Skin that was immersed in water for even a short time became soft and crinkly, even though thick calluses had built up from doing the same work dry. The skin at the joints of the fingers cracked and never healed until drier conditions prevailed.

Leisure activities

Fishing, when the weather was favourable, seems to be the one pastime common to my storytellers, but in truth it was not so much a pastime as a necessity, to augment shipboard food supplies.

I have been told by more than one informant that one Sunday pastime was a contest, usually between the youngest crew members, to get from one end of the ship to the other in the fastest time without setting foot on deck. The contestants were required to climb the jigger rigging and slide down the topmast stay to the mizzen top, climb to the mizzen mast head and slide down the royal stay to the main top and again to the fore mast head. The final descent was down the fore royal stay to the jib boom and then back onto the fo'c'sle head. It was not always a straight slide down, as these stays had staysails set on them. A more arduous version was to go in the opposite direction up the royal stays, hand over hand. Some skippers frowned on this activity, as an accident would leave the ship short handed, but others encouraged it, as it developed a sense of confidence, especially in first voyagers. It seemed to take place more on Finnish ships. Safety harnesses were unheard of.

There were other contests that generally related to the strength and fitness and balance developed from the work required to handle a large sailing ship. In *Lawhill* there was a seaman who always walked along the top of the yards from one end to the other, without holding on to anything, rather than along the footrope. Weight lifting with improvised weights was another contest; one story told of the ship's anvil being lifted over the head by the more robust seamen. Indian arm-wrestling and boxing were universal favourites.

The long hours of heavy work made sleeping the first priority in time off, with Sunday the only day free to wash and mend clothes, read, play cards or make models of their ship. Few social activities could be indulged in, given the small amount of free time available, but Eb Anderson relates that particularly in British ships a time-honoured custom was the 'spinning of yarns'. The complete absence of radio, newspapers or any communication with the outside world created the need for another dimension in the seaman's life, and the spinning of yarns provided this. The seaman's ever-changing world gave him many experiences to relate and places to describe. Spinning yarns was usually indulged in at meal times or during the evening watches if there was no deck work to be carried out. The watch would gather on the main hatch if the weather was warm or under the fo'c'sle head in cold weather.

Stories might then be told of past ships and shipmates, ports and their attractions, girls and storms. The supernatural featured in some of these stories, while the superstitious beliefs of sailors also stemmed from or were cultivated in these tales. Fo'c'sles often had a master storyteller whose tales outshone all the others. There is no doubt that even though they were all based on fact a certain degree of manipulation took place to help the tale along.

The Sleeping Apprentice

It was the tropic calm—a brazen day:
Spread-eagled on the fo'c'sle head, he lay
As the Archangel Michael must have slept
When tired with victory—high on some windswept
Pinnacle crag of heaven. Fathoms deep
His soul was washed by deep sea tides of sleep;
His sun-gold body and his golden head
Were motionless upon his rigid bed.
Through all the four-hour watch, so quiet he lay,
And yet—his mind was countless miles away:
He thought he saw blonde girls with long, white legs,
And drank pale beer, and ate grilled ham and eggs.

Mary Lang

Shantying

Much has been written about the singing of shanties and as the practice was dying out in the latter years covered by this book, only a fairly broad reference is possible. *Shanties and Sailors' Songs*, by Stan Hugill, is an excellent work on the subject. Singing shanties was more frequently mentioned by those from British ships. It depended entirely on having someone in the crew who fancied himself as a shanty singer, although once started the crew would join in. Shanties were traditional folk song melodies taken to sea and re-worded many times over to reflect the work carried out, for example, as halyard shanties and capstan shanties, each being used to wrench the last bit of effort out of those engaged in a heavy task. The words were sometimes made up on the spot; some reflected the complaints the crew had built up during the voyage and the dislike held for some officers or the owners. Others had strong sexual references and were quite explicit. The shanty sung with most gusto by the crew of a homeward bound ship was 'Call All Hands to Man the Capstan'.

Call all hands to man the capstan.
See the cable runs down clear.
Heave away and with a will, boys,
For old England we will steer.

Off Cape Horn on a winter's morning
Setting sails in ice and snow,
Heave away and with a will, boys,
Hoist away and let her go.

The word 'England' would be replaced by 'Hamburg' or 'homeland' depending on the nationality of the ship.

Accidents, injury and sickness

The nature of work in the sail-driven ship exposed the seaman to great danger and there was a dearth of adequate treatment if injury did occur. Surprisingly, the hundreds who informed me witnessed only a few serious accidents and deaths, although Alan Villiers, in *The War with Cape Horn*, states that in the period 1900–1911, in British ships alone, 10,000 seamen lost their lives. Many of these deaths would probably have resulted from ships foundering, running into icebergs and other events that claimed an entire crew. However, there were many who met with accidental death in falls from aloft or being washed overboard, the latter being more common.

The Cape Horn Breed by Captain H. S. Jones gives a graphic account of the tragic voyage from London to Pisagua in 1905 of the British ship *British Isles*. Not only does he describe the attempt to round Cape Horn from east to west, against the worst gales experienced for many years, he also describes the accidents that resulted in the death of six of her crew and the injury of many more. One of those severely injured was a seaman known by his shipmates as Jerry the Greek. He had his leg crushed in a wash port and for weeks endured agonies lashed in his bunk while gangrene slowly took over. Finally the master, Captain Barker, amputated his leg on the fo'c'sle table, without anaesthetic, cauterising the stump with a red-hot poker. Jerry the Greek was one of the lucky ones. He survived.

The following description by Colin Pelham of an accident in the Erikson barque *Killoran* in 1927 would be typical of many in which a fall from aloft did not result in death.

I suppose the most upsetting episode of the entire voyage has taken place. I was free watch and asleep and my mate Toby, was in the other watch. About 8 bells (4 pm) I was awakened with the advice that I should go aft, as Toby had had an accident. Seamen are not permitted aft of the mainmast unless on duty, so after obtaining permission from the officer of the watch, I was shown to the officer's quarters and into the first mate's cabin, which he had vacated. In the bunk was Toby. He had fallen from aloft when a footrope had given away about 30 feet up and fortunately beside the mainmast. Had he been on the yardarm he would certainly have been lost overboard. He had broken his left thigh about 4 inches above the knee, and was destined to spend the remainder of the voyage, until he was put ashore to the Royal Cornish Sailors Hospital in Falmouth, confined to his bunk. The ship carried scant medical supplies and portions had to be sawn out of the side of the bunk to make splints and some signalling flags were pressed into service as bandages. Even the urine bottle was an old whisky bottle, far too small to be used effectively. Toby eventually recovered and returned to Australia but walked with a limp for the rest of his life.

Sam Elfik told me of a similar injury in the ship *Garthwray*, adding a few comments that reflect the attitude towards injury that persisted until sail vanished from the seas.

One of our apprentices fell down the hold and broke both thighs. We could do nothing but pull them out straight and splint them up—without anaesthetic. I had the job of looking after him but there was not much I could do but bring him food, wipe his arse and put his prick in a bottle when he needed it. When we reached port the doctor said that ashore such an injury would have resulted in both legs being amputated. He later recovered and played football for Swansea.

Medical treatment was pretty standard at sea. There was a kit and a book called *The Ship Master's Medical Guide*. It identified various symptoms and required certain mixtures to be made from ingredient A, B or C, etc. Of course anyone reporting sick was told by the Captain that they didn't have enough work to do and were given a dose of black draught or castor oil and packed off for'ard and back to work. We all seemed to recover okay. Toothache was taken care of by the carpenter who pulled teeth without anaesthetic as you sat on a spare spar lashed along the main deck. We all developed an ability to survive, that could not have occurred ashore.

Captain Jack Walker told me of accident and sickness in the John Stewart barque *Amulree*, during his time in her as an AB between 1913 and 1917:

In Dunkirk we loaded large cast iron pipes for Buenos Aires where they were intended for a large sewerage project there. They were about 5 feet [1.5 metres] in diameter and they loaded a smaller one inside. These pipes nearly finished us off, as later at sea some of them broke loose. We were in serious trouble as they were quite capable of piercing the ship's steel hull. It was highly dangerous for us to go below and secure them but somehow we managed to get additional chains over them without anyone getting killed. We thought one seaman had copped it though, as he was between a large pipe and the ship's side when the pipe rolled. He just managed to duck down and he was saved by the space where the pipe bridged between the side of the ship and another pipe.

As soon as we reached Buenos Aires and went ashore, we usually ended up in one of the local whorehouses. Not for the usual reason but a cheap meal could be obtained there and we never had much money. There was a place I remember, quite huge, like a large hall, employing about 90 prostitutes. There was an upstairs balcony right around the inside and the girls' rooms opened on to this. In the centre were tables where cheap food and liquor was served. The girls wandered around in amongst the tables, trying to entice customers upstairs. There were several policemen at the entrance who searched everyone who entered for knives and other weapons. Each girl had a certificate stating that a doctor had examined her in the last 24 hours, but apparently this could not be relied upon as one of our apprentices ended up with a dose of syphilis. Much later in our voyaging we loaded rice in Rangoon for Liverpool. It was here that some of our crew came down with Beri Beri. On the way home more of the crew became sick and it was increasingly difficult to work the ship. One of the apprentices became very sick, as he was the one with syphilis. The skipper had been treating him with the prescribed mixture out of the *Ship Master's Medical Guide*, a mercurial compound called '606', but he was getting no better. So we put into the island of St. Helena, where the apprentice was left at the tiny hospital there. The skipper left 6 bags of rice out of our cargo as payment!

Eberhardt Wulf, seaman in the Laeisz 'P' Liner *Passat*, described a most upsetting incident when one of his shipmates fell overboard out of the rigging:

We were stowing a lower t'gallant sail which indicates that there was a very strong wind, when Joseph—I forget his other name, fell backwards, off the yard and into the sea. He came to the surface and appeared not to be injured by the fall. The ship was travelling about 12 knots before a big following sea and it was obvious that it was impossible to heave to [to] try to pick him up, without risk to the ship. All we could do was to watch his head getting smaller as the ship went on. His instinct for survival caused him to try to swim after the ship. It was a horrible scene and one I will never forget!

Another story that had a happier outcome, but indicates the lack of concern for injury, comes from Captain Eben Anderson, at that time (1914) an apprentice in *Hougomont*:

It was nearing the end of the 8 pm–12 pm watch and the mate called the 'policeman' to attend to something in the rigging. The seaman finished his task but missed his footing and fell about 10 metres to the deck, luckily striking the lines leading down to the fife rail. This broke his fall and he staggered to his feet. The mate called out, 'Are you all right?' and the seaman mumbled, 'I think so.' 'Well you had better go and call the watch then,' replied the mate.

Fred Maerz, a seaman in the German four-masted barque *Lisbeth*, told me of a close shave for one of his shipmates when his ship was loading wheat in Sydney in 1924.

A young seaman was aloft painting a royal yard, about 180 feet [55 metres] above the deck. As was the custom, the paint pot and brush had a lanyard attached and secured to a convenient place so that the user could have one hand free with which to hang on. He was sitting on the footrope painting the underside of the yard. Somehow he lost his grip and fell. Incredibly his leg became entangled in the paint pot lanyard and he hung there with only a half hitch between him and oblivion. I was working lower down on the mast and I yelled out not to struggle, otherwise the thin lanyard could break or shake loose and I went up to help him. I somehow got another rope around him and he was able to regain his hold. Naturally there was a lot of paint spilt but as we were on the yardarm, it went into the harbour. Had it hit the decks the mate would have given him a dressing down for being so careless and he would have had to clean it all up. He still got his dressing down for wasting the paint!

In 1932 Johannes Schwarz was a young seaman in the German four-masted barque *Priwall*, now in the Australian grain trade as a result of the drop in demand for West Coast nitrates. In December *Priwall* was at anchor off Port Victoria. I thank Beryl Neumann, secretary of the Central Yorke Peninsula National Trust, for these historical details contained in a small monograph she wrote about the incident:

Schwartz was aloft painting the jigger mast when he fell and was killed. On Monday 12 December, his body was brought to the jetty in a small boat and a company of cadets marched behind the hearse along the hot dusty road to the cemetery. Local people showed their sympathy by joining in the procession. The service was conducted in German by the Lutheran Pastor from South Kilkerran, J. P. Sabel. When the service ended the seamen moved around the grave and sang, 'Ich hat einen Kamaraden' ('I Had a Comrade'), a song often sung by them at sea. Twelve months later *Priwall* came again to Port Victoria and the Captain carried with him a little fir tree given to him by the boy's parents, to be planted by the grave. In the mid summer heat the tree soon died. The small wooden cross, rotted away over the years and the grave became overgrown until 1962 when Mrs. Selma Davies of Port Victoria organised a fund to restore the grave and erect a proper headstone.

I was in Port Victoria during the Cape Horners Congress in Adelaide in 1979. Part of the day's activities was a visit to the grave of Johannes Schwarz. The local minister conducted a brief service and then the German members of the group, of whom there were several from *Priwall* in 1932, one by one started singing 'Deutschland, Deutschland Uber Alles'. Already charged with the emotion of reunion with old friends and shipmates that day, those present all shed a tear not only for Johannes but also for an era long gone.

The Drowned Boy

A ship sailed over me yesterday,
And not so many ships come this way
As when I was a Sailor boy.
I like to see them pass overhead—
Great old ships, with their great sails spread,
And the waves dancing round for joy.

When I see them coming I swiftly rise
To the foam, and I once looked into the eyes
Of a boy on the fo'c'sle head.
He was staring hard right into the sea,
And his great blue eyes were fixed on me,
But he couldn't see me, I am dead.

I'd like to be back in a ship again;
In one of the poor old ships that remain
To come sailing round the Horn.
I'd like some tobacco, some talk and some fun
And I'd like to hear a good yarn spun
Of the days before I was born.

It's not bad here, but it's lonely to be
The only boy in this part of the sea.
(I was washed overboard alone.)
And as the Sea drowned me, she sang in my ear:
'I'll make you a Merman, my dear!'
And she keeps me here for her own.

Sometimes I go to the Ramirez Rocks—
But I'd like to go to the London Docks
And have a girl, and some drink.
The Sea's a lady—she's good to me,
But most of the time she just seems to be
Waiting for ships to sink.

Oh, a Merman's life is not too bad, at all;

There's nothing to worry about, at all,
And some of the time it's joy.
But I'm not quite used to a Merman's ways,
And I often think of the good old days
When I was a Sailor boy.

Mary Lang

Fights and violence

Because sailing ships were at sea for long periods, and because of many other factors, such as a multitude of nationalities being thrown together, poor food, the fact that a seaman not pulling his weight would be the target of both verbal and physical abuse, fights were common. All my storytellers talk about fighting and it was expected by the officers, who in many cases did not try too hard to stop it. Bob Russell in *Passat* in 1949 had a fight with another shipmate, with the crew milling around urging on one or the other. Bob said that he thought he had the better of his opponent when the skipper, Captain Hägerstrand, who had been watching for some time, finally said, 'That's enough, Russell, I think he has had enough now!'

It was a fact of life that some officers enforced discipline with their fists, particularly new second mates. Some have told me that it was expected, that unless the officer 'broke someone's head' early in the voyage he would command no respect for the rest of the voyage.

Jim Gearing-Thomas, a seaman in the Erikson ships *Olivebank* and *Pamir* in the mid thirties, told me of an incident in which he was involved.

> I was at the helm at the time and a fight broke out on the main deck. The mate and master were watching its progress from the poop and I was trying to see what was happening. In so doing I let the ship get off course which caused the leeches of some upper sails to flap. The skipper strode over to me and let me have a mighty blow to the side of my face. He looked into my face and said, 'Ven you are steering my ship, you will ploddy well steer it!' I saw stars and lost interest in the fight.

Peter Davies, an English boy who sailed in several Erikson ships in the thirties, was on his way to join the four-masted barque *Herzogin Cecilie* in 1934 with several other members of her crew. They contrived to arrive late, in the hope that she would sail without them. They thought that they could then get in the crew of another Erikson ship in port at the same time. The reason for this was that they did not relish sailing with Sven Eriksson as master, as he had a bad temper and had a reputation for violence. Peter said:

> It turned out that she did not sail when expected and we had to join her anyway. We were met at the gangway by Pamela Eriksson, wife of the skipper, who showed us our quarters and said that Sven was furious at our late arrival. He was quite an objectionable person and insisted that we called him 'sir' and not to speak to him unless he spoke first. He was very handy with his fists and I saw him hit seamen for quite trivial reasons. One time I saw him screaming at a seaman at the for'ard end of the long poop. The seaman appeared to answer back, so Sven picked him up bodily and threw him over the

railing down on to the foredeck. How he was not seriously injured, I don't know. Sadly the same seaman was one of those killed when *Herzogin Cecilie*'s boiler blew up in Belfast in 1935.

Shipwreck

I have been told of dismastings, strandings where the ship got off at high tide and cases where a sandbank was nudged without damage. Peter Davies described to me the stranding of *Herzogin Cecilie* in 1936. She went aground at Salcombe, not far from Falmouth, but there was no loss of life. It was thought that she could be saved but in the end she became a total loss. Anything that was useable was stripped and taken back to Mariehamn.

Out of the many who have given me their stories there was only one who experienced a fatal shipwreck and in the circumstances was lucky to live through it. Bill Young, then a 19-year-old apprentice in the British four-masted barque *Swanhilda*, gave me an incredible account of how this ship went ashore on the north-west coast of Staten Island, not far from Cape Horn, in 1910. He was one of five survivors of a crew of 29. It was another case of a sailing ship finding herself on a lee shore. *Swanhilda* was on her way to the West Coast and her master Captain Pyne had decided to go through the Straits of Le Maire rather than rounding Staten Island to the east. The ship was unable to weather Cape San Antonio and drove ashore. One lifeboat was lost in the breakers. The other boat was being lowered when one fall became jammed and the boat up-ended, throwing everyone into the sea except Bill. He managed to get another apprentice into the boat but it struck rocks 300 yards from shore. Even though he was weighed down by heavy clothing and the water was freezing he managed to swim ashore. He happened to be a member of the Croydon Dolphins Swimming Club, and this probably saved his life. Captain Pyne and his wife were drowned. The five survivors were eventually picked up by an Argentine freighter. (I have not been able to find out whether Captain Pyne was related to the Captain Pyne referred to in Chapter 3.). Bill settled in Western Australia and became a dairy farmer.

The albatross

A book about the life in the last sailing ships would not be complete without reference to the albatross. The long Southern Ocean run, to and from Australian ports, gave wind ship seamen the chance to become acquainted with, if not enraptured by, this bird. These magnificent seabirds were regarded with great reverence by everyone with whom I have spoken, even though they were ensnared for sport and even killed on occasions, for food or for body parts that would later become a trophy from the voyage. The huge webbed feet became tobacco pouches and the hollow wing bones became pipe stems. I have seen walking sticks made from a shark's backbone with the large hooked beak of the albatross used as the handle. As a food they were not successful, as the flesh was strong and fishy in flavour. Generally seamen were reluctant to harm them as the superstition persisted that the spirits of dead sailors resided in the albatross.

The method used to catch them was universal. A hollow steel triangle, 70–100 mm (2¾–4 inches) long, was attached to a line with a piece of cork to make it float. This was baited with a piece of salt meat and trailed astern—a common pastime when weather permitted. The albatross, always on the lookout for food, snapped this up and its hooked beak became wedged into the V of the triangle. It was important to keep tension on the line otherwise the bird could flap free. When the albatross was hauled on board it provided an opportunity for seamen to be photographed with them. They often became seasick, disgorging undigested fish over the deck. Eb Anderson's comments reflect most stories told to me about albatross.

> They flew alongside for days down in the Roaring Forties. Occasionally they would swoop down to have a closer look at us and appear to take an interest in what was happening on deck, almost with a disapproving look. Then they would fly ahead of the ship effortlessly, as if to show their superiority and mastery over the wind and then wheel around and take up station abeam again. They hardly flapped their wings, just a movement now and then to bank or change position. There were many types but were usually white underneath with grey, brown or black on the top or leading edge of the wings. The maximum wingspan recorded was over five metres but I never saw one over four. They appeared to sleep on the surface of the sea and to take off, had to run along the surface with their huge webbed feet, making a pounding noise that could be heard half a mile away.

Max Wood, a seaman in the first outward passage of *Passat* after the war, told me a similar story:

> I can recall an occasion when I was on a royal yard, stowing sail. This huge albatross came up from astern and kept level with me only a few metres away. He was travelling the same speed as the ship and was hardly moving his wings. We were both about 180 feet [55 metres] up and it was a strange feeling to be up there with this bird watching me closely. It is said that the soul of a dead sailor is in each albatross and I had the feeling that this one was watching to see if I was making a good stow.

While having a reputation as a master of flight, the albatross was not infallible. This story was told to me by Bill Boyd, once second mate in the little intercolonial topsail schooner *Huia*. I met Bill in a waterfront pub in Auckland where a photograph of *Huia* on the wall got us talking. 'You know, I sailed in her back in the forties,' he said. 'I was second mate.' I pointed out that I knew her well. As a kid, I used to row out to her when she anchored in Sydney Harbour. I always try to jot down conversations with seafarers such as Bill but on this occasion I was without paper and pencil. The conversation went on with the names of sailing ships passing to and fro. But I remember his comments about the albatross that inhabit the southern Tasman Sea. He said they could often recognise the same birds from a previous crossing.

> One big fellow would always be with us almost as if he was waiting for us to appear. He would swoop down to pick up scraps from the galley, flying in circles around us, almost

as if he was showing off. He tricked himself on one occasion though. We had just gone about and he glided down very close just to leeward. We were close hauled, with the mainsail sheeted well home. The albatross came up from astern and flew into our wind shadow. He immediately lost all lift and beat his wings furiously but collapsed unceremoniously into the sea. You should have seen the surprised look on his face. He almost looked embarrassed!

The respect felt for this great bird is best summarised in this poem by Captain Eben Anderson.

At the Gate

I humbly beg and pray that I shall be forgiven
for being over proud of having sailed the seas
in sail, and steam and vessels diesel driven
and other sins. When at your gate, Saint Peter, please
have pity on an old sea dog and let me into Heaven.

This favour if you cannot see your way to do
then may my soul become a wandering albatross,
an ancient superstition, yet it could be true.
A better fate by far than the muddy Styx to cross
is gliding over Southern Seas and round Cape Horn too.

Eben Anderson

3 THE LIMEJUICERS:
BRITISH AND AUSTRALASIAN SAIL

Archibald Russell

Most of the stories that have been told of life in the last British sailing ships, the limejuicers, have a ring of similarity but the narratives of Captain Eben Anderson have a particular potency. This grand old sailor man died several years ago at the age of 96, and our friendship spanned 25 years. He provided me with a priceless link with the last years of British sail. I have also included stories from some of my Australian and New Zealand informants in this chapter.

When young Eben Anderson signed his apprenticeship indentures in the offices of John Hardie & Co., shipowners of Glasgow, he commenced a maritime career that lasted 50 years. Eb was typical of thousands of British lads who went to sea under the system of apprenticeship that was unique to the British mercantile marine. He experienced life in the half deck of a limejuicer from 1912, at the end of a decade that witnessed, at sea, the toughest conditions that would ever be endured by working man.

There are not many people left who can recall British square-rigged sail. Even though the largest sail tonnage that would exist in the world was owned and operated in Britain, it had all but gone by the early twenties.

The maritime apprenticeship system in Britain allowed shipowners to employ six or more lads in a ship for a period of four years without paying any wages. Supposedly the apprentice was taught the profession of mercantile marine officer, but sadly the theoretical aspect of the calling was usually left to the individual to pick up the best way he could, by attending shore classes in navigation at the end of a voyage. The practical side of seamanship was soon learnt, as four hours on and four hours off, in a working week of 72 hours, gave the apprentice much exposure. This 72-hour week could be stretched to 100 hours when 'all hands' was called. Even though many have condemned the system, none of those interviewed who served as apprentices in British ships look back with regret. In spite of the poor food barely complying with Board of Trade regulations, primitive quarters and no wages, they found in general that the British ship master was fair and kindly towards the crew. In American ships, by contrast, the pay, food and amenities were many times superior but discipline and the treatment of the crew was usually harsh and physical violence common.

Captain Anderson described his early life in Glasgow and his years in sail in many of the discussions I enjoyed with him over the years. He was a great storyteller and brought the past right up to the present rather than taking me, the listener, back in time. Therefore I have worded some of his reminiscences in the first person.

Eb, what made you go to sea?

A pause, and a positive, 'I think it's in your blood, no other reason but that you just want to do it. My first job was in a Glasgow law office. I had to take documents around the city, but I spent more time down around the docks, looking at the ships, than I spent doing my job and I got the sack. My father was manager of the Carron Iron Works, famous for the carronade, the weapon used at sea in the age of fighting sail, and I then got a job with him. I worked with a rigger, an old sailing ship man. Our job was doing maintenance work around the furnaces. The old sailor and his stories more or less sewed the whole thing up as far as I was concerned and I made up my mind I was going to sea.'

What year was that?

'1912.'

How did life in 1912 compare with today? I imagine the sea and ships were an important factor in those days, and it was an easy matter to go to sea.

'Oh yes, there were hundreds of sailing ships around then. When I put it up to my father about going to sea, he set about getting me apprenticed. Life in Glasgow was much the same as anywhere else I suppose—a bit more disciplined, but it was just as badly organised as it is today,' Eb chuckled.

How many hours did one work per week, I mean, ashore?

Well, you started at six in the morning and worked until six in the evening, and on Saturday until 12 noon. You had Sunday off.'

That's about 66 hours a week. What was an average week's wage?

'Well,' said Eb, thinking deeply, 'a labourer received one pound per week.'

Which shipping company did you join?

'Well, my father knew someone in the Anchor Line, so he took me to see the Marine Superintendent. He kept telling me all about their steamers and then emphasised, "Of course, I served my time in sail." That finished me with them and I decided that I would go in sail. So we went to Hardie & Co. who had many sailing ships, including *Hougomont*, *Killoran*, *Kilmeny* and *Archibald Russell*. This latter ship had only just been built. I joined the four-masted barque *Hougomont* on four-year indentures.'

What premium was required?

'My father paid 35 pounds, out of which I received back 25 pounds as wages over the next four years. We had to provide our own bedding, clothing and eating gear as well as soap and matches. There were six apprentices and we were housed in the after deckhouse. The accommodation for apprentices was traditionally called the half deck. It was about 3 metres by 2.5 metres, and situated in the wettest part of the ship. There were two-tiered bunks, four fore and aft and two athwartships, with a narrow plank along the bulkhead acting as a table. The only furniture was our sea chests, which took up most of the remaining deck space. We really belonged to the after guard [captain and mates], but the food and work was exactly the same as the seamen for'ard, although the mates often dreamed up extra tasks for us to make sure we were never idle.

'We got no special instruction in navigation or anything like that. We worked four hours on and had four hours off, which was common to most ships at that time. So that we did not have the same watch every day they changed every night in the dog watches.

These were two-hour watches from 4–6 pm and 6–8 pm. Of course we worked longer hours than this, as any heavy work such as taking in sail or tacking ship was done at the change of watch when all hands were on deck. In an emergency the watch below was called and this time was never made up, the called-out watch having to fall out on deck at the allotted time.

'The first-year apprentices were given the worst jobs in the ship. Cleaning out the toilets and the pigsty were always left to first voyagers together with other tasks that were irksome but essential. One of these was sorting potatoes. These were kept in the 'tween decks and several times they had to be gone through to remove those that had gone bad. The smell was revolting especially in the confined space below without fresh air.

'I once asked the mate if there was a specific job I could do when the ship was going about, instead of tailing on to the braces behind everyone else. I used the cook as an example, who had an important job when going about. The fore sheets were secured to bitts adjacent to the galley in the for'ard deckhouse. The cook's job was to throw the coils off at the appropriate time. He thought for a moment and then announced, "Yes, you can change over the piss chute!" This was a wooden trough fitted into the for'ard mooring port and acted as a urinal. It obviously had to be on the lee side and when the ship went about it was changed over to the other side. The mate had this made by the carpenter to reduce the time it took to attend to this need and to stop the seaman spending more time than necessary in the lavatories that were under the fo'c'sle head.'

Where did your first voyage take you?

'Iquique in Chile.'

What cargo?

'We loaded coal at Port Talbot, Wales, and had to go around Cape Horn to get there. The passage took 110 days.'

How long was the actual rounding of the Horn?

'We took five weeks to get from just south of the Horn to 80°W longitude in order to get a clear run up the coast, a distance of about 450 nautical miles. In Iquique we discharged the coal and loaded ballast for the next leg to Portland, Oregon.'

I suppose you loaded timber there?

'No, wheat.'

Where for?

'Dublin.'

How long were you away from home on this voyage?

'A little over a year. It took six months to get from Portland round the Horn to Dublin. It was now 1913. It was while we were in Portland that two of our apprentices carried out an act of revenge on one of the older boys. It appears that the three had been cadets in the stationary training ship *Conway*. The senior one had been responsible for these two receiving a lashing for some breach of discipline. I remember his name was Dent—Digby Dent. They contrived to join *Hougomont* to get their own back. Before we left Portland they confronted Dent and told him to clear out, otherwise he would not survive the voyage home. He knew they were serious and we never saw him again.'

Where did you go next?

'Well, after arriving in Dublin the crew was paid off and we apprentices had a six-week break during which time I got a job at the Carron Ironworks again. I then rejoined *Hougomont* and we went again to Wales—Barry Docks—and loaded coal again, this time for Montevideo in Uruguay.'

What cargo did you load there?

'We couldn't get any cargo so we loaded ballast and were ordered to Port Adelaide. We went via the Cape of Good Hope and through the Roaring Forties. Adelaide was my first landfall on the Australian continent. I was rather taken with the Australian way of life and I suppose this visit had a lot to do with my eventual permanent residence here.

'We discharged our ballast in Adelaide and it was here that there was an incident that could have had serious consequences. Two members of the crew entered the saloon and demanded to see the master. They had been ashore and were drunk. They had heated words with him over some grievance and one of them picked up the saloon lamp and smashed it against the mirror over the saloon sideboard. Captain McDonald took his revolver out of the drawer and shot one of the men in the arm. The other got such a shock he pissed and shit himself. McDonald was placed under open arrest and had to stay ashore in a hotel. I escaped a lot of work on board during this time, as I had to act as messenger, going between the ship and hotel with papers and correspondence. I managed to get a few free lunches by timing my arrival at the hotel around this time. At the hearing McDonald was acquitted and the two seamen paid off.

'We divested ourselves of another apprentice in Adelaide. He was homosexual and the only time I have ever encountered this in all my years at sea. We had a suspicion that he had some sort of relationship with the bosun. If any of us had to work alone with either of them we made sure we had a marlinspike handy. To confirm our suspicions we set a trap for him. The other apprentices pretended to be asleep one night and I was selected to put the hard word on him. I offered him three helpings of the marmalade tart that the cook made on infrequent occasions, and when he agreed we all pounced on him, removed his trousers and covered his balls with marmalade. We gave him hell after that and before we sailed he jumped ship.

'They had a unique system at Port Adelaide for unloading our ballast. There was the usual single whip rigged to a yardarm, but instead of going down to a winch it was harnessed to a horse. All day the horse plodded backwards and forwards hauling out the ballast in a wicker basket. He knew exactly when to stop and when to go backwards. We loaded bagged wheat and sailed to Queenstown [Ireland] for orders via Cape Horn. From Queenstown we were ordered to Le Havre to discharge, and it was while we were here that the First World War broke out. I asked to be discharged from the ship and I joined the British Army.'

Why did you join up and not stay with the ship?

'Well, there was a lot of patriotic fervour about the whole thing and I didn't think we would win if I didn't help,' Eb chuckled. 'Actually, I enquired about the Navy but one had to sign on for eight years and the Army was just for the duration.'

You came out of the Army with a Military Medal, didn't you?

'Yes, but I don't know that I did anything outstanding. I was a machine gunner and pinned down a German advance which allowed our chaps to get organised.'

Then you went back to sea?

'Yes, I joined the Hardie barque *Killoran* as second mate.'

How did you get a job as second mate when you were so young and after only two and a half years of your apprenticeship served?

'Well, Hardies thought that my time in the Army counted for something and said that if I sat for my second mate's certificate they would give me a job. So I went to technical college for several months to swot up on navigation for the exam. I then went back to Hardies and joined *Killoran*. She was commanded by Captain Pyne. We once again headed for Swansea, Wales, and another cargo of coal, this time for Buenos Aires.

What cargo did you pick up here?

'We loaded linseed in bags for Antwerp. It was a fairly uneventful voyage both ways, apart from skirmishes with Captain Pyne. It was fairly common for ship masters to have a down on second mates. I'll give you an example. At noon each day the captain and mate would take a sight to get our noon position. As second mate, I would take my sextant up to the poop to take a sight too, mainly for the practice. Invariably Captain Pyne would find something for me to do such as, "Ah mister, that lower topsail brace looks a bit slack to me, you had better get it sweated up." And so just before the sun got on to the meridian I would have to put my sextant away and get the mob on to sweat up the brace or whatever it was that he nominated. He wasn't an easy man to get on with, although it was partly my fault as I wasn't the sort of bloke to take too many kicks in the rump. There were the odd occasions when I was on watch on the poop when he would walk up and down with me and tell me the story of his life, usually ending up speaking derogatorily about his wife or daughters. He was that sort of bloke.

'I got on particularly well with the mate. His name was Harry Freyne and came from the west of Ireland. He was a good bloke. Poor old Pyne had lost his previous ship, the *Dienmont*, not one of Hardie's. He was in the Bay of Biscay and he got becalmed on a lee shore in a big swell and was carried ashore. The anchors wouldn't hold and she was a total loss. He was exonerated though.'

A long silence and a smile: 'An amusing incident occurred on the way home. We had to go to the Western Isles for orders on the return leg from Buenos Aires. We were sailing along at a good bat and Pyne decided not to enter port but to pick up our orders on the run. We hoisted our signal numbers and the signal station hoisted the signal, "We have orders for you". We put up our answering pennant, after looking it up in the book, and they hoisted the signal, "You are to proceed to ————". By the time we had hoisted our answering pennant and looked it up in the book, we had sailed right past and were too far off to read it. We had to wear ship and go back to see what it was. We found out it was Antwerp.

'We picked up the pilot off Dungeness. He was a funny bloke. He kept us very busy, taking in sail, shortening down and setting sail and one thing and another. I'll admit he had his problems in as much as that part of the North Sea hadn't had all the mines cleared up from the war, but I don't think it was good seamanship on his part, or the old man's for that matter, as he should have intervened. Anyhow he got us to leeward of our port and he had to put us into Rotterdam. He then had to get a tug to tow us to Antwerp.

'I paid off here and went back to Glasgow to see the owners. They said, "Why are you back?" I said that I would not sail under Pyne again as we didn't seem to hit it off too well. I asked them if they had another ship, otherwise I would have to go somewhere else. They said I could go as second mate in the barque *Kilmeny*, which I did. I met Pyne some time later in Antwerp and he was quite upset that I had left *Killoran*. I told him I could not take any more of his needling, but he was mainly concerned that my replacement wasn't much of a sailor. He said, "That man they sent to replace you couldn't stay awake. I was wishing you were back all the time." I asked the name of my replacement and I remembered him as an AB. I said, "He would go to sleep chipping rust!" Pyne and I still remained on friendly terms. An example of another skirmish we had was as follows. One night he asked me to do a star sight. We had had two or three days of cloudy weather which prevented sun sights. Pyne said, "You can take a star sight can't you Anderson?" "Yes, of course I can Captain."

"Well, get your sextant and take one." "I can't, it's too dark."

"What do you mean it's too dark? The stars don't come out in daylight!" I replied, "I know Captain, but you can only take a star sight at dusk or dawn as you can't see the horizon at night. If I get called at 6 am I will do it then." He dropped the subject then. You see he had never learned how to do it himself.

'Another time, a new ship's gig had been delivered to the ship. It was my job to get it hauled from the wharf to its position on the deckhouse. It was only a light boat so I had two seamen on a capstan with a single whip rigged to a yardarm. The single whip would have then been led to the deck capstan. Pyne was watching me from the poop and called out, "That's no good, and you need a gun tackle [a more powerful combination of blocks] for that job." Knowing better than to argue, I replied, "Very well Captain", and on rigging the gun tackle, we hoisted the gig to the yardarm. When we slacked off, the weight of the gig was insufficient to overcome the friction in the powerful tackle and the gig remained suspended in the air. We had to send a man aloft with the original tackle to get the boat down. Pyne stayed out of my way for several days after that.'

Later in his career, Eb Anderson wrote the poem 'Head Wind' about *Killoran*. It hints at the conflict between master and second mate, sparked in this case by the frustration of head winds. The name *Killoran*, derived from the Gaelic term for church, allows Eb to draw a parallel between the pastor and his captain. The poem's reference to the movement of the upper clouds does not convey the wrath that would have descended on Eb, for unsolicited comments to the master of a ship were frowned upon and a second mate always waited until spoken to.

Head Wind

Does adverse weather ever irk
The Pastor of yon wayside kirk
Enough to make his imprecations
Undermine its firm foundations
While Elders, Beadles, strive in vain
A sense of order to maintain?
Not him. With faith for fairer weather
He and his flock they pray together.

Our barque *Killoran*, all sails set,
Homeward bound from the River Plate
Close hauled, a sight to please the eye.
Did Angels watch her from On High?
Head winds, not strong, about force four,
They'd plagued us for a week or more,
Persistent, drove the Old Man frantic
As North we beat in South Atlantic.
Striving, hoping soon to find
The South-East Trades and peace of mind.

We sweated up by day, by night,
But could we please him? Nought was right.
'The upper clouds move from the West,'
I mentioned, as a matter of interest.
'Mister,' he replied with a frosty stare,
'We're down here. We're not up there.'

I've wondered since, oh where, oh where?
While I'm down here, is he up there?
I've wondered often, dear oh dear,
Is he down there while I'm up here?

We'll meet perchance some day somewhere.
Let's pray that day the wind holds fair.

Eben Anderson

Our conversation continued.

When did you join Kilmeny, *Eb?*

'It was 1919 and I joined her in Antwerp. We went to Halifax, Nova Scotia, in ballast. To cross the Atlantic from east to west in a sailing ship it was customary to head well down to the southwest to avoid the strong prevailing westerly winds of the north Atlantic and to pick up the North-East Trade Winds. You then headed north. The skipper on this trip was Captain Auld—Tommy Auld. I got on all right with him although there was an amusing incident on our first day out that could have ended in disaster. We were headed down channel and I was on watch. The Captain was below at the time. The lookout reported a light ahead. I could see it was a lighthouse or some such beacon, so I called the Captain.

"There's a four-flash light fine on the starboard bow sir." "There's no such light in the English Channel," replied Auld.

"Well, we must be in some other channel sir, because there is a four flash light coming up fast. You had better come up and see." Auld came up cursing, but as soon as he saw the light he ordered us about and it was a very near thing. We had almost entered Falmouth Harbour and could have run aground. We were so close that the pilot came off as he thought we were entering Port.'

Eben Anderson claimed *Kilmeny* as his favourite ship, as the two masters he sailed with in her were competent seamen and respected by officers and crew. From Halifax, *Kilmeny* loaded a cargo of timber for Liverpool. She turned in a very good time for this passage. As was the custom with a timber cargo, being light, it was also stowed on deck, chained down, almost to the top of the deckhouse. Access was gained by leaving a passage or space around the doors and fife rails at the base of the masts. Temporary wooden pin rails were constructed in the shrouds and backstays for the running rigging that normally terminated at the rail and these lines were worked from the top of the cargo. As a timber-laden ship drew less water and work took place some 8 feet (2.5 metres) above the deck, such a passage was usually drier for the crew but also a lot more dangerous, due to the possibility of the timber shifting and the absence of railing around the outside of the ship. Makeshift wooden or rope railings were rigged but it was possible for a seaman to fall through.

Kilmeny, along with hundreds of other sailing ships, was living on borrowed time. As the world demand for shipping declined after World War I, ships were laid up without work. *Kilmeny* lay in Liverpool for several months waiting for a cargo. Finally she left in ballast, under the command of Captain George Fullilove, for Sabine Pass, a small up-river port on the Sabine River near Galveston, Texas. Here she loaded bulk sulphur. Before this cargo was finally discharged in Melbourne, it was nearly responsible for her demise, on two counts.

Sulphur is a very dense material. Long before her hull space was filled the Plimsoll marks on her sides signalled that her cargo-carrying capacity had been reached, but there was nothing to indicate that she now had a very low centre of gravity. A windjammer needs cargo or ballast to remain upright. Too little and she heels over readily, with the wind in the sails, and once over returns slowly, when the wind lightens. Sailors described a ship so loaded as being 'cranky'. The opposite occurs when a ship has a full heavy cargo, when a drop in the wind causes her to return very rapidly to an even keel and even beyond, creating a heavy rolling motion. Sailors describe a ship so loaded as being 'stiff'. One method used to raise the centre of gravity was to bury empty casks low down in the cargo and to build the cargo into a mound.

It wasn't long after *Kilmeny* put to sea that stiffness became apparent. In sailors' jargon, she 'nearly rolled the sticks out of her'. As she moved down the Atlantic and into the Southern Ocean towards Australia, her cargo settled and the stiffness worsened. To overcome this, the crew was sent below to move some of the sulphur up and into the 'tween decks. By this time the rolling had increased the slackness in the stays, so much so that preventer gear was rigged to take out the slackness. Blocks were seized to each backstay about halfway up. A line was rove through these blocks from port to starboard and hove down on deck.

But the damage had been done. A circumferential crack which went halfway around the mast was found in the steel main lower masthead. A preventer chain was rigged from the port main rail up over the mast cap and down to the starboard rail and tightened by a rigging screw. It was decided to put into Fremantle rather than risk sailing on to Melbourne. Happily the mast held and Eben had the job of dismantling the mast and getting it repaired. It was quite possible for a sailing ship's crew to rig or rig down their masts and yards without outside assistance. In this case, the main mast and yards were dismantled by the crew, thereby saving the owners much expense, and the lower mast lifted out by shore crane. Eb related:

> It was then found that there was a second crack in the mast about 200 mm below the first, running half way around the mast from the opposite direction, hidden by the bights of the shrouds. I will never cease to wonder how it stayed together until we reached Fremantle. It was during this prolonged stay that I sat for and passed my mate's certificate. We went on to Melbourne and our second emergency occurred, while we were discharging the sulphur cargo. A fire started in the hold, probably from a cigarette dropped by a stevedore. Anyone familiar with burning sulphur would appreciate that, if not contained, it would be impossible to get anywhere near the fire, due to the pungent sulphur dioxide fumes generated. Luckily sulphur burns slowly and we managed to rig a pump and extinguish it. We used fresh water from the quayside, as salt water would have ruined the cargo. We now loaded her return cargo of wool, hides and rabbit skins.

This cargo was referred to as a 'clipper cargo', from the days when the great wool clippers of the 1880s and 1890s brought immigrants, machinery and Scotch whisky from Great Britain to colonial Australia and took back the season's wool clip and its by-products.

Maybe the sea gods felt sorry for this old hooker and gave her this cargo as a reward for all her tribulations, for it was light and allowed her to sail her best. Maybe the sea gods knew that this voyage was *Kilmeny*'s swan song and at the end of it she would be broken up. Freed of the dead weight of the cargo that almost crippled her, *Kilmeny* gave her crew a voyage to remember—89 days to Falmouth and another two days to London's River.

Eben Anderson's poem 'Southern Ocean Symphony' is the best way to describe this last voyage. Bear in mind that anything under 100 days was considered a good passage. To achieve a passage of 89 days, there would be less than 30 days of powerful sailing to the Horn down in the Roaring Forties—hard, wet and cold—then a good slant up past the Falklands and into the glorious South-East Trades, always remembered fondly by sailing ship crews. The equatorial calms would have been encountered, but not the weeks and weeks of wallowing and slatting that so often caused impatience and frustration. Then into the North-East Trades and finally the westerlies of the North Atlantic to bring her to Falmouth.

Southern Ocean Symphony

A middle watch I well remember,
Fifteen hundred easting miles to run
To Cape Horn, th'eleventh of September,
Nineteen hundred and twenty-one.
Kilmeny, bald-headed, three-masted barque,
One four six nine tons net register,
Transformed to a bounding Aeolian Harp,
By the northwest gale that pressed her.
With practised hand it thrummed and thrummed,
On every backstay, every shroud,
While the running gear occasional drummed.
And the sea swished sweet and loud.
And to this from up aloft,
Some noises more remote,
And rhythmic from the hull so oft,
A deep protesting note.
The time provided by the roll,
With tonal variation,
Vibrant, warming to the soul,
A glorious orchestration.

Eben Anderson

Kilmeny tied up in Surrey Commercial Dock, London, just astern of the famous clipper *Cutty Sark*, now rigged as a barquentine. She never went to sea again and inevitably went to the shipbreakers. Eben remained in *Kilmeny* for about a month as watchman. The only other person on board was the master. Eben spent this time writing to other shipping companies and shortly afterwards started his career in steam with the Eagle Oil Transport Company, as third mate in the London-registered tanker *San Tiburco*.

The gruelling east to west rounding of Cape Horn took a high toll on ships and their crews compared to the west to east rounding. Eben Anderson was on his first voyage as an apprentice in the four-masted barque *Hougomont* when she took five weeks to traverse the distance between Lat. 50°S in the Atlantic to 50°S in the Pacific. Only those few alive today who have made this same journey in a heavily laden square-rigged ship can truly appreciate Eb's words on the subject.

Milestone

Mention headland, ness or promontory,
Any point of land, and note his scorn.
Of course it needs no commentary
He's been round Cape Horn.
West to East—well, fair enough,
But t'other way is sterner stuff,
To batter round from East to West.
No need to ask, he's stood the test,
The wet arse cut to Nature's plan
Whereby a boy becomes a man.
The narrow seas and oceans wide,
He's crossed them, took them in his stride.
The gales, the calms, the bloody fog,
All recorded in the log.
Why should other mortals care?
She was his ship. To get her there
He pulled his weight, but let's be fair
Could it be she took him there?

Eben Anderson

Bob McNeale was another limejuicer apprentice, going to sea at about the same time as Eben Anderson in the full-rigged ship *Queen Elizabeth*. His story gives an uninterrupted account of the voyaging of a typical sailing tramp and the cargoes carried early in the twentieth century. He offered to write for me a condensed version of his experiences, which I have reproduced exactly—a rather documentary description of a series of windjammer voyages around the world, it is typical of many of the stories I have been told and outlines the nomadic nature of the sailing ship's life in this period.

I was born in East Ham Essex on 12 November 1894. My father was in command of a seagoing tug around the British Isles, the Continent and as far south as Madeira. During school holidays my mother and sister used to go with him down 'channel' seeking sailing ships wanting a tow. After leaving school in 1911, I served under my father as Boy (cook) and deck hand and was told that if I wanted to go to sea then it was to be in sail and not chipping bloody rust in a steamship. I joined *Queen Elizabeth*, a three-masted ship of 1699 tons net, built in 1889 by McMillan & Sons at Dumbarton, Scotland. Her official number was 97586. I joined the ship at Alexander Dock, Hull on 4 July 1911, having signed ordinary indentures with the managing owners Blackmore & Co., of 5 East India Avenue, London, at the princely sum of five pounds the first year, six pounds second year, eight pounds third year and ten pounds the fourth year. I would get three pounds ten shillings a month as an AB should my apprenticeship be completed before reaching our homeport. These wages came out of the premium of fifty pounds that my father paid to get me apprenticed.

My first voyage was from Hull to a place near Gravesend to load ballast consisting of chalk, and left on 11 August for New York where we arrived on 7 September, where we docked at Bayonne to discharge the ballast and load case oil [two square cans in a wooden case] of kerosene, naphthalene and all the flammable oil you could imagine. We would take this to Sydney, Australia and Wellington, New Zealand. While we were in New York the Missions to Seamen presented us with a paddle organ. We left New York on 17 October arriving in Wellington on 1 March 1912 via the Cape of Good Hope and the Roaring Forties. We discharged part of the cargo into lighters and headed to Sydney on 1 March, arriving on 11 March, berthing at the Vacuum Oil Co. wharf at Hunters Hill.

We were delighted to find the 'wharfies' on strike for another farthing per hour, so we had three extra days in port. My main memories of Sydney are unfortunately connected with the police. I was arrested for playing 'two up' at the Woolwich pub, but let go and told to get back to my ship. Another time I was waiting outside the GPO in Martin Place for a shipmate and a policeman threatened to arrest me for loitering, as 'this is where the bad women frequent'. After the case oil was discharged we were towed to Pyrmont to the wheat wharves next to the bridge and loaded bagged grain for the UK or the Continent. Before we left Sydney we heard of the *Titanic* tragedy. The trip home was uneventful and we received our orders at the Fastnet Rock to proceed to Sunderland to discharge.

My second voyage commenced on 19 September 1912 when we left Sunderland in ballast and under tow for Newport, South Wales, arriving there 4 days later to load coal for Montevideo. We arrived in Montevideo 49 days out and anchored inside the breakwater. We had the worst electric storm I have ever seen while there. We apprentices had shore leave for one day and we missed the last ferry out to the ship. We slept on board the barque *Birkdale* in one of her lifeboats as she was alongside the wharf. The Old Man was furious when we got back to the ship as he thought we had been in the 'red light district'.

After discharging our coal we left Montevideo in ballast for Cape Borda for orders. There not being any orders we proceeded to Port Adelaide where the crew mutinied due to the poor state of the lifeboats which filled with water when lowered overboard. I might add that this always occurred to boats that had been out of the water for some time. The mutineers were taken to court and fined one month's pay. I had the address of some cousins and the Old Man gave me two days off to visit them. They showed me all over the beautiful city in a buggy and later had a sumptuous dinner and a wonderful sleep in a soft bed.

We received orders to proceed to Port Victoria to load grain for the UK. We anchored about three miles out into Spencer Gulf where we discharged our ballast. This was all done by the crew, who had to shovel about 400 tons of rubble into cane baskets and tip them overboard. The bagged grain was brought out to us in ketches. We apprentices were taken ashore one night by the ship chandlers (Trehearn & Co) and spent a happy singsong evening with them.

We left Port Victoria on 29 April 1913 and the Old Man decided to go to Falmouth for orders. In all his years as master he had always made the Fastnet Rock on the south of Ireland his point to pick up orders. On this occasion he decided to go to Falmouth. We were ordered to Limerick on the River Shannon to discharge. We had to tack out of Falmouth and head towards Limerick, which we made on 18 September 1913. We had to lighten ship at Wray Castle owing to being too deep to cross the sill at the dock. We apprentices were sent home but were hurriedly recalled to load stores for our third voyage after ten days.

We left Limerick on 6 October, 1913, in ballast for New York to load case oil for Melbourne. We arrived 18 days later and tied up in the Erie Basin, Brooklyn, not far from the *Annie M. Reid*. We left New York on 22 December 1913 with a full cargo for Melbourne, arriving 10 April 1914 and after discharge, towed over to Williamstown to load grain for Torne, Chile, where we anchored on 26 June 1914. We found it to be a small hamlet of about twenty shacks at the northern end of Talcahuana Bay.

All cargo was discharged into lighters and it was while we were here that the First World War broke out. Chile had many connections with Germany and we expected to be interned but we received orders to proceed to Portland, Oregon, to load grain for the UK or the Continent. We left Torne on 31 August 1914 and on the way met up with a small naval force of British and Japanese warships. Japan was an ally in that war. We passed quite close to HMS *Newcastle*. We dipped our ensign but they ignored it. It was however acknowledged by a Japanese cruiser.

We arrived at Portland on 24 October 1914, and were towed 99 miles up the Willamette River by the stern-wheel tug *Oklahoma*, discharging our ballast at Lynton. I will always remember the magnificent pine trees covering the hills on either side right from the water's edge. The day before we sailed we were invited to a party at the Flying Angel Club. We were fully loaded and at a buoy in the stream and the mate refused permission for us to go ashore. However a couple of steamship apprentices came alongside in a small punt and suggested, if we were game they would pick us up after dark. So Sandford who didn't want to go, kept the mate in conversation while we slid down the anchor chain, onto the buoy and into the punt, which landed us on a lot of floating logs, which had to be crossed before land was reached. We were lucky to get ashore without getting wet. Then a walk of three miles to get to the party. We had to get back the same way, which we did, in the early hours of the morning.

The next day, 10 November 1914, we were towed down to Astoria to commence our long haul around the Horn and home. We anchored here with a Norwegian barque and one of Milne's 'Inver' ships, the *Invercauld*, waiting for the tide so that we could be towed over the bar. Both left one day ahead of us and both were sunk by enemy action, the Norwegian off the Horn and the *Invercauld* off Pernambuco, Brazil, by armed German raiders. The crew of *Invercauld* was landed in Brazil. The *Queen Elizabeth* got through to Fastnet for orders and proceeded to Dublin where we docked at the North Wall on 3 April, 1915.

My fourth and last voyage in sail was short, leaving Dublin in ballast on the 8 May 1915 for Parrsboro in the Basin of Mines, Bay of Fundy, to load lumber for Liverpool. We arrived at Parrsboro on 25 June, after setbacks in the bay, which has a tidal rise and fall of 13 metres. While loading we would find our ship high and dry on the mud alongside the jetty at low tide. We left Parrsboro on 7 August and nothing remarkable happened on the way home apart from having to keep a lookout for U-boats. We arrived Liverpool 6 September 1915, and having completed my indenture plus two months as AB, said goodbye to sail. I was to sit for my 2nd mate's certificate in London with the promise that if I passed I would get the 2nd mate's job in *Queen Elizabeth*. Fortunately I failed to pass the eyesight test [pinholes of light in a dark room] and could not sit for the examination. I used the word 'fortunately', because on her next voyage, *Queen Elizabeth* was lost in the Western approaches, with all hands. I did pass the test later on and became an officer in steamships. I later joined the Chinese Maritime Customs Service and then became Harbour Master at Hoichow, Amoy, and Swato between 1932 and 1940 …

[In *Queen Elizabeth*] the Old Man was a Captain Samuel H. Quale, a strict but fair and honest sort of bloke. We apprentices thought a lot of him. The mate was called Hill and a real bastard. The only time he ever said anything kind to me was when he sent me aloft to loose the mizzen topgallant. I had just put my left foot on the footrope, my right hand was still on the shroud and I was about to grab the jackstay when down she [the yard] went. The chain halyard had carried away. I could have very easily been killed. Hill yelled out, 'Are you all right my boy, are you all right?' The 2nd mate was called Butcher from my hometown, which did not do me much good. Senior Apprentice Ray Vanderword from Westcliff, Essex, whose father owned a number of Thames barges, was made acting 3rd mate. Blackmore & Co. was too lousy to sign on a Bosun. The other Apprentices were Sid Sandford, Bill Luck, and Harold Aitken all from Gravesend, Les

Upton from Basingstock and myself. Harold Aitken jumped ship in New York. On our second voyage we had a different Mate, McCallum, who died from cancer and was buried at sea in St.Vincents Gulf. A chap called Evans from Wales replaced him on our third voyage. Other Apprentices that joined during my time were, Frank East and two whose first names escape me, Billet and Scott. The last mentioned being the son of the Commissioner of London Police.

Australian Rod Munn described his time in the Australian-owned barque *Rothesay Bay* and the British full-rigged ship *Wray Castle*, later renamed *Garthwray*. Rod was a typical AB from the twenties. He spent most of his life at sea and under sail in many a ship not mentioned here. He was the type of seaman that would have been held in high esteem and relied upon by his shipmates, especially stowing a topsail in a gale. Like Eben Anderson he had the ability to bring the past right up to the present. I have many pages of his exploits which he recorded over the years and wish there was room to include more. He typed out the following account, part of a valuable chronicle from the age of sail, on an old-fashioned typewriter.

There she lay [in Sydney Harbour], a beautiful green-hulled ship, my home for the next year, although at this stage I did not know how long I was to spend in her. She was the barque *Rothesay Bay*, owned by the timber merchants Vanderfield and Reid. I went aboard with my donkey's breakfast, knife, fork, spoon and a cup. On going down into the half deck, I found three other boys already stowing their gear. We spent the rest of the day getting acquainted. It was 17 February 1921. Next day our training commenced. Our first job was to raise the ensign and house flag. Next we had to go aloft and loose the upper sails so they could dry out from rain or night dew and in the afternoon we had to go up and stow them again. This procedure lasted about five weeks while we waited for a cargo. One of us was duty boatman for the evening after tea. We were anchored off the CSR wharf, not far from the Glebe Island Bridge, and the steps we used were just by the bridge. We had to ferry the crew ashore and on their return, bring them back to the ship, visitors also. Eric Livingstone, one of my shipmates, brought aboard a set of boxing gloves and a gramophone. Music and boxing were enjoyed in the dogwatches for the whole trip. The half deck was full of bugs and we had to use our sheath knives to try to squash them in the cracks. The fight was hopeless. Our wages were three pounds a month and all found. This meant they fed us but our bedding and working clothes were our own responsibility.

Our first voyage was to Adelaide. We were towed to sea by the tug *Hero*, and were cast off outside the heads. When all sails were set and things settled down, we boys were sent on all sorts of fruitless missions, searching for non-existent things in non-existent places, for the next few hours. The ABs and officers were all in the joke, and would direct us all over the ship, aloft and alow.

My first taste of authority came the first night out. Toohey, the second mate, told me to do something, and did not like the way I responded. He sent me aloft to the main royal, and told not to come down until he said so. It was quite cold and to prevent myself falling to the deck, I lashed myself to the royal mast. At the midnight change of watch I could not be found. The search was on and it was thought I might have fallen overboard. Then Toohey remembered he had sent me aloft and a rescue party arrived.

Apart from working the ship there were no unusual incidents, except I was seasick in varying degrees all the way to Adelaide. We were in Adelaide for several weeks, and during this time we boys were kept busy, scraping the teak railings and woodwork around the poop. We also polished the compass and all the brass fittings. As the cargo was unloaded and the ship rose out of the water, we were given chipping hammers, scrapers and paint, placed in a punt and had to clean and paint below the water line. One day someone put a chipping hammer through the hull plating and this finished chipping for a while. A wooden frame was constructed between the ribs each side of the hole and a cement block was poured, covering the hole. It was quite effective and no water leaked for the whole trip. Our next destination was Auckland. About two days out I was allowed to go lee wheel. This was a position taken by those who were being taught to steer. I had to put a rope loop over my shoulder as a sudden kick of the wheel could throw one completely over it. After several days I was allowed to take a regular trick by myself.

We thought we would make Auckland before Christmas, but headwinds most of the way prevented this. Eventually we sighted Three Kings, and spent Christmas just off Auckland. We had no special food to celebrate, just our normal fare. In Auckland, the six-masted barquentine *E. R. Sterling* was berthed just along the wharf from us. Some of us tried to pay off and join her, but skipper MacGuinness would not hear of it. We left Auckland and returned to our homeport, Sydney. Altogether it was another pleasant trip, with nothing exceptional happening.

We paid off on 15 February 1922 and several ABs and myself joined the three-masted British full rigger *Garthwray* for a voyage to Valparaiso.

Garthwray was owned by the Marine Navigation Company under the chairmanship of Sir William Garthwaite and had been acquired in 1917. Formerly the *Wray Castle*, her name was changed in Lourenço Marques in 1920 in line with Garthwaite's custom of prefixing the first part of his name. I have been told many stories about Sir William Garthwaite, who had visions of a fleet of cargo-carrying training ships for Britain. He believed in the value of sail training and ran his fleet with this supposedly as the main aim, although at the same time the low wages paid, and the premiums collected from those trying to gain a sail endorsement, gave him the opportunity to run a profitable enterprise. His sailing ships were the last to fly the Red Ensign and though they were registered in Montreal he was considered to be the last British sailing ship owner.

I have been fortunate enough to meet up with two other seamen from parts of *Garthwray*'s nomadic voyage, Sam Elfik, AB, and John Williams, mate. Sam gave me this brief but telling account of his time in this ship and his impressions of Sir William Garthwaite.

It was a bloody hard life and I didn't go to sea with any notions that it was romantic or that sailing ships attracted me because of their beauty. It was my desire to do my bit, as the First World War was in progress and I was too young to join the Army. The ship was old, rusty and I believe Garthwaite's endeavours to continue running sailing ships were prompted not by sentiment but the fact that old sailing ships were cheap to buy and, if running costs were cut to the bone, could still make a profit. Mind you, they were a beautiful sight under full sail and I never regret my time in them. The fact that I am 86 years old and still healthy, I put down to my early life at sea. The food was terrible. These days you could not feed it to the pigs, but it was plain and contained no preservatives or chemicals. The heavy labour of working a sailing ship made us fit and strong. Even though the first thoughts of the seaman on reaching port was to visit the nearest brothel and then to go and get drunk, the absence of alcohol for months on end was probably another factor in our overall fitness. For example, the carpenter in *Wray Castle* was 72 years old, yet every day he went aloft on each mast and oiled all the blocks, sheaves and tracks, climbing about like a monkey.

There were all sorts of characters in the crew and situations you had to cope with. We had a Russian Finn in the crew who was a surly type and he was aloft working on the royal yard. The mate ordered me aloft to help him. This was the first time I had been aloft and I climbed gingerly up to where he was working. I enquired, 'How can I help you?' In reply he pulled his knife and took a swipe at me. I made it down to the deck pretty fast and the mate said, 'What are you doing down here?' I told him what had happened and he said, 'Just get a belaying pin and give him a few swipes around the head, that should fix him!' I was then 16 and this was just one example of the raw nature of life in a wind ship.

Sam told me that Garthwaite was a 'tight-arsed old bastard', an opinion formed not only from his time in his ship but as a result of asking for another berth when he paid off at the end of the voyage. The request was made so that the required sea time to sit for second mate's certificate could be accumulated.

I went to see Garthwaite in his London office and asked if he had a berth for third mate. He said, 'Yes, you can go in the *Garthpool.*' When I asked him what the wage was, he exclaimed, 'What, you want to get paid? I thought you just wanted to get sea time!'

John Williams, Sam's shipmate in the *Garthwray*, told me that Sam was one of the best seamen he had come across in all his years at sea. He said that old Garthwaite did not know what a good man he could have lost. John Williams, later knighted and a recipient of an OBE for his achievements in marine salvage operations, is best known for his recovery of a consignment of eight and a half tons of gold bullion from the steamship *Niagara*, which struck a mine and sank off New Zealand early in World War II.

Captain Ted Wright of Stockton, New South Wales, also told some amusing stories about the Garth ships. In the bar of the waterfront Mercantile Hotel in George Street, Sydney, Ted related:

When I was in *Garthpool* we were berthed in New York and *Garthwray* was moored astern of us. We witnessed many amusing incidents involving *Garthwray*'s skipper's wife, who sailed with her husband [Captain Frampton]. Mrs Frampton considered herself the unofficial captain. She 'adopted' all of the apprentices that joined *Garthwray* and forced 'motherly' care on them. She made them attend a service on Sundays and was always onto them about wearing clean clothes. She did all their laundering but deducted a fee out of their almost negligible wages. She would stand at the gangway and stop the boys going ashore to sample some of New York's 'pleasures'. However they climbed out along their jib boom, which was over our stern, and escaped down a rope left hanging there.

When Captain Frampton went ashore on ship's business he would stop at one of the waterfront pubs on the way back to the ship. She knew this and went looking for him from one pub to the next and hauled him back to the ship. Another time when leaving Adelaide it was decided to take the ship through Bass Strait. Captain Frampton was below, sick, at the time and the Strait was usually avoided in favour of heading south around Tasmania. Mrs Frampton came on deck and announced that she would take over the ship and take her through the Strait. The mate rightly stood his ground and after a great deal of argument, told Mrs Frampton off in well-chosen sailor's words.

Rod Munn told me that in spite of all this *Garthwray* was a happy ship and it was partly due to the presence of Mrs Frampton on board. He had a lot more to say:

We joined *Garthwray* in Newcastle, New South Wales, where she had just loaded a cargo of coal. It was a fairly uneventful trip apart from the time that the cook, a Hindu, went berserk and was chasing everyone out of the galley with a meat cleaver. After some persuasion I managed to settle him down and things returned to normal. The Boston baked beans he cooked, were the best I had ever tasted. One of the crew, whose father was a fingerprint expert in the NSW Police, intended going for his ticket and used to shoot the sun every day when the skipper took his sight at noon. We called him 'Sextant Bill' and he was on his way to Denmark to marry a girl there.

One day out of Newcastle we got a taste of why British ships are called 'limeys'. In the dogwatch the third mate strides along the deck with a notebook and halts at the fresh water pump, which is always kept locked. All hands line up with utensils to hold water, the allowance being set down by the Board of Trade. Each man gives a set quota to the cook. He then takes what he wants for his daily use, part of which is used to dilute his daily allowance of lime juice, which has to be consumed in front of the third mate. Surplus water is noted in the book and is credited to the seaman for future use, such as the weekly bath or clothes washing.

One day in mollymawk territory, some of the crew who knew of such things set to work to make a gadget to catch one. A V of shiny metal around which was sewn a strip of meat was tied to a line and towed astern. It was not long before one was caught. They have a hook on the end of their beak and when they dive on the shiny metal it gets caught and they cannot get free unless the line is slacked. After hauling them on board we took some photographs and let them loose.

Getting down towards the Roaring Forties, in one 4–6 watch we logged 12 knots. The ship was sizzling along, lee scuppers just above water level. This was moving but it didn't last long. The skipper came up after tea and pulled in a few sails. Sinclair, the mate, whose watch it was, would have carried on regardless, but as the wind really freshened during the night it was fortunate the skipper took this action. After 80 days we arrived at Valparaiso. We did not berth because there is no wharf there. This was because of the terrific windstorms called *pamperos*. The night we arrived we took in sail and just drifted until morning when the tug came out. We were surprised to see the Australian flag fluttering from her mast. We were told an Australian owned it.

By now we were like monkeys in the rigging and always slid down the backstays instead of coming down the ratlines. Our hands were hardened from handling ropes and our feet were also hard as we only wore shoes in bad weather.

We anchored several miles off shore, putting out two anchors for'ard and one astern. Being close to the monsoon season our next job was to take down the royal and topgallant yards. In due course the baggers arrived, the donkey engine started up and the main yard cockbilled to act as a crane. A line was rove through its sheave, a cargo hook attached and unloading commenced. Another line called a bull rope was attached to the hook and belayed on deck. When the basket was lowered the bull rope held it in the correct position over a barge, which was alongside. The method of transport from ship to shore was by rowing, usually in the ship's gig. Competition between the boatmen was very keen and we would often engage in impromptu races with other ship's boats. It was our job to row the master ashore when he had to conduct ship's business.

Our second mate was an excellent seaman but never sober after his first weekend ashore. He was a commander in the navy during the 1914–1918 war and this probably affected him. The first thing he did on going ashore was to rent a horse and pay a boy to mind it as he went around the various hotels and bars. He would get so full that he had difficulty staying on the horse, falling over one side and then the other. One evening he came to the fo'c'sle door calling all hands on deck and shouting to loose the mainsail and topsails. He ranted and raved when no one moved and Sinclair came out and calmed him down. On another occasion the Chilean Air Force was exercising at night and he thought he was back in the war. He told me to get a hurricane lamp. He placed it on the rail, took off his jacket and began sending Morse signals by opening and closing the jacket. When he was drunk he used to become incontinent and the steward refused to attend to him. A row followed and Sinclair knocked him out. That was the finish and he was paid off.

The Captain had his wife and young daughter, Ena, on board. She had been born at sea. She had some chickens on the boat deck and we used to play tricks on her by placing carefully peeled and shaped potatoes in the egg box. On another occasion we made them drunk by putting *pisco*, the local brew, in their water.

All my *Rothesay Bay* mates paid off here, as we were not returning to Australia but were going on to England for a three-year refit. Our visit here was enjoyable enough although communication was difficult at times. One day when we ran out of money we dug out a five-pound Bebarfald [Sydney department store] furniture voucher. We took this to a moneylender and got the full five-pound value in pesos. Another time Sextant Bill and I tried out a lifeboat and were lucky to get back to the ship due to the poor performance of the regulation sail.

Discharging finished, our t'gallant and royal yards were put back aloft and we were on our way to Taltal to load saltpetre for England. There was a very sad sight in Valparaiso. During the war a dozen or more beautiful German three and four masters were interned there. Many of them still lay at anchor while some were high and dry, driven ashore by *pamperos*. It is said that the Germans put acid at the base of the masts to make them unusable.

Our replacement crew was unbelievable. A young Indian who would not go aloft, an old Maltese about 80 and an English third mate from an English shipping line who was not much use. Our new cook was a Swede, known as the 'flying cook'. The only seaman was a Chileño (we called him Chile). The Maltese was filthy and had to be scrubbed and was found to be crawling with head lice. We removed these with kerosene and sailcloth.

On our way to Taltal the order was given 'Clean the bilges'. What a dirty stinking job this was, but we lived through it. There were many jobs abhorred by seamen and this was one of them. Arriving at Taltal we anchored several miles offshore. As we had no money no one went ashore except Chile. My particular job was to tally the saltpetre as it came aboard. Every afternoon after knock-off most of us went swimming using the painting punt. This was brought to a halt one day when we were confronted by marine creatures which we later found out were sea lions. Taltal was very dry. The oldest inhabitant there had never seen rain.

One weekend Chile came aboard in a bad mood and abused Taffy. Taffy was Welsh and he had an inseparable mate, Ginger, from Liverpool. They were both getting on in years. A challenge to a knife fight was made and readily accepted. Chile was fighting mad and Ginger and Taffy, thanks to *pisco*, were only just able to stand up. The set-up was agreed upon. Chile was to stand at the break of the fo'c'sle and Taffy and Ginger opposite the deckhouse. I had to sit on the deckhouse and referee. Chile, knife in hand, thundered down the deck on unsteady legs. Ginger was swaying on deck, probably seeing several Chiles and wondering which one to tackle. Chile bore down the deck, yelling in Chilean and English, missed Ginger with his knife but knocked him into the scuppers where he remained. A similar fate befell Taffy. It took some hard talking and a jar of pickles to quieten Chile, who immediately went ashore again. He was, from the day he boarded the ship, carrying a chip on his shoulder about not being British. In the end I convinced him that while he was signed on a British ship he was British. Chile was a powerful man and a good sailor. He was the only fellow I met who could tie a Turk's-head. He used to tie them so quickly that you could not follow him. Everyone tried. At last I got the idea to colour each strand differently and so I was able to follow the twists. Chile could not believe that I had mastered it and it made us mates, sailor wise. For recreation we all sewed kitbags out of old sailcloth. I made one six feet long. We also plaited sennit of all kinds and made sandals, mats and all kinds of things out of canvas, rope and yarn.

At last loading was finished and we were on our way again, this time to England around the mighty Horn. Sailing was normal. As we left the fine weather latitudes we changed our light sails for storm canvas. The good weather was now finished and we were experiencing gales and big seas. Our hands had become sore and raw from salt-water cracks around the finger joints. This always happened after a sustained period of handling wet ropes in bad weather. We now saw albatross and other large birds. Also we were amazed to see little black birds bobbing around on the huge waves. They were 'Mother Carey's chickens' [storm-petrels] and it seemed impossible that they could survive. In rounding the Horn we went well to the south and while we didn't see any icebergs we could smell the ice.

On turning north we ran into the biggest electrical storm I have ever seen. The lightning was vivid and lit up the night sky. It ran down the steel rigging and into the sea. At the commencement of this storm we took the royals in. The royals were always the work of the ordinary seamen and deck boys. I used to make a practice of being first into the rigging, as I preferred to be on the yardarm rather than on a footrope with the others. On this occasion no one followed me and I had to stow the sail on my own.

Continuing north we had to change our storm sails for our light weather canvas again. Large sharks now appeared along with the attendant pilot fish. Also we were now in bonito territory. This was the only type of fishing I did not mind. The method was to use a large hook with a piece of white rag, and a length of wire connected to a thin rope line. We would dangle this on top of the waves from the bowsprit. An immediate catch was certain. A man on the fo'c'sle head then hauled in the fish. The story goes that a ship's crew was poisoned by this fish, so they are always boiled with a silver coin in the water. If it turns black then the fish is poisonous. Flying fish had now appeared, often flying on board striking sails or rigging and falling to the deck. We welcomed them as a tasty addition to our ship's fare. They were capable of hitting a seaman a severe blow.

Waterspouts were also occurring and some of the crew were concerned that we could run into one. In the doldrums we experienced a flat swell with the sea like glass. The ship was rolling both ways and the lower sails had to be raised to stop them slatting about and getting chafed. The skipper constantly paced the poop whistling for a wind. Every time the sea rippled it was an indication that it could turn into a breeze and the yards were hauled around to catch it. It would then fall off and come from another direction and the yards would have to be hauled around again. This was routine procedure for several weeks until we got into the North-East Trades.

Just before we hit the trades we had a freak storm and the third mate was thrown clean over the wheel. This called for another helmsman called lee wheel. Once we got into the North-East Trades, apart from sweating up the braces each day, the ship sailed herself and we had no work with the sails. All hands were kept busy painting and generally cleaning up the ship for our arrival in England. The wooden royal and topgallant masts were scraped and oiled. One day a large passenger liner passed us and circled us twice, probable giving her passengers a good look at us.

We made Falmouth early one morning and there were six or more Royal Navy warships at anchor there. We went to a mooring to await orders. They came after two days—'go to Leith'. Off Dungeness a tug came alongside and wanted to tow us to Leith but the skipper declined, saying he would see him outside the Dover Straits. The meeting never eventuated. We were becalmed in the thickest fog I have ever seen. You could not see more than a yard in front of you and we were right in the middle of the shipping lanes from London to the Continent. There were horns and sirens screeching all around us and we expected to be cut in half at any moment. Our own little hand-operated foghorn could only be heard a few hundred yards away and we were in this situation for about a day. When a breeze sprang up and dispersed the fog it turned into a gale. Visibility was very poor and when we made a landfall the skipper was not sure if it was Leith and decided to put out to sea again to wait for visibility to improve. Our second mate, Sinclair, was of the opinion that we had made Leith.

Trouble now really started for us. The ship was becoming sluggish and would not respond readily to the helm. It was apparent we were taking in water. In a few hours *Garthwray*, our beautiful sleek ship, was now an uncontrollable piece of steel. We could not tack and it took hours to wear ship. She was just wallowing in the trough of the waves. On one inshore tack, just south of Aberdeen, we tried to wear and she was very close to the cliffs before she responded. Visibility was now good and having returned to a seaward tack, we just wallowed around. The next morning, coming on deck at the change of watch at 4 am, we found the ship reduced to lower topsails and the royal and topgallant backstays secured with chains to take the slack out of them. The gale lasted for about a week. The fo'c'sle head was covered with ice and too dangerous to stand on. The lookout had to be kept from the top of the deckhouse. On coming off watch it took about half an hour of pain before we thawed out. Our clothes never dried out. One day Cooky got caught. On opening the galley door a wall of water rushed in, cleaning everything out. It put out the galley fire and pots and pans were washed along the deck.

The Northern Lights had now appeared, with wide parallel streaks of light filling the sky. I was nearly washed overboard one day. Some lines had come adrift from their belaying pins and I had to recoil them. The deck was permanently full of water about two feet deep. The terrific force of water swirling across the deck with each roll swept me off my feet and very nearly over the rail. I just managed to catch the tail end of a rope and was able to save myself. At last the storm subsided and we could see the lights of many ships on the horizon.

We sent up rocket after rocket but nothing happened. In the morning a trawler came alongside and put a line aboard to tow us in. They had seen our rockets but as they were trawling could not come to our aid. We were stopped by the swirl when we turned the corner at Aberdeen. A second trawler put a line aboard but was still unable to make headway. We had to be taken back along the north coast to Cromarty Firth, where we anchored at Invergordon. Eventually a pump arrived on a tug but it was not powerful enough and we had to wait for another one to arrive, which was able to pump us dry. The trouble that caused us to take on water was found to be a three-inch pipe, which we used to pump water to wash down the decks. It had rusted through.

All we could see of Invergordon were a few houses covered with snow. We did not attempt to go ashore, probably our experience with the ship's boat at Valparaiso had something to do with it. Before long we were off, under tow again and finally arrived at Leith where we paid off. The skipper offered to get me a job standing by and learning the rigging trade but we were all thankful to be ashore. After a stop at a ship chandlers to buy new clothes we went on to Liverpool, then went our various ways.

When I started tracking down the last mariners who'd served in the world's remaining sailing ships, I never thought I would meet up with anyone who sailed in three very famous ships, two of them clippers well known in the Australian emigrant and wool trade—*Antiope*, *Hesperus* and *Mount Stewart* (mentioned in Chapter 4, The French Bounty Ships).

I commented earlier that seamen, at least those in British ships, were considered by some to be at the lower end of the social scale. One would not expect to find a person living in a waterfront apartment at Point Piper, an exclusive suburb on Sydney Harbour, who'd started his career in a sailing ship.

Bob Hewitt, retired managing director of the Eastern Stevedoring Company, Malaya, told me of his colourful career from the time he signed on as indentured apprentice in the well-known sailing ship *Antiope* in 1918. This full-rigged ship was built for the rice millers Heap & Sons in 1866 and employed in taking general cargo from the United Kingdom to Melbourne and returning via Calcutta or Rangoon with rice. Basil Lubbock writes of her subsequent voyaging under various owners in his *Last of the Windjammers*, describing two serious mishaps, each of which could have finished her off. In 1908 a coal cargo shifted and she ended up on her beam ends. The only action possible was for the crew to shovel it back. While they were below in the dust-filled blackness of the rolling hull, facing what must have appeared to be an impossible task, the thought must have crossed their minds that the nickname given to their ship, *'Anti-Hope'*, was quite appropriate.

Like many other retired ships, *Antiope* was given a reprieve by World War I. In 1915, after some years as a coal hulk, she was re-rigged, this time as a barque. Her new owner was the Otago Iron Rolling Mills of New Zealand. In bad weather off Bluff Harbour, while under tow, she went ashore and it was only her iron hull that saved her. Pumped out and refloated, she was again refitted and young Bob Hewitt joined her for her next voyage:

> I signed on *Antiope* on 10 December, 1918. Our first voyage took us to San Francisco, where we loaded case oil, up the Sacramento River, for Wellington. The skipper was Captain Campbell, the mate was Mr Mcdonnell and the second mate was Eric Hay. We then went to Suva, Fiji, where we loaded copra for Rotterdam. The skipper, this trip, was Captain Broadhouse and the mate Mr Wylie. We had eight apprentices in the crew, eight ABs and two ordinary seamen. In Suva the galley boy and steward deserted and were replaced by two Indians. The Indian steward had a bunk in the pantry, which was situated under the poop near the lazarette.
>
> The weekly food ration for the apprentices included one small can of condensed milk, which never lasted more that two days. Being the junior and also the smallest apprentice, I was frequently nominated to raid the officers' pantry at night, to replenish our milk supply. Needless to say this required some skill and the prospect of being caught filled me with dread. It necessitated crawling on my hands and knees, past the officers' cabins, to the pantry, searching in the dark for the milk and transferring some of it into my container, hoping all the time I would not waken the steward. The officers discovered the discrepancy, blaming the steward and giving him hell. He came into the half deck, complaining he had been accused of stealing the milk, but never once did he mention that he knew the culprit. It was early one stormy morning off Cape Horn, when the steward came into the half deck and wakened me. 'I have come to say goodbye,' he said. 'I know you steal the milk, but don't worry, I like you and I want to give you my boots!' A few minutes later he jumped overboard. I was still half asleep and did not realise what it was all about until I heard the cry 'Man overboard, all hands on deck!' We were running before a gale and could not heave to or wear ship—even if it had been the captain. There was no way we could save him. He was lost at sea.
>
> We spent several months in Rotterdam before going to Vyborg in Finland [now Russia]. We were constantly hungry. The salt beef which was issued to us was inedible. It was so salty that we had to tow it astern in a bag for several hours before we could eat it. It was here another apprentice, Bob Rimmer, and I, jumped ship. We swam out to an American steamship, *Lake Gratis*, and stowed away. This ship was loading pit props for British mines and had a deck cargo about 20 feet [6 metres] high. She had a heavy list and we were able to climb aboard through a mooring port. We hid in the lazarette, under some sails and even though the Authorities came aboard, they failed to find us.
>
> When we got out into the North Sea, the deck cargo shifted and we went right over on to our beam-ends. The ship was in imminent danger of foundering. We got out through a porthole and could stand on the ship's side. The deck cargo was held down with a

series of cleats and we ran along the ship's side letting them off. This allowed the deck cargo to fall into the sea and the ship righted herself. A German tug towed us into Kiel.

From being stowaways we were now heroes. The Germans offered us positions in the North Sea pilot boats, but the American skipper would not hear of it and signed us on as ABs and took us on to England. Our wage was $60 per month and paid to us in gold sovereigns. We returned to Finland for another cargo of timber. The old *Antiope* took a cargo of timber to Delagoa Bay in Portuguese Africa and it was here that she caught fire and was burnt out. Her iron hull was still there only a few years ago.

Back in the UK there had been a long strike and we sailed on to Brest, France. There were many US ships here out of work. Another US ship full of coal came and bunkered us all and we left for the US in the middle of 1921. There was much unemployment in the US at this time and ships hard to get. The Sailor's Home in South Street was standing room only. I was lucky to get a ship-keeping job at Hampton Roads, North Virginia, breaking ice off the hulls of laid-up ships. Then after returning to New York I joined the US ship *Kansas* as an AB for a voyage to Adelaide via the Panama Canal.

Back in Australia I went back into sail in the trans-Tasman trade. I sailed in the *Northern Chief*, a barquentine, and the barques *White Pine* and *James Craig*. I sailed in the latter on what turned out to be her last voyage. We went from Auckland to Melbourne arriving there in nine days. Within sight of Melbourne heads the wind changed and we ended up well south of Tasmania, which added another 30 days to our voyage. Another voyage was planned to Africa but this fell through and she was taken to Hobart where she was hulked.

Bob went on to become second mate in the Union Steamship Co. before swallowing the anchor and going into the stevedoring business.

A chance comment by a young lady during a talk I was delivering on sailing ships brought me in touch with Bill Beadly, a professional seaman who sailed before the mast in both sail and steam during the 1920s. She volunteered, 'My father sailed in the *Hesperus*!' I first thought she must mean her grandfather or some other *Hesperus*, some coaster perhaps, not the crack clipper of the 1870s. When I met and questioned her father, I recorded the following story of his time under sail.

I joined the ship *Silvana* at Birkenhead in 1921. I had previously been an apprentice with the Morocco Steamship Co. but cleared out because of the low wages. As it turned out I would have been better off financially staying with them, but then I would never have had the chance to sail under canvas in this famous ship.

Silvana, a full-rigged ship, was seeing out her final years under the Red Ensign. She had been better known as the famous emigrant clipper *Hesperus,* built in 1873, and incredibly has found a place in this book in spite of the 130 years that have elapsed since her maiden voyage. This was helped by a period under Devitt & Moore ownership and 20 years under Russian ownership as a training ship, when she was re-rigged and refurbished. Built from iron, the almost indestructible material that preceded the more readily oxidised steel, *Hesperus,* under the ownership of Anderson & Anderson, proprietors of the Orient Line for 16 years, carried thousands of emigrants to Australia in the 1870s and 1880s. For a further ten years Devitt & Moore ran her out to Australia with 40 or so paying cadets, which added to the earnings from her paying passengers and general cargo. Devitt

& Moore sold her to the Russians in 1899. Under the new name of *Grand Duchess Maria Nikolaevna* and the ownership of the Odessa Navigation School, she trained White Russian seamen until World War I. During the war she was laid up in the Danish port of Fredrickshaven, later sailing under the White Russian flag until purchased by the British & Foreign Trading Association and renamed *Silvana*. She was broken up in 1924. Bill continues:

> I joined her as AB and we sailed to Santo Pola, Spain, to load a cargo of salt for Buenos Aires. The skipper's name was Souta, and I never got on with him although I liked the second mate, a chap called McNabb. We shipped quite a few Liverpool Irish in the crew and being a Pom I didn't get on with them. I preferred to associate with the Russians who were still in the crew. The owners were a mean lot and we ran short of food on the way out. The old man had taken two pigs on board for fresh meat, as was the custom. The skipper had other ideas and tried to sell them in Buenos Aires. The Customs got wind of it and ordered them destroyed. With no such thing as refrigeration, we had to eat them straightaway and only had one meal from them. On the way up the River Plate we ran on to a sandbank with all sails set. There was no damage but we had to sit there for two weeks until there was a favourable tide to float us off.
>
> We spent two months in Buenos Aires and finally loaded maize for Falmouth for orders. When we arrived in Falmouth we discovered the company was in financial difficulties and there was no money to pay our wages. The crew went ashore to complain to the union. We were told to go back to the ship as she had orders to unload at Bordeaux. Even when we had discharged the cargo there was still no money to pay us. We were in a foreign country and penniless. We were sent home by the British consul as distressed British subjects. Back in the UK, I went to see the Seamen's Union and spoke to Havelock Wilson, the founder. I learned that ten pounds were coming to me but I only received four pounds out of this as the union deducted my dues first and my lodgings cost 30 shillings. Havelock Wilson had an agreement with the shipowners to the effect that there would be no strikes if only British seamen were employed and he advised me to go and look for another job.
>
> The mate, a Mr Morris, found that his wife had received no allotment while he was away. He was so depressed that he committed suicide. I went back in steam and for a while served in the Great Lakes steamers. In New York I worked in the Baltimore and Ohio Tug Co. I then crewed on large yachts sailing out of New York and Newport, the most notable being the four-masted schooner *Katura*, owned by the Secretary of the Navy, Robert E. Todd. I then sailed in the Venezuelan barquentine *Gabiota*, from New York to Venezuela with general cargo. We returned in ballast but with 200 longhorn cattle for Crenpuego, Cuba.
>
> In steam again and was nearly lost in the tanker *Baton Rouge* when caught in a hurricane off Bermuda. In Australia I spent some time in a topsail schooner, sailing between Melbourne and Hobart. She was the *Joe Sims* and her skipper was Ray Heather whose brother was skipper of the *Alma Doepel*. I then swallowed the anchor and became the lighthouse keeper at South Head Signal Station in Port Jackson until 1958 when I retired.

Thomas Law & Co. of Glasgow, a well-known British shipping company, operated a large fleet of sailing ships well into the twentieth century. They were known colloquially as the 'Shire Line' from their practice of naming their ships after Scottish shires. Their last sailer was the four-masted barque *Elginshire*, built in 1889 and broken up in 1923.

I have been fortunate to have found a seaman who sailed in one of their ships. Archie McArthur joined the four-masted barque *Kinross-Shire* in Sydney Harbour in 1916 for a voyage to Falmouth for orders. He relates:

My first sight of *Kinross-Shire* was from the launch taking me out to join her as she lay at anchor off Kirribilli Point. She looked huge to me as the three previous ships I had served in were of a much lesser tonnage. They were the barques *Joseph Craig* and *Manurewa* and the barquentine *Lindstol*, all around 700 tons. Two days after joining her we had all sails bent and we were towed out of the harbour on 8 April 1916, headed towards Falmouth for orders around Cape Horn. The crew was a truly cosmopolitan lot; in fact an Irishman and myself were the only two British members of the crew. Captain Murchie was a Scot from the Isle of Arran. We had fine weather for the first few days after leaving Sydney and made good progress under full sail. *Kinross-Shire* was bald headed, meaning she carried no royals.

We were to appreciate this a few days later when we ran into really heavy weather south of New Zealand. We had left Sydney with our wash ports only opened half way and with the sea that was running it was obvious they needed to be opened to their full extent. So all hands were called to do this job at 8 am one morning. By this time, the seas were breaking right across the decks and the crew refused to tackle the job. It involved considerable risk, in knocking out the wedges, which held the doors half closed. The two mates, two apprentices and myself did the job plus one other AB who was a Russian Finn, and the only real friend I had amongst the crew.

From then on we received special treatment. Later the weather became worse and the ship had to heave to, as despite the fact that we had a fair wind our captain felt that the risk of broaching to in mountainous following seas was too great. It was 16 days before the weather conditions abated sufficiently to resume her course. During this time our conditions were appalling, for we had to exist without hot meals, as the galley was continually awash.

Eventually we rounded the Horn and headed north into much fairer weather and from then on conditions improved. We had no knowledge of how the war was progressing, for we had no radio. Our passage through the tropics was uneventful and we did not run into any bad weather until we approached the British Isles. It was easier to make Queenstown for our orders, as it was more suited to our course. When we arrived and the pilot boarded, the first thing he asked the Captain was why the boats were not swung out!

Captain Murchie asked, 'Why?' The pilot replied, 'Don't you know that 40 ships were sunk last week by enemy submarines in the vicinity of the English Channel?'

We had been at sea for 155 days and had no idea of any danger from enemy submarines. So the next day our lifeboats were given a thorough check over, provisions replaced as necessary and all boats swung out. We did not get ashore in Cork Harbour but did appreciate the fresh Irish butter and potatoes we bought from the bumboats that plied their trade there.

The senior apprentice who had been acting as third mate left us here. Because of my previous sea time Captain Murchie offered me his job but my rank of AB remained unchanged on the ship's articles as the law required that a certain number of ABs were carried.

The orders came for us to discharge our cargo in St Nazaire and on the fourth day after our arrival, we were towed out of port and set sail for our destination. We met with very heavy weather on the way but this was good, as no submarine could have operated in such weather. Eight days after our departure, the pilot boarded and we were towed into the River Loire and tied up in St Nazaire Harbour. I realised for the first time that we were in a serious conflict as the labour provided for the discharge of cargo was with German prisoners of war.

After our cargo was discharged, I was given the job of taking the crew to Liverpool, for that is where they signed on. They travelled under a Board of Trade agreement and were given an advance of a few pounds and would receive the balance on signing off. I was in complete charge of them and held one passport in which all their names were recorded. It proved quite a job, as it took two days to go by train to St Malo, where we had to board a cross Channel steamer. We stayed overnight in Rennes and I had great difficulty rounding them up from the local brothels. It was with great relief that I signed them all off, after arriving in Liverpool.

As if the normal hazards of serving in a sailing ship were not enough, the possibility of being sunk by enemy action during World War I added another element of danger for all seamen in this period. The following accounts of enemy sinkings represent only a fraction of the fate which befell hundreds of sailing ships during this conflict, for due to their lack of manoeuvrability they were easy prey for U-boats.

Captain J. Murray Lindsay told me of the sinking of his ship *Bengairn* on a voyage from Seattle towards Queenstown in 1916. *Bengairn*'s course crossed that of a German U-boat and the only possible action was for the crew to lower the boats and watch their ship sunk by gunfire. Generally it took only one or two shells, as the sailing ship, with only two watertight bulkheads and no positive buoyancy, would sink within minutes. Many ships' crews were not picked up or failed to reach land and perished, but *Bengairn*'s crew was picked up by a British warship.

If the U-boat had been at sea for a long time, her crew would take what provisions they needed from the sailer's meagre supply; the chronometers and officers' sextants would become trophies and, of course, the ship's papers were taken to prove the kill. There were cases recorded of violence, but usually the sinking was carried out in a matter of fact manner with the U-boat's commander wishing the sailing ship master, 'Good luck and I hope you get picked up soon.'

A rather amusing incident was related by *Pommern* sailor, Bengt Söderlund, about one of his skippers whose ship was boarded by a U-boat crew. The U-boat commander went down into the saloon and helped himself to a glass of the skipper's whisky. 'I'm sorry I have to sink your ship Captain, but would you like to have a glass of whisky with me first?' The irate skipper told Bengt, 'The bastard was bloody well offering me a glass of my own whisky. Of course I refused and it was the only time in my life that I have ever knocked back a drink!'

Captain Artur Söderlund, long-time master of the four-masted barque *Lawhill*, told the following story to my good friend Dennis Adams. Söderlund was a seaman in a small Norwegian barque early in World War I when it encountered a German U-boat. There were bullets flying everywhere and some of the rigging fell on deck. Söderlund ran to the lifeboat falls and was hit on the head by some timber from the boat deck. Dennis remembers the scars 23 years later. The U-boat came alongside and some crew scrambled on board to get what they needed in the way of food. The pig was quickly slaughtered and taken aboard the U-boat. Before getting into the boats the Norwegian master was asked by the U-boat commander, 'Why were you so long in Falmouth?' 'How did you know I was in Falmouth?' asked the Norwegian master. 'I saw you there,' said the German captain.

The Norwegian master would not believe this but the German replied, 'I saw you in the hotel and you complained about the coffee being cold!' Evidently this was correct. The German captain had come ashore in a dinghy one night. This was often done in order to pick up conversations about shipping movements and no doubt have a drink or two.

The barque's boats reached the Cornish coast two days later.

The last merchant square riggers to fly the Red Ensign of the British mercantile marine were owned by John Stewart & Co. of London. (The ships of Englishman Sir William Garthwaite were registered in Canada.) John Stewart & Co. owned a total of 28 sailing ships between 1877, when the company was formed, and 1928, when their last sailing vessel, the full-rigged ship *William Mitchell*, was sold to the shipbreakers.

Finishing her working life two years earlier was another Stewart ship, *Monkbarns*. It was 9 July 1926 when she backed her main yards with Dungeness abeam, and picked up the pilot and the tow that would take her to Gravesend and the end of her sailing days. On board was a young man who was educated and started his sea career in far-off Tasmania, eight years earlier. His name was Dudley Turner and as the result of many conversations and much reading of his meticulously kept diary, I am able to describe some of the colourful events from her last voyage. Some of Dudley's experiences prior to going deep water are no less interesting. A schoolmate of his called Montgomery later became the famous general of World War II. Dudley first went to sea at the age of 16, in the small three-masted schooner *Alma Doepel*. This vessel is noteworthy in that she survived in trade, albeit as a motor vessel, until the 1970s, and has now been restored as a sail-training vessel. Dudley told me of his first years at sea in this ship.

> My uncle took me to see Henry Jones with a view to getting me a position in one of his ships. He was a real gentleman and highly respected around Hobart. He owned the IXL jam factory and had other business interests such as timber. The story goes that he started his business empire by mixing up jam in his household copper [wash tub]. He said that I could join the *Alma Doepel* on the Melbourne run, which I did in 1918. She had four seamen, a cook and mate in the crew. The skipper's name was Harry Heather (pronounced Heether) and he was something of a legend on this coast. He was an exceptional seaman, although he only had a coastal ticket. We called it a 'blowfly' ticket. He had the nickname Spring Bay Harry from his practice of putting into one of the small east coast ports whenever he thought bad weather was coming. He had a sixth sense in this regard.
>
> The mate, Harry Brown, who had a foreign going master's ticket, was rather scornful of this and reckoned that we should have ridden out the storm at sea. The old man's judgement was correct and we never sustained any damage. Of course there may have been an ulterior motive as whenever we were holed up in one of these ports the skipper would go ashore and catch the train back home for a few days.
>
> I never noticed any charts or formal navigation, taking place. When we sailed from Hobart we turned left and headed off to Melbourne. We always got there. We often took 12 x 12 inch (300 x 300 mm) hardwood flitches to Melbourne as well as canned jam. We brought back general cargo. The hull had two centreboards, one for'ard and one aft, that we lowered when sailing. The deck and most of the fittings were painted a port wine colour, which was pretty standard for many ships on the coast.

We had a 100 hp Frisco oil engine that was only used for entering or leaving port and even though I was engaged as a seaman, I acted as engineer on these occasions. The engine flywheel had a series of holes around the outside and a tommy bar was inserted to kick the engine over. It often backfired, throwing the tommy bar out with great force, enough to embed itself in the hull planking.

When berthing, the skipper yelled orders to the engine room through an open hatch. It was difficult to hear him, so I got the idea to rig up an electric bell. One ring slow ahead, two rings full ahead and three rings full astern. We were in Port Phillip, heading for Victoria dock. When we were getting close to the wharf, I got two rings. I thought it a bit strange but orders are orders and I pushed the throttle full ahead. We crashed into the wharf, carrying away our dolphin striker and bobstay. The skipper had his orders mixed up but of course he blamed me. Another idea I had was to use a small radio that I had to receive weather reports. As radio was in its infancy at that time, we were the only ship on this coast with this luxury.

The skipper and most of the crew were hard drinkers. I remember one trip from Hobart to Tarana when the whole crew was drunk and I was the only sober one on board. I was left at the wheel all night while everyone sobered up below. The mate, an exceptional seaman who had been in the Australian barque *Wild Wave*, told me of a previous voyage when *Alma Doepel* brought a wine cargo from Adelaide. Everyone got stuck into the wine and did not keep an eye on the weather. They were hit by a sudden squall and most of the sails were carried away. Harry and the crew had to sew a few sails from wheat bags that they were also carrying, to enable them to reach their destination.

After a few years in a small tramp steamer, Dudley joined the full-rigged ship *Monkbarns* in Sydney. Dudley told me that this was the fourth of three Pacific crossings to the West Coast with coal from Newcastle that *Monkbarns* made after sailing from Birkenhead in 1923 with a cargo of rock salt for Sydney. In the South Atlantic she met with severe weather that put her on her beam-ends and caused her cargo to shift, together with much damage about her decks. Unable to right herself, *Monkbarns* wallowed at an angle of 40 degrees with her lee rail under. Carrying no radio to call for assistance, the only action was to get below and shovel the cargo back, an enormous task. As the storm was still raging the hatches had to be left battened down. The seas breaking on board threatened to breach the hatches and send the ship to the bottom. While most of the crew was below the remainder were securing broken gear on deck and making fast sail aloft. A young apprentice named Sibun, who was aloft securing a topgallant, fell into the sea and was lost. It was impossible to manoeuvre the ship and all boats had been damaged in the storm. *Monkbarns* put into Cape Town in distress and three weeks later set off for Sydney. Dudley continued his story:

We were towed up the coast to Newcastle, as was often the custom. It was only 60 miles and not worth trying to sail. We loaded coal at the Dyke and on 14 July 1925, sailed for Callao in Peru. After an uneventful passage of 60 days we arrived at Callao and discharged our coal. With us in port was the four-masted barque *Garthpool*, 83 days out of Melbourne.

We received orders to proceed south to Valparaiso, where we loaded a cargo of guano out of the Finnish barque *Queen of Scots*, which had been dismasted off Cape Horn. This cargo would be one of the worst to carry due to the pungent odour of ammonia. It didn't seem to worry the local stevedores but it made my nose bleed and the crew hated working the stuff. It took about two months to transfer the cargo as it had set rock hard, and we left for London on 20 January 1926. At 5 am a tug came alongside with the pilot, and all hands turned to unmoor ship. We had previously hove up the starboard anchor, all we had to do was to get in the wires from the buoy aft, as the tugboat unshackled our cable and hove up our port anchor for us. Another tug towed us outside the breakwater where we made fast, awaiting our anchor from the other tug and also the old man with the ship's papers. The tug came out after dinner and the mate decided not to pass the anchor chain through the hawse pipe and down into the chain locker, but to flake it along the deck, so that we could scrape and tar it on the voyage home. It was a terrible job dragging that heavy cable out along the deck.

At 6 pm the skipper arrived with the papers and we cast off the buoy and were towed to sea. As the wind was fair, topsails were set and the tug cast off as we got more sail on the ship. She stood by until we were well under weigh, then blew three long blasts on her whistle as a farewell signal and waddled back into the harbour. The steamship *Poplar Branch* passed us and her crowd gave three cheers for the homeward-bounder. We gave them three cheers in return and dipped our ensign in farewell. The old hooker must have looked beautiful from the shore, heading for the golden sunset with the wake frothing astern and ever increasing as we got the rags on her. All sails were set except the royals. By dusk everything was shipshape and all hands settled down for the long passage to London.

The diary that Dudley kept is probably the best I have read. Written in a school exercise book, which was usual, it contained day-by-day entries and comments regarding sailing conditions and the working of a deep-water sailing ship. It also stated the ship's position day by day. This may not seem significant but it was information not readily available to those who resided for'ard of the main mast. Dudley used to bribe the steward with a few cigarettes daily to take a look at the logbook. This diary has many graphic and poetic descriptions of parts of the voyage, which obviously made an impression on this young seaman. An early entry describes an idyllic trade winds evening, a later one the evening of this voyage as his ship is towed up the Thames to the end of her sailing days. An accident aloft is recorded graphically but in matter-of-fact terms, and I have chosen it to portray yet another aspect of sailing ship travail.

The work of repairing damage aloft was just another task that the windjammer seaman accepted as routine. Consider, however, the fact that this work took place 30 to 40 metres above deck with the masts describing an arc of perhaps 40 degrees with each roll. The only equipment available was simple hand tools. This was not a feat that would be acclaimed when *Monkbarns'* owners read the voyage report. It was a commonplace job of work that windjammer crews tackled without question. The qualification necessary for the job was simply AB—able-bodied seaman. Dudley recorded this incident with no more emphasis than other routine tasks, in everyday sailor's terms. The layman may find it confusing but if followed through carefully it describes all the actions necessary to make good the damage.

February 14th 1926, Lat 57°S, Long 65° W, 4.30 am Moderate breeze, showery and cold. Our watch had just turned in when there was a crash and a thud aloft. I jumped out on deck and there was the main upper topsail yard resting on the crane of the lower topsail yard and the topsail flapping itself to pieces. The tie had carried away which let the yard down by the run and carried away both lifts.

'All hands' was immediately called and on going aloft, we found the weight of the upper topsail yard had broken the pin bar in the lower topsail crane. It was a terrible job securing the yard and sail and getting the halyards rove off again. We had to clew up the lower topgallant to get a gantline aloft onto the cap. We then had to overhaul the halyards well and bend the gantline to the tie, a couple of fathoms from where it carried away. We then hove away on the gantline which was rove through the tie and led through the sheave at the topmast head, down through the block on the yard and re-bent on the gantline. We hove away until the end of the tie was at the mast head, shackled on. We then found that the pin bar in the lower topsail yard crane was broken in three pieces, so that the yard was likely to fall on deck at any moment. We got two good tackles on from each side of the cap to the yardarms and hove them taut. Hoisting the upper topsail yard a little we then got a fish tackle from the cap to the lower topsail yard amidships with a good strop, also a wire from the yard to the fo'c'sle head capstan which took the weight from the bar so we could knock it out. We substituted a piece of gangway stanchion, as we had no spare.

We then came up the gear and rove the yardarm tackles to a strop around the mast to prevent the yard jerking about. It would have been safer to do this as soon as we found out that the pin was broken. We also put a couple of wire strops around the yard and mast. We finished the job at 8 pm and reset the sails, having been aloft all day with the exception of a few minutes for dinner. Quite a pleasant way to spend a Sunday.

The fact that this incident took place on a Sunday meant that this day of leisure was lost and never made up.

A shipmate of Dudley's on this voyage was Ian Russell of Wellington, New Zealand. He relates the following events from earlier voyages he made in the intercolonial ships of New Zealand:

My first voyage was in the barque *White Pine*, formerly *Quathlamba*, an iron barque built in Aberdeen in 1879. I joined her as deck boy at Auckland in 1921. The master was Captain T. Proctor. After a slow passage of 21 days, we discharged our timber and were towed to Newcastle. We loaded coal for Brushgrove and Grafton, and after discharging this we loaded hardwood poles for Wellington. The three-masted schooner *Valmarie* left the previous day, also for Wellington, and we were anxious to see if we would beat her. However *Valmarie*, under Captain Schulbet, stranded on Farewell Spit when 15 days out. She was abandoned but was subsequently sold to a W. Lane, boat builder, for 100 pounds. He salvaged her and her cargo. She was renamed *Mapu* and afterwards finished up as a coal hulk at Nelson.

White Pine arrived after a passage of 17 days and sailed right to her anchorage. From Wellington we sailed to Greymouth with a small quantity of machinery, hardwood and ballast. After a stormy passage of 14 days we arrived off the breakwater but the bar was not navigable. We stood off in company with two W.S.S. Co. steamers for 24 hours, when the signal was given to enter. All sail was set and we headed in with a moderate fair wind. The signal, however, was meant for the steamers, and was changed to 'bar dangerous'. Captain Proctor ignored the signal, as he could not stop, and despite a lot of yawing, berthed safely between the two steamers. The Harbour paddle-wheel tug did not come out to assist in any way. A large crowd had gathered on the wharf and the Chairman of the Harbour board called for three cheers for our Captain and ship. We loaded a full cargo of rimu and pine for Sydney and arrived after a voyage of 16 days, sailing to our anchorage in Double Bay.

After discharging, the ship was sold to James Patterson & Co. of Melbourne to be used as a coal hulk. We sailed for Melbourne and after a passage of five days sailed through Port Phillip heads into the west channel, where we anchored due to a thick fog. We were then picked up by the tug *James Patterson* and towed to our berth in the Yarra River on 13 June 1922. I was kept working on *White Pine* with the carpenter for a month while she was being rigged down and converted into a hulk. Mr Fillies, the manager of James Patterson & Co., gave me a job on the tug *G. Patterson* as extra hand when she towed the barque *Shandon* to Adelaide. I was kept on the tug for several months until I signed on the Finnish full-rigged ship *Milverton* in October 1922.

Milverton was berthed in Victoria Dock and was loading wheat and wool. While in Melbourne the entire Finnish crew, with the exception of the six apprentices and sail maker, deserted. Eventually 15 ABs and two ordinary seamen were signed on. After loading, *Milverton* was towed to an anchorage off Williamstown and remained there for 14 days. The mate took advantage of this time to instruct the new crew in sail handling and where the various lines were belayed. Very few of the new hands had been in sail before and two were beachcombers. Eventually we were towed through Port Phillip heads and arrived in London after an uneventful passage of 90 days. This was an excellent passage time considering the inexperienced crew and the fact that the running gear was in poor condition and was constantly carrying away.

The Finns were excellent seamen but were handicapped in having to run the ship on a shoestring. On one occasion the spanker boom span carried away and the boom landed on the wheel, carrying away part of the rim and several spokes. Fortunately no one was hurt. The mate got one of the apprentices to remake the broken parts, and a good job he made of it. I can't recall the captain's name but he used to make excellent sheath knives out of old files.

Lionel Walker, an apprentice in *William Mitchell*, Britain's last commercial sailing ship, was transferred to *Monkbarns* in 1919 for a voyage to Buenos Aires. His comments put an interesting slant on the closing years of British sail.

I travelled to Ireland to join *Monkbarns* at Cork. She was in dry dock and some of the crew had hoisted a large Jolly Roger over the dock at Passage West and really caused a stir with the Sinn Fein movement. I remember one night walking along the wharf when a knife was thrust at my throat and I was asked, 'For God or Country?' I don't think the King of England would have been impressed with my answer that night.

While still in dry dock the carpenter went missing after going ashore for a few drinks. After much searching he was found in the net under the gangway fast asleep. It probably saved his life. While in Ireland we were invited to peace celebrations by the Royal Navy at Haughbollin. We decided to go in the ship's boat. Unfortunately none of us made it as the boat we lowered sank as it had been out of the water too long. We had to be towed back to the ship.

We sailed in ballast to Buenos Aires and returned with bagged linseed. When being unloaded we found that the stevedores were stealing the linseed. I was sent to confront them but several drew their knives and ran their fingers along the blades. I retreated and told the mate, who went down the hold but when confronted by a burly stevedore, just wished them good evening and left them to it.

Monkbarns was re-rigged at Cardiff and then took a coal cargo to Las Palmas in the Canary Islands. We unloaded the coal close to where a group of women were packing onions. We started throwing small lumps of coal at them and very soon they retaliated by throwing onions back at us. Very soon we had enough onions for the entire trip. We then sailed for Newcastle, New South Wales. When we were running the easting down in the Roaring Forties, we lost the fore and main topgallant masts. I was told by the 2nd mate to go and tell the skipper, Captain Davies. I went to his cabin and woke him up and was abused for dripping salt water all over his carpet. I apologised and in the same breath I told him we had just lost the fore topgallant mast over the side. As the deep furrows on his brow grew deeper I headed for the door and as soon as I was a safe distance added, 'and the main also'!

We loaded coal in Newcastle for Iquique but had to wait four months for new masts to be made in Sydney and sent up. When we arrived in Iquique we found there was a smallpox epidemic ashore and no one was allowed to leave or board the ship. I was made night watchman and given a heavy revolver and told not to let anyone on board, I wasn't nervous, but an oilskin coat hanging on deck to dry ended up with three bullet holes in it.

We loaded nitrate for Belgium, stopping at Falmouth for final orders. We were towed 50 miles to Zeebrugge. I left *Monkbarns* here as I had an atrophied optic nerve. It was thought that a prolonged trick at the wheel in icy conditions off the Horn caused it and I was told to keep away from cold conditions. During the same time another apprentice, Frank Wallace, had his hand jammed in a block and it was so cold that he didn't know he had three crushed fingers. When he returned to England the fingers were amputated. The need to stay out of cold conditions led to my returning to Australia where I finally settled.

I am including some exploits from Lionel's later life. While outside the definition of this book, they illustrate how these early years under sail led on, for many, to rewarding careers.

When I settled in Australia I spent five years in coastal ships, namely *Aeon, Period, Iron Chief, Iron Prince* and *Merriwa*. I then went to the Solomon Islands where I chartered schooners from Lever Bros. I recruited native labour for them at 12 pounds a head and returning them for two pounds a head after they had served their time. The last of the Blackbirders?

I spent 15 years in the Solomons and then became master of the Burns Philp ship *Rogeia*, known as the Bougainville mail boat. After that I was master of the *Malaguna*. I left the Solomons in 1940 and returned to Australia where I was involved with the RAAF, training crash boat crews between Sydney and Newcastle. I well remember the Japanese attack on Newcastle. We were instructed to 'search and destroy'. We had one 1914 machine gun on board!

When the Japanese occupied the Solomons, I was seconded to the Navy with the rank of lieutenant and acted as liaison officer with the US forces, as my knowledge of the area was invaluable. I made many sweeps with US Navy PT boats and shared a tent with a young US Navy officer, John F. Kennedy.

Also apprenticed in *Monkbarns* at the same time as Lionel Walker was Harry Fountain. He has given an excellent description of a fragment in the life of a limejuice apprentice and a look at the Port of Newcastle, New South Wales, in the twenties.

Our daily and nightly life at sea was inexorable. We were either on watch on deck or watch below every four hours, excepting in the dogwatches when we carried out the same routine for two hours. This was the tempo of our life in fine weather. In heavy weather there could be no routine. Life was ruled by the real emergencies of the hour as the urgent necessity of tacking and wearing ship, taking in or setting sail demanded the handling of many sails, meant a job for all hands, sometimes for a long spell. There were many times of heavy stress when no man could stay below, all stood by on the relative safety of the poop.

To us apprentices in the half deck were added the extra jobs, duties that had been handed down as tradition or more probably by necessity. We must do all our standing by abaft the mainmast and not with the crew. We were keepers of the ship's time, strikers of the appropriate bells on the poop to be answered by the lookout for'ard. (What a sleepy struggle this was in the warm weather of the trade winds.) All the work connected with flags and signalling was our province, heaving the log at eight bells and finally but not the least important was seeing that the binnacle lights were kept burning bright, a task which varied much with the quality of oil and the type of lamp. This job was that of the youngest apprentice on watch and in some jaundiced quarter this humble but necessary duty was put forward as the reason for young apprentices having to endure the taunt of 'light the binnacle boy'! It became a sort of challenge thrown at the young seagoing gentleman when ashore in his brass buttons, mainly in the colonial ports of Australia, New Zealand and South Africa. The reaction to it varied as to who made the saucy jibe. It was sometimes made by a bevy of knowing maidens or a cheeky larrikin. If the latter the matter was dealt with as promptly as possible and ending in broken heads and if the former, then 'circumstances altered cases'.

The Colonials were very friendly and ship conscious. Many were the homes thrown open to us then. The 'old country' was always spoken of as 'home' and talked about a great deal, even by those born here. It was our common background. The most attractive and best known of the Australian ports around this time was Newcastle. So attractive, that some apprentices jumped ship. Blue eyes and golden hair plus the attractions of high wages proved to be their 'Lorelei'.

Newcastle was the place for square-rigged ships to assemble for coal cargoes, mostly destined for the West Coast. Ships would lie across the Hunter River at Stockton, discharging their ballast at the dolphins until such time as their turn came to proceed along the Dyke to go under the tips. Not many square riggers were there in those days—along with us were *Kircudbrightshire*, *Garthsnaid*, *Archibald Russell*, *Mount Stewart*, *Vimiera* and *Hougomont*, along with a few flags from other nations. The most outstanding of these was the American *James J. Rolph*, and two pretty little New Zealand barques, *Rona* and *Raupo*. We, in *Monkbarns*, were there in the Hunter River for quite some time waiting for our masts, after our dismasting off the Kerguelen Islands. In all, we were about 11 weeks in Newcastle.

It was customary for the Captain to dole out to the apprentices on Saturday night, the sum of two shillings and sixpence or if the amount was recoverable from our premiums or parents, five shillings. With that sum in our pockets, at that age we owned the world, or at least Newcastle, for the evening. With so little liberty the beach was at any time an adventure to be enjoyed. Allowing for say, seven British sailing ships in the harbour with an average of 10 apprentices each, meant that 70 young hopefuls of like mind would converge on the main thoroughfare, Hunter Street. We seemed to spend most of our time and money in the Niagara Cafe. On Sundays we were taken care of by the Missions to Seamen, which was a good strong influence on wild young apprentices during the protracted stay in port. The padre was a fine fellow, Hare or O'Hare was his name. He organised many activities and provided lively young ladies to accompany us on picnics over in Stockton. Concerts were got up, revealing hidden talent amongst us. There were mouth organ, mandolin and singing recitals but sea shanties were taboo, partly because they were considered 'shop' but also because many of the versions would not have done in front of the ladies. We would walk miles back to the ship late at night or early in the morning, stumbling over the roughly laid railway lines along the Dyke, its wooden jetties littered with timber, wire hawsers and iron ballast tubs as there was very little lighting. You had to be very sure of where your ship lay, if she was on the outside tier and out of sight. Soon the time came when the ship was loaded and from the tips we were towed out to the farewell buoys to bend our sails and make ready for sea. Our day for departure came with real regrets, even if this was not shared by the larrikins of Hunter Street. There were broken heads and hearts on both sides. Fair enough! So we sailed for our next port—Iquique.

The last pages of Dudley Turner's diary are a fitting close to this chapter on British sail. I take up his words as his ship, *Monkbarns*, approaches soundings off the mouth of the English Channel at the end of her final voyage. The air of expectation that developed during the last days of a voyage was experienced by seafarers of all nations. The first sight of one's homeland after a prolonged voyage has been described as an unforgettable experience. The Lizard or its light was usually the first glimpse of land for the windjammer sailor since he left the other side of the Earth, and even though the crews in British ships were of mixed nationalities, this landfall always caused much excitement. The hardships of the voyage were usually forgotten from this point on.

June 24th, Lat 48° 29'N, Long 11° 45' W Wind dead muzzler again. Made fast the fore and main upper t'gallants and outer jib.

June 26th 11 am spoke to S.S. *Port Denison.* Wore ship at 11 am and 12 am.

June 28th Wind fresh but still easterly. Obtained G.M.T. from S.S. *Ashworth.*

June 30th Wind very light. A big steamer crossed our astern, probably one of the White Star ships, but too far away to make out her name.

July 3rd 1 am. Thick fog and foghorn going until 8 am when it cleared off. Passed a spar buoy adrift and at 2 pm a number of steam drifters. Becalmed all night, thick fog with occasional showers.

July 5th Wind light but fair. Took cast of the lead at 9.15 am and got bottom at 90 fathoms.

July 6th Ran over a drift net but did not damage it much. At noon the wind freshened and the main and mizzen topmast staysails were set.

July 7th 2 am picked up the Lizard light. 10.30 am the lookout reported land on the port bow and there was a wild rush to get the first glimpse of England. Even the watch tumbled out rubbing their eyes.

July 8th 8 am off Portland Bill, distance 12 miles. At 9 am it got very foggy but lifted during the afternoon watch. We are reduced to rice, tea and a little jam and bread and have not had a smoke for weeks, which makes matters a lot worse. As we are so near home, the skipper does not want to stop another ship for stores.

July 9th 3 pm Beachy Head abeam. 8.30 pm Dungeness abeam, backed the main yards and picked up the pilot and tug. All hands aloft putting a good harbour stow on the sails for the last time after a tedious passage from Rio.

July 10th Anchored off Gravesend and fresh meat and vegetables were taken on board. What a meal after rice!

July 11th 6 am all hands turned to, to take the turns out of the cables. Commenced heaving up the anchor at about 8.30 am, to the shanty 'Rolling Home' followed by 'Leave Her, Johnny, Leave Her'.
All hands joined in with a will, even the pilot, so that the echo went ringing over the river and a large crowd gathered on the shore to listen. It must have reminded many an old timer of the good old days of sail. The pilot even grabbed a capstan bar and tramped around with us singing 'In Amsterdam There Lived a Maid', etc. By dinnertime the tug had us in charge again and at 4 pm we were moored up to the buoys in the River Thames. The day we had been all looking forward to all these months had arrived at last. The Mate's last order was the customary 'That'll do you men!' After the Customs, Doctor and

Owner had gone ashore, all the ABs received 'channel money' [a few pounds to pay for lodgings, etc. ashore, until the ship paid off]. We were all soon ashore with our bags.

But what will happen to our old ship, now that she is safely home? Will she ever go crashing through the roaring forties again or know the splendour of those tropical nights, when the breeze sighs softly through the rigging? I wonder!

Dudley closed his diary with the words of an old sea shanty that he no doubt would have sung on many occasions.

Oh I think my song is rather long
Roll the cotton down,
Oh just one more pull and then belay
Oh roll the cotton down.

4 THE FRENCH BOUNTY SHIPS

Eugene Schneider

It is impossible in the space of one chapter to do true justice to the story of the last French ships driven by sail. French ships had an obvious presence on the trade routes and ports frequented by sailing ships in the latter years and outlived the last British sailers in trade by half a decade. Due to the fact that they rarely employed foreigners in their crews, not a lot is known about the way the ships were run and not a lot has been written about them, at least in the English language. Alan Villiers and Henri Picard collaborated on *The Bounty Ships of France*, which contains excellent data, especially regarding the ships built at the turn of the century. Villiers' dislike of British shipowners, revealed in his previous books, is evident in this book too, and if anything he paints too glowing a picture of the French sailing ships, although there is no doubt that conditions in them were superior to other sailers of the day.

Henri Picard, who was a seaman in the barque *Bretagne*, has helped me with much information and I recommend this book for further reading; Basil Lubbock also describes these French ships in his *Nitrate Clippers*. I have also been fortunate in obtaining first-hand accounts and comments from some of the remaining Cape Horn seamen in France.

Along with the Laeisz 'P' Liners, the French ships possessed an aura or mystique that most seamen of the day spoke of. They were worthy partners in the last act of the pageant of commercial sail. If the 'P' Liners represented the peak of development that could be achieved by technical thoroughness, then the French ships were examples of what could be achieved with an ample amount of money. This is not intended to diminish the worthiness of the French seamen, shipbuilders or shipowners, but reflects the fact that in France the financial uncertainty of operating, let alone building, sailing ships at the end of the nineteenth century was removed by government subsidy.

In 1881 the French government passed its first Bounty Laws, which provided a building subsidy of 60 francs per net ton and an operational subsidy of 1.5 francs per ton per 1000 miles sailed. In 1893 the bounty was increased to 65 francs per gross ton and 1.7 francs per ton per 1000 miles sailed. The government was not so much interested in building fine ships as building up a large reserve of sail-trained seamen that would form the back-up for its navy if required. The scheme went further, in that French maritime law provided that their merchant ships were crewed only by French nationals, and crew vacancies in foreign ports had to be filled with consular approval. Pensions were available to French seamen after 25 years of service, a benefit unheard of in British ships, and the scale of provisions decreed reflected the traditional French attitude to food and wine.

An important element of the revised bounty law of 1893 was the inclusion of gross tonnage in the formula for determining the extent of the subsidy. Tonnage is calculated from the cubic measurement of the ship's hull divided by a factor of 100. Gross tonnage is the total cubic capacity of the ship, including non-cargo spaces such as water tanks, crews, quarters, galley, etcetera. Net tonnage is the remaining space, taken up by cargo. Shipowners could now provide larger crew accommodation and include this space in their claim for the subsidy. This use of the rule gave a benefit beyond the comfort it provided for the crew. The extra space was achieved by lengthening fo'c'sle and poop decks to a point where in some ships they almost met. This reduced to a minimum the amount of water that a heavily laden ship could scoop up, making working on deck in heavy weather much safer and drier. These improved conditions in no way softened the French seaman, however—the task of taking in a topsail in a gale was not diminished by subsidy.

In praise of the British windjammer seaman of early this century, the work he performed—exactly the same as done by his French counterpart—might have been more easily coped with if preceded by a few meals from a French galley eaten in a mess room and not off his sea chest; this might have prevented some of the 27,000 desertions recorded from British ships.

The foremost and best remembered shipowner in France was Anton Dominique Bordes of Dunkirk, whose company A. D. Bordes, like F. Laeisz of Hamburg, had large interests in South American nitrates. Their ships were built with this trade in mind, and with it the west about rounding of Cape Horn, and were operated until the mid twenties. Sailing ships of different origins had readily recognisable features, and this was certainly true of French ships. Hull shape, sail profiles, and the fact that they were mostly painted pale grey added to the aura that surrounded them. It is said that the colour French grey comes from the shade used on these ships. Some had the row of decorative painted ports as favoured by the British, but the manner in which they were painted gave them a 'French look'.

One of the best descriptions I have of life in a French windjammer comes from Captain A. Jeannin, of Baisguillaume, France, who spent 52 years at sea. Young Jeannin joined the four-masted barque *Dunkerque* in 1919, under Captain Jean Forgeard, for a round voyage to Chile for nitrates. Apprentices were not usually carried in French ships. A lad wishing to make the sea his career signed on as a boy, and his first job was usually in the cabin aft where he assisted the steward and looked after the pigs or other livestock. Some work on deck and aloft was required as well. I have assembled this account from Jeannin's letters to me.

We took on provisions at La Pallice and sailed on 8 October, 1919. It was the custom for seamen to go on a drinking spree on the last day ashore, and this ended up with a five-franc fine. Traditionally the dockside police who rounded us up became just as drunk, as we would not go back to the ship unless the police joined us in our last rounds. We called the police *brasses carrés* because of the two-pointed cocked hats they wore. When we were all aboard, we were towed into the bay where we anchored for a few hours so that the crew could sober up. We raised anchor with our steam driven windlass aided by about 10 seamen manning the capstan. Off the Golfe de Gascogne [Bay of Biscay] the sea was very rough with an enormous swell. The winds were very strong from the west. Off Portugal we were slowed down by light winds and then head winds.

Then came the North-East Trades, blessed by seamen, warm, hot, a clear sky and an abundant supply of fish. There was little work required in trimming the sails, and we could always get a good sleep, disturbed only by the sound of a flying fish landing on deck. The crew tried to catch them before the cat, which was on watch also. A good-sized fish offered to the captain brought the reward of extra wine. If there were a number of fish the men on watch got a double ration. For the poor steward it was the beginning of the 'extra wine'. The 'fishermen' also asked him to fry the fish for them.

Young Jeannin's job at this stage was titled *le combusier* (steward's mate). The nickname given by the crew was 'officer in charge of the chicken coop'.

As well as looking after the hens and pigs, I was in charge of the stores, all the time, whether on duty or not. I distributed them to the cook and the men. I could always count on a seaman helping with the pigs for an extra quart of wine. I never worked for less than 15 hours per day in good weather, even more in bad weather. I had my own cabin and ate in the officers' mess aft, even though I was classed as a seaman.

My pay was less than that of an ordinary seaman, but at the captain's discretion I could receive a bonus at the end of the voyage, perhaps. To get this bonus I had to please the captain, who in turn had to watch the expenses for the owners. But the crew always expected extra provisions. For example, a barrel of wine was supposed to yield 900 quarts of wine, but the seamen always expected a generous serve. Also all favours by the crew to the steward were 'paid for' by a quart of wine. The payment for the care of the pigs was an example of this. The Captain had the answer. When filling a 20-litre demijohn, he said to put in 2 litres of fresh water and 1 litre of sea water, and then top up with 17 litres of wine. He claimed the salt water was good for digestion, especially on a diet of beans, potatoes and salted meat. He also had a solution for rancid barrels of salted meat. Open a fresh barrel but serve a little rancid meat with it, 'to economise'.

Jeannin makes many comments about food, a major factor distinguishing life in French ships from others of this period. The most notable difference was the provision of wine, and the complete acceptance by maritime authorities, shipowners and masters, of alcohol consumption by the crew as long as it was drunk in a more or less ordered manner. Jeannin's description of the food in the *Dunkerque* is fairly typical of what I was told by other French seamen. The quantity and quality was a definite result of the extra money made available through the subsidies, although it varied somewhat according to the nature of the skipper and the attitude of the owners. It is doubtful if a French bounty ship ever ran short of provisions, as did many limejuicers. While of better quality, the ingredients were not very different from those making up the bill of fare in ships from other countries, due mainly to the universal lack of refrigeration, but the addition of wine no doubt compensated for most of the shortcomings. In spite of the fact that the food was much superior to that found in British ships, and most considered it acceptable, it was never over-praised, perhaps an illustration of the age-old sailor's prerogative, the right to complain about the food.

A typical week's menu, according to Jeannin, was:

Crew
Breakfast: Black coffee and biscuits
Lunch: Monday, Tuesday, Wednesday: Salt pork and boiled potatoes
Thursday, Saturday: Canned beef stew and fried potatoes
Friday: Cod or sardines and boiled potatoes
Sundays: Beef stew or corned beef and fried potatoes
Evening meal: Bread (baked on board), jam and coffee
Bread was baked twice a week but it was often as hard as a rock.

Wine was issued each day, one quart per seaman and two quarts for the master. [The quart was a quarter litre, not an Imperial quart.]

Officers received the same food as crew but with extra, or alternatives such as other canned meat, vegetables and fruit, omelette made from eggs preserved in lime, chicken and rice.

Officers also got dessert—cheese or nuts, dried fruit and raisins, sometimes baked rice and milk.

Wine as desired, but controlled by the Captain, who knew that his first mate liked it a little too much.

… Fish were caught when in temperate or tropic regions, and if the ship was not going faster than 3 or 4 knots. In the cold southern latitudes we caught albatross and mollymawks and found that the thighs and breasts made a good stew with pork and onions. Potatoes were the only fresh food on board after the first 10 days at sea. The steward and I had to constantly sort and remove shoots, which grew very quickly in the tropics.

Fresh water was stored in large metal tanks between decks that were padlocked. The carpenter filled a barrel on deck each morning, which was available to the crew for drinking only. On Sundays, a ration of a bucket of water was issued, for each seaman, for personal cleanliness and clothes washing. The officers were allowed a small jug of water per day, and the steward and I were allowed a slightly bigger jug but we used this for bribes. The Captain was not better off. He had a bathtub but had to use sea water. We made use of rain in the tropics to wash clothes and ourselves—running around naked on deck—and collected drinking water in oiled canvas bags, which were almost waterproof. There was a boiler on board that could be used to distil fresh water from sea water, but I never saw it used, as fuel was too costly.

There were only two beds with a spring mattress—the captain's and the mate's. For the rest of us there was a wooden base with a canvas bag filled with seaweed or straw. We had to supply our own blankets, and any sailor who did not supply enough for cold regions never undressed. The owners gave little thought to the comfort of the crew.

Each man received three months pay in advance. He had to pay up his board ashore and buy bedding, clothes, oilskins, boots and woollens. Sometimes it was the landlady who made the purchases for him, and often found passages for them. They also provided many home comforts. When nearing the Equator there was little wind, and we had to work hard, day and night, trimming the sails to take advantage of any wind. We had to watch for waterspouts but soon the South-East Trades came and a good run south. Near the Equator we sighted the four-masted barque *Loire* under Captain Jean Cheventon—another Bordes vessel, which had left Dunkirk two days before us. One month later, in bad weather, south of the Falklands, we sighted her again ahead of us. We put on as much sail as we dared and found we were catching up. At daybreak we found she was out of sight and wondered if she was ahead or behind. Our skipper said little Jean Cheventon will not 'have' big Jean Forgeard, so the race was on, and maximum sail was carried.

Twenty days later, after only 74 days at sea, *Dunkerque* reached Taltal and left for Iquique the following day. *Loire* was beaten soundly, arriving five days later. We had changed to heavier canvas for rounding the Horn, which we accomplished in five days. The seas were not too heavy and winds were favourable most of the time, as it was summer, and we saw no icebergs.

I had an accident at this time, which could have been serious. I fell from the 'tween decks into the coal bunker and twisted my shoulder badly. I was looking for a hank of twine in the dark and the hatch cover had not been properly closed. The Captain gave me permission not to go aloft for two days.

In Iquique the loading took a long time as the bags of saltpetre had to be loaded from barges alongside, as we were out in the bay. The Chilean stevedores worked hard and long without fatigue and our crew did not go ashore apart from the Captain and the steward. We appreciated the uninterrupted night's sleep while in port, after the watches at sea. The only diversion while here was to watch the frolics of the sea lions or the sea calves as we called them, and the hundreds of pelicans, which dived on schools of fish.

I accompanied the steward ashore, for stores, every second or third day, in one of the ship's boats, with two oarsmen chosen from the most sober of the seamen. The Captain accompanied me on the first trip to show me what to buy. I was entrusted with funds, which I had to account for to the last cent. By 'cooking the books' a little I was able to give the oarsmen a good reward. The Captain was not naive; he had been a steward himself once!

The captains entertained each other while in Iquique. I was the *maitre d'hotel* in the *Dunkerque* because the cabin boy was rather uncouth, in spite of reprimands from captain and steward. I always listened with all ears while the captains recounted their experiences. Captain Cheventon of the *Loire* made a bet that he would beat *Dunkerque* home to France, even if he dismasted his ship. But we beat them by eight days. After dinner the captains would go ashore and a race would result between the boats from each ship. I overheard someone in the crew saying they were going ashore to 'see women'.

On the eve of our departure there was the traditional ceremony of the Southern Cross. The ship's carpenter made a large wooden cross decorated with many paraffin lamps. It was slowly hoisted aloft. The crew sang joyfully at the top of their voices. The crews of all the other moored ships, some 30 or so, joined in and ship's bells rang out. Thus as each ship departed it was wished *bon voyage*. The Southern Cross was lowered and when it reached deck it was toasted with a double issue of wine.

Before leaving Iquique the Captain had told me to buy some red peppers [chillies], as they were a good disguise for the taste of salt pork as it became older. He told me how to pickle them in vinegar. On the voyage home, during a meal, the Captain asked me to get a bottle of the red peppers I had preserved. But there was a catastrophe. The peppers had absorbed much of the vinegar and the top half of the jar was nothing but mould! To overcome the problem I removed the mould from the tops of two jars and created a new jar of good peppers from the unspoilt contents. In the store we kept a pail where weevilly biscuits were soaked, along with some bran, for our handsome pig 'Prince' who was fattening up well. What a good place to dispose of the mouldy peppers. My fellow sailor François Alain, who was in charge of feeding Prince, collected the mush. He was back in a hurry. 'The pig is sick,' he said. 'He rushed at his food as usual but he suddenly came to a dead stop and is now lying in a corner, his mouth wide open, and he won't stop groaning.' Not thinking about the peppers, I confirmed the situation and hurried to tell the Captain that the pig was ill. He decided to have it slaughtered immediately before it died. It was not until later that I remembered the peppers. I tasted the pigswill and it was enough to burn your insides out. For me there was no longer any mystery about Prince's illness! For him it was only an execution a little premature, because the end was near anyway. The next day pork chops! I ate mine with gusto while the Captain and mate tackled them gingerly not knowing if the pig had some terrible disease. The Captain, looking at me, said, 'It's good to be young, at his age one eats anything!' I never let on about the peppers.

In Chile we purchased 20 hens to replenish our stock. We had hardly left port when three died. The Captain noticed that each had a sort of abscess in the corner of one eye. Any of the remainder with the same symptoms was isolated and the eye bathed with carbolic solution. Not an easy job and quite laughable, but no more deaths. But some were blind in that eye. I was now the veterinarian! I had to continue to check the hens each day, and happened to notice that there were more eggs laid than gathered. So François and I discreetly watched—it was the Captain who helped himself! Not suspecting anything, the Captain announced at the dinner table that the crew must surely have been stealing the eggs. I dared to say that I had discovered the culprit and that the thefts would soon stop. He hid his face in his serviette and no more eggs disappeared.

The second mate had a pet white rabbit on board, making its third voyage. Weather permitting, it would be on watch with its master and its first action at the beginning of each watch was to jump onto the hatch of the companionway, when its master leaned there by design, and search in his coat pocket for a carrot or potato. Also, when the mate sat down to a meal, Johnny Rabbit came out and sat down beside him.

He sat respectfully on the table until he was served a saucer of red wine. A well-mannered alcoholic rabbit—where else could one find such a thing, but on a French Cape Horn sailing ship! However, he wasn't appreciated when he chewed ropes and they broke without warning.

One night when I was sleeping soundly, I was awakened by a severe pain in my big toe. A huge rat had been gnawing my toenail and had drawn blood. Another time I was aloft unbending the sheet of a lower topsail so it could be changed. To do this I had to stand at the end of the mainyard about 15 metres above the water and six metres out from the side of the ship. There wasn't much to hang onto. I looked down and saw a large hammerhead shark swimming right below me. They have a reputation of being very ferocious. I yelled out and the Captain who was on the poop heard me. He got a rifle from the charthouse—we carried several to deal with floating mines left over from the war. He fired two or three shots and the monster disappeared. The Captain told me to come down and stop work. 'Go and have a drop of brandy,' he said. 'You are quite green, and no wonder.' We often saw whales, porpoises and dolphins that gambolled under our stern, even at maximum speed.

What a strange zoo was *Dunkerque*. One Sunday six of us decided to have a competition to see who could go from the end of the jib boom to the other end of the poop without putting a foot on deck. What acrobatics there were aloft in the rigging! Four of us succeeded and I came in second, beaten by a *matelot leger* [seaman], a small thickset Breton as agile as a monkey. The Captain welcomed us on the poop with a bottle of white Bordeaux.

The ship's company comprised 35 men. We nicknamed the captain 'Grand Mât', meaning 'main mast'. The term for the first mate was 2nd captain, and the second and third mates were called lieutenants. The junior one of these took his watch with the first mate. In addition we had five petty officers: a boatswain nicknamed 'Bosco', a second-class petty officer, a master carpenter, a master engineer and a cook nicknamed 'Le Coq' (Rooster). We had 26 men in the crew: 22 seamen (20 ABs or ordinary seamen, a steward and a steward's mate, also classified as seamen), two 16-year-old apprentices and two ship's boys aged 13 and 14 years—one was assigned to the galley and the Captain, while the other looked after the officers and the cabins aft. The 22 seamen were divided into two watches and were housed in the deckhouses for'ard of the mizzenmast.

Two seamen were the official sail makers. During the day they repaired the sails which had been torn or damaged by the wind, and made new sails from new canvas carried for this purpose. It was the Captain himself who cut the new sails made on board.

There was a seaman allocated to each square-rigged mast (we called him a top-man) per watch — port and starboard, a total of six men. They were responsible for all the rigging on their mast. The remaining five or six seamen in each watch (there was at least one helmsman and one lookout) were occupied with washing the deck, work aloft at tasks found by the topman, upkeep of equipment, chipping rust and painting.

On Sunday the only work was washing the deck and the work necessary to navigate the ship. Everyone attended to their personal needs, bathing, washing clothes, mending, as well as hobbies such as model ships in bottles, making walking sticks from the backbones of sharks, tobacco pouches and coat hooks from the webbed feet and beaks of albatross.

In fine weather, music (accordion) and dancing on deck helped pass the time. When it rained or the wind was strong we played cards or slept. We slept at every opportunity, as the work was hard and we spent 10 hours on duty one day and 14 the next. In heavy weather when the ship was being tacked or sail being taken in we worked longer until the job was done. There was no overtime for this. On these occasions meals were hurried or missed altogether.

To illustrate the exhaustion we experienced—during a period of bad weather there was a lull and a young seaman leaned on a winch and immediately fell asleep. The deck was awash and he was in danger of being picked up by a wave and swept away. Without waking him, two other seamen lashed him to the winch and he continued to sleep in spite of the water, which washed to and fro, dragging his legs freely with the movement. As we approached the English Channel we found difficulty in manoeuvring. The Captain rarely left the poop and for three days did not undress. Two liners brushed us on a dark night—probably they did not see our weak navigation lights.

When we arrived home the Captain paid up the crew and gave each one a certificate. He gave me my bonus of 50 francs per month with the curt note, 'You earned it'. My certificate said that I was an intelligent young man, a conscientious, hard worker, and fulfilled my role as steward's mate. He shook my hand, something he had never done before and said, 'Good luck in your practical exam. You may have thought I was tough on you but it is necessary to make a man of you.'

After World War I *Dunkerque* was laid up out of work in the seaport of Dunkirk and in 1924 was towed to Swansea, Wales, with an Italian crew. She never sailed again. With her coal cargo she was towed to Italy where she was broken up. Captain Jeannin's comments reflect most of those made by others who sailed in the French ships and who spoke to me of their experiences: Captain E. Bergen LePlay in the barque *General de Sonis* and the four-masted barque *Tijuca*, Henri Picard in the barque *Bretagne*, Captain Le Bourdais in the four-masted barque *Wulfran Puget*, along with Georges Pachot on the same voyage.

All the French sailors I spoke to gave almost stock answers to my questions about the life, food and conditions in their beautiful ships:

'Yes, I loved the life, the happiest period in my life.'

'I did it for the adventure and to see new places.'

'My family were all seafarers and had a tradition in the Newfoundland ships.'

'Food, yes it was better than other ships and we always had plenty.'

'Food was acceptable but we had beans too often.'

'I enjoyed the canned beef stew, it was delicious.'

'The daily ration of wine was expected and we did not consider it a luxury.'

'The officers were always kindly, tough yes, but they had all started at the same place we had, as ship's boys.'

Among the exclusive band of women who sailed in the Cape Horn sailing ships was Mme Hervy-Delanoe from Dinan, France, who as a young girl sailed in the barques *Le Pilier* during the war and *Laënnec* in 1920, both commanded by her father, Captain Emile Delanoe. In 1922 *Laënnec* was sold to Germany who used her as the training ship *Oldenberg*. Today she is still afloat as the Finnish school ship *Suomen Joutsen*.

George Pachot's reminiscences of French sail were unique in that he was a radio operator in the four-masted barque *Wulfran Puget* for a voyage from Dunkirk to Iquique in 1924. Radio was rarely carried by sailing ships but its use became law for all French ships over 2500 tons. Two other seamen—one of whom later became a director of A. D. Bordes, François Le Bordais, and Captain Perdraut, President of the French Cape Horners—have also provided interesting material, both having sailed in this same ship.

George Pachot was not a sailor and did not have the desire to be one. Keen on travel and with an interest in the comparatively new development of radio, he went to sea as a radio officer, and his observations were perhaps sharpened by the fact that he was not involved in the day-to-day working of the ship. It was the custom for the radio officer to arrange for the installation of the equipment himself and George describes his meeting up with the ship that was to be his home for almost a year:

I left my home in Paris, never having been further than Orleans, taking with me all the radio equipment which was supplied by the Radio Industry Company (now Thomson CC at Dunkirk).

Wulfran Puget had been laid up for four years along with two others, *Valparaiso* and *Montmorency*. I was quite disappointed. She was dirty, dilapidated and covered with rust. I went aboard and met Captain Rieux and Second Captain (Mate) Samezin. The Captain, whom the crew called 'Le Pacha' or 'Le Grand Mât', was a courteous, cultivated man, who usually wore hunting clothes.

I was responsible for installing the radio equipment and getting it going. There was a receiver, transmitter and generating set. I was amazed at the agility of the crew as they installed the antennas aloft, attached to metal loops on each of the four masts.

Two fellow shipmates arrived, François Le Bordais who was 3rd Lieutenant and *cambusier* (officer in charge of chicken coop) and Maurice Berthes, 2nd Lieutenant. We were about the same age and became good friends.

We departed on 9 May 1924, with most of our crew loaded on board drunk. They brought with them a stray dog and cat together with much illicit alcohol. It was the custom, while we were at anchor in the bay, for boats rented by the local brothels to come alongside selling liquor. It was taken on board in a basket lowered over the side. The mate allowed them to be loaded but confiscated the lot. The owner's name was attached to the bottle and small amounts were dispensed throughout the voyage. There were 43 crew members in all.

We had no outward cargo, only ballast, which was 1500 tonnes of building rubble.

As radio operator I did not stand watches, but worked eight hours a day. I was on call at any time for navigation needs. During bad weather I listened for distress signals and these were often heard, but being a sailing ship we could not manoeuvre to go to their assistance.

I was always in contact with shore radio stations along the way, to give our position and to receive messages from the owner, A. D. Bordes. I could receive signals from the Eiffel Tower when we were over 4000 miles south of the Azores. My most important job was to contact as many ships as possible, which were ahead of us, in order to find out the weather conditions. This was very important for a sailing ship. I was able to give the 'Pasha' a lot of useful information. He also required me to get time signals so that he could correct our chronometers to determine the longitude. The Captain was rather touchy about his navigation. It was the custom at midday for the officers to determine the ship's position using the sextant. Many times the three officers agreed on a position different from that of the 'Pasha'. But he always recorded his own position in the log and ignored that of his officers. This wasn't important in mid ocean but a different matter near the coast.

One morning three or four of the watch were late in reporting for duty and they were visibly drunk. The door of the storeroom had been forced during the night. François noticed that an empty demijohn, about 30-litre capacity, which had contained oil, had disappeared, and the pumping equipment for the wine was in disorder. The thieves had firstly taken a good drink on the spot, and then in the dark had filled the demijohn for the other men in the watch, spilling a lot on the deck. The demijohn was found under a pile of rope with about 10 litres remaining with a layer of oil on top. As these men had an issue of a quarter litre with each meal it did not take much more to make them quite drunk. The penalty was to be deprived of wine until the amount equalled what had been stolen. Then they had to drink the wine with the oil in it.

In the Doldrums we had plenty of chance to catch sharks. They were easy to catch as they pounced on anything that fell into the sea. We tried eating the shark flesh but it was no good. However, when caught they often disgorged the contents of their stomachs, which included small fish that had just been swallowed. These were quite good to eat. When the ship started moving again we could not catch sharks but there were other fish that we could catch such as tuna, dolphin and bonito. The fishing technique was quite different. At 3 or 4 knots it was simple. A big double hook 100 mm (4 inches) long was decorated with the dried stems from garlic, or just a piece of white material, to represent a fish. It was trailed at the end of a line about 200 metres long and the other end was secured to a *cabillot* (belaying pin). Another 50 metres were coiled down on board, tied by a piece of sail thread to one of the observation platforms on the poop. At the slightest tug on the line the thin thread would break and the helmsman rang the bell furiously. Everyone came running to land the catch. One fish we did not catch was one that swallowed our log spinner. This was a solid bullet-shaped cylinder of brass with helical vanes on it, about the size of a champagne bottle. It spun at the end of a line and registered our speed and distance run on an instrument mounted on the poop rail. It must have been a large fish or shark as the line was bitten through. We caught tuna from the jib boom by skimming a piece of white material on the hook along the surface of the waves. It was not without its hazards, as when caught the fish dived at an incredible speed. A seaman next to me, when hooking a large fish, allowed the line to wind around his right index finger and the top joint was cut off like a blow from an axe. We caught the fish but the poor fellow was out of action for 20 days. The exocet (flying fish) were easily caught, especially when the ship was low in the water with the full load of saltpetre. We searched around the decks every morning and often saw schools of 200 or more flying through the air, often striking the side of the ship.

We had an excellent cook who was also a good baker and pastrycook even with limited means. The officers had fresh bread every day and cakes on Sundays, although the crew only had fresh bread on Sundays and had to eat sea biscuits during the week.

Drinking water was always available but we only received half a bucket of extra water on Sundays to wash in or wash our clothes, so rain was always welcome.

The officers' toilet was at the break of the poop, a small compartment about a metre square. There was a plank with a hole cut in it over a pan that was directly connected to the outside of the ship. In big seas, water was forced up the pipe, drenching the occupant, not only with sea water.

The crew's toilet was under the fo'c'sle head and was a long plank with holes in it over a trough that sloped towards the stern with the sheer of the deck. A pipe led from this trough to the side of the ship. It was a communal toilet.

On Sundays the only work performed was that necessary for navigating the ship. Maurice and François often came to the radio room, where there was a couch, and secretly ate pastry and drank a bottle of wine, smuggled in by François, from reserve stock. The empty bottle was dropped out the porthole with a message in it. The pastries were made secretly by the cook in return for favours from François in the way of extra wine. He frequently made visits to the storeroom to ask for an onion or some other item, and under his apron was an empty bottle that would be full on his return to the galley.

We sighted Iquique on 7 September 1924. There was only a wooden wharf and a Wild West type of town. The roads were dirt and horses were the main form of transport. All ships stayed at anchor in the bay where there was a constant heavy swell. It took one week to unload the ballast using steam winches and the engineer was kept busy with breakdowns. Barges came alongside with the 100 kg bags of saltpetre and the cargo was loaded by specialists so that it would not move during the return passage. As radio operator I was not required to work in port and spent my time fishing and catching crabs.

Mail was brought on board and all but two seamen received letters. After the ballast was unloaded we would clean barnacles off the hull using a flat-bottomed punt. This punt was locked up on deck at night to stop the seamen from going ashore. This resulted from an incident in which a seaman from a German ship had been drowned during a trip ashore. The weather had turned nasty and the boat ended up on the rocks.

The fish and bird population of this coast was huge. Flocks of birds over the ship cast a shadow and one day the 'Pasha' shot six ducks with one shot. Fish could be scooped out of the sea using the grating from one of the lifeboats. There were coastal vessels trading down the coast between Panama and Valparaiso and were much like a travelling bazaar. All sorts of goods could be bought from them. We all bought a large stock of food.

Before leaving Iquique our 2nd captain Samezin was transferred to the *Montmorency* as captain and their 2nd captain Faureeu came to us. This was because their captain had died south of the Horn. We left Iquique on 27 September 1924, towed out to sea by a tug but were then becalmed for 20 days. On 5 November 1924 we rounded Cape Horn in heavy weather and on 13 December 1924 we crossed the Equator. There was no crossing the line ceremony on either crossing. We heard our first signals from the Eiffel Tower on the 31 December 1924, at a distance of 2500 miles.

At the entrance to the English Channel we were hit by a severe storm and the ship and her gear was badly damaged. We lost all sails and it was impossible to get out on deck. We had to send out an SOS distress signal. We managed to limp into Dunkirk on 21 January 1925 and the ship was so damaged that it was not considered worth while it to keep her in commission and she was broken up.

It was 50 years before I saw my shipmates Maurice and François again. I met them in 1975 at the 30th Congress of AICH at St Malo. Captain Rieux had died several months earlier at the age of 95. Maurice died two years later.

One of the few foreign seamen to sail in the French bounty ships has given me a brief description of his experience in the four-masted barque *Richelieu*. This was preceded by a voyage commencing in 1924 around Cape Horn from Newcastle, New South Wales, to Iquique with coal and thence to St Nazaire with nitrate in the famous old wool clipper *Mount Stewart*. It is incredible that this seaman, Gordon Chapman, was able to tell me of his experiences in the last voyage of this ship, one of the last two built for the wool trade in 1891. She was sold to the shipbreakers at the end of the voyage and Gordon, a young ship's boy, had to find a vessel heading for home. Pre-empting a decision to send him home by passenger ship, Gordon requested that he be allowed to join *Richelieu*, which was moored alongside *Mount Stewart* in Nantes. *Richelieu* at that time was a near new ship, and was about to make her first voyage. She had been ordered by F. Laeisz in 1916 but not completed until 1919, when she was taken over by the Allies as part of war reparations. Laeisz had intended her to be named *Pola* but she never sailed under this name. She was handed back to France in 1921, and operated by Les Navires Ecoles Français.

Captain W. E. Colm of *Mount Stewart* and *Richelieu*'s master, Captain Populaire, discussed Chapman's request and on 17 November 1924 Gordon joined the French ship:

On 18 November, 1924, I took my cedar sea chest, which had also been my father's, and walked up the gangway to start a new chapter in my life. The experience was quite novel and getting to know these new shipmates was interesting. Some were friendly and easy to get to know while others were a little more reserved. General conditions were very much in contrast with other ships. Meals of a much better standard and better accommodation too. Of all things, a piano in the accommodation of *élevés* [trainees]. This was an unheard-of refinement. On some occasions the British national anthem was played following the French anthem, which was quite an act of courtesy. The time came for sailing and *Richelieu* was taken from Nantes to St Nazaire, and taken by ocean tug into the Bay of Biscay. It was a stormy afternoon when entering the Bay of Biscay, with a short steep sea. Being in ballast *Richelieu* became very lively and the motion was quite jerky. Sails were set to help the tug along. After some time under tow the splice in the wire towline started to draw, and more sail was made immediately.

Away *Richelieu* went on her voyage to Australia to load wheat. During the operation of getting more sail set, a headsail took charge. When the downhaul was let go, the sail flew up the stay of its own accord, over-running the halyard which became foul. To clear it, a seaman was lowered down the stay, and the sail hauled down. The mess was cleared up and the sail properly set. The canvas was almost new and had hardly been used. That night I was sent to the wheel to assist the helmsman who was having a struggle and thus the voyage commenced. The voyage to Australia was pleasant. Much was learned of a seafaring life, the art and skill, all of which add to the making of a sailor. The voyage took 85 days mostly of fine weather but occasionally we had a few days of storm. A lot of ice was encountered after the longitude of the Cape of Good Hope but it was all drift ice and small icebergs. Eventually we arrived at Port Lincoln and arrangements were made to discharge ballast, and load wheat.

As only French nationals were permitted to sail in French ships I had to leave her in Port Lincoln, but it did not occur at once. I spent some pleasant days rowing the gig across the bay to the small jetty and returning with bales of burlap with which to wrap the bare steel in the holds.

Gordon made further voyages under sail in the four-masted schooner *Holmswood* and the barque *Louise Theriault*. He topped off his time in sail when he joined Alan Villiers in 1937 in his full rigger *Joseph Conrad* as first mate on the final leg of this ship's three-year world-encircling voyage from Auckland to New York.

Richelieu left Port Lincoln on 4 April 1925 and delivered her grain to Liverpool on 22 July 1925. Returning to Brest she then sailed for Baltimore where she loaded 3134 tonnes of pitch. During loading, an explosion occurred, followed by a fire that completely destroyed her, fortunately with no loss of life.

5 GERMAN SAIL AND THE 'P' LINERS

Passat

Without doubt, the most successful fleet of sail-driven ships ever assembled under one flag were those operated by Ferdinand Laeisz of Germany. While the diversity and total tonnage of ships under British ownership was never equalled by any other nation, few sailing ships were built in Britain that could equal the size, power and strength of the Laeisz 'P' Liners, as they were called. The company's tradition of having their ships' names start with the letter P led to the nickname 'Flying P Line', which referred to the speed and power of the ships as much as to their names.

The story of these ships and the company that owned and operated them is impossible to cover here. Much of it is told in the book *A Century and a Quarter of Reederei F. Laeisz*, by Dr H. C. Rohrbach, Captain J. Herman Piening and Captain A. E. Schmidt. Basil Lubbock also describes them in his *Nitrate Clippers*. The most recent book about them is *Die Flying P Liner* by Peter Klingbeil.

The Laeisz company started out as humble hat makers in 1825. Progressing into general trade, insurance, mining and shipping over the next 100 years, the Laeisz empire set the stage for the final development of the engineless, sail-driven ship, long after the clipper era had peaked and long after the triple-expansion steam engine began sending its vibrations through the hulls of most of the ships emerging from the Clyde.

The interests that Laeisz had in South America were centred in Chile and the saltpetre that was mined there. Along the West Coast, inland of the Cordilleras an arid desert region exists, rich in a mineral known as *caliche*. Processed, it became saltpetre or sodium nitrate, was bagged and transported to the coast and the queues of ships offloading ballast, general cargo or coal. Saltpetre, used for centuries as one of the ingredients of gunpowder, had an important secondary use as a fertiliser, due to its high nitrogen content. When Ferdinand Laeisz Senior died in 1887, his sons Carl Heinrich and Carl Ferdinand took over the company. Recognising the potential of the sodium nitrate trade, they started building up their fleet of sailing ships with the latest in iron ships from Great Britain. However, the company wanted something special in their ships and all subsequent vessels were built in Germany, at the yards of Blohm & Voss or Tecklenborg, to their specifications.

By 1905 the formula had been perfected. The steel four-masted barque had emerged more than 15 years earlier and provided economies over the three-masted full-rigged ship, which was the sailing workhorse of the preceding half-century. By the turn of the century, Britain had built thousands of steel sailing ships but none of them matched the specifications laid down by Laeisz—heavy steel standing and running gear, triple topmast backstays, double topmast cap stays, Jarvis brace winches (designed in Great Britain) and halyard winches, steel masts and yards with double jackstays and the now standard Liverpool house, which gave increased accommodation for the larger crews carried, and reduced the amount of water a heavily laden ship could scoop up. Laeisz ships also featured balanced rudders, which took some of the kick out of the wheel in heavy weather. Steering was from amidships and consisted of double wheels that four men could operate at the one time if necessary.

And then there was the Laeisz directive to their masters and crews. This stated that the performance of their ships was predictable and repeatable. The company made it quite clear that nothing was spared in the fitting out and provisioning of their ships and so there was no excuse for long passages. This did not imply harsh discipline or that they expected more than the crews could give. It merely reflected the Teutonic thoroughness that permeated the company from boardroom to fo'c'sle. The most up-to-date charts, meteorological information and navigation instruments and aids were provided. (In British ships these all had to be supplied by the master.) When radio became a reality it was installed in their ships. Preliminary shore training was required before a boy could sign on and then only after a rigorous medical examination. In Germany, unlike Great Britain, the calling of seaman was respected and carried with pride. Laeisz was also one of the first companies to take heed of the early stirrings of the maritime unions, even in the 1890s.

In the years leading up to World War I, Laeisz owned a total of 34 sailing vessels and eight steamships. Twenty-five of these were built specially for the company, including the mighty five-masted ship *Preussen*, the largest sailing ship ever built. *Preussen* was 407 feet (124 metres) long, almost half the length of the *Queen Mary*. They also had the five-masted barque *Potosi*.

Ten sailing ships were commissioned after the turn of the century. *Preussen* 1902, *Pangani* 1902, *Petschilli* 1903, *Pamir* 1905, *Penang* 1905, *Peking* 1911 and *Passat* 1911, were built before the war, *Priwall* 1919, *Pola* 1920 and *Padua* 1926, after it. It was quite ironic that after the Armistice was signed, Laeisz was to lose all their vessels as reparations to Britain, France, Italy and Greece. Apart from France these countries had no desire to run sailing ships and by 1924 Laeisz had bought back *Priwall*, *Pinnas*, *Peking*, *Passat*, *Parma* and *Pamir*, then built *Padua* in 1926.

To make up for the declining trade in West Coast nitrates after the introduction of synthetic nitrates, the Laeisz ships entered the Australian grain trade, subsidised by their large complement of cadet seamen, but one by one their postwar fleet diminished. *Pinnas* dismasted in 1929; *Parma*, *Passat*, *Pamir* and *Peking* sold in the depressed days of the early thirties. By the outbreak of World War II, Laeisz operated *Padua* and *Priwall* alone.

I contacted an ex-crewmember, Robert Berlin, who then lived in South Australia. A very old man, his main observation was that the youth of today could do with a long voyage around Cape Horn to take their minds off the diversions that exist in modern society.

Other large German shipping companies also deserve mention—F. A. Vinnen & Co. of Bremen and the Rickmers Company. The latter built as well as operated sailing ships. I have managed to track down a seaman, later an officer, who sailed under the Vinnen flag but have never found any from Rickmers, at least in ships still owned by Rickmers. It was comparatively easy to find ex-Laeisz mariners as they operated sailing ships up to 1939.

I recall sitting in the living room of the then president of the German Cape Horners Association, Captain Bernhard Masson, in 1987, drinking beer with no less than seven German captains who all served in Laeisz sailing ships in the twenties and thirties. A day later I attended a *Stammtisch* in a cafe in Blankenese, a waterfront district of Hamburg that had once been a notorious 'sailor town', with over 40 ex-Laeisz mariners, all veterans of Cape Horn. Their memories of their time under sail were not allowed to fade as they had these Sunday morning gatherings every week. The past mission of sail training for the future of German maritime strength had been fulfilled, in that most of the men I met on those occasions had gone on to command in the mercantile marine and the navy. In our little gathering at Bernhard's apartment there were also two former U-boat skippers and a Luftwaffe pilot! The following first-hand accounts come from seamen who sailed in the Laeisz vessels in the post 1914–1918 years.

Helmut Schwabe was a German boy who sailed in the four-masted barque *Padua*, joining her on 10 July 1929. This was the fifth voyage of the newest sailing ship in the world. Many years had passed since the last batch of sailers had been built for Laeisz, but *Padua* was almost identical. Whatever was built into her represented the sum total of the knowledge that sailing ship builders had accumulated since the dawn of maritime history. She was the last commercial square-rigged sailing ship ever to be built.

The merchant fleet of Laeisz was run on almost naval lines. The company was highly selective in the crews they employed, particularly in the latter years when young aspiring mariners found the opportunity to gain sail training rapidly diminishing. Just as Eben Anderson was typical of the many lads who went into British sail, so Helmut Schwabe was typical of the young Germans who chose the sea for their career. He described his time in *Padua* thus:

> At the age of 15, I spent a Sunday with my family in the fishing port of Cuxhaven at the mouth of the River Elbe. Standing on the jetty with many other onlookers, we watched the traffic on the river and ships coming in from the North Sea, when a great white full-rigged ship appeared over the horizon. She was a training ship of the merchant marine. As she passed us under full sail her crew, on deck and in the rigging, cheered and waved in response to our waves and I knew then that this was what I wanted to do in

later life. I turned to my father and said, 'That's what I want to do!' He just nodded but my mother said, 'No!'

Later my father made an appointment with a seaman's doctor to check if I was fit for a career at sea. Colour blindness would have excluded me right from the start. The result was A1 for sea service. A week later, I started a three-month course at a seamen's school in Finkenwaerder in preparation for the real thing. We learned discipline, no back answering, how to look after ourselves and how to get along with others. We hand-washed our clothes in a bucket and slept in a hammock. We were taught seamanship and boat drill, although it took a while for our blistered hands to harden to allow us to fully enjoy the daily rowing. We learned the compass card, how to steer a ship by compass, the rule of the road, Morse code, signal flags and knots and splices. We also learned how to handle sails on a small square-rigged ship set in a concrete slab, which proved very useful later.

Before applying for a job I had to have written permission from my father to go to sea, as I was still a minor. Dad made two conditions. No opium or other drugs and no tattoos. I kept them both faithfully.

With my certificate from the seamen's school, I applied for a berth as a boy cadet in one of the nitrate ships owned by Laeisz of Hamburg. On 10 July I signed ship's articles and went by motor launch with other new cadets, out to join the four-masted barque *Padua*, which was under the command of Captain Piening. From the distance she looked fine and graceful and as we got nearer she was awe-inspiring. We marvelled at the height of the masts, the size of the spars and the complication of ropes. She was quite new, having been built by Tecklenborg in Vegesack, Bremerhaven, in 1926.

On board the chief and second mates sized us up as we filed past with our tightly packed kit bags and were showed our accommodation under the poop deck aft. There were fixed double bunks with only enough room to pass between them. A mess room with tables and benches screwed to the deck, cupboards on the wall for our eating utensils and pots for fetching our food from the galley, which was amidships. Kerosene lamps in gimbals were used for lighting.

After tea we were allowed into the rigging under the guidance of the older boys and were told not to take any risks or to show off. It was a heady sensation to look down at the deck and other ships from so high up.

Next day we were kept busy helping with the loading of cargo. This consisted of bags of cement from a barge alongside. We had to load these bags into a cargo net, which was hoisted on board. It was hard work and we learned how to conserve our energy during the day.

The next day another boy and I were promoted to gangway guard, to announce visitors and others to the officer in charge. We were in uniform and had to stay clean, but not idle. It was our task to keep all the brass work around the high deck [Liverpool house] and the charthouse, compass housing, ship's bell, etc. in the highest possible sparkle. We used oil, sandstone, a piece of canvas and our elbow grease. A light dusting of powdered French chalk that removed all traces of oil and it came up like new.

It was also our job to hoist the House Flag (a red FL on a white background) and the National flag at 8 am sharp and simultaneously. The flags were neatly rolled up, one loose end tucked under, hoisted beforehand and securely belayed. At 8 am a sharp tug, which frees the jammed loop, and the flag should unfurl nicely in the morning breeze. It should, but one day it didn't. The sharp tug brought down the halyard end instead, leaving the rolled-up flag still up under the truck, and me in quite a predicament. My world almost came to a standstill, 180 feet between the flag and me. I took the end of the halyard clear of all the standing rigging and other obstructions and proceeded to climb up with it. Okay until I reached the end of the ratlines, but not quite there yet. I shinned up the bare mast head, got hold of the rolled-up flag, and brought it down to a safer place to re-knot it, when I heard an angry whistle blast and saw an arm-waving officer calling me down in no uncertain words. I received an instant lesson on trussing up ensigns, plus a dressing-down about unauthorised climbing to the top of the mast, as if anything had happened to me, the third mate said, it would have landed him in gaol.

For a couple of days we were sent over to another company ship, *Parma*, to chip rust in her holds. When I climbed down into the hold, I saw in the semi-darkness a figure lying motionless on the bottom of the hold and I reported it. In short, I found a boy, who had been a schoolmate, dead from an accidental fall, and it shook me up considerably. As a witness I had to appear in court and at the funeral I was a pallbearer. It was terribly sad.

Back in *Padua* the loading was almost completed. We had 4320 tons of mixed cargo. On deck the sails were taken from the sail locker and hoisted to the yards for bending. The provisions came on board and were stowed away. The water tanks were filled and the pumps padlocked. From now on water was rationed. Finally the hatches were closed, covered with heavy tarpaulins and battened down.

Then came the last night ashore. My mother cooked my favourite meal and I drank lots of milk, which I would miss for many months. My friends called to have a farewell drink, in fact more than one. On board, everything was made ready for departure. The ocean-going tug *Seefalk* [*Sea Hawk*] took us on his hook and towed us down the river Elbe. We cheered the well-wishers on shore as long as we could see and hear them.

The crew, numbering 71, was on deck, which included 40 old and new cadets. The mate and second mate picked the two watches for the voyage. The mate the port, and the second the starboard watch. The hours on duty went, one day, from midnight to 4 am, 8 to 12 noon, 6 pm to midnight, which was 14 hours. The next day, 4 am to 8 am, noon to 6 pm, which was 10 hours. The time was given by the ship's bells, one by the steering wheel and one on the fo'c'sle, every half hour. At the change of watch the crew lined up to port and starboard according to their watch and were accounted for. The officer of the watch gave the order 'relieve the wheel and lookout', and the watch went below.

In the next days we were trained and instructed by the ABs about our duties during different manoeuvres, to fit in as quickly as possible.

We were now past the island of Helgoland in the North Sea. Sails were set, starting with the topsails, until all 33 were set. The pilot left and the hawser was slipped when the tug could no longer keep up with us. A final wave here and there and *Padua* sailed with good speed towards Chile on the West Coast of South America. The anchors were brought on board and the gentle swaying caused some to become seasick but I was never sick at sea.

We learned to steer, first as offsiders, then on our own. With the wind abaft the beam we steered by the compass. If sailing into the wind we steered as close to the wind as possible, keeping the weather edge of the main royal flapping. This sail is tightly braced to the wind for this purpose as an early warning. The helmsman must always keep his eyes on this sail and after his trick at the wheel his neck would ache. On 22 July we passed Dover and the wind freshened from the west, dead against us, and we had to tack. Through the English Channel, we just had enough time between tacks to clear the decks of running rigging to get ready for the next one.

We had shipped some water on board which got through the chart room and down into the captain's and officers' cabins. A few of us boys were put to mopping it up into wooden pails. Passing through the chartroom with a full pail I slid on the slippery soles of my leather seaboots along the deck when the ship heeled over. The next thing I was picked up bodily by the Captain and set upon my feet again. He grumbled at all the spilt water and the fact that I had not found my sea legs yet. The next day the carpenter fitted rubber heels to the leather seaboots of all the new hands.

We reached the steady northeast trade winds and changed sails. This meant unbending our good heavy weather sails and replacing them with older, lighter sails. The standing and running gear was overhauled, renewed and tested. The wire ropes were tarred, and sails repaired. New ones were hand sewn. Learning was constant on the passage but it took some time before we were proficient and less of a worry to the Captain and his officers. One constant job for us boys was 'stopping' the buntlines on the sails. This was a line, which was fastened to the bottom of the sail, led over a block on the yard and down to the deck. It was used to haul the sail up to the yard. The wire buntline had to be slack so that it would not chafe the sail. Twine loops were fastened to the wire to take a small piece of wooden dowel that stopped the buntline from going through the block and kept it slack. The dowel would break with a hard pull from the deck.

The carpenter recaulked the deck seams and we holystoned it with sand and stone. When dry we oiled it with boiled linseed oil and sometimes there was enough left over for us to reproof our oilskins. On the fine tradewind nights we were taught more about the hundreds of ropes and at sundown everything was cleared away in case of an emergency.

On 25 August we crossed the Equator and had the usual crossing the line ceremony. All the new hands received a certificate from King Neptune to say that we had been admitted into his realm. In the region of doldrums we had plenty of rain which allowed everyone to have a really good clean-up. The South-East Trades took us further south. Sometimes we harpooned a dolphin. The meat was dark and oily but was a change. The watch below spent their time reading, yarning, mending, listening to gramophone records and making ship models.

Nearing 40° south latitude, the sails were changed again and the best ones bent for the heavy weather ahead. Also, nets were rigged between the open spaces between the standing rigging to stop sailors being washed overboard. *Padua* was readied for rounding the Horn.

One day when I was at the wheel the Captain was pacing the deck on the weather side. Suddenly something from above hit the deck with a thud. A shackle pin had made a dent in the deck less than a metre from him. All hell broke loose. The Captain had a very loud voice and he used it to summon every AB and to show them what had happened through carelessness. He gave them all a piece of his mind and ordered them up the masts and not to come down until everything had been checked and secured—everything!

On 24 September we passed Staten Island on the eastern side. It blew hard from the northwest. A dark cloud prompted the Captain to take in the upper sails but the order came too late. Coming out from the lee that the land offered, the situation fairly exploded in minutes to a full hurricane. *Padua* swept with great speed through the boiling sea, dragging the bulwark of the main deck through the foaming water. The three royals blew out with the sound of cannon shots. With both watches on deck, the sails were taken in. Under enormous wind pressure the hoisting yards would not come down by their own weight and we had to haul them down by the clew lines.

Heavily listing to port in the squall, a huge breaker caught a sailor on the fo'c'sle and carried him all the way along the foredeck to the main deck ladder. He was fished out of the bubbling water and put in a safe place still unconscious. He was lying there in his water-filled seaboots, his legs at a grotesque angle. We thought he had broken his legs too. Luckily this was not the case and after getting rid of swallowed water he came good again.

We were in the rigging for hours, battling the flapping canvas. We came through it with three sails lost and many more torn. We spent the night hove to under storm sails. The watch was ready behind the strong canvas fastened in the main rigging as shelter from wind and spray. Even so it was very miserable and our hands too numb to roll a smoke. When everything was under control again the order came, 'Splice the main brace!' All hands filed past the charthouse where the Captain stood, handing each a glass of rum as acknowledgment for the job well done. When it was my turn the Captain said to me, 'Haven't I just seen you a minute ago?' Of course he was joking and of course I would not have dared to front up a second time.

With daylight, sails were set again and we went on with the rounding of the Horn. The ear-splitting roar of the wind in the rigging and the crashing of the sea coming over the rail, filling the decks before finally running off through the wash ports, is something remembered for life!

The following Sunday I was just hauling up the container with the plum and dumpling soup through the galley skylight, when with a terrific thunderclap, the foresail blew out and was carried away in big strips. The Captain said to me, 'Put that away and go and lend a hand.' With plenty of water coming over, I got wet through and when I got aft with the soup I was abused for taking so long. I felt badly done by, as I was the only one dripping wet.

As we approached our destination, the anchors were put over the side ready for use. We arrived in Corral on 6 October and soon started to unload our cargo. The captain's gig was swung out and manned by four of us boys. We were the first in the crew to set foot in a foreign land. Two of us were allowed to look around, while two stayed with the boat in turn, until the Captain returned. He had given us some money and I bought some peaches with mine, using sign language for the first time. One dark night we had a long wait for the Captain. When he finally came he jumped into the boat with the order to get going, before he was properly settled in the stern to take the tiller. We soon reached top speed but were stopped dead, suddenly. We all came off the thwarts with the oars all over the place. With an almighty crash we had hit a moored launch full on. The Captain blamed the bright lamp in front of him.

We unloaded the remaining cargo at Valparaiso. The German Consul had a party arranged for us, which all enjoyed and appreciated very much. Through an arrangement the Chilean *carabineros* took unruly crew members back to the jetty and their boat instead of putting them in the calaboose, a concession for the Flying 'P' Liners.

The next port was Tocopilla, to load bagged nitrate, used in explosives and as a fertiliser. Longshoremen stowed it, each taking a 120 kg bag on his hip from a platform in the hold of the ship and dropping it exactly where it should go. The bags were piled in a pyramid in each hold where they settled into a solid mass.

We left Tocopilla on 13 November with a full load of nitrate for Europe. The ship was readied again for rounding the Horn. We encountered stormy weather which, coming mainly from the west, gave us a good shove along. Running before the wind, an extra man was needed at the wheel to counter the extra pressure on the rudder. When at the wheel on one occasion, I have recollections of a huge, green-blue, glassy mountain of water rising on our port quarter. On the crown a streaming mane of white froth carried away in spray. I think I missed a heartbeat at the thought of being completely engulfed by this, which would mean the end of us. But *Padua* heeled over hard, forced by this giant wave, which rolled away underneath us, lifting us high and then dumping us into the following trough with a terrible screeching of the wind in the rigging. The Captain came over to the steering wheel and explained the periodic formation of three especially large waves, which one must let go if any manoeuvres are to be attempted. But I think he was relieved that at that time there had been no mishap.

With the wind aft, we were running free and achieved very good speeds of over 16 knots. The ship just tore along and it was a very good sight and feeling. I preferred to be aloft in heavy weather rather on deck with seas constantly breaking on board. And the view from aloft! The labouring ship below and the seascape was superb. One had to see it to believe it!

On 9 December we stood by the Falkland Islands and at the beginning of February we arrived at our destination, Bruges, Belgium, where we discharged our cargo. We left

Bruges on 13 February 1930, and a few days later arrived back from where we had started, Hamburg, the whole voyage taking a little over seven months.

After another voyage under sail in the four-masted barque *Passat*, Helmut attended navigation school and then went as mate in Laeisz powered vessels until 1939, when he obtained his master's certificate. The war intervened and as a prisoner of war Helmut was finally interned in Australia. He made Tasmania his home, becoming naturalised in 1948.

Another German lad, Hans Renz, told me of his time with Laeisz and his voyage in the four-masted barque *Priwall*:

I served in four square riggers in all. As an apprentice or *Schiffjunge* in the *Prinzess Eitel Friedrich* and then *Grossherzog Friedrich August*, both school ships. After this, I had to enlist in the German Navy and, after the 1914 war, I was AB on various steamers until I joined the Laeisz Company and the four-masted barque *Priwall* in 1920. The Master was Captain Brockhoff, First Mate Topper, Second Mate Michaels and Third Mate Stammarjohan.

It was another typical Laeisz voyage to the West Coast but noteworthy in that it was the second voyage of the world's newest windjammer. Hans continues:

We took a general cargo to the West Coast and returned with a cargo of saltpetre to Hamburg. One of my duties was wireless operator, along with the third mate, but the set never worked properly. It was powered by a 1 hp kerosene motor. We had a normal voyage outward bound as well as homeward. Not record breaking but not a long passage either. About 85 days.

Passing Dover, we could still observe the remains of the five-masted ship *Preussen* where she had run aground, and on arrival at Valparaiso we saw the famous five-masted barque *Potosi* at anchor—at the time not seaworthy after five years of sitting out the war. Our first mate, Topper, had been in *Preussen* when she stranded.

As soon as we anchored at Valparaiso, a small sailing boat came towards the stern of *Priwall*. There were four or five giggling senoritas in it and we exchanged greetings. I shinned down a rope and the girls took fright and sailed off. I had to climb back on board, which was with some difficulty as I had burnt the skin off my legs in sliding down the rope. After three weeks discharging at Valparaiso, we sailed north to Iquique. Every day I had to go to the charthouse to have my leg treated by the 3rd mate. But it got worse and worse. So did the wind until it died altogether. This placed us in something of a predicament. The north-setting Humboldt Current helped us to our latitude but, once there, we needed wind to make port or we would drift too far to the north. The Captain was always in the charthouse when I went to get my leg treated. He called me a 'Jonah' and threatened to tear up his navigation charts. At the last minute, we got just the right wind, otherwise we would have drifted too far north and would have been forced to sail away from the coast, head south and make a new approach. My leg didn't improve and I ended up in Iquique Hospital until the day we sailed.

Several men deserted here and were replaced when we sailed for home. Only one of them was an experienced sailing ship sailor. Idleness, enforced through the war years, in strange ports, caused many seamen to leave their ships and find work ashore. Our new AB told us his story. He too found work ashore in Valparaiso. He had been engaged to a girl from Saxony whose parents were quite well off. They wanted him to return to Germany, where he had been offered a position in his father-in-law's business. The AB's name was Karl Herbert and he showed us a passenger ticket in a steamer to Hamburg that the girl's parents had sent him. He decided to return home to get married but refused to use the ticket. He signed on the *Priwall* instead. It turned out to be a tragic decision. He was the best and most capable seaman *Priwall* had. Off the Azores, *Priwall* went through a hurricane and Karl Herbert fell out of the rigging and was killed. I was helmsman at the time. The mate was nearby, watching the compass and, as he walked past, he said to me, 'I just walked into something soft', shone his torch onto the deck and there was Karl Herbert. I shouted back that he would be dead, as I had seen him on the lower topgallant yard. He had fallen only a few metres in front of me but I had heard and seen nothing, due to the darkness and the screaming wind.

Three weeks later, mid January, we arrived at Cuxshaven and had to anchor for more than a week as the Elbe was frozen and ice bound, and tugs were not able to tow us into Hamburg. When we finally berthed, an elderly couple with a young girl, all in black, came on board. They were Karl Herbert's fiancée and her parents and had come to claim his body. The Captain had to tell them that there was no body, as he had been buried at sea. There was quite an upsetting scene that made a deep impression on all the crew.

I sailed in another square-rigged sailing ship, *Carl Vinnen*, in 1922-23, before sitting for my mate's ticket in Hamburg. I then joined the German Australian Steamship Company as 4th officer and, after two years in steam, I sat for my master's ticket. By 1927 I was 2nd mate but, as the maritime future did not look bright, I decided to accept the offer of my father-in-law, and come to Australia and settle on the land.

One of the ships purchased by F. Laeisz was the full-rigged *Fitzjames*, one of the last commercial full-rigged ships built. It is strange that Laeisz should buy such a ship when this rig had been superseded by the four-masted barque, of which they already had a large fleet. *Fitzjames* was built in 1902 by W. Hamilton of Port Glasgow for the London firm of W. Montgomery. Laeisz acquired her from them in 1911. She was renamed *Pinnas* and after the war was given to France as reparations. In 1922 Laeisz bought her back and returned her to the saltpetre trade. In 1929, on the outward voyage to the West Coast, she was dismasted and abandoned off Cape Horn. Ironically this was not caused by wind; rather by the lack of it. She had just passed through the Straits of Le Maire and off Cape Horn ran into hurricane force winds. While she could not make any westing against these winds, she was not at this stage in any danger. However, after several weeks of constant gale, the wind dropped, leaving a heavy swell. This caused *Pinnas* to roll heavily, up to 50 degrees in either direction, proving too much for her masts and rigging and causing her to be dismasted. The calm ended with a hailstorm and high winds, creating great difficulty for the crew as they worked to free their ship of the mass of wreckage.

The story is now taken up by Hans Mollitor of Malente-Krummsee in the north of Germany, second mate during the voyage and veteran of previous voyages in American sailing ships. Hans told me of many happenings during his time at sea and the story of *Pinnas* is incredible, as there was no loss of life or serious injury.

It was on our second voyage to the West Coast of South America around Cape Horn, in the ship *Pinnas*. We left Hamburg on 22 January 1929, with cement, coke and general cargo. The vessel was delayed almost four weeks in Hamburg Harbour due to extremely cold weather. The harbour was totally frozen over. I was 2nd officer. On the day of our departure two tugs towed the *Pinnas* down river and near Elbe 1 Lightship they were dismissed and our last voyage started. In the English Channel we tacked for many days and then entered the Bay of Biscay. From the northern to the southern hemisphere, as usual, we had all kinds of weather, and when we reached about 43° South we changed all sails and brought up all heavy weather canvas and prepared the vessel for Cape Horn. We rounded Cape Horn on 12 April 1929 after almost 14 days hard working with very strong weather.

The wind now dropped and *Pinnas* was rolling hard in extra high seas. Suddenly the fore and main masts broke about three feet above the deck. The foremast sails and steel yards crashed on to the deck. The mizzen to starboard sent the main mast to port. The mizzenmast cracked just above the top and the mizzen topsail and yards were hanging overboard on the starboard side. After all the rigging came down the vessel lost her stability and started to roll terribly and big seas came over from both sides. At first the situation seemed hopeless and we realised that nobody could help us in this sea. It was extremely dangerous to work on deck, not only from the heavy seas washing over the deck but all the rigging including wires, ropes, chain, remains of sails being pushed around by the sea. Most dangerous was the mizzenmast, which was rubbing on the ship's side and likely to break through the hull plating. With hammer and chisels the chief officer and myself worked on the broken mizzenmast, with a heavy wire leading to the capstan for'ard, and while we were hitting, the crew were manning the capstan.

After two days we managed to cut the steel mast and stays and it dropped into the sea. We now started to clear the deck because we found several holes in the main deck and the vessel was making water. Our pumps had been damaged when the masts fell. We also rigged an emergency aerial for the radio officer so he could send an SOS. During our dangerous work on deck an AB was smashed against the wreckage and his nose and jaw was broken. One could hardly recognise this man, as his face was so injured. I carried him to the after saloon to present him to the master, and he said to me, 'You are the doctor on board, try your best.' I managed to bring his broken jaw into the correct position, and fasten it with a bandage around his head. I fed him with a glass tube through a gap from a tooth he had lost.

On 24 April the radio officer had contact with the Chilean passenger ship *Alfonso*. She came from the north, bound for Punta Arenas. Two days later she came in sight, but the weather was still too rough for her to be able to help. The leaks in our decks were getting worse. The vessel was making more water and all lifeboats were smashed. The vessel had been drifting all these days closer to the rocks of Diego Ramirez. As continuing bad weather was reported, our master decided to abandon ship.

Alfonso was pumping oil on the sea to stop the waves breaking and so allow the lowering of a boat. The first boat was smashed against the ship's side, the second boat managed to get away safely. With two trips *Pinnas*'s crew was safely aboard the *Alfonso*. This was an excellent piece of seamanship.

No one saw the end of *Pinnas*. She was last seen drifting into a hailstorm, and as she was taking water into her hull it is assumed she sank shortly afterwards. *Alfonso* brought us to Punta Arenas, where most of our crew had to see the doctor due to injuries and salt water boils from the sea water. Fritz, the seaman with the broken jaw, went to hospital for an x-ray, and the doctor stated that I had done a perfect job so it was not necessary to break his jaw again. The crew was returned to Hamburg by a German cargo vessel.

Captain Bernhard Masson of Hamburg has given me this description of the traditional crossing of the line ceremony, or *Aquatortaufe*, as practised in German sailing ships. It was not greatly different from the procedure in ships of other nations, and reflects the traditional perceived importance of passing from the Northern into the Southern Hemisphere, and to a lesser extent back again. The practice was possible, because the point of crossing the Equator was in the belt of doldrums, the almost perpetual calms that existed adjacent to 0° latitude. The frivolities were dispensed with if bad weather occurred at this crossing. Bernhard joined the barque

Racing for Port Lincoln

Alan Villiers, in *Falmouth for Orders*, commented on an impromptu race between two four-masted barques, the Swedish *Beatrice* and the Finnish *Herzogin Cecilie*, between Melbourne and Port Lincoln: 'If a passenger ship had been in the vicinity of Cape Otway on the morning of Saturday, December 17, 1927, her passengers would have seen the sight of their lives; two great four-masted barques, relics of an age that has passed forever, racing under all sail to a stiff breeze. Both in ballast and high out of the water, it would have been extraordinary to see two sailing ships a mile or two apart, presenting a sight that only sailing ships can present. And no one was there to see it.' This last statement prompted me to place this event on canvas.

I have met many who sailed in *Herzogin Cecilie* but only one who sailed in *Beatrice*—Henry Nicholson, later master, and president of Cape Horners Australia. The master of *Herzogin Cecilie* on this voyage was Captain Ruben de Cloux, *Beatrice*'s master Harald Bruce. They became friends in Melbourne after discharging their cargoes and on learning that both would load wheat in Port Lincoln decided to make a race of it to Falmouth. They sailed on 19 January 1928, *Herzogin Cecilie* headed for Cape Horn, *Beatrice* for the Cape of Good Hope. *Herzogin Cecilie* arrived at Falmouth after a fast trip of 96 days, beating *Beatrice* by 18 days.

Beatrice was broken up in 1932; *Herzogin Cecilie* sailed in the grain trade until 1936, when she ran aground in Salcombe Bay, Devon. Her chart house is ashore nearby and her figurehead resides in the Ålands Sjofartsmuseum at Mariehamn.

Oil on canvas, 55 x 75 cm, in the collection of Jukka Hurme, Mariehamn

Plate XVII

Towards Falmouth

The year is 1933 as the four-masted auxiliary barque *Magdalene Vinnen* clears Sydney Harbour sailing towards Falmouth for orders with a full cargo of Australian wool. Built as a cargo-carrying training ship in 1921 for the Vinnen company of Bremen, she was the only sailing ship in the grain fleet with an auxiliary engine.

In 1937 the Nord Deutscher Lloyd Line bought her for use as a training ship. Renamed *Kommodore Johnsen*, she was sent out to Port Lincoln to load a grain cargo and again in 1939. This proved to be her last cargo. She was in Bremen at the outbreak of World War II and during the war made short training voyages in the Baltic. In 1945 Russia claimed her as a war prize and renamed her *Sedov*, using her as a pure training ship for the Department of Fisheries. Her 'tween decks were converted to accommodation, and a row of portholes pierces her sides. She is still in commission and to subsidise her running costs takes paying passengers.

The pilot steamer in the background is the *Captain Cook*, a familiar sight on Sydney Harbour. The small launch in the foreground is typical of the well-known fleet of workboats operated by Stannard Bros. They were used for a variety of tasks, in this case possibly hired by a newspaper photographer, for a sailing ship leaving Sydney in 1933 was a rare sight indeed.

Oil on canvas, 55 x 75 cm, in the collection of Alan Stannard, Sydney

Plate XVIII

Eastwards, Eastwards, Ever Eastwards

This painting of the barque *Penang* on the Australia run was inspired by the magnificence of a sunrise at sea, and some lines in the shanty 'Rolling Home', sung by the crews of sailing ships as they walked the capstan round: 'Eastwards, eastwards, ever eastwards, to the rising of the sun, / Our course is ever eastwards since our voyage has begun.'

Ships sailing from Europe or North America to Australia always travelled east to make best use of the prevailing winds. However, when working down through the Atlantic, the need to seek out fair winds meant that the sailer had some westing in her course, which took her over towards the coast of South America. Once in the globe-encircling westerlies of southern latitudes the sailing ship could travel many thousands of miles in fast time. On leaving Australia or New Zealand the sailer headed east again to return to Europe by way of Cape Horn.

Penang was bought by Gustaf Erikson in 1923, from which time she was used increasingly in the grain trade. She was torpedoed by the German U-boat *U140* in 1941 with the loss of all hands. *Penang* is depicted here prior to 1933, when she inherited the steel charthouse from *Hougomont* after that vessel was dismasted in the Great Australian Bight on her way to Spencer Gulf.

Oil on canvas, 30 x 40 cm, in the collection of Elfi Weiman, Munich

Plate XIX

Trade Wind

In 1911 Blohm & Voss of Hamburg built a four-masted barque for Laeisz which was named *Passat* (*Trade Wind*). This painting places her in the winds for which she was named. The wind strength is 15 to 20 knots, pushing up whitecaps and giving the sailer a good shove along, with the ubiquitous dolphins showing their paces and sharing in the exhilaration. All those who tell of their time in sail joyfully remember the trade winds—the warm sun, clear days and almost effortless sailing.

Of course there was no chance of lazing around in the sun, except on Sundays, and the working day progressed as usual. Adjustments to sheet and brace were at a minimum—but work required in the rigging and on the hull presented itself relentlessly. First of all, the heavy weather canvas used in the stormy North Atlantic and Southern Oceans was replaced with lighter, older sails. A four-masted barque usually had 18 square sails and about 13 staysails, and the process took several days. The sail maker took advantage of this weather, with new sails marked out on deck and old ones repaired. Aloft, rigging was replaced, stays painted, ratlines renewed and all gear inspected for damage or wear. The carpenter replaced split or damaged deck planks, pin rails and other woodwork and mixed the paint applied after the never-ending job of chipping rust.

After six years as an auxiliary sail-training ship, sailing to the east coast of South America, *Passat* was withdrawn from service in 1957, and now lies at Travemunde, Germany. She has recently been refurbished to A1 condition.

Oil on canvas, 55 x 75 cm, in the collection of Bob Russell, Sydney

Plate XX

The Duck Pond

On 26 January 1927 the *Sydney Morning Herald* shipping column reported: 'The German four-masted barque *Lisbeth* arrived at Sydney last night after a voyage of 58 days from Callao. She is now anchored in Watsons Bay awaiting pratique. The vessel which is in ballast had a fine but uneventful trip. She is commanded by Captain Hilgendorf, and is to load wheat in Sydney for the United Kingdom or Continent. It is expected that about 3000 tons will be lifted.'

Lisbeth loaded her grain in Cockle Bay in Darling Harbour, a part of Port Jackson, and is shown here leaving the bay. This part of the harbour was a hive of activity right up to the 1960s, with a large rail terminal handling wheat, wool and other rural produce, and millions of tonnes of coal for the power stations at nearby Pyrmont. Cockle Bay was almost landlocked, cut off from the main harbour by an opening bridge, with finger wharves where the coastal fleet unloaded cargo. It was nicknamed the 'Duck Pond' because there was little room to manoeuvre. Surrounding it were the multistorey wool stores of the large pastoral companies. Names like Dalgety, Goldsborough Mort, Australian Mercantile Land & Finance, Pitt Son & Badgery, still adorn these buildings, though now in disuse.

The hand on the fore royal yard is about to remove the Blue Peter, the flag traditionally flown from the foremast before departure to indicate, amongst other things, that a pilot was required. There is no doubt, however, despite the flag, that by 1927 the pilot would have been informed by telephone.

Oil on canvas, 55 x 75 cm, in the collection of Kevin Jones, Warwick Qld

Plate XXI

East of Eden

This painting portrays the steel barque *Kaiulani* off the New South Wales coast on the final leg of her historic voyage from Aberdeen, Washington, to Sydney in 1941–42, the last time the Stars and Stripes would fly from the gaff of a commercial square rigger. The American custom of hanging the ship's gig from stern davits can be seen, as can the spanker gaff set up from the mizzen lower mast cap rather than the futtock band. *Kaiulani* was built in 1899 by the down east shipbuilder Sewell & Co., at Bath, Maine, to the order of A. Hackfield, a German merchant and entrepreneur living in the Hawaiian Islands, and named after the granddaughter of King Kalakaua, the last king of Hawaii. *Kaiulani* spent most of her life in the Pacific, firstly in the sugar trade from Hawaii to the west coast of the United States, with voyages to Newcastle, New South Wales, for coal in the off-season. Sold to the Alaska Packers Association in 1920, her role changed along with her name, which became *Star of Finland*. In 1929 she was laid up in San Francisco until recommissioned in 1941 and given back her original name. She sailed around Cape Horn to Durban where she loaded a cargo of explosives for Sydney.

Japanese submarine activity and the attack on Sydney Harbour caused Captain Wigsten to head for Hobart instead, where the US Army requisitioned her for use as a store ship. *Kaiulani* was towed to Sydney and with following winds, set sails to help the tug along, overtaking her on many occasions. The lifeboat has been swung out in case a submarine is encountered.

Oil on canvas, 45 x 65 cm, in the collection of the artist

Plate XXII

Off the Dagger Rammereez

No longer a familiar sight to mariners are the uninhabited Diego Ramirez islands, a Chilean possession about 60 miles south-west of Cape Horn, actually the peaks of an undersea mountain range. They were a hazard to shipping, particularly at night or if several days of cloudy weather prevented a sight being taken. The windjammer seamen were either ignorant or scornful of the correct pronunciation of the name.

This four-masted full-rigged ship, *Falls of Clyde*, was built in 1879 by Russell & Co. at Glasgow for the Glasgow Falls Line, who named all their vessels after Scottish waterfalls and employed them in the India trade, taking out general cargo, steel products and cement and returning with jute or rice. She often went on to Australia, New Zealand, China and North America, and loaded many cargoes of wheat from the US west coast ports. In 1898 she was sold to Captain Matson of San Francisco, who put her into the Hawaii trade, carrying freight and passengers out and returning with sugar. In 1907 he sold her to the Associated Oil Co. of California and she became a sailing oil-tanker, still in the Hawaii trade. General Petroleum bought her in 1920 and she made just one more voyage under sail before being turned into an oil barge. After 37 years at Ketchikan, Alaska, she was towed to Honolulu to become a stationary exhibition for the Hawaii Maritime Center. Re-rigged as a four-masted ship, as she was originally, she is now listed in the National Register of Historic Places.

Oil on canvas, 55 x 75 cm, in the collection of the artist

Plate XXV

In the South-East Trades

The four-masted barque *Moshulu* powers through the South-East Trade Winds in the type of weather that made crews forget the hardships of more southern climes. She was built as the *Kurt* in 1904 by the British shipbuilder W. Hamilton for H. Siemers of Hamburg, who already had a fleet of steamships. One of the largest four-masted barques ever built, she measured 335 feet (102 metres) between perpendiculars. Siemers put her into the nitrate trade, her cargoes usually coal out and nitrate home. She was in Astoria, Oregon, when the United States entered World War I, and was seized by the US Shipping Board. Renamed *Moshulu*, a Native North American name, she traded to the Philippines, Australia and South Africa with lumber. Her return cargo was usually coal loaded in Newcastle, New South Wales. In 1921 she was sold to Charles Nelson & Co. of San Francisco and made several voyages before being laid up in Oakland, California, in 1922. She sailed to Melbourne in 1927 with lumber, returning to be laid up near Seattle until Gustaf Erikson bought her in 1935, re-rigged her and put her into the grain trade.

Her last commercial voyage was in 1940; she loaded grain in Buenos Aires for Farsund, in occupied Norway, where she was taken over by Germany. Rigged down, she saw out the war as a grain store ship. German shipowner Heinz Schliewen bought her with the intention of re-rigging her and putting her to work as a cargo-carrying cadet ship. This did not eventuate and she was bought by an American syndicate and towed to Philadelphia to become a floating restaurant. *Moshulu* is still afloat in this role.

Oil on canvas, 55 x 75 cm, in the collection of Stefan Eriksson, Mariehamn

Plate XXVI

On the Pacific Run

One of the last sailing ships built on the US Pacific coast, the five-masted schooner *Vigilant* (later renamed *City of Alberni*, then *Condor*) was typical of the numerous large wooden schooners built there in 1910–20. Launched in 1920 at the George F. Mathews shipyard at Hoquiam, Washington, for the E. K. Wood Lumber Company, she was 240 feet (75 metres) long. Her first voyage was to Sydney with timber. Being light, the timber was also carried on deck. Many features of these latter-day schooners resulted from this practice. The hoist of their sails and the height of their lower masts was such that the booms and gaffs could be set higher up the mast, although there was only about 4 feet clearance over the top of the deck load. The ship's boat was slung from stern davits as there was no room along the well deck. Sometimes an additional boat was carried lashed down on the poop.

It was unusual for these schooners to carry a gaff on the aftermost mast. A triangular leg o'mutton sail was set on a boom as this was easier to control when sailing downwind. They generally had a single yard on the foremast from which two square sails were set for downwind sailing. These were furled into the mast rather than the yard. They usually had a donkey-powered winch at the base of each mast to hoist the heavy gaffs.

Oil on canvas, 40 x 60 cm, in the collection of the artist

Plate XXVII

Down to Her Marks

It is 9 March 1948 in Port Victoria, and the ketch *Hawk* awaits the departure of the ketch *Falie* so she can bring the last load of bagged grain alongside the four-masted barque *Viking*. This will bring the total number of bags to 50,950—over 4000 tons—that *Viking* will take around Cape Horn to be unloaded in the Millwall Dock, London. The bags were hoisted on board and stowed by shore-based stevedores who had the job of dropping them exactly into place in the hold to form an interlocking pattern that would prevent the cargo shifting when at sea. Some bags were slit and loose grain allowed to fill the spaces.

Viking, pronounced 'Veeking' by the Finns, was built in Denmark in 1906 by Burmeister & Wain as a cargo-carrying training ship but in 1929 passed into the ownership of Gustaf Erikson. Her long poop deck, characteristic of training ships of the time, is obvious in this scene. Laid up in Mariehamn during World War II, she made just one voyage after the war. This took her from Mariehamn to East London in South Africa, Santos in Brazil and thence to Port Victoria. My great friend, Captain Ingemar Palmer of Mariehamn, was third mate on this voyage. Two other sailing ships were in Port Victoria at this time. The four-masted barque *Passat* is in the distance and the four-masted barque *Lawhill* is under sail — destination Beira, Portuguese East Africa.

Oil on canvas, 55 x 75 cm, in the collection of John Stanley, Sydney

Plate XXVIII

At the Ballast Grounds

The ship *Grace Harwar* lies at anchor off Wallaroo, South Australia, unloading ballast before returning to the jetty to load bagged grain. Alf Freestone, who sailed in this ship in 1929, describes the process in great detail in Chapter 7. These days, the dumping of ballast directly into the sea would not be allowed. I have been told of the cloudy appearance of water off these grain ports but now, 50 years since the last ballast was dumped, it quite clear.

Grace Harwar was unique in the grain fleet, being the only ship-rigged vessel. Ship-rigged vessels, built in large numbers in the nineteenth century, were superseded by the four-masted barque which needed no more crew but due to its greater length had up to 30 per cent more cargo capacity. *Grace Harwar* was one of Erikson's early acquisitions (1917) and she must have earned him money as he kept her until 1935. This voyage from Wallaroo was recorded on film by Alan Villiers, and also in print in *By Way of Cape Horn*, which describes many hardships during the long 128-day voyage to Queenstown for orders. On her final voyage in 1935, when she loaded wheat at Port Broughton, Spencer Gulf, for London, she made the quite good time of 98 days. She was towed from London to Charlestown, Firth of Forth, where she was broken up.

Oil on canvas, 50 x 70 cm, in the collection of the artist

Plate XXIX

Three Tall Ships: Grain Fleet Survivors at Port Victoria

It is 9 March 1948, and three four-masted barques are seen together for the last time. They are *Passat*, at anchor in the foreground, *Viking*, at anchor in the distance, and *Lawhill* under sail. It is incredible that three such vessels should have been found in the one place almost halfway through the twentieth century. *Passat* arrived from Port Swettenham in Malaya on 2 March. Her royal yards were taken down to improve stability while in ballast, but would have been replaced before setting off.

One can imagine that the boatload of her crew is heading ashore to the Wauraltee pub, a favourite gathering place. This pub still exists, and Port Victoria has not changed much. It is possible for the sailing ship devotee sitting in the pub to look out into the Gulf and imagine the grain ships out beyond the jetty and the loud laughter of seamen and farm labourers all around.

Passat made one more visit to Port Victoria, in 1949. She was then bought by Heinz Schliewen who ran her as an auxiliary training ship between Germany and South America until 1957. After *Viking* unloaded her grain in London's Millwall Dock she was sold to become a floating hotel and conference centre in Gothenburg, Sweden. *Lawhill* made seven voyages to Australia and two to South America between 1941 and 1948. Along with *Pamir*, sailing out of New Zealand, these two were the only large sailing ships to operate continuously throughout the war.

Oil on canvas, 55 x 75 cm, Australian Cape Horners Association, Adelaide

Plate XXX

Like a Bird Asleep

A line from Mary Lang's poem 'Parma', which appears in Chapter 7, inspired this painting of the four-masted barque *Parma*. Calms were encountered at various times during a round-the-world voyage, the most protracted periods occurring in the equatorial doldrums, where a ship might be frustratingly becalmed for three or four weeks, sometimes more. This created as much work as heavy weather. The slightest hint of wind required the yards to be trimmed, even though this catspaw might last for only a few minutes, or drop off and come from another direction, when the yards would have to be trimmed again. The courses were usually clewed up when there was no wind to prevent them from slatting about and becoming chafed. Sometimes, despite the lack of wind, a swell caused by a storm perhaps thousands of miles away could cause the ship to roll from side to side, to the point where it could be dismasted.

The old custom of whistling for a wind, whether believed in or not, was often practised. Many seamen have told me of the old man walking around the poop whistling quietly, in the hope of seeing the sea's glassy surface ruffled by a breeze that might signal the beginning of the trade winds. The superstition was often carried further—in heavy weather anyone whistling within earshot of the poop would be told to 'pipe down' for fear of increasing the wind even further.

Other parts of the world produced calms, but not as predictably as in the doldrums, and they were often harbingers of a storm. I have heard of calms off Cape Horn, even in midwinter, and it is certain that there would be no whistling in this case.

Oil on canvas, 40 x 60 cm, in the collection of Henrik Karlsson, Mariehamn

Plate XXXI

In the Gulf

The barque *Killoran* sets sail off Port Victoria in Spencer Gulf, with a heat haze building up astern. Her black hull indicates ownership by Gustaf Erikson, who bought her from Glasgow shipowners J. Hardie & Co. in 1924, when she had painted ports, a feature of many British-owned sailing ships.

Spencer Gulf had a long history of association with the sailing ship, brought about by its unique configuration, allowing ships to load deep within the grain-producing countryside. The towns and ports began developing from the mid 1800s, with produce and necessities being transported in the early days by hundreds of small schooners, ketches and barques from other parts of Australia and overseas. Sailing ships could make and leave anchorage, or leave their mooring at the long jetties that were a feature of some of the Gulf ports, without the aid of tugs. The first sailing ship to load a grain cargo from Port Victoria was the ship *Carlisle Castle*, in 1879.

Somewhat earlier, in 1859, copper was discovered at Wallaroo and nearby Moonta further up the Gulf. Initially the ore was shipped out, but in 1861 a smelter was built and refined copper was loaded as well. To run the smelter, coal was brought from Newcastle, New South Wales. To cater for this trade Captain Henry Simpson started a shipping company known unofficially as the 'Black Diamond Line'. These days bulk ships lie at the end of the grain conveyor at Wallaroo, far out in the bay, and in a matter of days are filled with more grain than the entire grain fleet would have loaded over three months.

Oil on canvas, 55 x 75 cm, in the collection of Celia and Philip Xeros, Wagga Wagga NSW

Plate XXXII

Bremen in March 1929 at the age of 15. This vessel was a cargo-carrying cadet ship owned by Nord Deutscher Lloyd.

Bremen was ice bound in Kiel Harbour, and was still fully loaded with saltpetre from the West Coast of South America. It was a hard winter and the sea was frozen completely. When the ice melted, a tug towed her to Danzig to discharge her cargo. I joined her in Bremen and we loaded drums here and in Hamburg and on 18 May 1929 we were towed into the North Sea.

Not long after sailing we had our first accident; a sailor fell from the rigging and was killed. On 24 May 1929, we passed the Lizard–Quessant line, and the Equator in middle of June. All sailors had a lot of work in front of them, because of the line crossing ceremony. Ropes with knots, dipped in tar, were needed for the baptism of new hands. Musical instruments were made. Drums and violins made from canvas, skirts for the 'Negroes' and long blonde hair for Thetis, made from rope. Her crown was made from margarine tins and the last thing was the baptismal font. The big day came on 16 June 1929, when King Neptune and Thetis came on board with their guards. Thetis with long blonde hair and crown, her bust stuffed with hemp, looked a real saucy lady. Of course we had an orchestra with a devil's violin—this you would find on every sailing ship—and an engine room telegraph made from wood standing next to the compass. Triton, with admiral's insignia, and binoculars made from two wine bottles, took over command from our captain. He pulled over the engine room telegraph to full speed ahead. Of course we had no engines and the whole thing was a joke. The ship's boys who had never crossed the Equator had to go for'ard then aft trying to avoid being hit by the 'Negroes' wielding the knotted ropes. Soon we had welts all over our bodies. Then we had to go to a horizontal bar for some pull-ups, and copped more hits with the rope if you failed to pull yourself up. Then came the blessing and we received some tablets that tasted like castor oil. Then we were lathered all over our face, and shaved with a long wooden razor, 1 metre long. Last of all we were painted on the chest with a large tar brush, and pushed backwards into a canvas trough of water. Two 'Negroes' held you under water for what seemed minutes, and then it was someone else's turn. This was a hard lesson but you need this treatment to help you survive around Cape Horn. In the afternoon we received cocoa and cake and everyone was happy except the boys. Still, it is a good memory even though it was hard and painful and the next trip was much easier and better.

[The ship-made instrument, the devil's violin] was made from an empty margarine can about 300 mm diameter, or a two-gallon petrol can. A broom handle was nailed across the can and strings stretched over the can from each end of the broom. Three or four metal discs (lids from the cans) were drilled in the centre with a hole and placed over the end of the broomstick. The instrument was played much like a bass fiddle, with the loose tin lids held at the top and prevented from sliding past the point of attachment of the strings. When a piece of wood (bow) was drawn over the string it caused the tin tops to vibrate and rattle.

My second voyage as a cadet in the barque *Bremen* commenced on 21 May 1930. We left Hamburg at 8.30 am and had a slight collision with the steamer *Cordelia* in the English Channel. This caused us no damage and the voyage went ahead as scheduled. On 29 May we passed the Lizard and on 27 June, the Equator. On 4 August we reached 50°S and planned to go through the Straits of Le Maire, but we had headwinds and fog. On this rounding we had constant headwinds and we could not get past Staten Island. Sails had to be set and furled at all times in hail and snow, and most of them were damaged by the storm. We could not make any westing and it took us 23 days 8 hours to round Cape Horn to the west. On 6 September we reached Talcahuano, San Antonio and Valparaiso, where we unloaded our cargo. On 11 October we left Valparaiso with sand ballast, and dropped anchor in the roadstead off Iquique. We then had to unload our ballast by hand, shovelling it into baskets and dropping it into the sea.

One evening after work I felt like a swim but swimming was strictly forbidden. As no officer was on deck I climbed down a rope ladder and swam around the ship. Next day we were chipping rust on the side of the ship and I looked down and saw a large shark. It scared the hell out of me and I never swam overside again. On 9 November we left Iquique with a full nitrate cargo. The four-masted barque *Priwall* left eight days later and passed us on 26 November, 31° 19' S, 18° 48' W (South Atlantic). But in Ghent she was only three days in front of us, arriving on 11 February 1931. We arrived on 14 February. Towards the end of the voyage our captain and some officers became sick and we were forced to call at the Azores. This gave us the opportunity to pick up fresh vegetables, lemons, eggs and meat from the shore in our lifeboats.

In the English Channel a collision occurred with a steamer crossing our course. We were holed above the waterline and had our bowsprit bent up. We knocked his funnel over. Luckily our foremast stayed intact even though our forestays were gone. On 13 February we reached Vlissingen and the next day berthed at Ghent where our saltpetre was unloaded.

While stories told by seamen from the Laeisz ships tend to dominate, I have included some others to illustrate that there were many other German sailing ships tramping the world's trade routes, trying to stay in business. A worthy inclusion to this chapter are the reminiscences of Australian Arthur Hennessy, who sailed as a boy in the German ship *Oliva* in 1914. His comments regarding the ship, master, officers and shipmates are noteworthy, and yet another illustration of the degree of professionalism possessed by those in the German mercantile marine. His description of life around the Gulf ports and the arrival of the five-masted barque *Potosi* at Valparaiso add additional flavour to his story.

I was always mad on the sea, I would walk around the wharves when I should have been at school, hoping for a captain who would have me as a crew member. Finally in late 1912, I went to sea in the ketches trading in Spencer Gulf and St Vincents Gulf in South Australia. These ketches would go ashore on the sandy beach at high tide, and at low tide, the farmers would drive their wagons to the ship side, load, and at high tide, the ship would refloat and away. On the ketches, living was very rough and ready, boiled beef hung in the rigging, after a few days as hard as a board. On return to Adelaide, there was usually a horse on the wharf, a whip slung from the gaff, a loop around the top third of a bag of wheat, the whip led through a snatch block made fast to the horse. The horse knew exactly when to start and stop. One had to have a strong back as we had no machinery except a hand winch. The crews were invariably runaway sailors, either German or Scandinavian. Port Adelaide in those days was full of them, and great men they were and the very best of migrants for this country.

From the little ships, I worked on the *Paringa* of the Adelaide Steamship Company, running to Port Lincoln, Port Augusta, etc. where there was always an amount of sandalwood to be loaded. We carried a full shipload of workers for the east-west railway, which was then being built. Port Augusta was a very lively place. The Gulf Steamship Company had a very fine steamer, the *Wandana*, in competition with the *Paringa*, and the *Morialta*. All ships did a round trip every week. We used to arrive Sunday morning and sail on Tuesday. I then sailed in the small steamers *Juno* and *Warrawee* of the Gulf Steamship Co.—the *Juno* to Edithburg and Ardrossen, usually staying overnight. *Warrawee* usually went to Kangaroo Island. For those days the pay was good, the food was very good, and able seamen got 16 pounds per month and ordinary seamen eight pounds.

Sailing ships were very plentiful in season and up and down the gulfs there would be 20 or more. Where we tied up in the *Paringa* at Port Augusta there was a bridge across the entrance to a large basin, which was usually full of sailing ships; most of the inward cargoes were timber, loaded from the Baltic and West Coast of North America. There used to be a large timber yard alongside the Basin. I got a job on the *Loch Torridon*, a four master. She had just arrived from the Baltic with timber. She was a Russian Finn, and a beautiful ship. A lot of the sailors had deserted and no wonder, their pay was three pounds a month.

Also there was the *James Craig* and *Laura Craig*, beautiful barques, very well kept up and less than half the size of the *Loch Torridon*. I think they went to New Zealand. This would be April or May 1914, however, my eldest brother made me leave and return home. But I would still walk around the wharves in Sydney hoping to get on a ship. I even went to Newcastle on the overnight ferry, the *Hunter*, leaving at midnight and arriving at 6 am, fare 25 cents, including a mug of tea and a thick slice of toast. She was crowded with sailors, etc.

Newcastle at that time, June 1914, was crowded with sailing ships. There must have been 60 or 70 ships all waiting to load coal and I tried them all with no luck. Stockton, where the ships were tied up, was a forest of masts, others loading at the Dyke, and a couple anchored in the river waiting for a wind. I hitched a ride back to Sydney on a collier, a '60-miler' they were called, as it is 60 miles from Sydney to Newcastle. In Sydney I tramped around the wharves where the sailing ships berthed, particularly Darling Harbour and the Wheat Terminal, where the sailers used to load. Amongst the German sailing ships loading at that time was the magnificent four-masted barque *Herzogin Sophie Charlotte*.

Eventually I got on board the German full-rigged ship *Oliva* and met the mate, a huge man with reddish hair and huge moustache, who spoke very little English. He took me to the captain, a short nuggetty man with pale blue eyes—funny how little things are impressed on one's mind. I landed the job, Captain Pehlreich took me to the German Consul and I was signed on as ordinary seaman at 30 marks a month. *Oliva* sailed from Sydney on a bright, sunny winter afternoon and I well remember the Manly ferries and yachts, waving us farewell. We dropped the tug about dusk, and I went aloft to loose the main royal, and could just then see the South Head Light through intermittent rainsqualls, as the weather started to break.

I felt very homesick, as I was just 14 years old and it was quite a few years before I saw Sydney again. I felt very out of place for a start, as there was very little English spoken. The Captain was fluent in English and Fritz Muller, later my best friend, had a few words. His vocabulary had greatly expanded by the time we reached Valparaiso. He was a fine lad and came from a good family. There was also an English AB who had signed on in Sydney, but he was in the starboard watch, I was in the port watch. I remember the mate very well indeed; he was a descendant of some remote Viking ancestor. He was a vital man with a terrific compelling personality, who could and did bellow like a bull if need be, a strict disciplinarian, and a great seaman. I had a very great respect for him as did everyone else, also a great deal of awe. When he commanded everybody jumped to it, and he was an unforgettable character.

The Captain was a different type, short, thickset and quick tempered, very much the captain of his ship, aloof, and to me, remote. He also was a very good seaman and knew his business thoroughly as he was to demonstrate later on, in the incessant gales we had to contend with in the Roaring Forties.

South of New Zealand we had a terrific gale, which sticks in my memory even today. The seas were terrifying and so bad, I was taken off lookout and onto the poop, where all hands were assembled; the main deck was a mass of broken water, and the white glare from the water made everything invisible. At the changing of the watch, the Captain issued a noggin of schnapps to all hands. That was the first time I had tasted it. The weather was really bad, enormous seas, snow, hail, and as the crew lived in the deckhouse, everything was wet, blankets, bunk, clothes, and as the boys had the lowest bunks near the door, as was the custom, we were really wet and miserable. After all, it was the middle of winter, and that kind of life to me in that period, seemed to be normal. Looking back I felt tremendously exhilarated and even now, I think it was worthwhile and would not have missed it. I think that was the worst gale I ever experienced and one of the memories that will live with me forever. Most of the crew thought the same.

The after guard were all very good seamen, the gear and sails were good. You felt confident aloft, no rotten footropes or gear. The foremast hands were all young fellows, and a few were naval reservists. All were good sailors and good types. The attitude in Germany to the sea appeared to be different from most other countries. They were a better class, and made the sea more of a profession than just a job. They were very decent and good shipmates. We boys were kept in our place, and had to show deference and respect to the ABs. I think it did us good and it is very different today. The youth in Australia and probably other countries too, could all do with discipline and restraint?

We arrived at Valparaiso, after a passage of 44 days. Early in the evening we anchored for the night, well offshore, probably 20 miles, because we could see the Andes in the distance. We sailed in to the bay next morning and to our anchorage in the rows of ships, quite a feat, as we did not have a tug. We discharged our wheat into barges, one bag at a time, very slow. We had no engine, in fact the only machinery aboard was the brace winches, which were good. Four men could do the work of a watch, bracing the yards around. She was the only ship I was in that was fitted with them. There were a large number of sailing ships there, including some of the 'P' Liners. The *Potosi*, a magnificent five-masted barque, arrived there from Hamburg a few weeks after the outbreak of the First World War. All the crew dressed in navy uniform, handled the ship very smartly and made a handsome showing. There were a lot of knowing critics among the many ships. There must have been 40 of them. I think the *Potosi*'s passage was 71 days from Hamburg and I don't think that anyone who saw her will ever forget the sight. She came in under full sail and only reduced at the last moment, she had a very big crew, who were exceedingly well trained.

Some weeks after the outbreak of war, Captain Oehlreich took me to the German Consul, where I received my discharge. He then took me to the British Consul, where I was signed on as ordinary seaman in the British four-masted barque *Crown of India*. I think Captain Oehlreich was a good decent human being, in doing what he did in getting me another ship, because there were a lot of men on the beach looking for ships, and it seemed to be the problem in all the West Coast ports. Looking back it was a bad place and time for a young boy to be adrift in any South American port.

Oliva was formerly the British ship *Ladye Doris*. She was a flyer and one of the fastest of the modern sailing ships. She was about 1600 tons, a real model, impossible to fault her. Gear, sails, rigging and the way she was run. She looked and behaved like a real lady. I was sorry to leave her.

On joining the *Crown of India*, we sailed in ballast to Portland, Oregon. We had bad weather off Astoria and in company with four other ships we beat back and forth for four days before we could cross the Columbia River bar, which had a bad reputation for wrecking ships. We towed 100 miles up the river to Portland, where we loaded wheat for Queenstown for orders; we sailed after Thanksgiving and had a good passage around Cape Horn of 121 days.

After arriving in Britain in the *Crown of India* Arthur Hennessy joined the British Army and survived the war. On discharge he joined the Royal Navy. He died on Christmas Day 1979 and as was his wish was buried at sea.

Otto Neumann, a retired German master mariner living in France, has given me great help in assembling the following description of life in several German ships, including the *Magdalene Vinnen*, an auxiliary four-masted barque built in 1921 and still sailing under the Russian flag as the training ship *Sedov*. The F. A. Vinnen Company fleet was run along similar lines to Laeisz. They relied on cargo to remain viable but catered to the need for Germany to build up her merchant and naval fleets by taking up to 50 boys per ship, who would subsequently enter the mercantile marine or navy as future officers. The Vinnen Company placed an order with Krupps Germania shipyard in Kiel to build five unconventional five-masted sailing vessels between 1921 and 1923. The word 'unconventional' is used, as there has never been a satisfactory description of their rig type. They were fore and aft rigged on each of the five masts but had three square topsails on the fore and 'middle' masts. To call them topsail schooners would imply that they were rigged with topsails on the fore mast only, like conventional topsail schooners. The lubberly-sounding word 'middle' to describe the third mast from the bow seemed to be used in German five-masted vessels, although in German it would have been *mittel*.

The year that Otto went to sea was 1922 and he joined the small ketch *Johanne*. This was a typical entry point for many of the northern European boys who aspired to a maritime career. I have been given many stories by those who experienced life in these small vessels. The life was incredibly hard and I must resist the temptation to include more stories from these ships. They deserve a separate book of their own. Otto's own words follow.

At Easter I left the grammar school at Stolz in Pomerania because I wanted to go to sea and become a captain. I was 16 years old and because of the war, undernourished, badly dressed and fitted out. With my parents' permission I went by myself the 800 km to Hamburg to look for an apprenticeship in a sailing vessel. I found *Johanne*, a small ketch of 130 tons, owned and skippered by a Peter Elfers. She traded around the North Sea and Baltic Sea, taking cargo from larger ships and delivering it to smaller ports. I had to cook, load cargo, batten down the hatches, heave up the anchor with a hand winch, set sail and take the helm, in fact everything that the captain wanted me to do, until we laid up for the winter on the mud bed of a tributary of the lower Elbe. His only praise when I left was, 'You can come back again next year'. I was in her for six months and the pay lasted for three days. It was inflation!

I then signed on a four-masted barque *Tamara XVI* and served about two years in this ship before joining the five-masted *Carl Vinnen*. I served about seven months in this ship before going into steamships, becoming 4th officer in the Hamburg-America Line ship *Hamburg*. I didn't enjoy the time I spent with this company, as I didn't like the hierarchy of a big company, so I left and in January 1929 rejoined the Vinnen Company as 2nd officer in the *Christel Vinnen*, another five master like the *Carl Vinnen*. I was now 23 years old. I joined the ship in Pellau/Konigsberg and changed into my passenger liner's uniform. The Captain and first officer were very amused at this. In Memel I heard the first officer say to the Captain, 'He knows what he is doing.' So I felt happy in my profession. I soon put this to the test when, on the way through the Kiel canal in the very cold winter of 1929 at minus 40°C, I had the five topmasts lowered to pass under the low bridge. I had them all up again in four hours and the first officer said it was a brilliant piece of seamanship.

We loaded cellulose balls for La Plata. In the North Sea we had bad weather and rode out the westerly storm, hove to over the Dogger Bank, in 24 metres [80 feet] of water. We put out a long cable as a drifting anchor from a hawse pipe. As I took over the long afternoon watch, the radio operator, Jansen, gave me the weather report he had just received. It said there was a bad storm north of Scotland moving north-east. The Captain and first officer were consulting in the chartroom and it was obvious they didn't know what to do about the weather. In seafaring school I had become very interested in meteorology and on the North Atlantic passenger liners I took all the meteorological readings by myself and telegraphed them on to America and Germany. In my opinion the weather had to clear. I dared to explain this to the Captain. I said that we should head for the Dover Channel and save ourselves many miles as well. He looked at me incredulously and said, 'But with this weather we don't even know our present position.' It was obvious that he did not know about radio position fixing. I said if we got three bearings by radio from England, Holland and Germany we would know the exact position of the ship. He asked, 'But what does that cost?' When I told him it was four marks fifty a bearing he said, 'I will pay for that out of my own pocket!' We set sail without the Captain consulting with the 1st officer.

When he came on deck for his watch, the ship was well on her way, the weather was clearing and we passed quickly into the Bay of Biscay. We had the fastest trip ever to La Plata. After almost two years in this ship, I went to Stettin seafaring school to get my captain's certificate. After six months' study, I got this certificate but now the depression was with us and I could only find work in a small three-masted schooner as an AB. In 1934 when the economic situation had improved, I was offered the position of 2nd officer in the Vinnen Company's largest sailing ship, *Magdalene Vinnen*. This ship had a 600 hp motor but it was used only for leaving and entering port and sometimes in calms. For the trip to Australia and back, which takes the average large sailing ship over 200 days, only 18 days fuel was taken on.

The training in *Magdalene Vinnen* was very intense, more so than in the average large sailing ship. On the outward voyage the permanent sailors spent a lot of their time teaching the boys. They had to master finding all the equipment in the dark, be able to steer and know the compass. They had to understand the manoeuvres in going about, be able to loose and furl the topgallant and royal sails, to be able to tie knots and splice ropes. In fact everything connected with seamanship. They were tested regularly in events that they would experience later on. On Saturdays the ship was cleaned, weather permitting. Everything was scrubbed and if rainwater was available we washed our clothes and ourselves. Water was strictly rationed and the 2nd officer was responsible for the 40 tonnes carried for the trip to Australia and back. In Spencer Gulf we loaded wheat from ketches and on the return journey the cargo shifted off the Azores. We took on a 30 degree list and I, with most of the crew, had to get below and lift the bags up to get the ship on an even keel once again. After 26 months I was offered the position of 1st officer but I declined as I wanted to return to school for my radio licence which I needed for my transfer to steamships.

The closing days for German commercial sail came with the final voyages of the four-masted barques *Priwall*, *Padua*, *Kommodore Johnsen* (ex *Magdalene Vinnen*) and *Admiral Karpfanger* (ex *L'Avenir*). The latter disappeared without trace in the Southern Ocean in 1939, as described in Chapter 7.

Padua made her last voyage as a grain ship when she loaded a cargo of grain at Port Lincoln and sailed for Europe on 5 July 1939. It was a particularly fast passage of 93 days. She discharged her cargo at Glasgow. *Kommodore Johnsen*, in Port Lincoln at the same time as *Padua*, left on 11 July. After a passage of 107 days she discharged her cargo in Cork.

Priwall was the last sailing ship to make the voyage between Europe and Chile. She sailed from Hamburg to Corral in 79 days from Dover, arriving on 10 August 1939. She then sailed up the coast to Valparaiso, arriving there the day before war broke out. She never saw Germany again. Chile took her over when war was declared on Germany and Japan. She was renamed *Lautaro* and painted white. She visited San Francisco in 1943 as a cargo-carrying training ship. In 1945 she caught fire off the coast of Peru and became a total loss. *Padua* and *Kommodore Johnsen* made training voyages throughout the war but were allocated to Russia on Germany's defeat. *Padua* was renamed *Kruzenshtern* and *Kommodore Johnsen* became *Sedov*, both are still afloat today in the roles of pure training ships.

The hiatus caused by the 1939 war and the postwar reconstruction of the German economy ended in 1950 when increasing maritime awareness caused some in Germany to recall their great maritime tradition and to reintroduce the concept kept alive by Laeisz, Vinnen and Nord Deutscher Lloyd of sail training for mercantile officers. The four-masted barques *Pamir* and *Passat* were already in the hands of a Belgian shipbreaker when Heinz Schliewen bought them, with the aim of putting them to sea as cargo-carrying training ships. This he succeeded in doing and, fitted with auxiliary engines, they made voyages during the 1950s to the east coast of South America until the tragic loss of *Pamir* in a hurricane off the Azores in 1957, with the loss of 80 lives. Only six survived. *Passat* was withdrawn from service and this is where it ended for German commercial sail.

A chance meeting with Carl-Otto Dummer in the Baltic town of Mariehamn in 1999 has allowed me to include this final story. He was one of *Pamir*'s survivors.

We were homeward bound for Hamburg! The mood of the 36 crew members and 50 cadets was fantastic, yes; it could not be better, because a good breeze meant a fast trip. But, at the change of watch the next morning at 8 am, even the last one of us should have recognised that the breeze had developed to a damn hard storm.

We in the galley desperately tried to fasten pots and pans on the stove so that meals could be prepared. On deck, the seamen tried to reduce sail, in order to keep the ship in the correct trim. The storm became worse, getting even more destructive, and turned into a hurricane. It was impossible to try to do anything in the galley and we had to put out the fire for safety reasons.

There were many sails torn and no one was allowed into the rigging, as there were so many wires and chains thrashing about. The whole crew was assembled on deck except for the radio operator and the cook's mate, who was translating orders between the Captain and the radio station. Life jackets were given out and a tarpaulin was fastened at the mizzenmast as a steering aid. I distributed bread and cigarettes.

Above all this was the roaring hurricane and everybody knew that we were right in its path. We could also hear the cracking of torn canvas and the hissing of wires and sheets in the rigging. The ship was now listing so heavily that the whole lee side up to the charthouse was under water. The ends of the yards were ploughing through the sea and the raging sea buried, destroyed and washed every thing before it.

This is when we became aware of our peril and the first SOS was sent out. Everyone, including the Captain and officers sat, hung or lay behind the bridge deck rail, staring paralysed at the rigging or into the breaking seas.

A sudden shock ran through the ship. The masts hit the water. The deck beneath our feet was torn away. The crew slid, tumbled and were thrown into the sea. *Pamir* had capsized! Now, the only thing that counted was trying to free oneself from the tangle of ropes sheets, rigging, ripped-off planks and human bodies.

I got tangled amongst ropes, hit comrades and the swirling waters tried to suck me down. Then almost suddenly every obstacle had disappeared. An undefinable noise behind me told me that *Pamir* had capsized totally and floated bottom up. After the roaring of the hurricane in the rigging the sound of the wind on the waves seemed to me like an unreal silence.

I looked around. Where were my comrades? Here and there I saw some heads sticking out of the sea. Where were the others?

Twenty-five men managed to get into one lifeboat and ten more into one that was damaged. After 54 hours, five of the ten had died from exposure, being immersed in water up their armpits in the damaged boat. They were picked up by the freighter *Saxon*. In the other lifeboat only one man survived. He was picked up by the US Coast Guard cutter *Absecon*.

6 NORTH AMERICAN SAIL

Moshulu

As has been written about the French, German and Scandinavian fleets of sail-driven ships, volumes could be written about the sailing ships that were built and operated in the United States and, to a lesser extent, Canada.

American shipbuilders made a 'giant step forward' when they developed the clippers of the 1840s and 1850s. These ships were fast and powerful and were successful because their hull lines were much finer than those of the apple-bowed British freighters of the early nineteenth century. They introduced hollow lines to their hulls, which were built largely from softwood. This made the ships lighter and faster, but had several disadvantages. The great size of their frames, usually white oak and hackmatack, and the thickness of their pitch pine hull planking reduced their cargo-carrying capacity, already eroded by their fine hollow lines. They also had a short life span, as they were driven hard and timber hulls were difficult to keep tight. This became a greater problem as the size and length of hulls increased. Crews were always wary of signing on in old wooden ships as they knew they would be in for long periods of pumping, especially in heavy weather when the timbers worked and let in water.

A great shipbuilding industry had developed on the east coast, particularly in the New England states, and produced many famous ships such as *Flying Cloud*, *James Baines*, *Sovereign of the Seas* and *Lightning*, the latter holding many records. She covered 436 miles in 24 hours on one occasion. The man responsible for these clippers, as they were called, was Donald McKay and many books cover his life and work.

When gold was discovered in California in 1849 the industry burgeoned, as the preferred method of 'going West' was around Cape Horn. While these ships through their speed were able to make westing around the Horn more quickly than the later full-lined British cargo carriers, there is no doubt their passengers wished they had braved the Indian attacks and other privations of a long wagon train journey. Nevertheless it was an established trade route for many decades.

When the last dog spike was driven into the east–west rail link, and the West was finally won, the clippers found new employment. They flocked to the growing ports of the Pacific North West, San Francisco, Seattle, Tacoma and the many smaller ports on Puget Sound and the Columbia River, to lift cargoes of grain for the east coast and further field to the United Kingdom and Europe. Then sawn timber emerged as the great export from the area. As new ships were built they tended to take on fuller lines to allow them to carry bigger grain cargoes, a trade which flourished from 1860 onwards. Basil Lubbock, in *The Down Easters*, describes the development of these American sailing ships and their builders. I do not intend to transcend Lubbock's book here, rather to set the stage for the stories and paintings in this chapter.

The term 'down easter' was used to describe the ships or, more correctly, the shipyards along the coast of Maine in what were known as the Down East Ports. At first many down east ships were acquired in the west, together with some famous limejuicers, but as the west coast ports developed, so did the need for their own ships and builders. Thus began a shipbuilding industry that rivalled that of the eastern states.

The outgoing trades that supported this growing fleet were bagged grain, sawn timber and later canned salmon and case oil. Inbound freight consisted of the multitude of items needed by a young growing economy—machinery, textiles, manufactured goods and, of course, liquor. Although most of these ships were built with a particular trade in mind, they were willing to load whatever offered in the latter years of sail, and sailed to many parts of the world. There was a ready market for grain in Europe, and the softwoods of the Pacific North West were in demand in Australia and South Africa. Case oil became an important export, initially to fuel lamps around the world, later the internal combustion engine.

Back on the east coast the square rigger was being replaced by the schooner for the ever-growing coastal trade, from which foreign ships were excluded. During the 1880s there was an economic slump which meant that three- and four-masted schooners were favoured over the more costly square-rigged ships, which also needed larger and more experienced crews, a trend also evident on the west coast.

By 1889 there was an upturn in demand, quickly taken up by the shipbuilding firm of Arthur Sewell & Co., which emerged as one of the most famous of the down east companies. They built many four-masted barques in the traditional timber, but departed from convention and turned to steel when they built the four-masted barque *Dirigo* in 1894. As the first steel sailing ship to be built in the United States, her name, meaning 'I lead', was aptly chosen. While it was logical to use the timber that was so plentiful in North America, it is strange that only 13 steel sailing ships were ever built there, 11 of them by Arthur Sewell & Co.

American ships developed a character that all seafarers were familiar with. A vessel hull down on the horizon could be identified as American by her white sails, which were made from cotton canvas rather than the hemp canvas used by other countries. American square riggers of the clipper and post-clipper period all tended to rig skysails. Even single topgallants persisted long after European ships began using double topgallants. In port, the American sailer could be distinguished by the absence of a spanker gaff, by her standing rigging set up on channels and, of course, the shapely wooden hull, transom stern and the bowsprit blending into the fo'c'sle head planking. There were many other features obvious to the seaman's eye that allowed him to make the instant observation, 'She's a Yankee.'

Foreign ships were prevented from operating in the US coastal trade which, it turned out, was best handled by the fore and aft rigged schooners that required smaller crews, and the progeny of the earlier creations of the down east yards and their west coast counterparts carried American sail through to the end in the 1920s. Two- and three-masted schooners were built by the hundreds, perhaps thousands, to meet the growth of industry and the demand for coal in the New England states. Much of this coal was loaded in Baltimore and Philadelphia, which only required a short coastal voyage. It was soon realised that larger ships would be more economical. This meant more masts, and the seafaring world's perception of the American sailing ship thus became that of the large multi-masted wooden schooner that not only carried heavy bulk cargo around the coast but became commonplace in ports around the world. This was particularly so for the ships build in the west as there was a world demand for the softwoods cut along the North West coast.

The numbers of large wooden schooners and barquentines built in the United States, at a time when British and European shipyards had all but stopped building sail-driven ships, is quite staggering. It is difficult to quote accurate statistics, however, as the research carried out by the recognised authorities on the subject uses somewhat different time periods, and sometimes east and west coast figures are combined.

After 1900, when Great Britain had ceased building large sailing ships—the last was the four-masted barque *Archibald Russell* in 1905—shipyards on the American North West coast were still building wooden sailers for the coastal and Pacific trade, over 100 of them between 1900 and 1910.

Incredibly, in the next decade, and particularly in 1917–18, over 170 large wooden schooners and barquentines were launched. The shortage of shipping caused by the war, plus the demand for building timber in Australia and South Africa, and the needs of the Hawaiian sugar mills and the Chilean railways for coal from Newcastle, New South Wales, promoted this activity. The breakdown of type of vessel is: 8 three-masted schooners, 49 four-masted schooners, 85 five-masted schooners, 3 six-masted schooners, 6 three-masted barquentines, 7 four-masted barquentines, 13 five-masted barquentines. Not all these ships sailed under American ownership. Over 80 sailed under the American flag, 54 were built for French interests, 18 for Norway and 23 for Canada. The remainder were Belgian, Australian and German owned.

Paul C. Morris, in his *American Sailing Coasters of the North Atlantic*, writes that on the east coast after 1910 there were 139 four-masted schooners built, out of which 109 were launched between 1917 and 1919. After 1900 there were 52 five-masted schooners built, 11 with six masts and one with seven. The latter was the huge steel *Thomas W. Lawson*, details of which can be found in so many other ship books that she will not be discussed here.

During World War I there were also dozens of wooden steamships built which became redundant when the war ended. Some were never fitted out with engines but were rigged as sailing ships. I have several stories from seamen who sailed in them.

Milford Loraway, an Australian seaman, as I got to know him revealed an amazing life story at sea in American sailing ships. Milford was a veteran of sail, having served in the Tasmanian ketch *Defender* in 1918, the three-masted schooners *Waimana* and *Rahra* in 1919, the steam auxiliary barquentine *Dart* in 1920, and the three-masted barquentine *Southern Cross* in 1921. Later in 1921 he joined the four-masted barque *Lawhill* for a voyage to Falmouth for orders under Captain De Cloux. He took this position as a replacement for Alan Villiers, who fell from aloft when this ship nudged a sandbank on her way to her anchorage at Port Lincoln. A long period of seafaring under the American flag allowed Milford to make these comments to me.

> I joined the six-masted *Oregon Fir*, later renamed *Helen B. Sterling*, in Melbourne in 1923 where she was discharging her timber cargo. She was on her maiden voyage. I signed on as AB and I sailed in her to Portland, Oregon. These American schooners were outstanding ships. There were hundreds of them all over the Pacific in the twenties. They were different from anything I had ever sailed in. We were treated like human beings and our wages were $75 a month. We even had our own mess room. Being fore and aft rigged there was not much work aloft apart from stowing the topsails. We had a donkey boiler and a steam winch for each mast, to hoist the heavy gaffs and their sails. We carried a yard on the foremast from which we set our foresail when the wind was fair. The ship would sail for days on end without touching the sheets and you could almost lash the wheel and leave it. We had good food, just salt meat and chicken but plenty of it. The captain's wife who sailed with him was very kind to the crew and gave us chocolates and biscuits every weekend.
>
> *Oregon Fir* had been built as a steamer but it was decided to convert her to a sailing ship before she was finished. This load supposedly paid for her. After discharging the timber in Melbourne we went to Newcastle to load coal. As there was a coal strike, we lay in Newcastle at Stockton for three months waiting for a cargo. During this time we had to dig the ballast out. It was stones dredged out of the Columbia River, where she had come from. Sailing ships were stretched out as far as you could see, three deep at the wharf. Our crew changed many times. They went ashore and got drunk, some cleared out and others ended up in jail. When we engaged more crew the same thing happened. We finally filled up with coal and headed off to Valparaiso. From here we went to Portland where I paid off. As a foreign seaman I had to pay head tax of $5. This was legal entry into America and it entitled me to sign on another American ship. I had a bit of a holiday and then looked for another ship. I signed on *Oregon Fir*'s sister ship *Oregon Pine*, later renamed *Dorothy H. Sterling*, bound for Melbourne with a cargo of timber. She was also on her maiden voyage, and she carried 4 million super feet of timber.

Milford's other experiences at sea, on the Great Lakes running bootleg liquor from Canada to the United States, and later during World War II, could fill a book, but his comments on these latter American schooners would be fairly typical.

Another seaman who speaks glowingly of these American ships is Sam Hort. He admits that some Yankee skippers and mates were harsh disciplinarians but if you worked hard, things were okay. Sam had started his sea career in 1917 when he joined the four-masted barque *Hougomont* in Sydney. He also served as second mate in the barquentines *Westfield* and *Forest Friend,* and the schooner *William H. Smith.* After a period ashore he went back to sea in the depressed days of 1927.

He joined *Fort Laramie* as second mate in Sydney when she was unloading her cargo of Douglas fir timber. She returned to the United States in ballast. *Fort Laramie* was a six masted schooner carrying a single yard on the foremast. Two square sails were set on this yard together with a raffee topsail. This was a triangular sail, hoisting to the fore topmast head. Her tonnage was 2200 and she was registered in San Francisco. She was laid down as one of the many wooden steamships built for wartime use and completed as sailing ships. Sam told me of this voyage on many occasions, always introducing another happening when I thought I had it all! His daughter Pat Stenner has kindly lent me a letter that Sam wrote to his brother while at sea, almost a diarised account. I have reproduced most of it. Sam mentions many incidents of broken gear, which became commonplace as these last sailing ships reached the ends of their lives. He also refers to conflict resulting from the skipper's wife being on board.

After dropping the pilot off Sydney we had dinner and came on deck and set the fore, main and mizzen plus fore staysail and jibs. We then let go the tug and we were on our way. The breeze was fresh NE which only allowed us to head SE so we did not set all sail until next day when the wind hauled to the north. Five days out we sighted Lord Howe Island. Now there is one thing this old scow won't do and that is sail 'on a wind' and there was a doubt that we could weather the island. So the Old Man decided to go around. It took nearly an hour to 'wear her'. We had to lower the spanker and set the square sail to get her to pay off. Anyway, we got her around and headed south. We were 12 days out, when we passed the North Island of New Zealand. We then got a decent SW breeze and averaged 205 miles per day, for the next four days. After that we had bad luck. We got an easterly breeze and had to run north. One night the roping on the spanker carried away and the sail tore from head to foot.

What we need is a crew of sailors! There are only 3 men of any account and the rest (5) are first trippers. Our carpenter is a wonderful all-round man and has a knack of keeping the gas engine going which saves us a lot of pulling and hauling as well as pumping ship.

When we were 28 days out we had further bad luck. We had 30 days of calms or light airs. We got no SE trade wind. Imagine 30 days to sail 1200 miles! We then picked up an ENE wind and crossed the Equator 61 days out on 9 December.

It was during this period of calms when I ran foul of the skipper's wife. She butted in on me when the cabin boy was giving me a lot of lip. It was more or less a joke between the boy and me but she was just outside the door listening. She was always eavesdropping. She came in and hollered at me to stop picking on the boy and of course I told her to mind her own business. I told her that as I was second mate it was not her place to encourage the cabin boy to give me cheek. She said, 'second mate my foot'. I said, 'maybe, but not a fool to let you tell me what to do'. So that ended it. I didn't speak to her for days.

Today is Sunday, 11 December It has been doldrums all day and it has been, booms over one side and then the other and one square sail in and the other out, nearly all day, but this afternoon we got a SE slant that allowed us to set everything. I have just come below at 10 minutes to midnight and the wind has lasted up to now. Our main worry is that we can weather the Hawaiian Islands. It is doubtful, as we will get the North-East Trades soon and they will surely run us down onto the islands, unless it is good and easterly. We are at Lat 4° 32' N and Long 151° 19' W and Hawaii is about Lat 14° N and Long 155° W, so we have only 200 miles easterly allowance in 550 miles of northerly sailing so our chances of getting to windward of the islands is very slim. It means the saving of 3 to 5 days if we can.

Well, 2 days later and the light east south easterly wind is still holding, with occasional calms but owing to a heavy head swell, we are making slow progress, even though every stitch of canvas is set. The Southern Cross is now almost touching the horizon and to the north we can see the Great Dipper constellation and the North Star. Soon the Southern Cross will be out of sight and we will have no stellar reminder of our home in the Southern Hemisphere.

I am having trouble with one of the men who has been sleeping on lookout. He also tries to steer with his back to the wind when it is squally.

15 December 66 days out. At 1 am today we clewed up the driver topsail to make the vessel steer better in the heavy squalls we are now having. I noticed a tear across the mainsail, so we lowered it and put in two cloths about 3 feet long. Then the mizzen topsail carried away, torn at its head. We made it fast and then clewed up the fore and jigger topsails. We worked right through and got the mainsail finished. It was dark and the 'old man' was sewing and could hardly see the sail as he is long sighted. It was my watch below but I said, 'I guess my eyes are better than yours, Captain, let me finish it.' Anyhow, I got a drink of whisky for it.

18 December, Sunday 69 days out. We are certainly having a rough trip, as last night the squalls were gale force. Luckily for me the mate had the long watch out and during this time the mainsail carried away. He then clewed up and made fast the topsails, jib topsail and spanker and it blew a gale all night. Of course a gale in this ship is not what it was like in *Hougomont*. We have dry decks and don't have to worry about getting washed all over the ship.

From 12 to 4 it was my watch, it blew hard and the Old Man was up until 2 am. We got yarning. I try to cheer him up, as I know the mate gets him nervous. He is always seeing things and seems to take the confidence out of anyone.

At daylight the mate unbent the busted mainsail and the driver and when I came on deck at 8 am I bent the driver for the mainsail. Then I saw a little hole in the mizzen so I lowered that for repairs. It is Sunday, but not for us. We have worked all day.

We are getting short of provisions and the skipper was talking of putting into Hilo for some grub but we can't make it now as we are going to leeward of the Hawaiian Islands. We sighted the islands of Hawaii and Maui and it is almost calm. At 2 pm the trade wind came in and it sure did hum. We took in the topsails and she is leaning over and doing 9 knots, with the wind just forward of the beam. If it increases we will probably have to reef down. We are going to run between the islands of Oahu and Kauai if possible. There are 45 miles between and this son of a gun sure needs plenty of room.

Good news too. The old woman has thawed out and is actually friendly.

In the afternoon an American submarine came alongside and asked what we were loaded with. As if they couldn't see we were in ballast!

We saw the loom of Honolulu's lights and it started to breeze up as we passed the island and we had to shorten sail. Next day we had to set them again. However that night we were obliged to shorten down again.

On Christmas morning it started to blow. At 7 am, bang, away went the foresail. In lowering it, the foot block unhooked and whizzed past my head and back again. I was lucky to escape, apart from getting my fingers squeezed up a bit. Then the jaw rope broke. This holds the jaws of the gaff up to the mast. The gaff unshipped itself and was charging about up in the air. Eventually we got it secured and we lowered all the lower sails.

At 10 am the wheel was relieved. It was Chileano's trick and he was 35 minutes late. He always was a lazy bad egg and I was wild. I belted hell out of him. There was blood everywhere and his face looked in pretty bad shape. He was laid up for 24 hours. That afternoon it blew a hurricane and I had Christmas dinner standing up. I had 3 spoonsful of cold soup, a cup of cocoa, 2 small pieces of cake and two sliced canned peaches. I also had a glass of the Mts' whisky.

The next day the wind calmed down and we tried to set sail. She rolled too much and carried away the jigger gaff. Sail was lowered again and we are running under our two square sails and the raffee. We have been working like hell, straightening up the decks, reshipping the fore gaff, bending a new foresail, changing the driver gaff, for which we haven't a sail, to the jigger. We only have one good sail and that is the mainsail. We have no sail bent on the driver and none to bend.

8 December Last night the glass fell again so we set the inner jib and took in the square sails and raffee. At noon the barometer was 29.45 inches, very low. At present it is raining with a light SE breeze and very far from being bad weather but it is about somewhere.

Grub is getting pretty short. Potatoes have all gone, and we have less than 200 lbs of flour. We are, however, within 1700 miles of our destination so with moderate luck we should be there in 10 days. For 10 days now we have had no bread. The cook was unable to make yeast without spuds, until the cabin boy made some and yesterday we had some fine bread and my belly is full now.

We have had good fair winds for a week but cannot run the risk of setting any more sails and we are averaging about 100 to 120 miles per day. We have enough wind to do 240 easily but our canvas is too rotten to stand any severe squalls, so we must leave them furled for safety sake. We are within 1200 miles of our destination now but unless the wind is lighter we must make slow progress.

2 January 1928 We are abreast of San Francisco now, about 400 miles away. The night before last with the glass at 29.25 we had several very bad squalls. We are under bare poles, with only the staysail set but even then I thought the sticks would come out of her. Facing the wind you couldn't breathe or open your eyes and she was logging 8 knots. There is a terrible cross-sea running and the ship rolls very heavily at times.

So this is our 89th day out. Two days ago the weather settled and we had one fine night, the first for a long time.

We will be about 500 miles off today. It has commenced to rain a little and so we clewed up the main topsail and then the square sail clew ring carried away so we made it fast. If this wind continues it will be no use to us as it will be a head wind in Puget Sound, down which we will have to sail 60 miles.

Today the barometer fell again. Yesterday and last night we had a SE gale. We ran it out under inner jib, staysail, reefed fore and mainsails. It was a cold miserable night, raining most of the time and I simply couldn't keep warm. I went below once and got an old pair of socks, which I put on my hands.

The mate and Old Man are still at loggerheads and I don't blame the Old Man either as the mate is a damned fool. The grub is getting light and a few times I have been as hungry as hell, but I suppose I will work the fat off.

It is now 8 January, 90 days out. We are less than 200 miles from Cape Flattery in a fresh SE breeze under staysail, reefed fore, main and jigger sails and if we sail right up to the land we run the risk of getting caught on a lee shore, or pushed to north of the Cape. A SE wind is a headwind down the Straits of Juan de Fuca. The only wind we can sail on, is SW.W to NW and it's no use depending on tug boats. Puget Sound is a very big place, running nearly 200 miles inland. Port Angeles is 60 miles from the entrance. Then with these rotten sails we have to be very careful, also we haven't had a sight in 3 days on account of fog and rain, so we are only running on dead reckoning, which is not very reliable around these parts due to many variable currents.

12 January 93 days out. We have had a few days of heavy fog. Last night we got a SW wind and after a lot of doubt and fright, the Old Man stood in under square sail and reefed mainsail. He is clearly worried and so is the mate. Well there was a good breeze early and SW too, but when I said it was SW he flatly denied it. Then when he was forced to admit it, after we wore ship, he said it was too foggy. Then we saw some steamers in the distance and so his last excuse gone, he stood in. Now this morning he is weeping because the wind is light and although we had only a fresh breeze, he said there was too much wind. He is certainly no man to navigate a ship.

Two nights back I took a Pole Star sight and got Lat 47° 522'N. I told him in the morning and said I hadn't worked one for years. He said he would show me and then he didn't know how to do it. After half an hour I went back and he said my sight was wrong. Of course captains are never wrong. So I worked it out again, two different ways and got the same result, proving him wrong. He hated to admit it and blamed his Almanac, which was 1924. Mine was 1927. It is almost the same but in the 1924 the astronomical day was from noon to noon and in the other it was midnight to midnight.

Then he said, 'By golly, you're some navigator,' and then asked me where I learnt it. You see, some of these fossils don't like the second mate to navigate as it could show up what bums they were. With luck we will be in tomorrow. The mate is trying to get soundings now but he didn't get any. He lost the bait once. That is the priming on the bottom of the lead to pick up a sample of the bottom.

Well it is now *Friday 13 January, 1928,* and we are now lying in Port Angeles after 94 days at sea. We made a good landfall yesterday in spite of poor observations and ran down the straits before a light westerly breeze and made anchorage at 11 am.

When we were in Sydney there was another sailing ship, the *Thistle*, with us in Blackwattle Bay. They had only half discharged their timber deck load as we left, and they beat us home. They were 70 days. The *Monitor*, another American sailing ship, left Newcastle just before us and was 74 days. They are lying here at anchor. There are just the three of us, *Monitor*, 5 masted barquentine, *Thistle*, 5 masted schooner and *Fort Laramie*, 6 masted schooner. So thereby ends the passage.

Alongside these American-built ships were many built elsewhere, mainly in the United Kingdom, and operated by west coast companies. Even though this large US sailing fleet increased during the World War I years, the number of shipping companies operating sailing ships rapidly diminished in the twenties as the world demand for shipping dried up. The large wooden-hulled sailing ships were hard to keep from leaking and they deteriorated quickly. The wooden sailing ship was the first to go. There was also a dearth of sail-trained seamen.

Like the last British shipowners, Garthwaite and Stewarts, a handful of American names will also live on. Along with Sewell & Co. and their steel sailers were a number of others who bought and operated ex-British ships and surviving down easters. Captain Matson, whose company went on to operate the well-known trans-Pacific liners, operated many sailing ships including the *Falls of Clyde*, now an exhibition ship in Honolulu. Captain Robert Dollar tried to keep the square rigger in business in the Pacific after the war with his last ships, *Dunsyre* and *Eclipse*. The latter he renamed *Janet Dollar*. As *Eclipse* she was better known for her time as a sailing oil-tanker. She was sister to *Arrow*, which was also built as a tanker and later became

Parma under the Laeisz flag. Captain Dollar also bought the four-masted barque *Hans*, which was interned in Santa Rosalia in Mexico, along with many other German ships, when the United States entered the war. She was renamed *Mary Dollar* but never sailed again as a four-masted barque. She was converted into the six-masted schooner *Tango* early in 1941. The Rolph Navigation and Coal Co. also deserves mention. Apart from a fleet of smaller wooden vessels they owned three well-known British-built ships that traded until the twenties: *Annie M. Reid*, *Celtic Monarch* and *Lord Shaftsbury*.

When the United States entered World War I, the US Shipping Board interned quite a few German ships that happened to be in port and operated them, mainly in the Pacific. They were first renamed after well-known American sailing ships of the past but subsequently after Native American tribes. Mrs Woodrow Wilson was responsible for this. There were three four-masted barques: *Kurt* became *Dreadnought* and then *Moshulu*, *Dalbek* became *Red Jacket* and then *Monongahela*, and *Ottawa* became *Flying Cloud* and then *Muscoota*. *Moshulu* is still afloat in Philadelphia as a floating restaurant. There were also three full-rigged ships, which became *Chillicothe*, *Tonawanda* and *Arapahoe*.

The best-remembered US shipowner, and the last to operate a large fleet of sailing vessels, was the Alaska Packers Association of San Francisco. They bought many famous ships to carry the season's salmon from their canneries in Alaska. Every year their ships set off from San Francisco with up to 200 fishermen on board and loaded with knocked-down wooden cases and tin plate to be made into cans. After buying a vessel named *Star of Russia*, they renamed each ship they bought using the prefix '*Star*', and lengthened the poop to accommodate the cannery workers taken north. In 1925 they still operated 32 square-rigged ships. The Sewell barque *Kaiulani* became *Star of Finland* but reverted to her former name when recommissioned at the beginning of World War II. Basil Lubbock describes this fleet in detail in *The Down Easters*.

The writers of the thirties had no way of knowing that *Kaiulani* would go to sea again as a commercial sailing ship when they described the full-rigged ship *Tusitala* as the last sailing ship to fly the Stars and Stripes. *Tusitala* is particularly worthy of mention, although most sailing ships that survived the twenties are unique for various reasons. Launched as *Inveruglas* in 1883 at Greenock, Scotland, she traded for 20 years under the Red Ensign. She then was bought by the well-known Sierra Line of Liverpool and renamed *Sierra Lucena*. Sold to Norway in 1903, she was renamed *Sophie* and had this name until 1923, when a group of New York businessmen, writers and artists took her over, renamed her *Tusitala* and kept her trading until 1932, almost for the sake of nostalgia. *Tusitala*, meaning 'storyteller' or 'teller of tales', was the name given by the Samoans to writer Robert Louis Stevenson, who spent many years in Samoa; the regard in which the New York group held him was further demonstrated by giving *Tusitala* his effigy as a figurehead. This group, the Two Hours for Lunch Club, was headed by noted humorist, poet and novelist Christopher Morley. They used the ship as a meeting place and headquarters; her saloon was decorated with extracts of the writings by members and noteworthy guests. This framed, handwritten letter from Joseph Conrad adorned a bulkhead in the saloon.

June 2, 1923, Effendi Hill, Oyster Bay Long Island, New York.

On leaving this hospitable country where the cream is excellent and the milk of human kindness apparently never ceases to flow, I assume an ancient mariner's privilege of sending to the owners and ship's company of the *Tusitala* my brotherly good wishes for fair winds and clear skies on all their voyages and may these be many.

And I would remind them to watch the weather, to keep the halyards clear for running, to remember that 'any fool can carry on, but only the wise man knows how to shorten sail in time'. And so on in the manner of ancient mariners the world over. But the vital truth of sea life is to be found in the ancient saying that it is 'the stout hearts that make the ship safe'. Having been brought up on it, I pass it on to them in all confidence and affection. *Joseph Conrad*

Hans Mollitor, a German lad who was building up his time in sail for his planned career as a mercantile marine officer, sailed in the American four-masted schooner *Kingsway*, in *Tusitala* and the Laeisz ship *Pinnas*. (He talks of the dismasting of *Pinnas* in Chapter 5.) He sailed in *Tusitala* in 1925, from New York through the Panama Canal to Honolulu. She carried a cargo of ammonium sulphate fertiliser, which was used in the sugar plantations. From Honolulu she sailed in ballast to Tacoma Harbor on Puget Sound. Here she loaded magnesite and timber for New York. Her master was Captain James Barker, who many years before had commanded the ill-fated full-rigger *British Isles*, mentioned in Chapter 2.

Hans said that the voyages were fairly uneventful, apart from the fact that few sailing ships ever used the Panama Canal. He said that the ship was well kept and the crew well fed. *Tusitala* and her crew were acclaimed when they reached Honolulu, as square riggers had almost disappeared from the Pacific. The same happened in Tacoma Harbor on the return journey. Hans gave me a yellowed clipping from a Honolulu paper that described her arrival:

> Another breath of sea romance blew across the harbor yesterday morning with the docking of the good ship *Tusitala*, full-rigged, three masted, steel windjammer, 71 days from New York via the canal.
>
> Rich in the traditions of an old master, Joseph Conrad, the *Tusitala* made her second bow to Honolulu yesterday, for it was almost a year ago that this fast disappearing type made her first appearance in this port and which, during her stay, entertained many prominent citizens including Governor Farrington, in the spacious saloon under her quarterdeck [poop]. As was the case a year ago the *Tusitala* carries a very prosaic cargo, consisting of 2400 tons of ammonium sulphate fertilizer consigned to the Pacific Guano and Fertilizer Co. Castle Cooke & Co. are her agents. She is operated by Tusitala Ltd. The vessel will remain here about two weeks when she will proceed to Seattle with 500 tons of scrap iron ballast to load a cargo for New York.

Another clipping proclaimed:

> A visible shadow of an era now past, that era when the sailing ship was the mistress of the sea, is the full-rigged ship *Tusitala*, last of her kind to sweep over the broad expanse of the seas with her sails spread and bellying to fitful gusts of the wind as she makes her way from port to port.
>
> She is the craft to whom the *Leviathan*, largest of modern day vessels and pride of American shipowners, and the fast mail boats on their way out of New York harbor to the United Kingdom and Europe, dipped their colors as a salute when they passed her,

as she was beginning her present voyage to this coast. It was a salute that did reverence to a vessel truly representative of a day gone by.

They were also moved to print the following excerpt from 'Tusitala's Christening Ode' by R. D. Turnbull:

> Down where the salt sea reaches
> Re-echo the gull's wild cry
> There's a gleaming hull, and the patterned spars
> Of a tall ship fill the sky.
>
> Oh more than a ship! For aboard her
> The lonely and friendless find
> Laughter—romance—adventure.
> And love, most nobly shrined!

Tusitala remained in commission until 1932 and was broken up in 1938.

Another well-known American sailing ship was *Edward Sewell,* one of the few US windjammers built from steel. Captain A. F. Raynaud of Seattle gave me the following first-hand account of his voyage in her, together with accounts of his voyages in the five-masted barquentines *Russell Haviside* and *Forest Dream.*

I shipped out in the *Edward Sewell* in 1914 after a long wait in Seattle for a berth. Times were hard, ships few and far between, and plenty of hands on the beach and in waterfront boarding houses. The *Edward Sewell* arrived at the Novelty Mill, a large grain elevator in west Seattle, and was chartered to load grain for Queenstown for orders. I was aboard at an early hour on a cold miserable day, with my hat in hand. Captain Quick was the only one on board, and when I asked for a berth he turned me down flat. The ship had been in San Francisco previously and I had worked on board her with a rigging gang from the Haviside Co. Captain Quick swore we had stolen his vessel's fish tackle, and we were nothing but a band of thieves, including me. A barge came alongside as he was berating me, and he stopped long enough for me to take the lines. As I left the ship, he called me back and told me to get to work and put my dunnage in the 'tween decks.

Captain Quick was quick by name and quick by nature. He was tall, slender had reddish hair and blue eyes and a commanding voice and he knew and so did you that he was Master in every respect. He was a prime seaman, excellent sail maker and a very keen businessman and devoted to his ship. He had been master for 20 years and knew every nut, bolt and rivet and piece of gear. He was very frugal in spending any money and always got full value from his crew, and merchants.

The ship fed well and the quality was good. There was only one time while I was in her that we ran short of food and had to subsist on lima beans, coffee and hard tack. I have never endured lima beans since. We loaded about 5500 tons of bagged grain and towed out of Seattle on the first sunny day in weeks. The crew was a typical deep water collection of various nationalities except for Germans. The war in Europe and the chance of getting caught was too great. There were only two native-born Americans, a young fellow from Bellingham, and me from San Francisco. Captain Quick was a blue nose from Nova Scotia, although a long time naturalized citizen of Maine. The Mate was a whitewashed Yankee from England and the Second Mate, a native of South Africa.

We set sail off Swiftsure Bank and the crew mustered aft to see what Maxie Levy and Billy Ryan, had sent aboard for prime seamen. They weren't too bad, most of them had been to sea before, and could steer, go aloft, and take in or set sail. It was watch and watch, and work six days a week, and hope for Sunday to be fairly free. Wages per month were $25 for ABs, $15 for Ordinary Seamen, $35 for the Bosun, $40 for the carpenter. The Mate got $75 and the Second Mate got $60.

As the ship's previous voyage had been a long one there were no leftover stores, so we had plenty of fresh grub, canned goods and vegetables. Food and fresh water were whacked out weekly and the usual arguments came up when it came to weighing it out. The steward claimed the bones should be included and fat and gristle were good to eat. At any rate we didn't go hungry and the pea soup was always thick and plenty of it. Hard tack was also plentiful, but no waste. Lime juice was issued soon after the fresh meat and vegetables were consumed, but it was more or less a voluntary drink at any time. British ships logged the issued and noted anyone who didn't take his shot.

Captain Quick had his wife and two daughters on board on this voyage. Susan was about 5 and Claribel about 3. They were a fine family and we never had any trouble with them. Too often there was a great deal of trouble when the wife tried to run the ship.

The vessel was painted white from truck to waterline, and kept in yacht-like condition. No rust or scale was allowed to form and the brasswork shone rain or shine. Decks were holystoned and kept tight, no leaks in the hold or in the deck heads of the houses or poop. Quarters were cleaned out every week and no dirty pictures were allowed. The only lights were kerosene lamps and they had to be kept in shape, clean globes, or no oil. The heads were scrubbed down every morning watch. The mates were kept alert by the old man, who was apt to come on deck at any time of the day or night, and check the course, the trim of the sails or whether the braces needed a pull or two. The ship was very tight and we seldom had to pump bilges, although we had to turn the pumps over just to keep them free. There was no auxiliary machinery, only the steam donkey engine and as soon as the last topsail or topgallant sail was set, and the anchor secured, the boiler was shut down, tubes and firebox cleaned, and then filled with water. The bearings were greased and the stack taken down and stowed in the donkey room. There was a Clayton fire-extinguishing machine on board; rather a complicated affair that used sulfur fumes to extinguish fire in a coal cargo. We tested it out to make sure it was in operating condition, but never had to put it to use. With grain, we had no problem but coal was tricky.

The crew got along very well and there was no fo'c'sle bully or hard cases and in spite of the mixed crowd, they worked together and the ship didn't suffer. The bosun was a big Finn and a good seaman who knew how to handle men, and that helped a great deal. The mate had been master in British ships, and was a good officer and navigator. The second mate hadn't been to sea for some time and tried hard to please the old man. He put up with a lot of criticism. He found out later that his eyesight was defective and after getting a pair of spectacles in Dublin, was able to trim sail quite well.

The voyage was probably an average one. We had a fair wind for most part in the Pacific, an easy rounding of Cape Horn, and varied weather in the South Atlantic. We saw very few vessels and only hove to for one—a small American whaling schooner. They warned us of German raiders. Later we learned the Germans had sunk the *William P. Frye*, another Sewell vessel.

The North Atlantic turned cold and miserable and when close to our destination, thick fog. We were hailed by a British destroyer who told us we were in the middle of a minefield, and advised that we turn around and go out the way we came in. We had a fair wind behind us and we had to keep going and made it without mishap. We arrived in

Dublin 135 days out. There we had the usual problems with the crew. The pubs were too close, the weather was bad, and it was hard to get the Irish to work and get the ship discharged. They did it with hand winches! We had a few deserters, but picked up a couple of stowaways and had a few more who wanted to get out of the war zone. I think we were all glad to leave the Emerald Isle. We had a rough and stormy trip to Norfolk, Virginia, where the crew paid off, and we had peace and quiet for two weeks. We loaded coal for Montevideo and had a full load. The crew was shipped from New York and didn't amount to much—too many greenhorns and a couple of schooner men.

The weather was good and we made a good passage of it until we were hit by a *pampero* just as we could see the lights of Montevideo. We lost a lot of sails and had the forepeak full of paint, as some drums got adrift. We were delayed in port by a revolution of some sort, and we had to keep below the bulwarks as bullets were flying all around for a few days. Then we towed to Santa Fe and loaded quebrache wood for New York. That wasn't too bad. Most of the crew deserted and the few that stayed were okay. We finished loading in Buenos Aires. We had a long passage home and ran short of grub, but did manage to put into the West Indies and pick up a few items but lima beans were still with us.

We arrived in New York on Christmas Eve and it blew for a week. It was bitterly cold with snow, and there was nobody on board except the two mates and me. The ship dragged towards the shore but our anchor held. We had no trouble except when we had to heave up, and that was the coldest, wettest job I ever had. The next voyage was a tow to Norfolk to load coal for Rio de Janeiro and then load coffee and linseed. The voyage and crew were about average and nothing much happened that didn't happen before. I was made Second Mate and felt pretty good about that. I then left the ship to return to San Francisco. I had enough time up to get a second mate's ticket in steam and was persuaded to go into the Pacific Mail Steamship Company. They operated a passenger service to the Orient. I just didn't like steam boats and passenger ships. America entered the war and I joined the Navy. My service was rather dull and certainly not heroic.

After the war I joined the five-masted barquentine *Russell Haviside* as Chief Mate. The vessel had a converted wooden hull, and was designed as a Ferriss type steamer, but as the war was over, there was no point in completing her as a steamship. The vessel was completing rigging when I joined her and the acting master was a fine old gentleman, Captain Davidson. We finished rigging and towed to Port Blakely, where we loaded lumber for Cape Town. The permanent master came aboard with his wife and they were both doubtful characters. They were a pair alike and I was tempted to leave the ship, but the chance of getting a master's berth with the company was good so I stayed. This character was known as Dog Face Johnson and it was a fitting name. He tried to be a bucko hard case skipper, but the crew refused to take him seriously. They were young greenhorns from the Government training school and while they didn't know much, if anything, they were willing. The second mate was a Californian Indian, William Seamore, a good seaman but barely literate. The older hands wouldn't stay in the vessel; they knew the old man and they smelt trouble. The second mate and I hoped for the best, as there wasn't anything we could do.

We had a full load of lumber, deck load and all, and left Port Blakely under tow to Port Townsend. We anchored and lay there a week. Why we did not know, except the sails were bent and the deck load secured. The owner finally sent a telegram to the skipper and suggested we get under weigh, which we did. We towed out and fortunately it was fine weather and we got sail on her without any trouble. Our hard case skipper stayed on the poop. We got a fine breeze and were making 10 knots by the log when I was told to shorten her down. Orders are orders but from then on it was nothing but arguments, fault finding and grief. Here was a new vessel, everything in order, and a fair wind. What more could one ask for! There was plenty of work, all new vessels need it, and we managed to teach the youngsters quite a lot. The older men that stayed were good. Nothing out of the ordinary happened. We painted the yards, bowsprit, deckhouses and rails, and we tarred down the rigging, but with a deck load you are limited.

Rounding Cape Horn was fine, no trouble and we hove to off Tristan da Cunha, a small group of islands that had been a British base in the Napoleonic Wars. There were about 50 or 60 people living on the islands then. They were an odd lot, spoke a rare brand of English and didn't smoke or drink. But they were good traders and they knew what they wanted. We had to watch them closely. They said they never stole anything from a ship but they took anything that was loose.

The boys traded gear for albatross-feathered hats, bags, etc. and thought they did really well. The boys were getting quite itchy and I asked one of them whether it was fleas, or bed bugs. But no, it was bird lice from the feathered hats. I told them to throw them overboard, but they were sure they could find a cure. They did. They put them in the galley stove oven when the cook turned in, thinking the heat would kill the lice. The cook turned out early, and completely unaware of the oven contents, stirred up the fire and soon had a terrible smell coming out of the galley. That was the end of the hats and bags, and the lice.

On our arrival in Cape Town there was more trouble. Our smart skipper failed to take a pilot and anchored in the wrong place. Two heavy fines ensued. Then we couldn't use our cargo gear and had to take the Port's expensive cranes. After that, crew trouble started, and the ship was plastered for debt. I'd had enough, and I wanted to pay off as there was a nice little barque called *Berlin* that wanted a mate, and was bound for New York. The skipper wouldn't cooperate. We finally discharged, picked up two stowaways and were off to Newcastle, New South Wales, to load coal for Chile. Things didn't quieten down and the voyage was miserable. Then we hit a Southerly Buster and it was a good one. It was my watch below, fine weather and the decks were being holystoned. Hard case came on deck and started a row with the second mate. Without any warning the blow hit us with all sail set and caught us aback. Fortunately the ship was new otherwise we would have lost the foremast, but sails were being blown out one after another. We were able to save the fore and afters but most of the square sails were gone. After we got squared away we headed for Newcastle again. The skipper decided to head through Bass Strait. That was something. Tack, tack, tack, and tack. It looked as though we would never make it. If we couldn't tack we had to wear ship. Finally we got through and arrived in Newcastle one hour before our charter expired.

We were detained because of the two stowaways. They were forbidden to enter Australia and were tossed in jail. Later they were put aboard a limejuicer bound around the Horn. One final row, and I packed my gear and was at the Consul's office and signed off. Dog Face had a hard time of it at Newcastle. He ended up with a whole new crew and before he left had picked up several more fines.

The five-masted barquentine *Forest Dream* was lying in Newcastle waiting for a mate for a voyage to Hawaii. Her skipper, Captain Wester, heard of me and after a short interview was signed on and had one of the best voyages in sail I ever had. *Forest Dream* like so many other vessels was designed as an auxiliary motor vessel but the motors were never installed. She was a little smaller than the *Russell Haviside* but faster, and easier to handle. Captain Wester had been in her for some time, and had made the vessel very comfortable for all hands. She was well found in every respect and the stores were not only plentiful but of good quality. We were soon under weigh and I found we had a top crew, everyone a proper seaman and willing to work. The second mate was a Dane and could do a little navigation so we were well fixed for sights. The carpenter was a huge Finn who was leaving Australia because he couldn't qualify as a citizen. He had a fearful row with the Immigration people and broke up a lot of furniture in the office when they told him he was an Oriental and couldn't become a citizen. Captain Wester saved him from a term in prison by shipping him in the *Forest Dream*.

The Captain was a very fine man to sail with, a first class seaman, navigator and very understanding of a sailor's ways and how to handle men. He was rather short and well filled out, as he always tried out the cook and steward before signing them on. His son, George Junior, was signed on as cabin boy, but it didn't make any difference to the old man. Junior was still cabin boy and took orders from the mates. The vessel was well laid out in the quarters and had electric lights in the saloon and galley. She was the first and only sailing ship I was in that had that luxury. We had to be careful about the lights. If you left one on and fell asleep or it wasn't being used, the old man would remove the bulb and you would be without light for a day or so. He even caught himself! Instead of watch and watch we had 3 fours and 2 sixes and that wasn't bad once you got used to it. A good five-hour sleep came in very handy. We fed very well, more variety than on the *Edward Sewell* and *Russell Haviside*. Fried eggs and bacon on Sunday, fruit soup on Thursday and fish balls (canned) on Friday. There were hot cakes and salted lamb (or mutton) several times a week!

The weather was ideal, sun, fair winds, and moderate seas. It was like a yachting party in a bay. The vessel heeled over on the starboard tack for days and we had to walk on the weather side most of the time. One morning the old man came to my cabin, and said, 'Mr Raynaud, you'd better get the lawnmower out and have the watch cut the grass.' It was a bit early for a drink and the old man looked sober, so I went on deck. The wind had eased a bit and the port side of the deck was now out of the water. The deck was covered with a heavy blanket of deep green weed, and the crew spent the whole day scraping it off. We then scrubbed it down with sand and lye. We arrived at Port Allen and moored to a buoy, where we discharged the coal into lighters. It was then transferred to small dump cars and railroaded to the sugar mill. The crew had to work cargo here, but were paid extra for it. This was rather unusual for those days. There was nowhere to go, and nothing much to do after working cargo all day, so we had very few problems until someone found the little Japanese Tea Room. They sold *okeleho* as well as tea. It was a long walk from the tea house to the sugar mill and that was on the top of a hill at the shore line.

Normally you walked down a very long flight of steps to the wharf, and then down a ladder to the boat. The boys went ashore Saturday night with an advance of $5 and imbibed a little too much okeleho. Some of them had a hard time walking. We heard a lot of shouting and went on deck to find out what was going on. It seems they needed help. The second mate and I took the boat and went ashore, where we found a number of fallen sailors. We lifted them to their feet and staggered to the mill. It was a problem to get them down that long flight of stairs. The second mate solved the problem. He got a sack of sugar, put it on the chute and watched it slide down to the dock. We hoisted a man aboard a sack, gave him a shove and away he went. It was a great success and we never lost a man. We got them all in the boat and on board before sunrise. After that no one walked down the stairs, but the mill people were not too happy to see so many sacks of sugar on the open dock. They put a watchman on to prevent any more sleigh rides. We discharged the coal, cleaned the hold and waited a few days hoping to get a cargo of sugar or pineapples, but Matson had a hold on everything so we shovelled in a few hundred tons of ballast, and headed for Grays Harbor.

The voyage home was all too short. We just had the vessel cleaned, painted and the masts oiled so we looked quite smart arriving in port. To my dismay there was a strike on in the lumber mills and the seamen's union had also called one. The vessel was laid up and we were paid off after we sent down all the sails, as it looked like a long hard winter. Captain Wester also took time off. He was a fine man to sail with. Captain Wester took the *Kate G. Pederson* to Australia. She picked up a load of coal at Newcastle, but the vessel leaked so badly he had to return to Newcastle to discharge, and take on enough ballast to get back to San Francisco. She made a record passage.

Sail was about finished in 1936 and it was too hard to keep employed and hope for a steady berth. It was a matter of survival, and go into steam, or look for something else to do. Shore jobs didn't appeal to me, although a few rigging jobs looked interesting. So it was steam boating for a while, with a short passage in the five-masted schooner *Undaunted,* a very uninteresting passage. I had many years in steam apart from a short passage in the schooner *C. A. Thayer* from Seattle to San Francisco.

As in World War I, the maritime losses that occurred during World War II as a result of enemy action, and the huge tonnage of war materials that had to be moved, meant that anything that floated could be used for some purpose, and some laid-up sailing ships were given a reprieve in this way. On the west coast of the United States there were still some of the Alaska Packers fleet rusting away, and a few others that had seen service in the Robert Dollar fleet. There were several well-known sailers amongst them, including the mighty *Daylight,* a one-time tanker owned by the Anglo American Oil Co. Re-rigged, each of these vessels made a voyage in the early war years, although at this stage the United States had not entered the war.

I am indebted to Captain Harold Huycke of Edmonds, Washington, an authority on this era, who has kindly provided me with information concerning the fate of the five ships that took part in this strange reincarnation.

Re-rigged as a six-masted auxiliary schooner, the steel vessel *Tango* had been the four-masted barque *Mary Dollar,* of the Robert Dollar Line. She had been built as the *Hans* in 1904, by William Hamilton of Glasgow, to the order of G. H. Siemers & Co. of Hamburg. She was sister to *Kurt* which later became *Moshulu,* one of Erikson's pre-war grain fleet. She left the Columbia River in April 1942, loaded with timber for South Africa around Cape Horn. From Durban she headed off to South America with a coal cargo, but caught fire and returned to Durban. Eventually she was bought by a Portuguese owner and renamed *Cidade do Porto.* She was broken up in Lisbon in 1948.

Star of Scotland was also rigged as a six-masted schooner in Los Angeles in 1941. Formerly the four-masted steel barque *Kenilworth,* she took a load of timber from Grays Harbor to Capetown in January 1942. She then loaded coal for South America but was sunk by the U-boat *U159* off the African coast in November 1942. The U-boat commander's name was Helmut Witte. Harold Huycke states that 35 years later, Captain Witte handed back to the owners *Star of Scotland'*s documents, taken at the time of her sinking.

The four-masted schooner *Commodore,* formerly *Blaatlund,* remained virtually unchanged from the time she was built in 1919 in Puget Sound near Seattle. She sailed from Port Angeles in December 1941 for Durban. The only wooden sailer in this group, she had problems on the way. Her master, Captain Charles Tulee, a naturalised German, and according to Sam Hort, a one-time shipmate of his, was a first-class seaman in every sense. He died from a brain tumour in Durban and the ship was sold to cover debts. She ended her days under the South African flag and was broken up in 1948.

Eighteen years after she was laid up by her last owner, J. Griffith & Sons of

Seattle, the famous four-masted barque *Daylight* put to sea again in 1943. Built in 1902 by Russell & Co. of Port Glasgow as an oil-tanker for the Anglo American Oil Co., she had five owners up to the time that Murray Simonsen bought her in 1943 and put her back in service under the Brazilian flag. If any of the seamen from her earlier years had seen her then, they would not have recognised her in this incarnation. The nearest description of her rig was barquentine, although she carried no gaff sails, only staysails. Above her fore lower topsail yard she carried a raffee upper topsail. Her masts were cut back to lower masts with pole topmasts. A midship deckhouse was extended to the bulwarks and a bridge built on top of this. Down aft she carried a smokestack which indicated she was now an auxiliary. She was a large ship, 351 feet (107 metres) long. Basil Lubbock gives a good description of her earlier days in his *Coolie Ships and Oil Sailers*.

Without a doubt the vessel most deserving of a place in this chapter is the barque *Kaiulani*. She went back to sea in the early years of the war, making a voyage from Grays Harbor, Washington, to Sydney in 1941. The voyage was noteworthy in that, unlike the other ships that were recommissioned at this time, she was engineless and retained her original square rig and the features of her previous employment. Her retirement, which commenced in 1930 when laid up by her last owners, the Alaska Packers Association, had been interrupted briefly in 1938 when she was used in the Gary Cooper motion picture *Souls at Sea*. An American syndicate led by shipowner Vincent Madrigal bought her in 1941 and registered her in Panama, which was often the practice if survey requirements could not easily be met.

I have been fortunate to obtain first-hand stories from two seamen who sailed in these ships—Colin Lockwood, an Australian, who served in *Daylight*, and American Gordon Riehl, who sailed in *Kaiulani*. Colin told me of the voyage that put him under masts and yards halfway through World War II and took him around Cape Horn:

> I joined the *Daylight* as an AB in Vancouver on 25 March 1943. We sailed for Port Alberni partly loaded with 100 lb bombs, ammunition and small arms, newsprint and cement. We topped up in Port Alberni with timber and then sailed for Cape Town via Cape Horn. Off San Pedro we anchored for four hours awaiting Admiralty Orders, which brought us up to date with the situation regarding shipping movements, both ours and the enemy. When orders were received we headed for Cape Horn. We experienced reasonable weather and arrived in Cape Town and discharged the timber and newsprint. We then sailed on to Durban, where we discharged the bombs and ammunition. Leaving Durban for Dar es Salaam and Mombassa, we were caught by very severe weather, sustaining much damage. With winds in excess of 100 miles per hour [160 km per hour] and big seas, 80 to 90 feet high [about 25 metres] we were forced to put back to Durban for repairs. Eventually *Daylight* left Durban for Dar es Salaam and Mombassa where we discharged the cement and ammunition. We left Mombassa in ballast—this being water in *Daylight*'s deep tanks—and headed back to Durban. While we were in Durban, the American schooner *Tango* ex *Mary Dollar* [of the Dollar Lines of San Francisco] arrived in port. We loaded coal in Durban for Rio de Janeiro and en route to that port we were nearly intercepted by a German armed merchant cruiser, but the Royal Navy intervened and we continued on to Rio de Janeiro, arriving there on 1 January 1944, where our cargo of coal was discharged. Articles for the ship on this voyage were from Vancouver to Vancouver, and to any port between latitude 60°N to 60°S. While in Rio the ship was sold to Wilson & Company. The crew was repatriated to

Vancouver via Trinidad and New York, going back as passengers on board the S.S. *Poconi*, a Lloyd Brasiliero passenger and cargo ship.

The voyage of *Kaiulani* is described by Gordon Riehl, who has given me a detailed description of his experiences and allowed me to read and quote from his well-kept diaries. I have kept the last sector from Hobart to Sydney intact, as it describes the last voyage ever to be made by a commercial sailing ship flying the American flag.

Our *Kaiulani* adventure took in roughly 15 months. She was registered in Panama, but was American owned. We signed on the ship in Aberdeen, Washington, in early September 1941. *Kaiulani* was towed up to Aberdeen from the San Francisco Bay area with a skeleton crew on board. We loaded Douglas fir lumber which took about one month. A deck load was also carried, 1,173,000 board feet in all. The ship's company was 20 persons and three cats, the crew consisting of a few 'old timers' and 10 young men, 'greenhorns'. We were towed out to sea, leaving Aberdeen on 25 September 1941, roughly two and half months before [America's entry into] World War II.

We had no electricity, no engine, no armor, no refrigeration and no ship's radio. We proceeded south heading for Cape Horn. We spent 17 days in the Doldrums, roughly west of the Panama area. Here Captain Hjalmar 'George' Wigsten developed blood poison from a 'rope burn', and we almost lost him. A short time after, the bosun also developed blood poison, but both survived. Because our kerosene was getting low, the Captain decided to go to Pitcairn Island to replenish our supply. We hove to, off Pitcairn for two days, taking on fresh fruit, live chickens, etc., and kerosene. A nurse on the island also attended to the captain's injury. Thence on to Cape Horn to the southeast. Fortunately for us it was summer time and at one stage we were actually becalmed.

We had left the USA on 25 September 1941. Roughly two and half months later found us at war with Japan. On a small battery-operated 'picnic type' radio that I had brought along, we faintly heard the news about the Japanese attack on Pearl Harbor, through the BBC. This was roughly a week after the war had started. We were southwest of Cape Horn when we heard the news. The Captain feared we might encounter some Japanese ships while rounding the Horn, so we dropped down to 59° South to avoid any such possibility. We had iceberg lookout to avoid the chance of any collision. We had good strong winds across the South Atlantic, around the Cape of Good Hope, to Durban. On approaching Durban's narrow harbor entrance, we inadvertently sailed over a minefield guarding the very narrow channel to the harbor inside. Durban was a major stop for all Allied shipping coming around the Cape, to and from Europe, the USA and Canada, etc., and to the Middle East.

Our lumber cargo was unloaded here. We took on a half cargo of cordite explosive for delivery to Sydney, Australia. We had good strong favorable winds on this leg of the voyage, taking 42 days from Durban to Australia. The Captain had purchased a small battery-powered domestic radio in Durban to keep us up on the war's progress for our sailing to Australia. We were in the same longitude as Perth on Australia's west coast, but way down south, when the Captain heard that Japanese submarines were operating off the east coast of Australia and that the Japanese had actually penetrated into Sydney Harbour and damaged shipping there. The *Kaiulani* being without armament would be inviting disaster to go near Sydney, so we went to Hobart, Tasmania, further to the south, to deliver our cargo. After unloading the cordite, we were unable to pick up another cargo.

After many weeks of idleness, Lieutenant Glover from the US Army small ships bought the ship from the Californian owners. The American flag once again flew on the *Kauilani*. The crew delivered the ship to the US Forces based in Sydney.

The towing north took approximately two weeks with no mishaps. We set sails along the way to assist the tug and often overtook her. It was here the *Kauilani* passage ended on 12 October 1942 and the crew paid off. Some remained in the area to join the US Forces and the remainder was transported back to the USA to Long Beach, California, in the ship *Wisconsin*.

I conclude this chapter with words taken from Gordon's diary as *Kaiulani* left Hobart for Sydney during October 1942. These words would be the last ever recorded about events on a commercial sailing ship flying the Stars and Stripes:

6 October 1942 Even though American owned we had been registered in Panama and flew their flag. But now we were making history by being the last commercial sailing ship to fly the American flag.

We had 14 in the crew. The skipper Captain Wigsten, Tom Soules, Paul Soules, James Walpole, Karl Kortum, Harry Dring, Jack Henriksen, Bill Bartz, John Newbuck, Willard (George) Jorstad, Kenneth Glasgow, Lindsay Masters, Chris Rasmussen and myself, Gordon Rheil. For the first time on our journey we have no mascots.

We left Hobart under tow about 6.30 pm. It was very calm and quiet except for our donkey engine.

It was puffing away and spouting steam and smoke, hoisting our anchor. Mr Goodman our new mate got off at the last moment as he didn't want to go to Sydney with the US Army's new low rate of pay, so we had to go without mates.

As we made a wide circle following the tug, I looked at the house where the Donald MacKays lived and saw someone waving a white towel. We waved back and also dipped our flag to them. Our tug belched black smoke, as we glided along behind it, leaving Hobart astern. It was sunset and a sad parting indeed after our three months stay. As we slipped past our agent, Mr Pope's place, the skipper had me dip our US flag three times in salute to him. We were at last leaving these friendly green hills and trees behind which would now only live in our memories. We chose watches at dusk.

Port Watch: Karl Kortum acting as mate chose Bill Bartz, Paul Soules, Jack Hendrikson, Willard Jorstad and John Newbuck.

Starboard Watch: Harry Dring acting as second mate chose Ken Glasgow, Jim Walpole Tom Soules, Lindsay Masters and myself.

The skipper had been drinking again and wanted to make a speech. But he didn't know what to say. 'It's the way we used to do it in the old days,' he explained.

Chris Rasmusson was our cook and he really put out the goods.

The skipper said to us, 'Just keep the ship neat and clean and you don't have to work. At night you can sleep on watch, but with your clothes on.' This was all very agreeable to us.

7 October, 1942 We had the sleepy 12 to 4 watch and this morning we could see the black outlines of the hills either side. We steered by a white light on the tug. Abaft the port beam the outline of the Tasman Peninsula and Tasman Island was discernable, with a narrow channel between them. We then turned the corner! A flat sea. Our 8 am–12 watch and we washed down and cleared up the decks. This afternoon the sea roughened and we pitched a little. A freshening breeze was coming out of the North.

The port watch swung the port lifeboat this afternoon and made her well fast. This was in case we encountered a Japanese submarine. The old man is limping about with a bad knee that he cracked when he fell over the windlass brake lever under the fo'c'sle head last night.

Karl Kortum said that the tug signalled 17 miles since 10 am. Not very good for eight hours steaming on a voyage of 600 miles. This morning we made one and a half miles in two hours.

8 October 1942 Our 4–8 and 12–6 watch. We just did a bit of cleaning up and steering and hauled up about 25 sacks of coal and dumped it in the donkey room bin.

It has been hazy all day and we can't see the shore at all. A stiff north wind blew from straight ahead. The tug was bouncing about but we rolled along gently, taking a few seas into the hawse pipes. My radio has gone dead, probably dead batteries.

9 October 1942 At sea, somewhere in the southwest Pacific. We had the sleepy 12–4 watch this am. The wind has veered around to about 2 points off the port bow and it looked for a while that we could set some staysails. It was an overcast night and quite cold. We all had our oilskins on as it had rained a lot in the port watch's 6–12 before us. I had first lookout on the fo'c'sle head and I snuggled up in the furled fore topmast staysail to get out of the wind. I slept in the wheelhouse in my standby hour and then had third wheel. She steered quite well. Our signalman, Lindsay, a 16-year-old from Hobart has been quite sick, heaving continuously, but keeping his watches, good fella!

Our 8–12 watch and we found the fore topmast staysail and mizzen topmast staysail set—the other watch's work. The wind had veered around to the west, coming onto our port beam, so we set the inner jib, spanker and the two lower topsails. We hoisted the inner jib but half way up it ripped at the leech from the flapping so we hauled it down again and Tom and I made it fast. At the change of watch at noon we, all hands, hoisted the main upper topsail. It was a good wind and the tug was glad, as they only have bunkers for six days. With all the head winds it was beginning to look bad for them and also us, as far as being pulled was concerned. At noon they signalled for our signalman and thanked us for setting the sails. We told them we were logging 6 knots and asked them if they could go faster as the tow line was dragging along abeam of our bows. They answered that they couldn't go faster. We thought of ribbing them and asking if they wanted a tow but our signalman thought it best not to. The beam sea made it more endurable for the tuggers as she didn't plough up and down as she did yesterday. We took sprays continuously over the weather side all morning.

It was a bit warmer today and the sun shone in a clear blue sky. We couldn't see the shoreline and we are now in the Tasman Sea.

We are observing our blackouts at night again with canvas covers on the skylights, etc. that the port watch rigged up. In our 12–4 watch the longboat got loose and jumped out of the chocks. We lashed her down before she could be stove in against the bitts in the waist. We also had to brace the yards square from on the starboard tack. Our new Hobart-made fore topmast staysail draws well! It's good to have some rags up and do a bit of sailing. I would like to get on to some other sailing ship after I get off this one, maybe!

10 October 1942 At sea, Saturday. We relied mostly on the tug today. Long greasy swells and calm weather were our lot. This afternoon, the wind being ahead, we [the starboard watch] furled the main upper and lower topsails and clewed up the fore lower topsail along with the fore and afters. On our 6–8 watch tonight it blew like hell but on the 4–8 the wind dropped and the seas were down and the sails just drawing. We washed down and set the main and fore topsail. The Australian mainland sighted. Tom played records on the main hatch, lovely weather now. Braced the yards hard on the starboard tack.

11 October 1942, Sunday Our sleep 12–4 and the damn port watch left the clewed up fore lower topsail for us to furl. It was pitch black (and a strict blackout) and we (4 of us) went aloft and furled it as best we could, cursing all the time. The wind was from dead ahead and our watch took in the inner jib, main topmast staysail and mizzen topmast staysail. We left the fore topmast staysail and spanker set as we figured that the wind would shift.

This morning in our 8–12 we swung the starboard lifeboat over the side and lashed it there. We took our time and spent practically the whole morning at it. We are going up the coast now about five miles off. There are green rolling hills and sandy beaches with birds crowing and flying about in our rigging. The sky is overcast and the sea a dull color. There is very little rolling and the sea quiet. We are going along at about 4 knots.

Last night the tug had out a smaller white light, as we are now getting into dangerous waters again.

The port watch set the fore lower topsail this afternoon. We played records in the fo'c'sle this afternoon in my watch below. At noon we passed Montague Island and have 150 miles to go, to Sydney and the end. The cook baked a special chocolate cake today for dinner.

We sighted a large whale just before noon today, spouting and rolling along. It was our 6–12 watch tonight and it was light until about 7.30 pm. I had first wheel and with sails filled with wind on our starboard beam she steered very easily, just a spoke now and again.

The port watch had set the fore lower and main upper and lower topsail and our starboard watch set the fore upper topsail while I was at the wheel. We all have channel fever and it wasn't at all surprising to see half the watch below, the cook and all of our watch, all walking and running around the capstan amid laughs and shouts as they hoisted the fore upper topsail. We all realize that it might be the last time sail is hoisted on *Kaiulani*—the last white wings set to the wind. We all admired the square sails and white canvas with prolonged glances. She's been our home for 13 months and it will be a sad parting when we leave her. Even the Old Man was stamping around the decks and reminiscing, and looking with sad eyes at the sails. 'Yes, it will be the last time we'll see this fellas, the last time,' he said. 'She'll be as good as broken up when we get to Sydney.'

He has spent 25 years in sail and loves every stitch of the canvas we have set. I'll never forget the words I once read. 'She steered like a dray and rolled like a pig, but as I walked away I turned and looked, and had a tear in my eye.' And so with us, we who have sailed her, loved her, cursed her. There are only 13 of the original 21 crew left—thirteen who stuck it out to the end, to work for a cause different from any we could have foreseen or expected.

Kaiulani—that name will stick with us as long as we live. It will live in our memories and haunt us to our dying day.

About 8.30 it poured cats and dogs and we roared along with a bone in our teeth. We were sailing quite fast and our chain tow line was dragging a bight about 20 yards back on the starboard side. We were sailing on our own, a beautiful sight! I went to the end of the bowsprit and admired the phosphorescent water breaking under our bows.

Later tonight the wind got stronger and the skipper came up, looked around and got a bit worried. He had us clew up and furl the fore and main lower topgallants and topsails. We had just got the bunt of the main lower topsail up when someone shouted it was 5 minutes to 12 so we slowed down so that the other watch would have to furl it. A squall hit us and we got a good wetting in about two minutes.

12 October 1942, Monday (Columbus Day) Our 4–8 watch and we got into our wet clothes again and came on deck to find that the port watch had set the fore upper topsail again and we were going like hell, it was blowing like hell and we were rolling like hell. Our starboard lifeboat supports carried away and it was in danger of being stove in as it was swinging about wildly. We hove the fore and after painters tight and threw a lashing around the rail and around a strong support in the boat which made her safer temporarily. I slept for about three hours in the wheelhouse and rather a disturbed sleep as the ship was rolling considerably. At 7.30 Harry called me to straighten up some lines on deck as the wind and seas coming over had washed and blown them to leeward, and what a mess they were!

Some heavy seas in the waist had floated the longboat that we had lashed and washed it against the hatch and bitts when it broke loose and stove in both sides. 'All hands' was called about 1 pm to stand by as we were getting pretty close to Sydney Heads and the Old Man wanted every one around. While I was at the wheel about 2 pm a couple of extra large seas came along and damn near washed away the two swung-out boats. This sea parted two of the three lashings on our starboard boat leaving it with only one lashing. Ken and Tom set about lashing it up again when another large sea came along, sending the ship rolling heavily. She then rolled to weather and dipped the boat under water, partly filling it with water. Then the ship snapped back up and the weight of the water-filled boat broke off both davits. Luckily the forward painter held and the boat was still upright. The skipper was nearby and he bent on a gantline to the painter and let the boat run out astern. This happened about 5 miles out of Sydney. Then the line snapped and the boat was adrift. We had to let it go.

It began raining about 2 pm and we took in the fore and main topmast staysails. We went through Sydney heads about 3 pm and the yellow cliffs were a welcome sight.

The large, beautiful, well-kept, clipper-bowed pilot steamer *Captain Cook* came to meet us just outside the heads, ploughing through high seas and rolling a lot but looking very graceful all the while. We must have looked quite strange to these Sydneyites. An American flag-flying vessel with one gun on the fo'c'sle and four on the poop came out also. We could see several large ferry boats rolling heavily inside the heads.

The pilot boat shouted some message to us but the skipper couldn't hear so they gave up. We went through the heads and the tug towed us to the right towards Manly into a little bay and circled around us for us to anchor. The pilot boat came close alongside and lowered a boat carrying the pilot to our ship. He didn't know we had not anchored and the ship drifted to leeward very close to the rocks. We dropped our port anchor. As we had used our starboard anchor chain for part of the tow line we could not drop our starboard anchor until we had dropped the tow and shackled it back on to the anchor and flaked it down for running. The tug tried to give us a line so they could tow us further away from the rocks and we could drop our starboard hook. We gave them two of our best wires but they broke. They finally pushed us to starboard and we let our anchor fly. We are in about 5 fathoms of water here. We finally knocked off at 6.30 pm, all tired and worn out. It was raining all afternoon. We all stood anchor watches of one hour during the night.

13 October 1942, Tuesday Sydney Harbour. The starboard watch turned to at 9 am and worked until noon. I worked in the galley most of the morning. The watch cleaned up the shelter deck and straightened everything back up to normal. The forepeak, with its paints, tars, lines, etc., the galley with its pots, pans and dishes and the food store were a mess from the excessive rolling yesterday.

Ferries were going past all day long to and from Manly. Tom had a bottle of gin and with some lime cordial from the cook we all had a drink, just enough for a glow. Watches continue. It was my night watch from 10 to 11 pm.

14 October 1942, Wednesday The wind has moderated but this afternoon it started to blow quite strong. About 11 am our tug *James Wallace* came alongside and asked if we had enough stores. They said that we would have to stay here until the gale moderated. They also told us that our lost lifeboat had been washed up on Coogee Beach just south of Sydney. Manly ferries are going by all the time. They are painted green and are well enclosed. Some of them have twin stacks and they are pointed both ends. Crossing the heads they roll like hell. They weren't running today as it was too rough.

15 October 1942, Thursday I was messman today and washed up the dishes then washed down the decks. I helped Tom put a splice in a wire for a mooring line. The wind is still blowing strongly. A three-masted schooner came through the heads today towed by a tanker. She looked as if she had been through a tough time in the gale. There was a lot of activity in and out of the harbour today. Several patrol boats and a couple of grey-painted passenger liners went out. The sun came out today and it is quite warm and it feels good. I have put away my sleeping bag.

16 October 1942, Friday This morning two tugs, *Warang* and *St Aristell*, came up and we started heaving up our anchors. *Warang* gave us his line and *St Aristell* was alongside on the port side. The pilot told us that he had brought in the Canadian five-masted schooner *City of Alberni* [ex *Vigilant*] the previous year. The weather has quietened down and it is now warm and sunny. We passed through the anti-submarine boom net that is across the harbor and saw the *Captain Cook* lying at anchor as well as two Liberty ships flying the American flag. They looked like good ships. We were towed past Woolloomooloo and a small island fort and saw the US army troopship *Mt Vernon* that had brought 2000 troops here. Then past Circular Quay with all its ferries. We then went under the Sydney Bridge with about 10 feet clearance. We tied up alongside a steamer with one anchor out. We all got dressed ready for shore and then a Navy tug came alongside and we had to get back into our working gear to move ship. We were moved over to Millers Point where the US Army's small ships headquarters were. There were two old sailing ships hulks there, the *Currajong* and the *Muscoota.*

I was at the helm and was the last person to steer the old ship to her berth.

I am privileged to have had the opportunity to read Gordon Rheil's diaries and I am indebted to him for sending them together with much other material from this voyage. I was particularly interested in his description of *Kaiulani*'s arrival in Sydney Harbour and the storm, as I can remember it vividly. Wartime secrecy prevented any mention of shipping movements in the press and I never knew what happened to *Kaiulani* when she was towed out of North Harbour.

The words of Captain Jim Gaby round off the life of this famous old windjammer. Cape Horn sailor, master, writer and patron of the Australian Cape Horners, Jim told me of his encounter with *Kaiulani* after her arrival in Sydney. The words he used in his book *The Restless Waterfront* are probably the last words that would be published about *Kaiulani*, at least while she was still an operational sailing ship. Jim was a wharf superintendent at that time.

Many of the big American Atlantic liners came to Sydney packed full of GIs. Vessels from the Great Lakes saw the open ocean and certainly, Sydney for the first time. Even one of the old wooden steam schooners that used to ply the California and Oregon coast tied up at one of our wharves. She was a nostalgic sight. I had been aboard her in San Francisco before World War I. But the most nostalgic sight of all opened out to me on my way around the Walsh Bay wharves one afternoon. There, towering high above the central wharf shed, were the lofty masts and spars of a good-sized, barque-rigged sailing ship. Fore and main royals, double t'gallants, double topsails and a long pole mizzen mast standing away back by itself were just something good to behold. They had an untidily trimmed look, and the ship badly wanted painting, but it was wartime, and I was ready to forgive.

Six years of my younger life bounced back fair and square. For six years I had lived in the shelter of masts and spars, and the sails that billowed from yards such as these had carried me over the oceans of the world. Yes, and even around Cape Horn. Before I left sail, I had the honour to be the first mate of a barque of similar size, and this chance encounter brought with it a warm feeling of nostalgia and satisfaction that had stayed with me all my life.

'Wonder what barque she is? What flag's she flying?' The anticipation of it all quickened my heartbeats. I approached, saddened for a moment by the overall untidiness.

All her sails were away in the sail locker, and Irish pennants were flying from everywhere. She was bluff in the bow, bluffer than any of my old 'barkees'. Her name was *Kaiulani,* but another name had been thinly over-painted and [was] still showing: *Star of Finland.*

I hadn't seen her before, but old shipmates had often told of the lovely *Kaiulani.*

A door from the deck to the saloon was invitingly open, so I walked through. The dull teak panelling gave it a dark, unfriendly character; there was no nice white, glossed paintwork and no brightness at all. The only light came from the poop skylight above. A heavily built man was sitting at the saloon table writing a letter.

'Good morning,' said I.

He looked up, and his look was as to an unwelcome intruder, which perhaps I was. 'Good day,' he replied.

'Would you be the captain?' I asked in my pleasantest tone to offset my intrusion.

'Ya, I'm the captain.'

His eye ran me over to determine the cut of my jib. I introduced myself and told him I was just another old square rigger sailor attracted by the sight of masts and spars.

'Where are you from?' I asked.

'We towed up from Hobart. Too many submarines about to sail up.'

'Where do you go from here?'

'Mister, I don't go anywhere else in this damn ballahouse. Some other poor son-of-a-bitch can take over my trouble.' He looked at me with fierce eyes. It wasn't a happy man's look at all. One more question remained.

'Who's relieving you?'

'Look, Mister, that's their business.' Then the thought struck him. 'You got a licence?'

'Yes!' I proudly told him about my flash certificate and that I had been mate of a barque about the same size and rig as the *Kaiulani.*

'What about you taking the job?' he shot at me. 'If you like, I'll tell the agent when I go up this morning. You'll get it, but you'd be crazy to take it.'

What a temptation! My life's ambition had been to be Master in sail. I would gladly have passed over the biggest liner for a command like this. But it had come along just ten years too late. Although wartime manpower rules forbade a man to leave a job, the rule was always waived for anyone who wanted to go to sea, so I really could have taken the ship. But I had almost reached my fifties, and to be honest with myself and my family, there was no future in it. Even the problem of a crew didn't frighten me, and I do think the *Kaiulani* would have done better out of Sydney. I had broken young steamboat men into sail before. All you looked for in them was guts and obedience. I told the Captain how much it appealed to me but that the circumstances weren't just right. I think he understood, but he was not really interested in finding a successor. You could see that he only wanted out. We chatted for another ten or fifteen minutes; then after another fond look around, I came ashore and thought of it all as just a nostalgic interlude.

What Jim didn't know was the fact that *Kaiulani* had been requisitioned by the US Army's small ships for use as a store ship. At that time anything that floated was being bought to support the Pacific campaign. A great friend, Jack Savage, an Australian who was first to be employed by the US Army in this activity, told me much about this almost unknown group. He went around and bought up all sorts of vessels—trawlers, yachts, whatever he could lay his hands on. Most were taken to Milne Bay, New Guinea, to provide coastal transportation for the Australian and American advance against the Japanese, and described superbly in *The Forgotten Fleet* by Bill Lunney.

Kaiulani never spread her wings again. She was dismantled and spar by spar she was stripped until there were only the three lower masts sticking out of the hull. After being rigged down she was towed to Milne Bay to replace the *Muscoota,* mentioned earlier by Gordon Rheil. *Muscoota* had been sunk, one report says by Japanese bombs, another by collision, and *Kaiulani* took up her new duty, as did many of her sisters, as a storage barge and fuel hulk. And that was the fate of the last square-rigged commercial sailing ship to fly the Stars and Stripes.

While *Kaiulani*'s career was ordinary, apart from being a fast vessel she should have achieved immortality and the status of a national monument as a superb example of the down east shipbuilder's art plus the fact that she was the only surviving steel sailing ship out of the few that were constructed in the United States. Other museum ships spread out around the United States—*Balclutha, Star of India, Moshulu, Falls of Clyde, Wavertree, Elissa*—were built in the United Kingdom, white *Peking* was built in Germany.

Captain Harold Huycke told me of *Kaiulani*'s ultimate fate:

> After the war, she was in the Philippines, and was sold to a Philippines company to transport logs and bulk cargoes. She was in pretty bad shape. A group was formed in the US who planned to restore her and sail her back to Washington, DC, via Cape Horn. It turned out that there was no dry dock available in the Philippines, and she was in such a bad state that it was decided to cut the hull into sections and ship them back for rebuilding in the US. The pieces arrived at Todd Shipyard in Seattle, and as with most schemes of this nature, funds did not materialise and Todd Shipyard told the group to take their scrap steel away.

The pieces were never welded together and *Kaiulani,* Child of Heaven, quietly disappeared from the face of the Earth.

7 THE GRAIN SHIPS AND THE ERIKSON ERA

Viking

The term 'grain ship' requires some comment. The transportation of grain from Australia and the stories from the Erikson ships are closely linked. However, grain from the west coast of North America also was a regular cargo for the world's windjammers, particularly those from Great Britain, in the late nineteenth and early twentieth centuries. The Erikson ships, while largely relying on Australian grain for their livelihood, had other cargoes that helped to pay the bills. Baltic timber often took them to South America and South Africa. Guano from the Seychelles was a convenient cargo as these islands were more or less on the way to Australia and there was a market for this fertiliser in Australia and New Zealand. But from the twenties and thirties most of the world's remaining sailing ships would arrive in Spencer Gulf from December into the New Year, when the millions of acres of cereal crops were being harvested in the surrounding countryside—and not only Erikson ships; the remnants of the French, German, Swedish and Danish fleets all loaded grain cargoes there.

While some sailing ships also loaded grain at Port Adelaide, Melbourne and Sydney, there were several reasons for Spencer Gulf being the centre for this trade, a major one being the lack of mechanised loading facilities. Manually loading a ship with up to 60,000 bags of grain took quite a long time, which steamships of much higher capital value could not afford. The time involved in a sailing ship voyaging to Australia and back to Europe, 200 days at best, did not allow more than one trip per year, so it did not much matter how long it took to load. Very low crew wages, coupled with the fact that many in the crew had paid a $100 premium as an apprentice for the voyage, meant that a large wage bill did not accrue as the sailer was slowly loaded. A good passage time to Europe might mean that on discharge of her cargo, usually in the United Kingdom or a Continental port, she might be able to return to the Baltic and load a cargo of timber for South America or South Africa on her way to Australia in time for the next season's crop.

There was another important factor. The Australian harvest, being six months out of phase with the Northern Hemisphere harvest, allowed the grain to be warehoused at no cost in the sailing ship's belly as she spent 100 days on the homeward run, and to arrive when the price on European markets was high.

The ports in Spencer Gulf are mentioned many times. Port Lincoln on the western shore performed a similar function to Falmouth, England, or Queenstown, Ireland. The latter two, conveniently situated near the entrance to the English Channel, made it easy for sailing ships coming in from the Atlantic to call in for their orders. It must be remembered that these sailing ships were without radio. The maritime laws of most countries did not require it, and it was an additional expense.

Port Lincoln was easily made as the sailer came in from the Great Australian Bight and from here many were sent on to the other Gulf ports—Port Victoria, Wallaroo, Port Broughton, Port Germein and Port Augusta. Sometimes the charter would be known before leaving Europe and the ships could sail right up to their port of loading. If not, the ships anchored offshore at the ballast grounds. If they were to load in Port Lincoln they dumped some of their ballast and then sailed in to the jetty. Perhaps the term 'drifted' is more appropriate, as only a few sails would be set, usually fore and afters. When some distance off they would be warped in, using lines taken ashore by local launches. With bagged wheat loaded to replace the dumped ballast, the ship would be sailed out again to the ballast grounds. On the east side of the jetty were two haul-off buoys that the sailer ran a line out to so she could be hauled clear before sailing off. However, the wind that took them clear of the jetty often came from the wrong direction to get them out of the Gulf. The ship would have to anchor and wait for a fair wind to get them south.

Gustaf Erikson's emergence in the thirties as the world's last sailing ship owner created a nexus between his ships and the Gulf and, indeed, the men, boys and a few girls of many nationalities that made up their crews.

The story of life in the Erikson ships must be preceded by a brief look at the history of the Åland Islands, home of the grain fleet and most of the seamen who sailed in it. Spread across the entrance to the Gulf of Bothnia in the North Baltic Sea is the Finnish Archipelago comprising 6654 islands. The largest is about 50 kilometres (30 miles) in length, many others only rocks with little vegetation. It is Finnish territory but possesses the autonomy of its own parliament. It is also a demilitarised zone and armed forces are not permitted. Going back in time Sweden and Finland were one country, and the cultural background of the Ålands is Swedish, as is the language spoken. The Vikings knew these islands well and there are many Ålanders today who claim Viking ancestry. They were initially a farming and fishing community, and somehow managed to grow crops in the short summer when there was no snow. Their seafaring traditions evolved around the need to move from island to island with seed, livestock and produce to trade with the mainland countries of the Baltic. The war of 1809 brought Finland and the Ålands under Russian control and Åland vessels were prevented from trading beyond the Baltic. Despite this, the Ålanders developed strong shipbuilding and seafaring skills, and when the trade laws were relaxed in 1856 they started building larger vessels and voyaged further afield, especially when the Baltic Sea froze over during the long winter months. Finland declared its independence in 1917, after the Russian Revolution. Mariehamn, named after Tzaritza Maria Alexandrovna, became the principal town and centre of commercial and social life of the Åland Islands. Åland now has its own flag, blue with a yellow cross and a narrower red cross superimposed over this, but their ships fly the white and blue flag of Finland.

Long before Gustaf Erikson emerged as the last and most famous of the sailing ship owners there were others who laid the foundations for what became, for the Ålands, a thriving industry. August Troberg, Robert Mattson and Matthias Lundqvist were shipping pioneers whose descendants still reside in Mariehamn. Their shareholders were the farmers, boatbuilders and everyday folk of the Ålands. Many smaller groups also had shares in the small wooden schooners they expertly built and operated. The full story behind the development of the Erikson fleet and others in the Ålands is told by Ålander Georg Kåhre in his book *The Last Tall Ships*; it is impossible to attempt, within the scope of this book, to give even a condensed overview of how this region became the last home of the sailing ship.

Gustaf Erikson went to sea, as did most of the boys from the Ålands, in the wooden sailing vessels that were built by the hundreds in this area. During World War I he moved from seafaring into shipowning. The high freight rates generated by the war made shipowning highly profitable and it was possible for a ship to pay for herself after only one voyage. After the war, in the early twenties, there was a shipping slump, and ships could be bought at almost scrap prices, particularly sailing ships. This again suited Erikson. The low freight rates now offering could be offset by the inherent Ålander culture of resourcefulness, thrift, the ability to survive on a shoestring. His ships were manned largely by boys, and wage levels were very low. As older ships became unserviceable they were stripped, and the spars, sails and fittings used again and again. Erikson made some good buys in the early twenties and some famous German and British sailers came under his flag.

In 1929, Britain's last sailing ship, *William Mitchell*, made her final voyage. The French had several still trading. Laeisz retained *Padua* and *Priwall*, and there were a few others—Finland's *Favell*, Sweden's *Abraham Rydberg* and *C. B. Pedersen*, and Denmark's five-masted barque *København*. There was also the German Vinnen fleet of auxiliary cargo-carrying training ships, which included the large four-masted barque *Magdalene Vinnen*. But by 1930 Gustaf Erikson had emerged as the world's largest sailing ship owner. Between the years 1913, when he bought his first sailing vessel, the barque *Tjerimai*, and 1942, when he bought his last, the three-masted schooner *Sirius*, he owned a total of 46 ships. In 1933, of the 22 large steel sailing ships which loaded grain in Australia, 13 were owned by Erikson. He took apprentices for $100 a voyage, while passengers could sail to Australia for $1 a day. The desire for a sail endorsement to their certificates attracted most of the aspiring young mercantile officers who made up the crews. The average age was a little over 20, although many of the Ålanders had been at sea in their small Baltic traders since they were ten years old. Erikson carried his own insurance and the provisions carried in his ships came from Shierbeck's, of Copenhagen. In the early days provisions came from the local farmers, many of whom were shareholders in these ships.

When World War II broke out, there were those who said the grain fleet was finished, and they were almost right. Thirteen sailers loaded grain in Spencer Gulf in 1939, of which ten were owned by Erikson; only four, all Erikson-owned, were trading after the war. Three of the 13 were sunk early in the war. *Pamir* arrived in New Zealand and *Lawhill* in South Africa just after the war started. At that stage Finland had an agreement with Germany and was not occupied, an alliance which resulted in their ships being regarded by the Allies as 'enemy', and thus *Pamir* and *Lawhill* were seized as war prizes. *Passat*, *Viking* and *Pommern* were laid up in Mariehamn during the war. *Moshulu* and *Winterhude* were taken over by Germany as store ships, and *Archibald Russell* remained in the United Kingdom at the end of her last voyage. At war's end it was decided to send *Viking* and *Passat* to sea again, and Gustaf Erikson personally put much effort into getting them seaworthy. *Pommern* needed too much work to pass survey, so all effort was concentrated on the other two.

Gustaf Erikson died in 1947 and passed on to his son Edgar the responsibility of being the last man on Earth to own and operate commercial square-rigged engineless sailing vessels. After sailing throughout the war under the New Zealand flag to the west coast of North America, *Pamir* made one trip to Sydney in 1947, then to the United Kingdom, returning to New Zealand in 1948. She was handed back to the Erikson fleet for the last grain ship voyage in 1949. *Passat* made two trips to Port Victoria, in 1947–48 and 1948–49. *Lawhill* voyaged all through the war between South Africa, South America and Australia and loaded grain in Port Victoria for the last time in 1948 for Beira, Portuguese East Africa (now Mozambique). *Viking* made voyages to South Africa, Brazil and Spencer Gulf in 1946–48.

By late 1949, Edgar Erikson had to face the cold economic fact that commercial sail was finished. Sentiment and nostalgia were costly emotions and thus *Pamir* and *Passat* were sold to a Belgian shipbreaker. They were onsold to German shipowner Heinz Schliewen, who turned them into auxiliary cargo-carrying training ships, once again under the German flag. *Viking* became a stationary seamen's school, and later a hotel and restaurant in Gothenburg. The Erikson family presented *Pommern* to the town of Mariehamn as a museum ship, where she stands today, and that was the end of the grain fleet!

Back in Port Victoria the railway lines on the jetty grew rusty and loose sheets of corrugated iron on the wharf building flapped in the wind. The old-timers at the Wauraltee pub talked of crops and drought and the sailers that used to appear each summer. And on the opposite side of the world the last real seamen on Earth would gather in Societetshuset and talk of their voyages to Spencer Gulf, of the hot Australian sun, friendly country girls, the cold beer from the Wauraltee pub and Kneebone's Cafe. Gustaf Erikson's ships will never be forgotten in this town as the streets now bear their names.

In 1986 I sat in the church on Norra Esplanadgatan, the church that shipowner August Troberg had built for the people of Mariehamn, for it happened that my arrival there had coincided with the day of Edgar Erikson's funeral. I pondered whether my chance visit to the Åland Islands at this time held some special significance. Earlier in the day I witnessed Edgar's casket being carried from the Erikson family home further down the street up to the church, by six men I guessed were old captains from the Erikson fleet. Specially spliced ropes supported the casket from the shoulders of the pallbearers. Townspeople lined the street to say their farewell to Edgar and with his passing to another link to the age of commercial sail.

Mariehamn today has much the same appearance as any other small country town, but few such towns have Mariehamn's record of achievement in the tough business of international shipping. *Pommern* stands proudly in the western harbour, where once ten or twelve large sailing ships could anchor for the late summer months. She is lovingly cared for, not only by those who remember, but by a new generation of young people aware of their heritage and intent on keeping the traditions of Åland seafaring alive. The maintenance work is carefully carried out to avoid changing anything that is a link with the past. Even the ballast, dredged from the Humber when she discharged her last cargo of Australian grain at Hull in 1939, is intact. Overlooking her from the foreshore is the Åland Maritime Museum. It is world class with, naturally enough, the best collection of artefacts from this era I have seen. All devotees of traditional sail should make a pilgrimage to this place. Like the streets of Port Victoria, taxis in Mariehamn bear the names of past sailing ships, instead of number plates.

On board *Pommern* — photographs by Alan Palmer, Mariehamn

Crew foc'sle in *Pommern*

Saloon (Captain and officers)

Master's cabin

Galley stove (coal or wood fired)

Donkey engine (oil)

Anchor winch

Halyard winches and Jarvis brace winch

Base of foremast with pig pen

Wheel box and poop skylight

The grain ships, Erikson's and a few others, have been a rich source of material. The stories chosen to portray this era represent only a fraction of what was offered, a broad selection of the important themes.

One of the earliest stories of life in the Erikson fleet comes from Colin Pelham of Adelaide, who sailed in the barque *Killoran* as ordinary seaman in 1927, from Port Lincoln towards Falmouth for orders and Rotterdam to discharge. Erikson bought *Killoran* from J. Hardie in 1924. Colin told me of several incidents which I have selected to introduce the picture of life in a grain ship.

In the doldrums, those windless areas just below and about the Equator, when I was off watch, I frequently climbed to the top of the mast and sat on the truck [the circular piece of timber on the top of the mast] and watched the sharks swimming around the ship. It was also an ideal place to see the miles and miles of windrows of yellow seaweed floating on the sea's surface. Many times there were turtles to be seen amongst it. There was little English spoken in the ship and then only when instructions had to be given to my shipmate Toby Christie or myself, the only English-speaking members of the crew. However, the rest of the crew spoke enough English to pull my leg many times.

Casperson was a man with a great sense of humour as was Hansen, a Norwegian from the starboard watch. They both conspired to trick me as to what would happen when we reached Cape Horn. I was told that I could write letters home for the boat would come out to us from Cape Horn with fresh fruit and vegetables, and to take back mail to my parents and friends in Australia. I only half believed them so I wrote no letters. When we were off the Horn the Captain, who was on the poop for only the second time since leaving Port Lincoln, called me from the main deck and with his telescope, pointed out the notorious Cape Horn to me. It was no more than a faint pencil mark on the horizon. So much for the fresh fruit and vegetables! Oddly enough our rounding was on a comparatively calm day, although just prior to and immediately afterwards we ran into really foul weather.

We had an AB, a Swede called Lindbergh, quite a decent fellow. He was in the starboard watch. Casperson and I were in the port watch. Lindbergh had an odd condition of sleeping with his eyes open. Actually they were closed when he went to sleep but as he slept deeper so they opened wider. It was thought he had some thyroid complaint. Like most of the crew in the forecastle in the warmer latitudes he slept naked. Of course being out of touch with the fairer sex, certain parts raised themselves during sleep. So it was with Lindbergh. Casperson, the Finn, being the practical joker that he always was, took a ball of spun yarn [hemp saturated with Stockholm tar, used to bind seizings and splices] and dropped a couple of half hitches over Lindbergh's erect penis. Casperson then tossed the ball of spun yarn out of forecastle over the combing and into the scuppers. Just then the second mate, Mattson, came along. He was a most difficult man even at his best. He picked up the ball and with a string of expletives in Finnish about the waste of spun yarn, commenced to wind it up. He made a few turns, then finding it would come no further thought it to be caught between the door of the forecastle and the coaming, he gave a tug and fortunately he only gave one tug. Lindbergh awoke with a yell and very nearly lost his penis. He never knew to the end of the voyage who was responsible for the prank. Luckily no great damage to his person occurred.

When we left Port Lincoln, my friends gave me two books to read. They were *Beau Geste* and *Beau Sabreur* by P. C. Wren, and had only recently been published. I was a greenhorn sailor and left them in the ledge above my bunk. I did not complete reading either, for toilet paper is not provided for the crew and I found the back pages of both books disappearing, apparently purloined by various crew members as they went forward to attend to their needs. The same thing happened to the soft weatherworn patches on the bottom of the foresail, when we were in tropical climes. The canvas eventually blocked up the pipe from the head to the ship's side and I, Peter as I was known, had the task of going over the side and clearing it. But that is another story!

When we tied up at Rotterdam I elected to remain on board as watchman as all other crew members including the officers decided to go ashore, apparently to live it up. After working for five months on a four hours on and four hours off basis it was nice to go to sleep knowing that I would not have to leave my bunk again until morning.

Captain F. Olsen of Albert Park, South Australia, told me of his years under sail, commencing with his time in the small Baltic schooner *Poseidon* at the end of World War I. He was one of hundreds of young Scandinavian boys who went to sea in these traders, travelling from the Baltic ports to the Mediterranean, Africa and the east coast of the Americas. He later joined the Danish four-masted barque *Viking* for two voyages to Port Victoria in 1923. His comments about his voyage in *Viking* are not all that dissimilar to many of the narratives I have recorded, but his descriptions of the activities of this port and its characters are significant and reveal some of the shore culture that was part of the grain ship saga.

The 'ketches' that Olsen and many of my other informants mention are well described in the book *Ketch Hand*, by Ron Theile, which tells of his experiences as a deck hand in these small ships around Spencer Gulf. They were not all ketch rigged, many being two- and three-masted schooners. In the early days they sailed out to the waiting sailing ships anchored offshore but in the latter years most were equipped with engines.

Port Victoria, along with the other Spencer Gulf ports, must have presented itself as a harsh, strange place to young Olsen and his shipmates, as it seemed to most of the seamen who came from the relative sophistication of the northern European and Baltic ports, with their mercantile activity and social influence. These ports existed mainly because of the grain that was grown over the thousands of square kilometres of dead flat country stretching inland from the shores of the Gulf. Every season the grain was harvested, bagged and stacked throughout the town, usually in the open, awaiting the sailers that relied on this cargo for their survival. The farmers of the region were thankful not to have the freight costs that would have seriously eroded their wheat cheques if their produce had to be transported overland to Port Adelaide.

A long jetty at the foot of the main street thrust itself out into deeper water where the small ketches were used to lighter the grain out to the sailers at anchor, anything up to a mile offshore. The bagged grain was handled many times between the time the farmer sewed up the heavy wheat sack with a longer version of the needle used by the sail makers of the grain ships, to when it was bedded down in the hold. The interface between the farmer and the grain ship sailor was the 'wheat lumper'. A time-honoured calling in the great wheat belts of the Australian continent, the lumper was a labourer who followed the harvest, or lived permanently in one of the wheat towns, and plied his trade of moving 180-pound (81 kg) bags of grain on his shoulders. In the Port Victoria district in the twenties the bags of grain were loaded onto a horse-drawn wagon or, if the farmer was more up to date, a Dodge or Chevrolet truck, and taken to the town. From the massive stacks that grew up all around the town the bags were then loaded onto another wagon and taken to the jetty. The jetty was equipped with flat horse-drawn wagons running on steel rail lines. The lumper transferred the bags onto this wagon and it was run out to the small ketches moored alongside. Gravity was used to slide the bags down a chute from the jetty into the hold. The ketch now took its cargo out to the sailer. Slings of bagged grain were hoisted aboard, using, if the crew was lucky, a diesel or steam powered winch. A lot of care was taken to stack the bags neatly to conserve space. The lumper's job had only just started once the first layer of bags had been placed, for it required up to 60,000 bags to fill the average sailing ship. The task of walking over this uneven surface with 180 pounds slung across the shoulders would not even be contemplated by today's stevedore, even if he found he could get one of these bags onto his back. The bags were dumped in rows, with each successive row at right angles so the bags locked into one another. Once the bag was dropped into place it was not touched or moved, so expert were these men at their work. These men had skills in common with the stevedores of the West Coast nitrate ports, where bagged nitrate was loaded in much the same way.

The other ports of Spencer Gulf, Port Augusta, Port Broughton, Port Germein, Port Lincoln, Port Pirie and Wallaroo, all played host to the sailers of the grain fleet; some of these ports had jetties with deeper water alongside which the sailer could load. The jetty at Port Germein was over a mile long.

Olsen describes Port Victoria and some of the local characters who, just as he did, left the grain fleet for the higher wages offering in Australia.

Fifty-six days out from Santos we arrived at Port Victoria in South Australia and dropped anchor at the ballast grounds. As we approached our anchorage we saw what appeared to be another big sailing ship at anchor. However, it turned out to be a French barque hard and fast on Wardang Island. She was beached here a couple of years ago and later caught fire, becoming a total loss. Her name was *Notre Dame d'Arvor*.

After we had discharged our ballast, *Viking* was worked into the inner anchorage. The bagged wheat was brought alongside in small ketches and schooners from the jetty or other ports in the Gulf. Four wheat lumpers lived on board *Viking* and stowed the full cargo of wheat, assisted by members of the crew, who would attend to the chutes and the up-ending of the bags. Quite a number of small ketches and schooners were registered in Port Adelaide, some 60 of them. They were mostly engaged in trade around the gulfs and lightering wheat and barley from the small out-ports to steamers and sailing ships in the main ports. A number of bigger schooners and ketches were also engaged in the Tasmanian timber trade. A big proportion of these small ships were crewed and skippered by runaway sailors. They had quite colourful names bestowed on them by the locals. Some of the names which come to mind are Cigar Wally, a Dane; Jubilee Johnson, a Swede; Experience Jack, a Swede; Roaring Peter, a Dane; Bosun Gus, a Russian Finn; German Max, the mad Dane and the Dago. Other names were Truthful Tom, so called for the careless way in which he handled same, also Ice-cream Charley, who always wore a white coat and trousers whenever he went ashore. Most of the men were hard-working and hard-drinking. Some of them stayed on in South Australia and raised families. Slim Jim, a Swede, left in an American schooner to make his fortune in American rum-running.

Port Victoria township had a wide main street with a pub on one side and a post office on the other. There were also the offices of wheat agents, several general stores, one or two soft drink shops and a billiards saloon and not much else. Most of the buildings were made from corrugated iron. I don't think I have seen whiter sand than that which made up the sand dunes south of the town. The main street was covered with white sandstone dust, and with no trees to be seen anywhere, looked a dusty hot place. The pub, the Wauraltee, did a roaring trade in spite of having to close at 6 pm. At five minutes to six the local policeman would place himself in the door of the front bar to make sure that no one committed the awful crime of drinking beer after 6 pm. The grain ship sailors usually with little cash did not frequent this pub as much as they would have liked but most have fond memories 50 years later.

Captain Olsen himself left *Viking* in Port Victoria and went into the Australian coastal trade. He settled in South Australia as did many of the grain ship sailors and ended his career as a Port Adelaide pilot.

Reminiscences by two seamen in the Finnish barque *Favell* and their voyage to the islands of Mauritius and Reunion in the Indian Ocean inspired me to paint *Favell* in a setting that was not usually enjoyed by grain ship sailors. This period in *Favell*'s life is told by George Häggstrom, who now lives in Helsinki, and Bertil Bengstrom of Melbourne, who served in the ship as cadets.

I joined the barque *Favell* in December 1923 in London and we sailed to Norway where we loaded a full cargo of D.B.B.—deals, battens and boards—for Port Adelaide. We were 124 days at sea. In Adelaide we loaded grain for France, via Falmouth for orders. The next loading port for Australia was Sikea in northern Sweden. We headed for Melbourne and another slow passage, arriving there in January 1926. In Melbourne we waited in vain for cargo to Europe. We stayed there for nearly four months and finally obtained a cargo of wheat flour for the islands of Mauritius and Reunion in the Indian Ocean. We loaded at Williamstown and while in Melbourne there were several other windjammers including the lovely Swedish four-masted barque *Beatrice.*

Our first port of call was Port des Galets, on the Island of Reunion. After some difficulties with the westerly gales south of Australia, we succeeded in rounding the most southwesterly part of the continent and then we were in the South-East Trades in the Indian Ocean. On the same day we killed our last pig taken on board in Copenhagen when leaving Europe. We had now started changing to our light weather sails and such an occasion had to be celebrated. We now had a steady wind on our port quarter, but had to remember that in the Indian Ocean this time of the year, March, was the time for tropical cyclones. About one week's sailing from Reunion, the Captain noticed the barometers were falling rapidly. It was very likely that we were now in the neighbourhood of a cyclone centre. He gave the order to shorten sail, so in a few hours the ship was carrying only staysails and lower topsails. The trade wind died and we were slowly rolling in a cloudy and strained atmosphere. In excitement we waited for the cyclone to arrive, all hands stood by but nothing happened.

After a few hours the barometers were rising and soon reached the normal pressure ruling in these tropical waters. On 30 April 1926 we dropped anchor in the roadstead of the town of Saint-Denis, Reunion. On the following day a boat came out to us carrying bad news. A few days before our arrival a cyclone had been moving across the island and destroyed Port des Galets including the channel to that port. A French steamer was shut up in the port, which could not be used for months, perhaps years. It was very likely that same cyclone was the one we were in touch with on the voyage. Using our lifeboats we started to make visits ashore. The population was a strange mixture of all coloured peoples including Chinese and Indian. Very few whites could be found. As the island belongs to France, these were all French. All coloured and whites speak the French language.

An immense quantity of sugar is produced and exported and fruits of all kinds could be bought for practically nothing. Bananas and pineapples are growing practically wild.

During the Napoleonic Wars this island was occupied by England, but after the wars it was handed back to France and was renamed Reunion. The old name was Isle de Bourbon.

One day a French steamer arrived from Mozambique and anchored in the roads near our ship. The whole cargo consisted of cattle of all kinds. As there was no quay on the island the cattle had to be discharged into the ocean and towed ashore. This was the way to empty the ship but nobody thought of the sharks, which were abundant in these tropical waters. The natives in the towing canoes had to leave many a roaring cow in a half-dead condition to the hungry monsters of the Indian Ocean. The agents for our cargo told us they had ordered barges from Europe in order to discharge our cargo, but nobody could tell us when they would arrive.

On the first of July we left Reunion and sailed to Port Louis, Mauritius. We dropped anchor in the inner harbour and next day a partly black gang started to unload that part of the cargo destined for Mauritius. In a few days we had finished unloading and a new time of waiting for news from Reunion commenced. We spent about 50 days in Port Louis altogether. We had plenty of time to get acquainted with the island and its inhabitants. On 23 June it was the birthday of the Prince of Wales and the Finnish midsummer, so we had a big feast together with the sailors from the American five-masted barquentine *Forest Dream* lying in the harbour. We had picnics at the famous Pamplemousses with tropical and botanical gardens. We played football with British soldiers on station on the island and sometimes our opponents were all black boys.

Once a week a big British liner called at the port and brought new Chinese colonists from Hong Kong. On the return trip she sometimes loaded dead Chinese in metal coffins to take back to China. In those days no Chinese in his right mind would be buried anywhere but on Chinese soil. On 14 July we celebrated the French national holiday by visiting the Opera House where the opera *La Vive Joyeusse* was the show for the day. Although Mauritius belonged to the British, the French language was mainly spoken. Today the island is independent.

On 17 August we sailed again to Reunion and anchored near the small town of Saint Paul. They had succeeded in obtaining a few barges so we commenced to unload our remaining cargo from Australia. At last on 22 September with black sand in our holds as ballast, we hoisted our sails and started the homeward voyage to Australia again. After four months and 22 days in port in these very interesting lovely islands, we now sailed down to the Roaring Forties singing at sheets and braces, 'for Australia's lovely daughters we are very fond of you'.

We returned to Port Adelaide for orders and then proceeded to Port Germein to load grain. After a long and stormy voyage around Cape Horn we arrived at Falmouth for orders after 159 days at sea. We discharged at Newcastle on Tyne. Very seldom did our ship visit her home port but this time we loaded coal for Helsingfors [Helsinki] where I left *Favell* and went to navigation school for my mate's ticket. I had been in *Favell* for 42 months, and during this time her master was Captain Karl Strömsten who also left the ship in Helsingfors and went into steam. The first mate Sten Lille became master until 1934, when she was broken up.

George Haggstrom's shipmate Bertil Bengstrom made one more voyage in *Favell*, sailing out to Melbourne where he jumped ship. He joined the Port Phillip Pilot Service where he stayed for the next 43 years and finished up Mate. George Haggstrom went on to become Master in various steamers and motorships, was teacher of navigation for eight years and Harbour Master of the Port of Helsinki, Finland, for 22 years.

While the well-known operators Erikson and Laeisz were mostly responsible for prolonging the last years of sail, there were still a few entrepreneurial syndicates spurred on by a business opportunity that required low capital investment and minimum running costs. There was a high risk, but it was possible to make a profit if everything went well and freights were available at a reasonable rate.

Such a venture took Enid Berntsen and her two small children around the world and around Cape Horn under canvas in the year 1923. She has given me a unique look into the operation of one of the last independently owned sailing ships, *Souvenir*. While *Souvenir* was not strictly in the grain fleet, this voyage took place at a time when Australian grain was always a hoped-for charter and the vessel's arrival in Adelaide could have resulted in a grain charter rather than the coal cargo she loaded in Newcastle, New South Wales. This vessel was one of the only two four-masted barques built in Holland. She was built as *Jeanette Françoise* in 1892; later, under German ownership, she became *Carl*. When World War I broke out she found herself in Antofagasta, Chile, and was interned there until after the war. Enid relates:

> There was a depression after the First World War and many of the small Norwegian shipping companies folded. My husband, who was master in one of these ships, found himself without a job. A friend, Olaf Kverndal, shipbroker of London, asked my husband whether he would be prepared to sail as master if he bought the barque *Jeanette Françoise*, which was lying in the harbour at Cotte, in the south of France. He would be allowed to take his family with him. It was some years since my husband had been in sail and only up to the rank of second mate, however, he jumped at the opportunity. The ship's name was changed to *Souvenir* and she was moved to Marseilles and stayed there for three months while being overhauled and equipped with sails (second-hand, I fear) bought in Spain.
>
> I journeyed from the north of England with a baby son of eight months and a daughter of 2½ years. I joined the ship in Marseilles, not having the slightest idea what I was in for. We waited, but no cargo was forthcoming, so we sailed in ballast for Campbellton, Canada. Incidentally, the master had no salary but was paid a percentage of the freight, which wasn't exactly profitable! We had made many friends in Marseilles and there was a big farewell party on board and an escort of small craft to see us off. The next day, to our embarrassment, we were still within sight and our friends came out again to wave to us. It took us a week to get through the Straits of Gibraltar, tacking back and forth, the cliffs of Morocco looming up at one side and the Rock of Gibraltar at the other.
>
> Eventually we made it and then the crew trouble commenced. We had the most motley collection on board, many of them landlubbers who became seasick and wouldn't work. A vicious Maltese, who was quick to use the knife but fortunately, had one redeeming feature; he loved children and became another person when he would talk to them.
>
> It was a happy day for us when we reached Campbellton and a kind family invited the children and me to stay ashore with them. Especially so, after the last night on board, when the drunken cook threw all the crockery, pots and pans overboard. Against my husband's wishes, we stayed ashore until sailing time as I refused to believe that the weather could change. It sure did and I will never forget the nightmare of trying to get on board from the tug in a huge swell. One of the mates was lashed to the side of the ship and the children literally thrown to him. When it came to my turn, I would never have made it but there was a scream of 'now', a push from behind and someone on the other side to grab me and haul me on board. The new crew was a great improvement, even though some of the poor beggers had been literally shanghaied. My husband had

taken a tour of the pubs and jails. Those in jail glad to be free and those who were dead drunk were hoisted on board in nets and woke up to find themselves at sea. I don't think there was any ill-feeling. We had a full cargo of timber from Canada to Australia, including deck cargo but as far as I remember, enough space on the main deck for the children to play in good weather.

Everyone asked me how I spent my time in the long months at sea. I was always busy, two children to look after, their clothes outgrown or worn out and I, who had never done any sewing before, found myself concocting attractive garments out of calico flour bags or bunting—the latter not very popular, too scrubby. When we arrived in Australia, I bought an old hand-sewing machine and materials so that, when we eventually arrived back home, the children had an attractive wardrobe, minus the flourbags. My main hobby was playing the piano, which I did for hours on end. I had bought an old piano in Marseilles for the princely sum of $30 and it gave us all endless pleasure. The most frustrating part of that voyage, as far as I was concerned, was being becalmed close to Tristan da Cunha. I was an avid reader of the Sailing Directions and dreamt of going ashore there, picking wild fruit and exploring the island. I begged my husband to put out a boat to enable us to do this but, naturally, he wouldn't hear of it—the wind might come up at any time.

Souvenir was a slow ship and not particularly lucky in getting a fair wind and it took us 135 days to reach Port Adelaide by the usual route, down to the Roaring Forties, close up to the Kerguelin Islands, where we had a wonderful view of the penguins. Port Adelaide was my very first glimpse of Australia and I loved this country from the first moment. The people were so kind and hospitable, the climate beautiful and my one ambition was to settle here, which we eventually did in 1927.

From Adelaide we went to Melbourne and then to Newcastle, New South Wales, where we loaded coal for Iquique, Chile. There were several other sailing ships in Newcastle at the time, amongst them *Annie II*, which followed us all the way to Europe. In Newcastle, the piano was moved out on deck and a Musical Comedy Company, currently playing at one of the theatres there, came on board and did the whole show for us on the main deck. I had commandeered the galley in off peak hours, two days previously, and prepared sufficient food to feed this large company, plus all the officers and masters of the other ships in port.

The voyage from Newcastle to Iquique was a nightmare. With a heavy cargo of coal, the rolling of the ship was terrific, and everyone was bruised and exhausted by the time we reached our destination two months later. The main deck was awash most of the time and it was an endurance test for the steward to transport food from the galley to the officers' mess aft, hanging on to a wire with one hand and a basket of food in the other. It was the custom in Norwegian ships for the master to eat alone in his quarters. This we did, each of us with a child on one's knee, trying to balance a plate and spoon to feed them. Quite a gymnastic feat!

I enjoyed our long stay in Iquique in spite of the sand and the fleas and lack of vegetation. We met an English couple with two small children, whose nurse was quite happy to entertain our two at the same time, leaving us free to do as we wished. As in most of these out-of-the-way places, we made good friends and had an enjoyable stay. The trip to and from the ship in various small boats was always pleasant. The sea lions intrigued me, popping up everywhere and staring with those great big eyes. As sailing time drew near, I became a bit apprehensive about the dreaded trip around the Horn. The skippers in port made it worse by telling my husband he couldn't think of taking the children and me with him but should send us overland. Anyhow, we duly sailed and I began to read the Sailing Directions to find out what the inhabitants were like on that southern tip in case of shipwreck and survival. I gathered they were quite unfriendly and supposedly cannibals, so it was not very reassuring. My little bag was always packed, ready with warm clothes and tins of milk for the children. The main sport on the whole of the 139-day trip to Rotterdam was seeing who could catch the most fleas. Apparently, they had come on board in the nitrate bags and the ship was infested with them. All bedding and blankets were taken out on deck each day and the crew had competitions to see who was the best flea-catcher. All pretty ghastly! We were nearing the Channel when we got rid of the last of them.

I can't brag about icebergs, gales or terrific seas, round the Horn. In fact, we had perfect weather. However, it was another story the next day when we got gales and mountainous seas and there were all hands on deck right through the black night. Before one sail could be made fast, another one ripped. The whole ship shook and it was a miracle that the masts remained standing. My duty was to stand in the chart room, doling out tots of rum as the crew filed past in their dripping oilskins and sou' westers. I met a captain in Norway recently, who sailed with us as AB on that trip and he insisted I had rounded the Horn twice. He said that particular storm blew us right back around the Horn and we had to re-round it.

With a few exceptions, my memories of the trip after that are pleasant ones. Lazy days in the doldrums, sunbathing on the main deck, children playing, chickens clucking, our little lamb prancing around, the sail maker mending sails and the gentle creak of the rigging. My poor husband didn't find those days so peaceful, spending the days pacing back and forth, looking heavenward and praying for wind!

One of the sports the crew had, during those days of calm, was to catch sharks and it was always exciting when one of these monsters was hauled up on deck. I came home with shark's teeth, a shark's backbone and other souvenirs the crew presented me. Something I really appreciated was when they climbed out onto the bowsprit and harpooned porpoises or *springer*, as they call them. It was good red meat which to me in those days, was as good as the most luscious steak. I haven't mentioned food before. I don't even like to think of it. Weevils in the soup, maggots in the flour, that awful salt beef and pork, and the canned foods in those days had a horrible preservative taste. It is difficult to think of life without refrigeration, especially looking back on those long trips. Waterglass was the only preservative of eggs in those days and, of course, not practical at sea. However, I found I could keep eggs for two months by wrapping each one in newspaper and packing them close together. The hens on board weren't very productive, I'm afraid their diet wasn't right either! If I thought a hen was about to lay an egg, I hovered around, ready to get it for my babies, terrified that someone else would get in first. The children were remarkably well on their poor diet, except that they were too fat through too many carbohydrates. It was difficult to control when, as soon as my back was turned, the cook fed them with pancakes at all hours of the day. The crew poured endless cups of cocoa into them and the children, being little gutsers, consumed the lot.

An amusing but sad incident happened one night in the tropics. Our quarters were unbearably hot, so my husband rigged up a canvas awning or screen out on deck. We slept in hammocks and the children on mattresses on deck. Several nights I was awakened with a start but I thought it was the children who were restless. However, I became suspicious so my husband and I changed hammocks and that night I was awakened by a loud thud on the deck and the side of the awning caving in. Loud voices, as my husband called to the officer on watch to come as a witness. He had knocked a man down. It appears that a sex-starved member of the crew had been playing with the Captain's leg. When the 4 am watch was called, the boy was missing. A quick search of the ship was to no avail. My husband knew full well that if there were a man overboard, it would be hopeless to get back on the same tack and find him. However, he put it to the officers and crew, whether he should put about, and they decided against it. At daylight, the search of the ship continued and, thank goodness, the boy was found, hiding in the hold amongst the cargo. The incident provided both comedy and drama for the crew on a long, wearisome trip but I was sorry for the boy concerned, who would never live it down.

One of the excitements was when we had a heavy rainstorm. Everyone rushed out with tubs, buckets and every available receptacle to catch precious water and have a good bath and washing day. My usual daily ration was a small wooden tub in which I bathed the children first and then my husband and I had our daily ablutions, after which I proceeded to wash the clothes and usually had to rinse in salt water. I sometimes think of this when I stand under a lovely hot shower and then press the button on my automatic washing machine. As we neared the Channel and were on the last lap of our journey, I once again became a little nervous and apprehensive. We were bound for Queenstown for orders and when we were in the direct shipping routes, we got heavy fog. The lifeboats were swung out, my little bag packed and ready, while our poor little siren made its weak little wail, which couldn't be heard more than a few yards away. We received our orders at Queenstown to proceed to Rotterdam and there was no holding my husband. Homeward bound, with all sails set right up to the royals, we raced through the passage between Lands End and the Scilly Isles, passing *Annie II* and arriving at Rotterdam one week ahead of her.

Enid's son, Michael, followed a seafaring career himself, sailing in Pacific trading schooners and becoming an officer in the Royal Australian Navy during World War II. He then went on to command in the merchant service, as master in BHP iron ore bulk ships.

Captain Nick Brink of Sydney, New South Wales, was an ordinary seaman in the barque *Winterhude*, in the years 1933–35. A Danish boy who had spent some time in steamers, plying the North Sea, he decided to write to Gustaf Erikson requesting a position in one of his ships. He was offered a position as apprentice at a premium of 50 pounds sterling, but chose to go as ordinary seaman at a monthly wage of 10 shillings. This was much lower than he had been earning in steamers but he was prepared to put up with low wages in order to get sail experience. *Winterhude* was in Glasgow and young Nick travelled there by train from London. After four weeks they left for Port Germein, South Australia.

Winterhude, according to Nick, was a heavy ship, meaning heavy in the steering. She had a single wheel and exceptionally long yards for her length and breadth. It took three men at the wheel to hold her in heavy weather. As do most seamen of the grain fleet, Nick has fond memories of the Gulf ports:

In Port Victoria we worked every day except Sunday, although we would have to wash down the decks and tidy up before we could go ashore. It took several hundred buckets of water to wash down the decks, and this had to be sea water, hauled up by hand, even though we had pumps We would row ashore to the Wauraltee pub on the waterfront at the end of the main street, known by grain fleet sailors the world over. Our weekly wage of two shillings and sixpence bought us a packet of Players cigarettes for sixpence, and a bottle of wine for two shillings. We would go down on to the beach and consume the results of our week's work in several hours.

We were lucky in that we didn't have to shovel out solid ballast, as in many of the other ships in the fleet. We had water ballast tanks capable of taking 900 tons of sea water. They were known as deep tanks and they stood on the ship's bottom, just abaft the main mast, coming just level with the 'tween deck beams. We had a donkey boiler and pump in the forward deckhouse, and this was used to discharge ballast. I was down below on one occasion, chipping rust on the top of the tank, and my chipping hammer went right through a rusty part in the steel. The mate repaired it by driving a wooden peg into the hole, and up-ending a small tin can of cement over the peg. The top of the tank was covered with these repairs. This was the usual method of repairing rust holes in the hull. Aloft we had a different method. If a chipping hammer went through a steel yard, a 'bandage' of sail canvas was wrapped around the yard, liberally covered with paint. The Lloyds surveyors in the latter days of sail were not too keen to go aloft to inspect the rigging, and such repairs always escaped notice.

We never had any money, and a minimum of clothes. We made our own clothes, mainly trousers and shirts, out of old sail cloth. We pulled apart our oldest garments, and used them as patterns. We became quite expert at this form of 'tailoring'. It's funny the things you remember. The crew's toilets, as in all ships, were under the fo'c'sle head. There was always an opportunity to take a prolonged break, out of sight of the mates when one needed to use it. So the carpenter made a wooden trough or chute, which went out through a wash port in the ship's bulwark. For some reason we named this device 'Lisa', and we had to use it for urinating, thus saving several minutes of time that could be used for work.

On our second voyage out of Port Germein, we found a stowaway on board. He was a big hulky Australian, and only possessed the clothes he stood up in. We had little spare clothes we could give him, and he went around Cape Horn in midwinter, with no oilskins or warm clothes. We called him George, and the mates made him work normal watches. But he would never go aloft above the courses. He amused us by claiming in his Australian drawl, when referring to the futtock shrouds, 'Hell, I can't get around the fuckin' corner!' At the end of the voyage in Swansea, Wales, the Captain allowed visitors to inspect the ship, and most of the crew befriended the local girls. The girl that George had taken a liking to, asked if she could climb the rigging, and asked George to go with her. She went nimbly up the main shrouds and swarmed over the futtocks effortlessly. This was too much for George, and he made a superhuman effort and followed her to the masthead. After this George was expected to work aloft with the rest of the crew.

From Swansea we sailed on to Mariehamn, where *Winterhude* laid up for the summer. George the stowaway ended up in a Finnish gaol for a short time, and then was allowed to go back to sea. The trip to Mariehamn was the fastest I can remember the ship sailing. Strong fair winds all the way. It took five days. In Mariehamn, the mate, two other seamen, and I removed the royal and topgallant yards to reduce weight aloft before going onto the slip at Nystad. After this I joined a work gang going around the Erikson fleet, doing maintenance on *Herzogin Cecilie, Killoran* and others. I lived ashore in a boarding house.

There was a definite social distinction between apprentices and seamen in the Erikson ships. Apprentices paid a premium to go to sea, but were given the worst jobs in the ship such as cleaning out the toilets, pig pens and washing up, etc., but were considered a step above the rest of us. There was a club in Mariehamn called Society, where all the prominent citizens spent the evenings. Apprentices were allowed into the club but not seamen. Below the club was the police station. It was here I spent my first night ashore, after trying unsuccessfully to get into the club. It cost me a 10-shilling fine—a month's wages.

We went out again to Spencer Gulf to load wheat at Port Germein. I remember the four-masted barque *L'Avenir* was moored on the other side of the long jetty. She was a superb vessel, with generators for electric light, and accommodation for 80 passengers or cadets. She even had a piano and a dance floor. She was all white, including the masts and yards. One night her captain threw a party for the shore people of Port Germein. Five crewmen were stationed at her gangway to stop the *Winterhude*'s crew from getting on board. But they didn't dare stop us, as they knew we would get them in the town, the next time we were all ashore.

When departing from Port Germein our skipper, Uno Mörn, put on a show for the town. He had all the yards hoisted, and sail loosened and partly sheeted home, and on the blast of a whistle, the mooring lines were let go, and the ship sailed off without a tug, and on her way. Of course the wind was offshore and not too strong.

On the homeward run, I was on the jib boom taking in the outer jib, as conditions were freshening, when we saw a big four master charging along with all sail set, outward bound, we assumed to Spencer Gulf. That evening we thought we saw the same ship and wondered how we could pass the same ship twice. Actually the ships were *Padua* and *Priwall*, sisters or near sisters, who had left Hamburg together and were making a race of it. Their passage times were 63 and 64 days, which shows how these superb 'P' Liners could keep almost steamer timetables.

This long letter from Claude Beneke from Townsville is reproduced in its entirety, as it describes a grain ship voyage in great detail. He includes everyday incidents as well as descriptions of the working of the ship. Claude sailed in the four-masted barque *L'Avenir* in 1937 from Port Victoria towards Falmouth for orders. He relates:

I first met Captain Nils Erikson of *L'Avenir* at the Shipping Agents, Crosby Mann, in Adelaide mid February 1937. He was a huge man, running on the fat side and, I understand, was well over 20 stone [280 pounds]. I have heard since that he was an excellent seaman but he was rather grumpy looking and one could see he was not the type to be trifled with in any way. The *Moshulu* was in Port Adelaide at this time and I was told it would be a good idea to go and look her over and get an idea what these sailing ships looked like. When I went aboard I was really thunderstruck. She seemed enormous, especially the masts. I began to have my doubts how I would cope with climbing them and becoming familiar with the masses of ropes, etc., and I really did have some misgivings about the whole adventure. A ship's clothing place in the city selected the gear that they thought would be advisable to have on the voyage, so I left it to them and, after buying a metal cabin trunk, paid the bill, packed up and was ready for action. I got a ride to Port Victoria with a trucking company and within a few hours, one of the boats from *L'Avenir* collected me and my gear at the jetty and took me out to the ship. Of course, I was the subject of great curiosity by all members of the crew and felt like a freak.

I was told to share a cabin with a Belgian AB named Robert Remacles. This was under the fo'c'sle head on the starboard side. There was a kind of metal cupboard to put my gear in and, again, I was under many eyes as I packed the stuff away. I really did, at this stage, feel utterly miserable and lonely and wished I had never heard of the ship. All the faces looked different from the ones I was used to seeing and they were chatting away in their own tongue, and I began to wonder what I had let myself in for. Anyway, after a few days, things got better. Remacles could speak English, there was a Scottish apprentice named Williamson and some other Swedish Finns who also were capable of the language. There was a German apprentice named Bever. He became a good friend later on, after we had a couple of confrontations, more of a wrestling match like kids did at school, than a fight. The same thing happened between Remacles and myself after we had been at sea about six weeks.

These confrontations had nothing to do with our work but were more of a clash of personalities between foreigners. I found that the southern Finns were more of our type but those in the crew from the north were totally different in temperament and appearance. They mostly spoke in Finnish, which I could never get the hang of, whereas the southern lot always used Swedish and some of them couldn't speak Finnish, which I thought strange at the time. Incidentally, all the shipboard orders were given in Swedish, which was difficult for some weeks but after that became no problem. After I had been aboard about a week, after our day's work was over, another first voyager and I decided to climb to the main royal and stand on the footrope. I know when we got there and we were puffing a bit, the rope was shaking. I think we were both trembling with excitement. After that I always found it never seemed as high when the sails were set as when the mast was bare.

It was the morning of 4 March when the big adventure started. We set sail, along with the *Pommern*, with Macrae and myself pulling ropes here and there and being of very little use. Watches were set with me in the port watch under the 1st and 3rd mates and Macrae in the starboard watch under the 2nd mate. On the morning of 5 May, we were out of sight of land, which we did not see again for 93 days, that being Lands End in the United Kingdom. That night we also lost sight of the *Pommern* and it was to be 70 days before we would see another ship or boat of any kind. It was about this time I started to feel a bit strange. The next three days it was sheer hell. I couldn't keep a thing down and there was nothing available that may have settled the stomach. It was a case of eating the ship's fare or going without. It made no difference anyway, as my system threw out even a cup of water as soon as it went down.

There was no such thing as having a bit of a lie-down during the watch. We had six little pigs in a cage in the well deck, which were to grow up and later be eaten at various stages in the Atlantic. It was the apprentices' job to get in with these, shut the door and proceed to scoop up their mess into a bucket, get out again, throw it over the side, scoop up some sea water with the bucket attached to a rope, then back in with the piggies and scrub out with a scrubbing brush. The pigs would be squealing, I would be throwing up and the mate looking on would be highly amused. No doubt he had been through it all in his early days. The seasickness seemed to pass all at once and I soon began to feel really well.

Even though the weather had not been too bad, I was still clumsy in making my way about the ship. One of my first worthwhile jobs was down in the forepeak with a lantern, chipping rust and red leading. Our salt beef was stored there and one time I stood on one of the wooden kegs that apparently had been opened. The lid tilted and my leg went down into the smelly brine. It had an awful smell but, when cooked, although salty, was quite nice. We only had it about twice a week. Two dishes we all enjoyed were pea soup followed by a large pancake. These were really tasty. We each collected our ration of sugar each week, a cup full, which was not enough. We had plenty of bread, also margarine. Coarse salt instead of fine, no pepper, sauces or jams or cheese, although, in the tropics, we were given a ration of jam, also lime juice. We had potatoes for about two months. These were cooked in sea water with their jackets on. Water was rationed of course, but in the cold weather, we weren't concerned with washing and when we made the tropics, it was great fun, if the opportunity arose, to strip off in a tropical downpour and really have a scrub down.

One thing I recall is that no member of the crew showed any sexual tendencies and there was no great talk of sex or what could happen when arriving in port. I think we lost interest because we really used up plenty of energy in our work and we never seemed to have enough sleep. There was no quarrelling and no favouritism shown by the mates to crew members. The apprentices, naturally, obeyed the few able seamen aboard and took notice of the ordinary seaman. After all, we had a lot to learn and we certainly looked forward to becoming useful members of the crew.

By the end of the first week, we were 47°S, 143°W and after being at sea two weeks, crossed the International Date Line at 51°S. By this time, both Macrae and I had learned to steer and also had helped in taking in and furling the royals and topgallants, as well as staysails. We were both really starting to enjoy ourselves and felt great. All was so peaceful in a way. No radio, didn't need to have money in one's pocket and looking at the sea in all its fury plus the feeling that we were doing something worthwhile. We were, by this time, becoming used to plenty of water on deck, fierce sleet storms with snow at times and always the mountainous following seas. Our mileage, measured by the log line, was usually over the 200 every 24 hours and did get up to 275 before rounding the Horn. *L'Avenir* had a double wheel on a raised platform between the main and mizzen mast and was exposed to all the elements. It was really heavy work trying to keep on course with these huge following seas, as the ship would swing as the crest of the wave ran underneath and it was quite an effort to get near the course before the next wave came. One time, when I was at the helm with the 1st mate standing by, a huge wave came underneath and, before the ship responded to the rudder, some of the following wave broke on the starboard side, taking away a couple of sections of railing and followed on by smashing in the side of a small deckhouse situated on the long poop deck. I was not reprimanded, so was not at fault apparently, or I would have heard all about it. *L'Avenir* was fitted out to take quite a few passengers and had lots of obstacles on deck, which made it difficult to work the sails, particularly in the dark.

The pigs seemed to grow at an alarming rate and, of course, by this time were penned under the fo'c'sle head and proceeded to stink us out for the rest of the voyage. The last was killed and eaten just before reaching Falmouth. Most of the sea gear I bought in Adelaide proved useless. I had to cut the tops off the sea boots, as they were too clumsy in the rigging. My first and only experience with the oilskin trousers was one rainy night, about a week after sailing, I was sent up the main mast to cut something or other and found I could hardly bend my knees and to get over the crosstrees, it took a superhuman effort. After using my knife, I found that, in trying to get it back in the sheath, I cut the cord holding up my trousers. The mate was yelling at me, wanting to know what I was doing, so I threw the knife over the side, got down somehow, with the trousers hanging down, and never wore them again. A Finn gave me a knife with a round-top sheath and, as the knife had a rounded handle, which wedged into the sheath, I had no further trouble. As for the waterproof material, I just wore the oilskin jacket and sou'wester and didn't worry about legs getting wet, and further cut the sea boots down to galoshes as they already had holes in them from sliding down the backstays.

The weather was the same all the way to Cape Horn. We had a couple of albatrosses with us day and night and all got much pleasure out of their graceful movement in flight. We gradually moved on a more southerly course, sometimes having a double lookout at night for icebergs, which did not appear. We had long since dispensed with the kerosene navigation lights, probably to save kerosene but, of course, they were hardly needed down there. The last two days before reaching Cape Horn, we were at 56°S and on 5 April, we were at 57° and that was the big day. It was a nice day weatherwise. Very big swell, not much wind, icy cold but with lots of blue sky and good visibility. I always recall that the sea was a particularly blackish kind of blue that day. The mate sent me up to the royal to see if land was visible but it was the same view as other days. No doubt we were too far south. We all appreciated setting a more northerly course and, within a few days, the weather was much warmer and not the great rolling waves we had previously experienced.

About the middle of April, we had a violent storm, lasting over three days. The previous night it was beginning to really blow and I remember it quite well as Williamson and I were sent aloft to furl the fore topgallant. We were sailing as close to the wind as possible, it blowing from the port side. It was raining heavily and the ship was pitching more than I had ever experienced. I might add that on a previous occasion I was stowing the flying jib, when the jib boom went way under water. I was surprised at the force as my feet went up in the air and it took quite an effort to hang on with my hands. Many seamen in the past have lost their lives by being washed off jib booms. Getting back to the story. To make matters worse, one of the buntlines had fouled and the sail wasn't clewed up properly in this section. Both Williamson and I screamed down to the deck for the watch to take the appropriate action but couldn't make ourselves heard. We set to and made a fair job of it but poor Williamson became violently ill and couldn't make it off the footrope. I couldn't leave him so stayed alongside and waited. We seemed to be pitching so violently I felt as if my stomach would come out of my mouth. Of course, I had thoughts that the mast would separate from the ship. Eventually, Williamson made good and we regained the deck, being one and a half hours on that yardarm. The mate wondered why we were so long about the job. That was really my worst ordeal in the rigging. I had been up helping cut down blown-out sails in the colder latitudes, which seemed to me a rather risky job, as the remnants, always wet and heavy, seemed bent on trying to knock one off the footrope. I had been underwater in the well deck, hanging on with all my might, also swept off my feet and half drowned on other parts of the deck, but this time, in the rigging with Williamson, was certainly my night of nights on that voyage. The morning after this episode, the wind really came in from the port side and, before midday, all sails were taken in except lower topsails and the odd staysail. The ship was brought as close to the wind as possible. During that day, the rudder line snapped and there were a few anxious moments before the emergency wheel could be pinned. The clamps wouldn't hold the rudder and it was belting from side to side, making quite a racket. The Captain was there and he certainly showed his concern. The wheel was eventually connected up and all was well. Years later, I heard *Moshulu* was nearly lost this way with a parting of a rudder cable. We had three days of this storm, with a bit of a lull the second day and then the third day again in all its fury. The ship seemed to be lying with the lee rail underwater all the time and no work could be done on deck. The wind was so fierce that it would flare the nose and mouth and it was impossible to stand. Lifeboat covers went and the screaming through the rigging with most sails furled was really something to be heard, to be believed. One good thing, it wasn't freezing cold. I think we were about 37°S or somewhere near that latitude. After the storm, all was plain sailing until we reached the United Kingdom. The weather gradually warmed up and life became most pleasant.

We had a problem with bed bugs. As they were dormant during the colder weather, the steel framework of the beds was taken out and jarred onto the well decks, then kerosene torches were applied to any crevices, both in the beds and the fittings, and this reduced their number. They still caused some of us some trouble but, in time, we didn't seem to notice their bites as much. The days to follow were really great. Dolphins and bonitos were swimming just ahead of the cutwater and lots of flying fish came aboard. The pigs were gradually killed off and we managed a couple of meals from each. We had good South-East Trades and there was no work of any consequence to be done with bracing, etc. A big day, of course, was the changing of the heavy canvas to lighter sails. The steel stays in the rigging were all greased down, which was a pleasant job but a bit dirty. After leaving the trades, we had the usual bracing around to catch any breeze that rippled across an otherwise glassy sea. We spent five days at 8°S of the Equator with sometimes no steerageway. The Captain became very surly during this period of no wind but most of the crew had no worries. Had a good scrubdown during the tropical downpours, swam over the side, and caught a large shark, which the remaining pigs ate. The German apprentice made a walking stick from the backbone, going to considerable trouble.

It was about 10 May when I was up the rigging one morning when my eyes swept the horizon to see if there were any ships and well ahead, was the outline of some sails with no hull visible. This caused great excitement, as it was our first view of any ship since leaving Australia. Some of the more experienced sailors identified it as the *Pommern* as it didn't carry royals. We lost sight of it the next day and when seen again she was anchored off Falmouth having beaten us by a day. We crossed the Equator on 13 May and were glad the King Neptune initiations were not held. We did not have many problems in catching the North-East Trades and had rather an uneventful voyage to Falmouth. We had nearly a week of fog before sighting Lands End and also saw a few steamers, most of them altering course to get a closer look and some exchanging conversation with our captain through megaphones. During the fog, I had my first experience with pumping the hand-operated foghorn. This was operated both day and night from the fo'c'sle head and gave a blast similar to a steamer. I seem to recall that this instrument gave some signal. For instance, two blasts if we were on the port tack, three if starboard and one if sailing before the wind, but am not sure.

There was great excitement when Lands End was sighted. About this time the last of the pigs was killed. This, to me, always seemed to be a gruesome affair. The pig, while being held in an upright position, was bashed on the head with a large hammer. It was then stabbed in the heart and a dish was held near the wound and caught the blood pumping out. That evening, blood pancakes were served up. The Finns were very fond of this dish but I only tried them once. They tasted like fried blood and had the same appearance. It was said that the skipper ate too many of these the night before reaching Falmouth and was seen throwing up over the poop railing. Whether true or not, it provided quite a bit of amusement.

On reaching Falmouth, we went on day work and what a blessing it was to be able to sleep all night. During the voyage, we were always up and dressed, also counted, at midnight and 4 am. There were some crew members exempt. These were the carpenter, sail maker and donkey man. Also, in the tropics, some of the ABs went on day work for a few weeks. We lay at Falmouth, some distance from shore, for about three weeks. Even though we didn't get ashore, it was a very enjoyable time. The weather was good and lots of pleasure craft would be sailing around the ship, having a good look and I, for one, felt quite proud of myself for having rounded the Horn in sail. Fresh food was again available and, of course, with mail and newspapers, we soon caught up with current events again. After three weeks, Gronqvist, self, Macrae and, I think, John Sommarström, the sail maker, and a legend in Erikson's ships, were transferred to the *Archibald Russell* as we heard the German government had bought *L'Avenir*. We hardly had time to say goodbyes and felt rather sad about the whole thing.

L'Avenir was really a lovely ship, she was said to be the best of all ships at that time to sail hard into the wind without making leeway. The masts, I think, were only in two sections, all steel, as were the yards. As I said before, the deck was rather cluttered up with fittings and later on I found ships like the *Archibald Russell* with the long open deck were more convenient for working sails, etc. *Archibald Russell* had brace and halyard winches, whereas *L'Avenir* lacked this equipment. The wheel, being open and exposed to the elements on *L'Avenir*, left much to be desired. It was freezing cold in the high latitudes and, apart from copping the wind, rain and sleet, there was always a good measure of spray thrown in to make it more uncomfortable. The rigging seemed to be in good order but, of course, some things came adrift, mainly in heavy weather. One very cold morning, two topgallant halyards parted. I had loosened the gaskets on one and was standing clear, amid the backstays, ready to overhaul the buntlines after the sail was set, when I got the biggest fright of all. The yard was almost hoisted when the halyard parted near the deck and it came crashing down. The whole mast shook and rattled and I slithered down a backstay to the deck in a state of shock. Needless to say, I was promptly ordered aloft again. Macrae had the same experience on one of the other topgallants the same morning and, of course, he didn't enjoy the experience.

There was accommodation in *L'Avenir* for quite a number of passengers but I never got a look into any of the cabins and did have a job one morning polishing the small ballroom floor. This was a very nice area, complete with small grand piano. Electric light was also fitted throughout but the crew never had power. There was a diesel engine and generator set in a waterproof compartment in the well deck and, as this would be in operation at various times, no doubt some power was available for the Captain and mates. We had three passengers who, I understand, paid 10 shillings a day. There was a Miss Gwen Edwards, a Miss Marjorie McPhee, both from Adelaide, and a retired Scottish banker who had done a number of voyages as passenger.

Looking back, it was really a marvellous experience. There were, of course, unpleasant jobs for the foreign apprentices, apart from cleaning the pigs. I must add that the young Finns also shared these jobs. One I didn't like was bringing the food from the galley and washing up. This came up about one week in three and a lot of it was done in one's free time. Another was carting the coal to the galley. The coal was kept in an airless type of locker and it wasn't the work involved but because we ended up like Negroes and it was so hard to get reasonably clean.

The apprentices and young Finns did all the high work in the rigging, like taking in royals and topgallants and of course, overhauling buntlines, undoing gaskets and recoiling them on all yards when sail was being set. We didn't mind this because the older hands had been through it all. I don't think there was any great danger in the rigging, as long as nothing came adrift. One had to be careful furling sail as it had a tendency to blow back into one's face but, then again, there seemed to be a good balance on the yardarm with the soles of the feet set firmly on the footrope. Of course, on the lower yards, when more blokes were furling, the height of this rope constantly changed. That old saying of 'one hand for the ship and one for self' wouldn't work on these ships. It would be as well to stay at home.

Finally, I would say she was a happy ship. There were no accidents or sickness on the voyage, no fights and hardly any arguments, no backchatting superiors and, most of the time, we felt so fit and well. Had a tot of grog about twice during the trip and that was usually after all hands were involved with the sails in bad weather. Cigarettes were available once a week and were deducted from our pay. We played a lot of cards but money was never used. One other thing I was always curious about was the fact that, in the southern latitudes, some sail was taken in after dark and set next morning. I must add that I never noticed anyone in the rigging without footwear. Some of us were playing around one Sunday in the tropics and were timing who could reach the royal in the quickest time. I tried it with bare feet and had tender feet for some days. Maybe if a ship were in tropical areas for a long period and one was used to being barefooted and the soles became hardened, footwear wouldn't be necessary.

After I left *L'Avenir*, the Germans renamed her *Admiral Karpfanger* and, in 1938, she was lost somewhere in the Southern Ocean with all hands. Bever, my friend, was a crew member and his father sent me a snapshot of him, early in 1939. They lived at Kolberg on the Baltic Coast. Bever looked very smart in his cadet uniform with *Admiral Karpfanger* on his sailor's cap.

The latter days of the square rigger, particularly those in the Erikson fleet, saw quite a few women make voyages in them as passengers. Doubtless the romance of sail had its effect, as it did with many of the men and boys who made up their crews. After the immigrant clippers of the nineteenth century disappeared, passengers usually travelled by steamship. The odd sailing ship master might have his wife with him but it was discouraged by most shipowners. Erikson was happy to take a few passengers in his ships—it might have made the difference between a voyage making a profit or not.

Some of these passengers were women, and I have been fortunate enough to meet up with some of them. Their stories highlight aspects of sailing ship life that are often ignored by male writers. Interesting comments come from Kay Bunnett of Melbourne, who as a 12-year-old girl in 1936 travelled to Falmouth from Spencer Gulf with her parents in the four-masted barque *L'Avenir*. Her words are important in that she has recorded impressions that were often seen but overlooked by those who travelled the leisurely and lonely route of the grain ship. She spoke of:

The enthrallment of watching dolphins at play, as they followed the ship, the Portuguese men-o-war with sail hoisted to windward, whales spouting, flying fish, and the never-to-be-forgotten sight of a ship in full sail by moonlight, phosphorus glowing like giant torches beneath the dark ocean, sprinkling the tossed sea with silver magic. An iceberg at sunrise only 15 miles away reflecting every colour imaginable.

Perhaps the best-known of the women who sailed in the square riggers is Pamela Bourne, who first voyaged in the four-masted barque *Herzogin Cecilie* in 1934 as a passenger and later became the wife of the master, Sven Eriksson (no relation of Gustaf Erikson). She continued to voyage with him until *Herzogin Cecilie* went aground in 1936. In my early readings of sailing ship literature I saw reference to this woman, read with great interest her books, and in 1946, when it was not known if the Erikson ships would set off once again for Spencer Gulf, I read an article she wrote for the *Sydney Morning Herald*, titled 'News of Åland's Tall Ships'. In it she wrote of *Pommern*, *Viking* and *Passat* still laid up in Mariehamn, queried if *Archibald Russell*, *Moshulu* and *Lawhill* would still sail again under the flag of Gustaf Erikson, and lamented the fate of *Killoran* and *Olivebank*, early casualties in the war. I met Pamela Eriksson in 1979 at the Cape Horners Congress in Adelaide and it was immediately apparent that she was quite different from other 70-year-old ladies of my acquaintance. At the banquet, ageing grain ship sailors lined up to dance with her. One perspiring captain said to me after dancing with her, 'You know, I have always loved that woman and I haven't seen her since my time in the *Duchess*.'

Inevitably, Pamela has now passed on but one of her books, *The Duchess*, describing her time in *Herzogin Cecilie*, lives on as an important chronicle of the last days of sail. 'Duchess' is the English translation of the German *Herzogin*.

Around the same time, 1934, another adventure-seeking young lady, Mary Lang, was writing down her impressions of life under sail in a diary from which she kindly gave me permission to quote. Growing up on a grazing property near Cooma, New South Wales, Mary possessed quite a literary talent. At the same time some of the publicity given to the grain ship voyages must have reached up into these southern foothills. Whatever the influence, this young lady made two voyages in sailing ships, one from Australia around Cape Horn in 1934, the other returning her to Australia in 1936. She wrote two books of poems. In them are some of the best elegies to the square-rigged sailing ship I have read, in which Mary reveals a deep love of the sea, its ways and its white-winged ships.

Thumbing through the first pages of the diary she kept when she sailed in *L'Avenir* in 1934, I see a comment that could have been written to describe this book and the paintings it contains: 'This voyage will be something for me to talk about when I am old, when the deep-sea sailing ship will only be something that lives in the pictures and writings of her worshippers, but no longer on the lonely ocean roads.'

Further into her diary she writes an excellent description of one of the most important jobs in a windjammer—sail making—and describes the crew members through the eyes of a young woman. The sail maker referred to was the legendary John Sommarström, whose name has been repeated many times over by my informants. He made his last voyage in sail in *Passat* in 1949.

In the afternoon I went to visit the sail maker who is the oldest man on board, and here there is no need for Esperanto, his English is so perfect. He works nine hours out of the twenty-four and of course takes no watches. He sits in a big empty hatchway amidships which must be rather dark on cloudy days. At the moment he is making an upper topgallant sail, and the whole of the deck is covered with humps of stiff canvas. 'That is half of it,' he tells me.

An upper topgallant takes about a month to make and is of number one canvas—very strong. The royal, the highest of sails, takes about two weeks, and number two canvas is used which is lighter. A lower topsail (bigger than a tennis court) is made of 00 canvas, its surface nearly as stiff as a board. The canvas comes in big rolls, 2 feet [600 mm] in width. The sails are all designed and drawn on paper at a scale of one inch to the foot. For neatness and exactness, they rival any architect's plans. Then the cloths are sewn together by hand, to the required design, with tarred twine and large three-cornered needles. The sail maker must sew many miles every year. In two years he has made twenty six sails.

Perhaps it is appropriate to relate the comment on the stiffness of sails to the task of taking them in, in storm conditions, in high latitudes. Rain and spray sodden sails become at least twice as heavy, and when frozen present a task that cannot be comprehended by anyone who has never been called upon to take one in. A wet mainsail can weigh over a tonne; the gossamer-like sails of a modern racing yacht offer no comparison. The bitter cold of these high latitudes which froze sodden sails and caused them to become board-like also created razor-sharp ice splinters that cut into the flesh as the seaman endeavoured to dig his fingers into a ballooning sail as it tried to knock him off the yard.

Mary continues:

Some days ago I had the idea of collecting the signatures of everyone on board on an old hat of mine, a hoary warrior, several years old. I brought it along to the sail room today in the expectation of some of the boys wandering in. Being a Saturday afternoon, many of the crew were wandering about having finished their work for the weekend and were filling the few minutes that remained until coffee time. They came in groups of twos and threes and on being asked to sign did so, with alacrity or protest, according to their nature. First came Aho, quiet and capable, always smiling, and rarely speaking. He wants to be a pilot. Then the young Finnish marquis, handsome, with blue-black hair, clean-cut features, and black melancholy eyes, strolled in with 'Big' Johnsson, one of the most promising of the apprentices, a tall blond boy of eighteen with kind blue eyes and a very gentle face. Then there was a great clattering down the stairs, and with a general clanging, banging, slithering, leaping and sliding, little Danish Harry burst in, making the maximum possible noise. He has perhaps the most winning personality of all the boys, little, lithe and quick, he is always cheerful and has a most enchanting smile. He is nineteen but looks younger, and will soon be an AB. I have never seen anyone with such a variety of garments, a different coloured pullover every day in the week, blue dungarees, patched with every conceivable coloured material; khaki trousers, black clerical pants that surely came out of the Ark. For headgear he wears either a tiny black beret perched right on the back of his tousled flaxen mop, or else an old Bill Sykes cap, pulled right over his ears, and hiding his twinkling eyes. When confronted with the hat he said he had six names, and should he put them all, please? Then a group of three sauntered in, 'black and white', a Belgian and the youngest on board having had his sixteenth birthday on the day we sailed. Albert, also Belgian, and the ship's joker. His round comical face under a thatch of very curly mouse-coloured hair. He always wears an expression of aggrieved resignation. He speaks six languages and I am told is a wit in all six. With the two Belgians, shambling after them comes an odd figure, the only English boy on board. Tall and strong, he has a too large head with a real shock of coarse hair, eyes almost invisible behind thick horn-rimmed glasses, his clothes are nothing but rags and tatters, showing great patches of skin on the iciest days. He has foul weather clothes, but not gibes, persuasions, not even orders will make him put them on. He wears always on his feet a pair of split canvas tennis shoes and no socks. He must have the constitution of an ox.

Later came in the oldest of the boys, Jorgensen, the Danish doctor. He is a fully qualified doctor, and was inspecting my fingers the other day. Then when it was only a few minutes till coffee, the white-haired boy of *L'Avenir*, Otto, whom everybody adores, came in. Only four boys are ABs and he is one of them and he is one of the best looking boys I have ever seen, certainly he shares with the tall willowy young apprentice Hjelt, the distinction of being the handsomest amongst twenty-five good looking boys.

Able Bodied Seaman

High perched aloft, he sews a damaged sail
A patch of weakness that the west wind knew;
It was the sport of last night's sudden gale,
But Otto's fingers strengthen it anew.

His gleaming arms are copper in the sun,
His crinkled curls are copper shavings, and
About his young lips, secret laughter's run
Though set face bends to watch his toiling hand.

His strong arm lifts in a symphonic sweep;
He moves like flowing music, but his eyes
Are still and calm as the blue-vaulted, deep,
Forever unperturbed Pacific skies.

Mary Lang

The sailing ship that returned Mary Lang to Spencer Gulf was the four-masted barque *Parma*. In the thirties there were few windjammers not owned and operated by Gustaf Erikson, especially one of the calibre of *Parma*. However, the syndicate that purchased her from Laeisz in 1931 included Erikson as a lesser shareholder. The other shareholders were Ruben de Cloux, a highly experienced and respected Erikson master, John Wennstrom, Isidor Eriksson, Alan Villiers and Algot Johansson. She was built as the *Arrow* in 1902 by A. Rodger & Co. of Port Glasgow and operated by the Anglo American Oil Company until 1911, when bought by Laeisz and renamed *Parma*. In 1919 she passed to Britain as war reparations. She was in Iquique at that time and was sailed back to Delfzijl in Holland. Britain had no use for her and Laeisz bought her back in November 1921 for 10,000 pounds. The syndicate that bought her from Laeisz in 1931 registered her in Mariehamn and she survived until 1936. Villiers talks of her making good money but her final voyage was made on a shoestring. A collision in 1936 caused damage that was too costly to repair and she was towed to Israel as a hulk where she was broken up. *Parma* holds the record of 83 days for a voyage from Port Victoria to Falmouth in 1933 under the legendary Ruben de Cloux. The final round voyage she made was to Spencer Gulf, returning to Falmouth in 1936.

Karl Karlsson was the skipper and *Parma* gave him some anxious moments, as well as several weeks of frustration, when she was ready to leave Barry roads, Wales. It was almost as if the old ship knew her end was near and contrived to prolong the commencement of this last voyage. The frustrations encountered in windjammers were usually associated with lack of wind, but in this case *Parma* was prevented from leaving port because of strong head winds. With both anchors out and dragging she was in imminent danger of running aground. The incident is described in this extract from Mary Lang's diary.

Day after day, night after night, *Parma* has ridden out these south-west gales with 130 fathoms of chain cable out on the starboard anchor, and 140 fathoms out on the port anchor, and dragging them savagely sometimes. We can't help thinking of the other Åland ships, battling around the north of Scotland in this weather, and we pray they'll be all right. Strangely, I haven't been at all bored. The Captain's sharp whimsical sense of humour has been a tremendous help, and now that these eight idle days are over, they have left only a confused memory of a great deal of laughter; even at the succession of south-westerlies, the mucky water, the sickening Breaksea Lightship, and the dirty tramp steamers that pass us so often.

The Captain has a 'girl friend'. There is a stove in the saloon, a creature infinitely capricious, which we have dubbed Herzogin Geraldine-Jemima, plain Gertie for short. Only the Captain understands her complex mentality, only he can wheedle her into staying alight, cajole her when she smokes crossly and blackly all over the saloon, soothe her when her funnel rattles in the south-westerlies. It has been much warmer, the last few days so we have let sleeping Gertie lie and have been warned on no account to rouse her when the spanker is set as it usually is when we are at sea. I wonder what state of shivering, we, her lackeys, will be driven to before the end of the voyage. We have all turned out our wardrobes, surveyed them and paraded them. The Captain has put my fur in his camphorwood chest, hung a brown skirt and velvet dress in his own wardrobe, and presented me with a pair of white trousers which he bought in New York in 1920. He has been glowing reminiscently ever since. He says the food is too good to last. We have had a really good selection of dishes at every meal so far, but his attitude is 'eat before the food gives out'. So we do eat.

In between the eating I have been in the 'tween decks with the boys, chipping rust, making chafing gear and discovering the crew. At first the boys were to me merely a confused jumble of black berets, blank faces, black trousers, strong arms, and hard stares, but various figures are beginning to stand out. There are 28 souls on board altogether, Captain, two passengers, three mates, cook, steward, and the crew. The steward has slanting, tawny eyes and has only been married five weeks; he used to be in the *Olivebank*. The cook is very fair, wears a white yachting cap, and plays the violin rather well in the evenings. There is an Estonian who has been in the Iceland herring fishing fleet and looks like someone from a Wild West film. Sometimes I catch sight of a handsome, willowy boy, with black almond eyes and a slow smile, but so far I have not been able to discover his name, nationality or status aboard. There are three tall Germans, one very lugubrious, a middle-aged bright-eyed carpenter, one very tall, brawny AB from Åland, with a kind face, a university student with a flaxen beard, Barker, a young English public school boy with extraordinary ideas of his own about most things. There are seven slanty-eyed Finns, one of whom looks like a baby Eskimo, and there is a passenger, Mr Potts, who goes very gingerly aloft. The first mate is very large, kindly and fair, and looks like an old baby. The second mate is very blond and wears a perpetually sarcastic curly smile, and has a slow walk. The third mate remains to me merely a voice. For the last four nights, I have had several minutes conversation with him before going to bed, for he is night watchman, but to my knowledge I have not seen him yet, and to me he remains merely a short, broad, dimly glimpsed figure and a shy voice. Probably before long I shall have sorted out the problem of names, nationalities, etc. and make a point of asking the Captain the name of every boy who comes to the saloon door for tobacco.

This morning the wind was found to be south by east. We prepared for sailing. The anchors were found to be fouled to the extent of there being 40 feet of the starboard chain entangled in the port anchor, so there was nothing to be done except keep steam in the donkey [engine] who is as capricious as Gertie, the stove, and not half as lovable, and spend a wild hour or so at midday, hauling on the signal, halyards and screwing one's eyes into a telescope focused on the Barry Signal station. We swore at them for not answering us at once, for we were asking them to order a tug from Avonmouth, where *Parma*'s owners have a contract. And they signalled that a tug is to be here at midnight, finally; a curious hour to send a tug, and we shall have wasted 16 hours of fair wind. However, we are in hopes of having all sail set by 8 am and leaving the filthy Barry Roads behind us forever. As the tug will be in here in two hours we are going to get a little sleep.

Sunday, November 3, 1935 The chapter and verse of today's misfortunes, are going to make gloomy writing. We are a very chastened trio at this moment. Even the lamp over the table has lost its accustomed sparkle or rather, glow. The Captain is sitting at the head of the table with his head in his hands and great lines under his eyes, for he was up at one this morning and has been on deck ever since, mostly in the rain and wind on the fo'c'sle head, and only coming below to gulp a couple of cold meals congealing in the dish, long after Mark and I had finished them. And the faithful Spot leans his head against his master's knees and is dejected too. It is all so dreary. We each had a glass of port a few minutes ago, to celebrate the rock bottom of disaster, but it has made us more instead of less gloomy.

To begin at the beginning; the tug arrived at a quarter past one, and as it was no use attempting to raise the anchors and chains until dawn came, the Captain told the tug to return at 6 am. This it did, and I got out of bed and went up on the fo'c'sle head. Steam was raised and they started heaving the port chain. The turns were stubborn but several came out, and we all began to feel more hopeful, but we feared what might be below the muddy water. By midday, we realised that we were in the devil of a fix. Thirty-five fathoms [210 feet] of the starboard chain were wound tightly, devilishly, and inextricably around the port anchor. Then the winch in the donkey room broke—a mere matter of fifty or sixty pounds to get repaired, but annoying enough on top of everything else. Then the port anchor chain broke off like a piece of string. By 1pm the tide had turned, and the feeble tug was hanging uselessly on our starboard bow. We gathered sternway, the tug could not hold us, and slowly, steadily we were drifting ashore. There was no hope of getting a rag of sail on her for she had her head to the wind, and before anything could be done, we would be on the rocks. The Captain came quickly aft. 'Get out B,' he shouted to Mark and me, 'we must get another tug, or we'll be on the rocks sure as death.' I fumbled in the signal locker, found B and Mark hoisted it. We watched anxiously through the glasses, and the Captain through a telescope. We could see the tug waiting in the dock basin, but she hoisted no signals. 'He's in church—singing hymns,' snorted the Mate.

The Captain never shifted his eyes from the tug, he was very still, but I heard him muttering stonily under his breath, 'She'll break her back, she'll break her back.' The minutes seemed very long, and no sign from the waiting tug. Then, with our stern close to the rocks, our own tug apparently opened out full throttle, and after a moment or two we could see that our sternway was checked. Then after a long time, it seemed we slowly began to gather headway. We took down our signal, and I found some relief in folding the flag up with extraordinary concentration. It had been a close thing. The afternoon dragged on wretchedly, worriedly, for our position was far from safe. It is extraordinary the way in which both Mark and I have identified our selves with *Parma* and her captain. The latter has a terrific load of responsibility on him, and whatever happens, he is sure to be blamed by the owners. Had we anticipated anything like this, we would have stayed in dock until the fair wind came, or taken a tug to Lundy Island. However, we chose, as we thought the cheapest course, to lie in the Roads until fair wind, and so save dock dues and tug expenses. How was anyone to know that where the Barry pilot said was good anchor bottom, was simply rock? How were we to know that our anchors could foul themselves to such an extent? The crew worked all day, their Sunday too, and now the results of their work are at the bottom of the sea.

At about 4 pm the tug skipper produced his megaphone and shouted something. It was hard to hear what he said, and we made him repeat it over and over again. At length the message became all too clear. We were to anchor again, as he had not enough coal to carry on. By this time, we had drifted halfway across the Bristol Channel, and with much cursing of everything in general, we had to drop both anchors again; and here we are, our fouled anchors down again, our day's work wasted, the anchor bottom an unknown quantity, the tug gone, a squall approaching, a heavy tide ebbing, and worst of all, the fair south-easterly still blowing, a wind which were it not for our fouled anchors, would soon take us clear of Europe. Heaven only knows how long it will be before we get another south-easterly, or any sort of fair wind.

As it is, there is nothing to do, except cut loose the anchors and buoy them and limp back tomorrow into Barry, which we thought we had left forever and ever, get the winch repaired, get two new anchors, get a tug to Lundy Island, all of which will cost about 400 pounds. And the shame of coming back to Barry again to be met by those grinning Welshmen, no doubt each of who will ask us why we have returned. The Captain says he will tell them he has come back for his broken wire cable. And to think of this beautiful wind blowing east-south-easterly now. We are all so gloomy that I think there is nothing more to be said or done, so we are going to bed, in the hope that things will look a little brighter in the morning.

This description of *Parma*'s problems with headwinds, fouled anchors and tugs running out of fuel is quite significant. It illustrates the utter helplessness of a sailing ship, commented upon early in this book. These types of mishap were not uncommon although to have them all happen at the same time was extremely bad luck.

One of the most excitement-causing events during a long windjammer voyage was the sighting of another ship. The Australian grain ships found themselves in a trade that took them to some of the loneliest areas of the world's oceans. Much of the long haul from the South Atlantic to the Australian grain ports and thence on towards Cape Horn was outside the normal shipping routes. Even in the South Atlantic their course took them off the beaten track. The sighting of a steamer gave the sailing ship master a chance to check his position and his chronometers and to request that the sighting be reported by radio to the owners. But the sighting of one of their own kind caused the most excitement, particularly on the homeward run. Sailing for Europe via the Cape of Good Hope, as some did, did not disqualify a ship from the so-called 'Grain Races' as there were no rules and no judges—passage time was the only yardstick, and the results only of interest to the participants. The spirit of the race prevailed even though the contestants were usually ill matched.

Further into her diary Mary Lang describes one such meeting on this outward voyage of *Parma* to Australia. Her position—halfway between South America and the African mainland, just north of the Equator.

Thursday 12 December 1935 21 days out, 2° 22' N, 20° 35' W. Such a tremendous excitement arrived last night—something so thrill making that I can hardly write coherently about it even now. We have been for several days on the starboard tack, and last night, just before eight bells, the watch put the ship about. The noise of shouting and running feet awakened me, and as I was lying drowsily on the settee, I saw the Captain cross the saloon in pyjamas and go up on deck. A few minutes later, I did the same thing. Emerging on the poop, I found everybody—or some people, craned over the starboard rail and watching a flashing light about three miles on our starboard bow. 'What is it?' I murmured sleepily, trying to push to a place in front. 'I think she's the *Lawhill*,' answered the Captain, making room for me. 'A sailing ship,' I screamed, and then was quite dumb, as I scanned the tall shadow that showed her to be a four-masted barque. We morsed a little: 'How many days?' 'Twenty-one.' 'Good race,' we replied. At the moment there didn't seem anything more to be said.

We had been on opposite tacks, and so had come together quite swiftly and not seen each other until we were quite close. After she had given us the information that she had seen *Killoran*, *Lawhill* said 'good night' to us and we went below again and turned in, expecting to see her again in the morning. Sure enough when the sun rose it showed her astern, for we had passed her to windward and we were very close together. After breakfast we were little more than three-quarters of a mile apart, and could see quite clearly without glasses, her captain and mate dressed all in white, standing at the break of the poop. Each of us ran up flags in salutation. The Boss wanted to add an old and horrid pair of trousers to the halyards to let them know they were beaten, but he thought better of it. We were sailing closer to the wind than she, and she went away to leeward. Papa, who was the mate in *Lawhill's* last voyage, says that while in a good stiff breeze, both ships sail equally well, *Parma* can undoubtedly sail closer to the wind than *Lawhill*.

When it got dark we began morsing again, *Lawhill* being about three miles abeam to leeward. She gave us the information that she is bound for Wallaroo, which if correct, means that she is already chartered and has received her orders, but as she sailed from Copenhagen 33 days ago, we can hardly credit the truth of this, and the Boss believes it to be only a leg pull. In fact he actually morsed back 'Baloney'!

Friday 13 December, 22nd day 0° 01' S, 22° 35' W, 160 miles run. At last, in spite of it being Friday the thirteenth or perhaps because of it, we have picked up South-East Trades, and our noon position showed us to be one minute south of the line. There is an extraordinary large swell today, coming down from the north-west. The Captain says they must be having a terrible Christmas gale up in the Western Ocean, for us to feel the swell right down here. It seems funny to think that these same waves were possibly giving trans-Atlantic liners a fierce buffeting yesterday; it is so sunny and peaceful here. Truly, the sea is a strange person.

That witch *Lawhill* is beating us! Early this morning, she was a long way off on the horizon to leeward, but later, she began to eat her way steadily into the wind and now she is almost dead ahead. Needless to say we are all furious.

I've had a very lazy day, but very enjoyable of course. In the afternoon after playing a little ping-pong, the Boss went out on the decks to see about cutting a new lower topsail. He, Papa Anderson and I (as offsider, wielding a blue chalk and rolling canvas and feeling important) spent the afternoon at work. I got an idea of the price of canvas and a suit of sails for a four-masted barque. Six bolts of canvas are needed for a lower topsail; there are about 44 yards [40 metres] in each bolt, and the price is two shillings and four pence per yard. I believe there are twelve bolts in a mainsail.

After knocking off time I was talking to Potts for a long time, mostly about photography and globetrotting, and then when it grew dusk I went up on the fo'c'sle head to have a look at the *Lawhill*, now a dim column of white, far ahead. I only hope we can catch her up again.

It should be evident that such a ship as *Parma* could cast a powerful spell over those who sailed in them. This was particularly so in the thirties when those who joined the sailing ship did so, not only for the job, or the passage to the other side of the Earth, but because of an indefinable emotion that was stirred by the sight of masts, yards and sails. As Mary told me of her adventures in this ship, I often suspected that it was not only *Parma* that had captured her affections. This young girl could not help being smitten by the handsome Carl Karlsson, master of the ship, but perhaps he was quite oblivious to it. Mary's poetic ability, already well developed prior to this voyage, allowed her to write these beautiful lines.

Parma

The music of her movement on the waters
Will echo in my soul until I die;
And was there ever one, of all the daughters
Of man, so beautiful as she—
The best loved of the sea?

The mermaids dived for jealousy
When she passed by, —dived deep as whales,
And, cold-eyed in green water caves,
They watched her shadow slide above the waves,
Darkening for an instant all their home.
When the Trade Wind filled her sails,
Second by second, a flower of foam
Blossomed anew around her bows.

Where the eternal Wester raves
In the Lonely South, she raced the waves
Swift as Atlanta, 'till the Sea
Lusted to claim her for his own.
He thrashed her decks, he tore her clothes,
He stole a sailor, but alone
He could not win her; he called the wind—
Told him to burst his lungs with blowing.
They left her naked. The sea was flowing
White on her decks; she was almost his bride,

But she jilted him—fled away in pride,
Of new canvas bent by her fighting crew,
She fled from the South, and a kinder wind blew
So that foam flowers bloomed at her bows again.

I have seen the sun burst through the mist
To watch her pass. The stars have kissed
Her mastheads on still, Tropic nights.
And I have seen how she has lain—
Like a bird asleep—daylong becalmed,
No longer cleaving the water, she,
The water crept by her tenderly,
And slowly as Eternity.

Along the waterfronts of towns,
I have seen old men gaze long at her
Till their eyes grew dim with memory
And I know their old hearts longed to be
Out on the elemental sea
With such another ship as she
To sail and love.

I have heard the Symphonies of man.
I have heard the Nightingales
And listened to them 'till night pales.
I have heard the long, harmonious roar
Of Pacific surf on a sandy shore,
I have heard the rivers run.

I have heard the melodies of the birds
And the Symphonies of man,
And I have heard the nightingales …
But the music of her movement on the waters
Will echo in my soul until I die.

Mary Lang
S/V *Parma*, Port Broughton, 1936

In the winter of 1986 I visited Mariehamn and walked about the decks of the four-masted barque *Pommern*, the last true example of a working windjammer left. She was built in Glasgow in 1903 as the *Mneme* by J. Reid & Co. for B. Wencke & Sohne of Hamburg. In 1905 she was sold to another Hamburg shipowner, Reederei A-G von 1896, but one year later came under the ownership of F. Laeisz and renamed *Pommern*. Laeisz ran her in the nitrate trade until World War I when she was interned at Valparaiso. After the war she was handed to Greece as reparations but was never used. In 1923 Gustaf Erikson bought her, and she sailed under his flag until 1939 when she was laid up because of the outbreak of World War II. She never made another commercial voyage.

As I walked around her decks, dodging lumps of snow falling from her yards, I tried to recall the stories I had been told by some who sailed in her—Alex Hurst, well-known author and publisher, Captain Don Munro from New Zealand and, only that day, Bengt Söderlund of Mariehamn. Mrs Iveson Bell of South Australia also gave me her impressions of life in this ship, as a passenger:

> Our voyage started on 24 March 1938 from Port Germein, after waiting at the anchorage for a suitable breeze to take us down the Gulf. My husband, the Rev. Albert Bell had always wanted to make a voyage in a windjammer and he inquired through the Erikson agent in Adelaide, Crosby Mann & Co. Some of the grain ship skippers would not take women, but Captain Karl Broman of *Pommern* agreed to take us, although I can't remember the actual fare. Payment was made at the end of the journey, as it was not known how many days it would take. It took 117 days. Everything possible was done to make us happy and comfortable. When we got down into the southern latitudes and the weather was getting colder, the stove was lit in the saloon, which made our cabin quite cosy. The food was good and plenty of it. Six pigs were carried for fresh meat, the first being killed for Easter. On this occasion Captain Broman dressed in his full uniform, which was appreciated by us.
>
> A friend had placed a mailbag on board for us containing 120 letters and small gifts from our friends. Each day my husband took out a letter or present, which made us feel as if we were not so far away from home. Someone had put Easter eggs in for us and we gave them to the Captain for his small son back in Finland.
>
> We had hail, rain and snow for Anzac Day and by 1 May the weather was very bad with big seas. There was plenty of water on deck, rushing in where it was not wanted, but our cabin under the poop remained dry throughout the journey. The doors leading from the deck were kept closed at all times, and the steward had to go up to the poop deck and down through the charthouse with all the meals. We spent many hours on the poop, watching the tremendous waves crash on board. Many times the men working on the main deck would disappear as the waves washed over. One Sunday a large wave hit the ship and I was thrown out of our cabin onto the saloon table. There was no real damage except I had to spend the next three days in my bunk. We reached Cape Horn 32 days out but could not see it due to bad visibility. Once around we were becalmed and in the iceberg region, although we did not sight any. The glass [barometer] had fallen lower than Captain Broman had ever seen, but no storm eventuated. The Captain told me that records show that a period each hundred days will be calm. We had more storms after this calm and heard the three whistles for 'all hands on deck' on more than one occasion. The Captain told me that some men had nearly been washed overboard, but all that went were two of the pigs [as noted earlier in Bengt Söderlund's account of this trip].
>
> Eventually we reached the South-East Trades and enjoyed the glorious weather. There was much to see, the sea seemed full of life and there were birds overhead most of the time. On 17 June we crossed the 'Line' but did not reach the Doldrums until 5° North. The 24th of June was midsummer holiday in Finland and so we had a sports day with all sorts of articles being brought forth so there were enough prizes for everyone. I did not have much to do with the crew, apart from the Captain and officers, as there was only one, a South African boy who could speak English. After the North-East Trades we had poor winds and we made very slow progress. The Captain was getting concerned that we

In Soundings

The term 'soundings' refers to the comparatively shallow waters above the continental shelf surrounding a continental land mass. The four-masted barquentine *Mozart* drifts along at the mouth of the English Channel with a fog just lifting and a tug ranging up to see if she would like to take a tow. *Mozart*, and her little written about sister, *Beethoven*, were built in 1904 at Port Glasgow by the Grangemouth Dockyard Co. for A. C. de Freitas of Hamburg. She was sold to another Hamburg firm, Schulter & Maack, in 1911. Hugo Lundqvist of Mariehamn bought her in 1922 and until she was broken up in 1935 she sailed mainly in the Australian grain trade.

Mozart was the only barquentine in the grain fleet. Barquentines were generally favoured for short hauls and coastal trading as they were easier to tack and required a smaller crew. Georg Kåhre, author of *The Last Tall Ships* (his brother Karl, one-time director of Ålands Maritime Museum, sailed in *Mozart*), states that for her size *Mozart* should have had five masts. This would have made her tall gaff-rigged sails narrower and more manageable. The heavy gaffs and their sails tended to cause much wear on rigging, and running before the wind she was hard to steer. The run through the Roaring Forties would have been especially difficult, as the wind direction varied frequently, from south-west to north-west. A square rigger would just have to adjust her yards as the wind changed, but with *Mozart*'s fore and aft sails a change of course would have been necessary to avoid a gybe.

Oil on canvas, 45 x 60 cm, in the collection of Birgitta Johansson, Mariehamn

Plate XXXIII

Towards Spencer Gulf

The four-masted barque *Pommern* slips through the waters of the Great Australian Bight. The last great sailing ships knew these waters well. The Roaring Forties would have taken *Pommern* from the South Atlantic, well south of the Cape of Good Hope, in good time until longitude 134°E was reached, when she headed north for the Gulf to call at Port Lincoln for orders. *Pommern*'s last voyage from Spencer Gulf was from Port Victoria, commencing on 20 March 1939. She arrived at Falmouth on 15 July and was ordered to Hull, where she discharged her cargo and loaded sand ballast dredged from the Humber River before sailing on to her home port of Mariehamn.

Pommern was laid up during the war and never went to sea again. She is still afloat in Mariehamn, moored beside the Åland Maritime Museum. When it was realised that she would never sail again, the Erikson family presented her to the town. *Pommern* is unique amongst museum ships in that no additions mar her authenticity apart from floodlighting and fire protection. The ballast that holds her upright is the sand she loaded in Hull, for even it was considered an important element of her time as a working sailer. While she spends most of her life tethered to the quayside in Mariehamn, *Pommern* is regularly towed to dry dock in Stockholm for inspection and maintenance, a few sails always set for the sake of nostalgia.

Oil on canvas, 55 x 75 cm, in the collection of the artist

Plate XXXIV

A Fine Quartering Wind

One of the best-remembered ships of the Erikson grain fleet, the four-masted barque *Lawhill* moves easily before a steady fair wind on her last voyage from Europe in 1940, the Finnish flags painted on her sides hopefully indicating her neutrality to marauding U-boats. '*Lucky Lawhill*' acquired her nickname for several reasons—she traded through two world wars unscathed, returned her purchase price to Erikson after her third voyage, and is also recorded as never killing a man, rare indeed in the days of sail—although I was told by Bill Demerall, a seaman in her crew, that a seaman returning on board in Cape Town fell into the harbour and drowned. Built in Dundee in 1892 for the jute trade, she had a near sister, *Juteopolis*.

This last outward voyage took her to the Seychelles to load guano for Auckland, then to Port Victoria to load grain for South Africa, arriving at East London in July 1941. By this time the treaty signed between Germany and Finland had made her an enemy vessel in the eyes of the Allies. She was seized as a war prize and thereafter traded between South Africa, South America and Australia. Most of her Finnish crew remained with her, including her master. Captain Söderlund had taken his wife Elize and daughter Doris on the 1940 voyage to escape the Russian invasion of Finland, and they remained on board for the next seven years.

Lawhill was not returned to Finland after the war and continued trading until 1948. Plans to convert her into a training ship did not eventuate and she was broken up in 1956.

Oil on canvas, 55 x 75 cm, in the collection of Trygve Eriksson, Mariehamn

Plate XXXV

Flying Fish Weather

The barque *Winterhude* moves along easily in 23°S Lat., in the type of weather that was some compensation for the hard times met with in higher latitudes. In the tropics a whole new world appeared, grey days and dark foam-streaked waves giving way to brilliant sun and deep blue seas. The term 'flying fish weather' resulted from the numbers of these fish found skimming the waves in these waters, often flying on board to add variety to basic fare. Each day presented marine animals to the wind ship sailor who, unlike those in powered vessels with thrumming engines and belching smokestack, had the opportunity to observe them in a leisurely manner. A pod of whales, unconcerned by the sailer slipping quietly by, provides a diversion for the free watch gathered on the fo'c'sle head. Most commonly encountered were the dolphins and porpoises that kept close company with the ship, swimming along in the bow wave but always able to keep ahead. Though their meat resembled steak, many seamen were reluctant to kill them. Sharks, however, were caught and killed without remorse. The jaws were carried home triumphantly, the backbone became a walking stick and the tail was nailed to the jib boom as a token of good luck and fair winds, mounted with the longer lobe uppermost. When a larger shark was caught, its tail replaced the first. The hot weather also incubated thousands of the bed bugs and cockroaches that seem to have resided in ships since man first put to sea.

Oil on canvas, 55 x 75 cm, in the collection of the artist

Plate XXXVI

Reunion Anchorage

Reminiscences from George Häggstrom and Bertil Bengstrom, seamen in the Finnish barque *Favell*, of their voyage to the islands of Mauritius and Reunion in the Indian Ocean inspired this painting of her at Reunion in 1926, peacefully at anchor in a setting often dreamed about by sailors on the Cape Horn run. At the beginning of the twentieth century, an important trade in sugar developed with these islands, backed by a demand for coal to fuel the sugar mills and general cargoes of essential items to keep the isolated population going.

Favell was built on spec by Charles Hill & Sons of Bristol in 1895, the last square-rigged vessel to emerge from that port. The decision to build such a vessel, without a definite order, must have caused shareholders some concern, especially when a buyer was not immediately forthcoming. However, the company was as much at home operating ships as building them, and ran their new ship for several years. Named after Charles Hill's daughter, *Favell* took shape under a glass-roofed shed. Launched bow first, she was also unique in that she still crossed single topgallants, when this had been superseded by the more manageable double topgallants many years before. Her name remained unchanged through four changes of ownership. She tramped around until 1910, when she was bought by Finska Skolskepps Rederiet (Finnish Schoolship Company), a subsidiary of the Finnish Steamship Line. *Favell* continued in trade, loading grain in Spencer Gulf each year until 1934, when she was broken up.

Oil on canvas, 45 x 60 cm, in the collection of the artist

Plate XXXVII

In the Chops of the Channel

The four-masted barque *Abraham Rydberg*, pictured here taking a tow, was one of the few sailers on the Australia run not owned by Gustaf Erikson. She was operated by the Abraham Rydberg Association, a Swedish sail-training institute, which had two earlier vessels with this name. She was built in 1892 by C. Connell of Glasgow for A. Nelson of Honolulu, who named her *Hawaiian Isles*. She was sold to the Alaska Packers Association in 1909 and renamed *Star of Greenland*. In 1929 she was sold to the Abraham Rydberg Association. She had many features that allowed instant recognition even from a long way off. She was the only four-masted barque in the grain fleet with single topgallants; she used a triangular main course and cro'jack on many occasions; she had a Liverpool house and was painted grey.

Abraham Rydberg was a regular visitor to the Gulf in the thirties, always returning to Europe via the Cape of Good Hope. She sailed well into World War II, and although owned by a neutral country, lived dangerously until 1943, trading between North and South America. Bought by a Portuguese company and renamed *Foz do Douro*, she made several more voyages to the United States before being rigged down and fitted with an engine. I saw her in Sydney Harbour shortly after the war. Even though she looked strange, with her lower masts and cut-off bowsprit, she was quite recognisable. She was still in Lloyds Register in 1950 and presumably was broken up shortly after this.

Oil on canvas, 45 x 60 cm, in the collection of the artist

Plate XXXVIII

The Road to Cape Horn

In the Southern Ocean, the four-masted barque *L'Avenir* is being pushed along by a strong north-west wind. She was built in 1908 by Rickmers AG to the order of the Belgian Maritime Association as a cargo-carrying training ship. Her name means 'the future' or 'what is to come', representing her owners' expectations of a continuing supply of sail-trained seamen. In 1932 Gustaf Erikson bought her for the grain trade. She retained her all-white colour scheme and earned the title 'Erikson's yacht'. He utilised the extra accommodation under the long poop taking passengers on the Australia run and for summer cruises around the Baltic. The pianist and composer Percy Grainger made a voyage in her from Spencer Gulf to Falmouth in 1934. There is also a story of a permanent passenger who found sailing back and forth between Australia and Europe cheaper at a dollar a day than living in a boarding house.

In 1937 Erikson sold *L'Avenir* to Deutsches Schulschiff Verein, sponsored by Hapag Lloyd, who ran her once again as a training ship with the name *Admiral Karpfanger*. On 8 February 1938 she sailed from Port Germein with a full cargo of bagged wheat. Her last radio report, on 12 April, placed her well on the way to Cape Horn. Nothing was ever heard of her after this. The most likely cause of her loss was thought to be broaching to with a heavy following sea. An encounter with an iceberg was also possible. The only wreckage found was a lifeboat and a door, washed up on the Chilean island of Navarino near Cape Horn.

Oil on canvas, 45 x 60 cm, in the collection of the artist

Plate XXXIX

The Last Grain Race

In the sleepy little Spencer Gulf town of Port Victoria, 29 May 1949 came and went with seemingly little to distinguish it from other days. However, an important event was about to be enacted. A vessel laden with 60,000 bags of barley slid quietly away from the shore. There was no throb of engines, just the shouts from her crew, the sounds of sheaves in wooden blocks and the slatting of great sails being swung to the wind. The four-masted barque *Pamir*, after 44 years sailing the oceans, was commencing her last voyage as an engineless sailing ship, around Cape Horn towards Falmouth for orders. Sailing two days later was the four-masted barque *Passat*, shown in the distance, with the same destination. This denoted the end of Spencer Gulf's association with the grain ships and the end of the commercial sailing ship.

When they completed this voyage *Pamir* and *Passat* were laid up at Penarth, Wales, as grain storage ships before being sold to the shipbreakers. They received a reprieve, however, being converted to auxiliary cargo-carrying training ships and sailing between Germany and South America until 1957, when *Pamir* was overwhelmed in a hurricane in the North Atlantic.

More than 50 years later, *Passat* has been completely refurbished to A1 condition, and again will sail the seas, 90 years after she was built. This painting was commissioned by Åland Post for a stamp to commemorate the 50th anniversary of the last commercial sailing ship voyage.

Oil on canvas, 50 x 75 cm, Åland Post, Mariehamn

Plate XL

The Last Rounding

Pamir rounds Cape Horn on 11 July 1949. This four-masted barque was built in 1905 in Hamburg by Blohm & Voss for the German firm of F. Laeisz for the nitrate trade. In 1931 she was bought by Gustaf Erikson, whose company relied on the grain trade with Australia for most of their cargoes. In 1941 *Pamir* arrived in Wellington, New Zealand, and was seized as a war prize. Under the New Zealand flag she traded across the Pacific to the United States and Canada, made one trip to Sydney in 1947 and one around Cape Horn to the United Kingdom in 1948. In 1949 she was returned to Finnish ownership, sailing to Port Victoria and loading a grain cargo along with *Passat*. Their destination Falmouth for orders, *Pamir* departed on 29 May, *Passat* on 1 June. *Passat* rounded Cape Horn on 9 July, *Pamir* two days later, the last rounding of Cape Horn by a commercial sailing ship. A certain amount of licence has been taken here as *Pamir* actually made the rounding in darkness. Keith McKoy, a seaman in her crew, told me that at daybreak the sky assumed a strange yellow hue as depicted here.

Pamir, returned to German ownership, later voyaged to the east coast of South America as an auxiliary training ship. Her tragic end came in 1957 when she was overwhelmed by a hurricane in the Atlantic, with the loss of 80 of her crew of 86.

Oil on canvas, 55 x 75 cm, Åland Maritime Museum, Mariehamn

Plate XLI

End of the Voyage

A pilot cutter meets up with the barque *Kilmeny* at the end of her final voyage, described in the words of Eb Anderson, her second mate on this voyage, in Chapter 3. *Kilmeny* was typical of hundreds of small barques built at the end of the nineteenth century and used for world tramping. She remained in trade until 1921, when her owners J. Hardie sold her for scrap.

Kilmeny was somewhat unusual in that she was rigged without royal yards, in sailor's jargon a 'bald-headed bastard'. The absence of royals may have offended the eye, but her second mate claimed her as his favourite ship. To compensate for their lack, the upper and lower topgallant sails were wider and deeper. Eb claimed that this gave *Kilmeny* more speed, as it allowed a greater area of canvas to be set without the leverage caused by the royals, which were another 10 feet above the deck.

The painted ports favoured by British shipowners are evident here. They were always painted black, below the bulwark strake, on a white background, above a band of light grey that terminated at the load waterline above the red boot topping. On one occasion *Kilmeny* appeared to be painted yellow. While at Sabine Pass waiting to load sulphur, the crew was employed in painting her hull. The paint of those days took several days to dry, and the cloud of yellow dust that enveloped the ship as the bulk sulphur was dumped into her hold stuck to it, giving her a bright golden hue.

Oil on canvas, 55 x 75 cm, in the collection of Dr Fiona Boyd and Dr Peter McGeoch, Lake Macquarie NSW

Plate XLII

Wallaroo, Spencer Gulf, in the early part of the twentieth century.   Courtesy Jason Hopton

Port Victoria jetty in the early 1930s with ketches alongside and windjammers out to sea. Courtesy Port Victoria Maritime Museum

A ketch loading bagged grain at Port Victoria. Courtesy Port Victoria Maritime Museum

Grain stacks around the township of Port Victoria. Courtesy Port Victoria Maritime Museum

(*Left*) Loading grain on board *Lawhill*, 1937.   Courtesy J. Hourriere

Ketch *Coringle* with a deck load of bagged barley for *Pamir*, 1949.   Courtesy Port Victoria Maritime Museum

Plate XLIII

A sling of bagged grain goes into *Pamir*'s hold, 1949.
Courtesy Port Victoria Maritime Museum

Axel Stenross's boatshed and slipway, *c.*1937.
Courtesy Axel Stenross Maritime Museum

Shovelling ballast in *Lawhill*; a typical windjammer crew,
1937. Courtesy J. Hourriere

A basket of ballast goes overside. *Herzogin Cecilie*, outside
Boston Island, Port Lincoln, 1934. Courtesy Neil Cormack

Keeping the sea water out of your sea boots!
Courtesy J. Hourierre

(*Left*) Shifted ballast meant trouble for the barque
Bretagne at Port Newcastle, New South Wales, in
1915. Courtesy Henri Picard

It looks easy in port! Unbending sail on board *Herzogin Cecilie*, 1933.
Courtesy Jason Hopton

Brian 'Pinocchio' Peters at the wheel in
Passat, 1949.   Courtesy Brian Peters

(*Below left*) 'Walking the capstan round' in *Lawhill*, 1937.
Courtesy J. Hourierre

Who is in whose territory? Paik the German shepherd faces
off an albatross aboard *Herzogin Cecilie* in the Southern
Ocean. Courtesy Jason Hopton

(*Left*) The *Amulree*'s
'catch of the day'!
Courtesy Captain Jack Walker

(*Far left*) The crew's urinal;
the 'piss chute' onboard
Pommern. Robert Carter

Plate XLV

Port Lincoln jetty. *Pamir* and *Passat* in port together, 1939.
Courtesy Axel Stenross Museum

Life in a sailer was a dangerous
calling. A seaman killed in a fall
from aloft goes to his rest.
Olivebank, 12 July 1927.
Courtesy Jason Hopton

The very last grain race. *Pamir* under sail and *Passat* at anchor,
Port Victoria, 29 May 1949. Courtesy Fay Simms

Cape Horner monument at Port Victoria, erected in
1959. Courtesy Jason Hopton

The last two! *Pamir* and *Passat* at Penarth, Wales, 1949.
Photographer unknown

Plate XLVI

Captains Hägerstrand and Björkveldt and *Pamir* crew member
AB Roy Pilling, Port Victoria, 1949.
Courtesy Port Victoria Maritime Museum

The Wauraltee pub, Port Victoria, in 1949. Happily, it looks
the same today! Courtesy Port Victoria Maritime Museum

Moshulu, now a floating restaurant in Philadelphia.
Robert Carter

Memorial to drowned sailors on the waterfront in
Mariehamn; *Pommern* lies alongside.   Robert Carter

Pommern in the Western Harbour, Mariehamn, as she is today.
Robert Carter

Balclutha at San Francisco Maritime National Historic Park.
Courtesy Andrew Carter

Plate XLVII

The restored barque *Elissa* slips through the waters of the Gulf of Mexico. Courtesy Texas Seaport Museum

Wavertree and *Peking* at South Street Maritime Museum, New York. Robert Carter

Star of India sailing on San Diego Bay. Courtesy San Diego Maritime Museum

Sedov ex *Kommodore Johnsen* ex *Magdalene Vinnen* in Wilhelmshaven. Courtesy Michael Grauer

(Left) Falls of Clyde at Hawaii Maritime Center. Robert Carter

Plate XLVIII

would run out of food. One day we sighted a ship so we sent a boat over to buy some stores. The boat came back with provisions, newspapers and a bottle of French Benedictine for 'the lady passenger'. We read about happenings in the world, and realised that we were so happy at sea that the outside world was forgotten. The news was brought back that the four-masted barque *Admiral Karpfanger* had been lost and the barque *Penang* had been towed into Dunedin, New Zealand, with damage to her rigging

We were shocked to hear about *Admiral Karpfanger* as the Captain said she had passed them in the Gulf outward bound as *Pommern* was coming in. He said she looked too heavy in the head.

We passed many more steamers who came close to have a look at us but would say nothing. The officers in one German ship gave us the Nazi salute as they passed. After four months and two days we sailed very slowly into Falmouth. We left *Pommern* here and were very sad when the time came to say goodbye. *Pommern* made one more trip to Spencer Gulf but we were not back in time to meet up with Captain Broman. We never saw him again. He spoke very little English and was a very fine type of man.

I first read about the Erikson ship *Grace Harwar* in a *National Geographic* magazine dated February 1931. It was about 11 years old when I came across it in a second-hand bookshop and was perhaps the first piece of literature I was to read on the subject of the deepwater sailing ship. Written by Alan Villiers, it described her 1929 voyage from Wallaroo in South Australia to Queenstown (Cobh) in Ireland; a voyage that claimed the life of one of her crew and nearly claimed two more. Villiers, an Australian seaman turned journalist was, at that time, gaining a reputation for his books and articles on sailing ships. He signed on *Grace Harwar*, along with fellow journalist Ronald Walker, for the purpose of making a documentary film of the voyage. It did not proceed as planned. Ronald Walker was killed down in the Southern Ocean when a halyard broke and a yard fell on him. The voyage dragged on for 136 long days. There were many setbacks and hardships: a man overboard, an attempted suicide by a deranged second mate, a leak that required continuous pumping, and shortages of food, water and tobacco to cap it all off.

Villiers was a veteran of square-rigged sail and Cape Horn roundings, having sailed in *Herzogin Cecilie, Lawhill, Bellands* and *James Craig* in previous years. No doubt the voyage had its effect, even on this hardened sailor, for some of his words in the book he subsequently wrote, *By Way of Cape Horn*, were condemnatory and resentful as he spoke of 'that wretched voyage'.

In spite of this, Villiers' love for sailing ships, which would only be understood by those similarly impassioned, was not dulled, as he became a part-owner of the four-masted barque *Parma* in 1933 and two years later was to buy the little Danish full rigger *Georg Stage*, which he renamed *Joseph Conrad*. He circumnavigated the world over a period of three years with paying cadets. This he described in his book, *The Cruise of the Conrad.*

Grace Harwar, as history reveals, was not a lucky ship, and Villiers relates a number of unfortunate incidents in his book. A collision with a steamer in Falmouth Bay and another outside the Clyde, dismasted several times, hurricanes and men overboard. It all added up to a bad record, and made her a 'jinx ship', as seamen would say. But she lived from 1889 to 1935, and 46 years is a long time for a windjammer with a bad name.

Along with Villiers and Walker, for that 1929 voyage, were three other young Australians, Alf, Ray and Jim, making five Australians out of a working crew of 13. William Alfred (Alf) Freestone, known as Rolf by the Finnish crew, emerged from the past when I tracked him down on the North Coast of New South Wales 50 years later. I detected that, as a greenhorn, he must have found the voyage hard and unbearable at times. Sadly, we never had the chance to become fully acquainted, as he died not long after I found him. But he left a diary, a tidy scrawl in a cheap notebook, now yellowed; to the imaginative it conjures up visions of the young 20-year-old in his corner bunk in the half light of the fo'c'sle lamp, writing down the strange and alien events that this old windjammer was imposing on him, every day.

The part of Alf's diary I have selected covers not the Southern Ocean storms or other graphic parts of the voyage, as Villiers' book does that, but describes the pre-voyage preparations and readying for sea of a grain ship, a part of the life ignored by many who have informed me about their voyages but nevertheless significant.

I take up Alf's story on the page dated March 15, Friday, 1929: 'The desire, that had been swaying me for a least a year or more, at last got the better of me. This desire was to round Cape Horn in a sailing ship. Many other lads had been, so at last, I made up my mind to go.' This opening statement could have been taken from almost any one of the diaries I read while researching this book. Alf lived in Port Lincoln on the south-western shore of Spencer Gulf and travelled to Wallaroo on the eastern shore to join his sailing ship. The four-masted barque *Hougomont* was loading in Port Lincoln but for some reason Alf chose to go in the ship *Grace Harwar*, along with another boy from Port Lincoln, Ray Millard.

> We went on board and were interviewed by Captain Svensson. He told us we could start in the morning and could get ourselves settled in the fo'c'sle. The wage was four pounds per month. Previously I had been earning four pounds per week. Once our luggage was on board, we went to the fo'c'sle to meet the crew. The Captain had told us that we would find two more Australians on board; one was Ronald Walker and the other Alan Villiers and they hailed from Tasmania. I had met Villiers' brother, Frank, in Port Lincoln and he had joined *Hougomont*. Villiers and Walker had joined with the purpose of making a moving picture of the trip around Cape Horn. [It appeared on the screen under the title *Windjammer*.] When we put in our appearance in the fo'c'sle, we inquired about these two chaps. This presented grounds for conversation. Villiers could speak Swedish fairly well and he translated our particulars to them. I selected an upper bunk in a corner, which was a little more private than the others and luckily, the lower bunk was unoccupied and I could stow my sea chest there.

> *Friday, 21 March* I was roused up at 6.30 am by the watchman. I rose up and washed, ready for breakfast. The weather was fine and it seemed very romantic, stepping out of the fo'c'sle into the stillness of the morning to see the masts and rigging towering aloft for the first time. After breakfast, the second mate came along and turned us to. My first job was to pick the good patches off old sails. After this, I was taken below to the 'tween decks and told to bag up some stuff, which looked like dirt. It was guano and smelt so strongly of ammonia it made me sick. After dinner, I was put to binding the ironwork in

the hold with sacking in readiness for the grain cargo. It was then that I learnt that we had been tricked, as we had not yet discharged our ballast. This meant that we would not be sailing for a month or more. The idea of signing us on so early was to dig out the ballast as nearly all the old crew had paid off.

Sat. 22 March No work today as it was a Finnish holiday. There was an English chap on board, named Jim Evans. He had been in Australia for some time. He had sailed in the four-masted barque, *Olivebank*, the time Tyler was killed. Jim advised me to go aloft and get accustomed to the rigging, which I did.

Monday, 25 March 'Rise up, rise up!' 'What's the time?' I asked. '5 am, hurry up, as we sail right away.'
    This was a surprise but I fell in with the plan readily. This was my first experience of helping to put a ship to sea. A sailing ship at that! I was sent aloft on the mizzen mast with Jim Evans to loose the topgallant and topsails. This was my first lesson in letting go sails. We sailed out about three miles, by the wind, and then dropped anchor. It was about 10 am before we had breakfast. After breakfast, we had to turn to, to shovel ballast. Luckily it was straight sand and not too hard to work. We were employed thus until two bells—5 pm, when we knocked off. It was strange how these sailing ships like to prolong working days on occasions like this as one cannot claim overtime on sailing days.

Tuesday, 26 March Shovelling ballast again from 7 am until 5 pm, except a period that I had to carry water to top up the cook's water tank.

Wednesday, 27 March The Captain came along and asked us if we would work overtime, as they were anxious to get the ballast out. He said he would pay us a shilling an hour. Having nothing else to do and being anxious to get to sea, we readily consented, although the pay did not attract us. We worked the ballast from 7 am to 6 pm and got one hour overtime. The ballast was hoisted from the hold in canvas baskets. These were hitched to a diesel winch and, once on deck, a hand hooked another line onto the base. They were then swung out over the side and up-ended.

Thursday, 28 March Once more we settled down to a day's work on the ballast. Today we only worked ordinary hours, as tomorrow is Good Friday. My turn came to wash up the dishes. I tossed Ronald Walker to see who should do them this week or next. He won the toss and decided to wait a week. I thought at first he would dodge them altogether. A few gentle hints brought him into line. To while away the evening, I wrote some letters to my friends in Port Lincoln.

Friday, 29 March Good Friday. We were asked if we would work all day. There being nothing else to do, as we couldn't get ashore, we said yes. We were pleased indeed to strike the bottom of the ship, thus telling us our task was nearly over. The ballast having gone, it was necessary to clean out the hold, which was by no means a clean job. There was guano and such like in all the cracks. When guano is wet, the smell would knock one flat. We were earning a shilling an hour all day so we could not growl.

Saturday, 30 March Easter Saturday. During the morning, we continued cleaning out the hold. We had shifted 600 tons of ballast between nine of us. In the afternoon the decks were washed and I received the job of cleaning out the fo'c'sle.

Sunday, 31 March Easter Sunday. Having nothing to do, I decided to do my washing. I had not spent an Easter like this before in my life. So quiet, nowhere to go except around the decks. The Captain was ashore and I envied him, as it was the rule for me to go picnicking at Easter time.

Monday, 1 April The Captain came aboard in the morning and as the wind was slightly favourable, he decided to sail in alongside the wharf. This meant that the anchor had to be weighed. After we had set a few sails, we set about connecting up the capstan to the windlass under the fo'c'sle head. Special bars were fixed into the windlass and a rope run around them to the motor winch. This idea worked well for a time, then some of the bars broke. This meant we had to wind it by hand. Steel bars were inserted into the windlass and, with six men on one side and six on the other; we had to work it by an up and down motion. This was indeed backbreaking work. The chain came in inch by inch and seemed endless. I was lucky enough to miss being sent to stow the cable. At last it was up and then we discovered that the wind had changed for we had been too long. After sailing one mile, we were forced to drop anchor and take in the sails. All that work for nothing! But that is often the case in a sailing ship.

Tuesday, 2 April The wind was still unfavourable so we had to lie at anchor. While we were at anchor, we cleaned the bilges. This was a dirty job. I had to get down underneath the water tanks and bale out the stinking water.

Wednesday, 3 April All the deck supports and ironwork had to be bound with sacking. This occupied part of the morning. The wind being slightly in our favour, the Captain decided to have another try to get alongside. Once again we weighed that dreadful anchor. Setting sail, we thought, at last we would be alongside. Again we were disappointed for we only got within about half a mile of the wharf and down went the pick again. We approached the Mate and went ashore that evening in the motorboat. It was good to get on land again, although we had to wait until one o'clock in the morning to get back on board again.

Thursday, 4 April 'Rise up, Rise up.' It was 4.30 am and I have only just gone to sleep. Never mind, we go alongside this morning. First came that confounded anchor. When that was weighed and the chain stowed, the pilot gave orders to his launch to take the line ashore. This they made fast to the wharf, the other end being made fast to the capstan forward. Heave ho, boys. Round and round we went with the capstan, straining and pushing as hard as we could. By this means we had to draw *Grace* alongside. This took until about 8.30 am, inch by inch she came, slow but sure. I was just about sick of the sight of the fellow's boots on the bar in front of me. Then they took another line from aft. Up until this time, the sea was calm and no wind. Then came a strong wind to make things worse. We had to strain against this as well as pull the ship through the water. Once alongside, we fell to finishing the holds for the wheat cargo. It was past 10 am when we received breakfast. At 5 pm, we finished up for the day.

For the next week, we chipped rust on the hull and painted with red lead. Other jobs, such as loading the coal for the galley, dressing the deck with linseed oil and Stockholm tar and, of all things, stowing the captain's car in the 'tween decks! It appears that Captain Svensson had bought a car while in America.

Wednesday, 17 April At last the great day had arrived. After doing several odd jobs during the day, 5.30 pm arrived. Orders came to get her under weigh. I was exceedingly pleased and sprang to with a will. Shall I ever forget that evening? The anchors weighed, aloft in the rigging I had the task of letting go the sails. Great silver wings, spreading before the beautiful sunset. From the mizzen topsail yard I commanded a wonderful view of the receding landscape. I thought, *What a wonderful country of open spaces; when shall I see you again, land of my birth?*

Seven o'clock—six bells, saw all the necessary jobs done, anchors drawn up, sails set and lamps burning bright. Then came the task of picking watches. All hands went to the main hatch. Roy was picked for starboard and I for port. Port watch went below. The drawing for places at the wheel came next. I drew fourth wheel. This meant second lookout. Well, *Grace* put her nose down the Gulf with a fair wind. Thankful we all were to be, at last, on our great journey to Falmouth.

Grace Harwar took her grain to Falmouth and on to Glasgow to discharge. Alf Freestone left her in Glasgow and the ship went off to La Guaira with patent fuel loaded in Swansea, Wales. With no charter from here, she returned to her home port, Mariehamn, to await more favourable times. It was now 1930 and times were bad, not only for sailing ships. However, in 1931 a charter was obtained to take a cargo of sulphate of ammonia from Middlesborough to Mauritius. Her skipper was Gunnar Boman, who took over from Captain Svensson after the 1929 voyage.

John Thode, a young New Zealander, joined *Grace Harwar* in Auckland when she arrived on the second leg of the voyage. He tells us:

I joined *Grace Harwar* in Auckland in February 1932. She had just brought a full cargo of guano from Juan de Nova, a small island in the Mozambique Channel. The earlier part of the voyage had taken her from her homeport, Mariehamn, on May 13, 1931. She was drydocked at Southbank and then went to Middlesborough in June, where she was loaded with 2,500 tons of sulphate of ammonia.

On September 13, she arrived at Port Louis, Mauritius, where she discharged the sulphate. From there, she went to Nossi Be [in Madagascar] for orders and sailed for Juan de Nova Island, arriving there 20 November. On February 2, 1932, she arrived in Auckland. After discharging the guano at Kings Wharf, 800 tons of earth and rubble ballast were loaded. Of course, some of the ballast was taken on before discharging all of the guano. Four of us joined in Auckland, including a cook and steward, both of whom paid off in South Australia. My mate, Cedric Constance from Otahuhu, and myself, both had considerable experience behind us. Cedric had sailed in the Melbourne yacht *Oimara* in the first Trans-Tasman Yacht Race in 1931. I had a position in the *Rangi*, our family boat 1920–1929, so we were not absolutely green.

On Monday, 22 February 1932, we sailed from Auckland for Port Victoria, South Australia. The master was Captain Gunnar Boman. The crew comprised the master and two mates, carpenter, sail maker, sail maker's mate, 12 fo'c'sle hands, of which two were ABs and 10 were ordinary seamen and boys, a cook, steward and one passenger for Port Victoria.

On 20 March, we anchored at the Port Victoria ballast grounds. We lay in Port Victoria for six weeks, discharging the ballast and loading bagged wheat. We moved closer inshore on April 13 and completed loading 35,439 bags (3,500 tons) on April 29. On Sunday, 1 May, 1932, we sailed for Falmouth for orders. Two new hands signed on. One ex *Favell* to replace the steward and an ordinary seaman ex *Viking*. An American passenger, Charles Gulden of New York, also joined us. He was to have joined *Hougomont* for the voyage to Europe but she had been dismasted in the Great Australian Bight. After rounding the south of Tasmania, the westerlies took charge and varied north-west to south-west but always fair and strengthening. For four weeks we made grand progress—one day's run of 252 miles and 1,009 miles in five days. Then we ran into light airs, fogs and easterlies. One entry in my log, June 15, states: Beating between 55 and 57 degrees South longitude about 78 West. Rounded Cape Horn 55 days out, after weeks of beating against head winds and reaching nearly 60 degrees South! Very cold, midwinter conditions!

The cargo shifted and the ship was in grave danger for several days. On top of this, three of the main weather shrouds carried away. We had to heave them down with chain stoppers and luff tackles. In these instances, the Old Man was very generous with his white Mauritius rum and we chewed wheat for sustenance—the galley being washed out. Once around the Horn, we headed away to the north-east, seeking the South-East Trades. They came in good time and life became much more pleasant. The passage north up the Atlantic was in the accepted pattern, South-East Trades, Doldrums, North-East Trades, Westerlies, for the final leg to the Channel. Charles Gulden, Cedric Constance and I left her in Falmouth. Cedric went home by the passenger ship *Majestic* and Charles and I went on to London. I tried to sign on for another voyage in sail, as I needed 12 months to get a square rig endorsement when I gained my second mate's certificate. However, I was not successful, as I could not raise the 50 pounds premium required. *Grace Harwar* was ordered to London where she discharged her wheat and then returned to Mariehamn.

In 1885 a young Scot named Andrew Weir decided he would leave the bank in which he worked and go into the shipping business. He must have had a good credit rating, for he bought his first ship at the age of 21. This vessel was *Willowbank* and the suffix to her name set a pattern that has continued to the present day. Andrew Weir's fleet of sailing ships was the largest that ever existed under the Red Ensign, and over the next 25 years he owned and operated a total of 44 large sailing vessels. They, along with the fleet of steamships that he began to acquire from 1896, formed the beginnings of the company that survived four depressions, two world wars and in 1985 celebrated its 100th anniversary. Weir's selection of names for his ships resulted in the formation of the Bank Line Limited, and it is still possible to walk along the waterfronts of Port Jackson, New York or Liverpool and read on today's ships the names of *Willowbank*, *Clydebank* and *Ivybank*, inherited from their sisters of the past.

The last Weir sailing ship, built in 1892 at the Glasgow Yards of Mackie & Thomson, was the four-masted barque *Olivebank*. She left Weir ownership in 1913 and her name was changed to *Caledonia* by her new owner, E. Monson of Tvedestrand in Norway. She stayed under the Norwegian flag while passing through five changes of ownership, until Gustaf Erikson bought her in 1924 and gave her back her original name.

She tramped around, loaded grain in Geelong in 1924 and Port Victoria in 1925. In 1927 she loaded grain at Port Lincoln and amongst the new hands signed on to replace the deserters was a young man called Bill Smith. Bill was a telegraphist at Port Lincoln and wanted to go to sea as a wireless operator. As this type of position was scarce in Australia he planned to go to the United Kingdom and *Olivebank* made it possible for him. He had some experience in the small schooners and ketches around the Gulf and so was signed on as ordinary seaman. Bill continues the story:

> I joined *Olivebank* at Port Lincoln, South Australia on 6 April, 1927. She was already loaded with 4500 tons of wheat and lying at anchor about two miles out in Boston Bay waiting for stores and more crew, being the last ship to load that year. The Captain could only get four men in Port Lincoln, so he had to go to Port Adelaide to try and get more crew. He managed to get two able seamen from the *Garthpool* and two off the beach. The Captain left instructions for the ship's lifeboat to be at the jetty when the passenger boat arrived from Port Adelaide so that the men could be taken straight out to the ship, the

reason being [that] captains of other ships had brought men over from Port Adelaide while their ship was still at the jetty and next morning they were gone, as all they wanted was a free trip to Port Lincoln and a booze-up on the passenger boat. When they arrived on board three of them had sea-bags with their belongings; the fourth, a little Scotsman five foot tall and 62 years of age who boasted that he had been in most jails around the world and said the Australian jails were the best, dumped a small bundle tied up in a red pocket handkerchief on the fo'c'sle table and said, 'There is my dunnage', being all he had. Luckily, we had a good slop-chest aboard where he could buy clothes otherwise I don't know how he expected to do a trip around Cape Horn in what he stood up in. We ended up with a crew of 22 and that included the Captain, three mates, bosun, donkey man, cook, steward, three able seamen, five ordinary seamen and six Lithuanian apprentices, a very small crew for a large and heavy ship like *Olivebank*. It was all manpower, and we had no luxuries like brace, winches, etc.

Tuesday afternoon, 12 April, the Pilot came aboard and took us out into Spencer Gulf at the back of Boston Island where we remained for 14 days waiting for a fair wind. I guess our friends in Port Lincoln thought we were well on our way to Cape Horn. Just before the Pilot left he singled me out and shook hands, wished me luck and told me to be careful aloft and said don't forget, one hand for yourself and one for the ship. I wondered why an ex-sailing ship captain should say that but many years later I learnt why. He had a son who was killed when he fell from aloft.

While we were still in Spencer Gulf waiting for a fair wind we had run out of fresh meat and vegetables and were on salt horse. I never did know if it was horse or beef. Most of our stores had to come from Port Adelaide, and I think we got what they could not sell. The potatoes had started to grow, we had to lay them out on sawdust in the 'tween decks so that they were not touching each other to try and prevent them from going rotten but they only lasted about two months. The Captain would not accept the butter when it arrived, as it wasn't fit to eat, so he bought up all the butter he could get in Port Lincoln, which wasn't nearly enough. There were several beekeepers near Port Lincoln so he took honey instead. We had two live pigs on board and killed one when about six weeks out and the other when about three months out. It was quite a treat after salt junk. I shall never forget the first pig we killed. The cook was there with a bowl to catch the blood and the steward with an eggbeater to prevent the blood from congealing. I didn't attach much importance to that, as I knew the Germans and Scandinavians used to make black puddings, etc. However, for our evening meal there were slabs of meat, which I thought was the pig's liver, floating in the gravy. I helped myself to my share and afterwards remarked that it was the best liver I had ever tasted. It was then that one of the Finnish boys said it was 'no libber' but was pig's blood pancakes. The cook apparently mixed up a batter with the blood and fried it, it was delicious and I really thought it was liver but was glad I didn't know what it was before I had eaten it or I might have missed out on something that was very nice. On the whole, I think we fared very well considering we were 166 days at sea, the last six weeks our diet consisting mainly of peas, rice and pancakes but we had a very good cook. I consider we were fed better than we were on some of the Bristol Channel tramps running to Brazil and back, when we were only three weeks at sea each way.

We eventually got under way about 6 pm on 26 April, we had a good strong breeze and set all sails, by midnight the wind had freshened considerably and we had to shorten sail, the main reason being, the ship's bottom was so dirty with barnacles and marine growth we could not make full use of very strong winds as it was over two years since she had been in a dry dock, and quite a considerable amount of that time was spent at anchor in tropical waters. We eventually got down into the Forties, but instead of getting the strong westerlies we were getting easterly winds, which persisted, practically all the way to the Horn, and this was very unusual for that time of the year. Down in these regions it was freezing cold and very miserable, the nights were long and the daylight very short (about 8 am to 4 pm). It was somewhere down south between New Zealand and Cape Horn that I had a very frightening experience. One night about 6 pm and very dark I had to go aft to get some bread from the steward. I kept under the lifeline all the way as we were shipping some huge seas, but I had to leave the lifeline to go to the steward's door. He passed out two loaves and told me not to get them wet, as they were the last as it had been too rough for the cook to bake bread. I stopped to put the bread into my oilskin jacket when over came a huge sea. I had no protection and I was too far away to grab the lifeline. The sea just picked me up and the last I remembered was being washed between the jigger mast and the poop deck bulkhead. Where I went from there I don't know, it is a terrible sensation to think the end has come, especially when you are only 20. At first I worried for my mother, as they would never have found me in those mountainous seas and on such a very dark night. I seemed to have been in the water for a very long time, then I hit something and hung on with all my strength and when I regained my senses I found I was clutching the bitts [mooring bollards]. After I had recovered enough I made straight for the lifeline and when I got back to the fo'c'sle I was abused for being so long. All they were concerned about was the bread, but alas, when I tried to retrieve it from under my oilskin it was well and truly saturated with sea water and unfit in more ways than one for human consumption. I had been in the water for about 25 minutes, I don't know if I had been on board for the whole of this time or whether I had been washed overboard and back again. I really thought I had, otherwise, it would have been impossible to be washed up and down the deck for that length of time without bashing into something sooner than I did. Discussing it later with one of the ABs he told me that he had seen a man washed overboard and washed back again. We will never know.

The usual run to the Horn is approximately 30 days, but we took 60 days and rounded the Horn on 23 June. After we got around Cape Horn and started heading north-east we were surrounded by icebergs, which was also very unusual. Being midwinter they are then usually in the packs. It is in the summer that they start breaking up and floating about and becoming a danger to shipping. We were surrounded by them for over a week, some of them were huge and they are nasty things to tangle with. At night visibility was very bad and the period of daylight down there was very short, in daylight we could see the bergs but what we couldn't see was the ice just below the surface. We had some very close shaves, but luckily, we eventually got clear of them and started to make our way up into better weather.

It was then that we had the misfortune to lose one of our boys. He was one of the Lithuanian apprentices. It appears he had been working on the jigger mast and had fallen about 100 feet. He was killed instantly and it was just as well, as we could not have done anything for him. Three ABs washed him and sewed him up in canvas, which was weighted down with chains. The body was placed on a hatch board and placed in the donkey house. Holes in the donkey house had to be sealed up to keep the rats out. The ship was alive with them. I think everyone was stunned with shock, and apart from the officer of the watch and the man at the wheel, no one did any work for the rest of the day. Next morning was a beautiful day, and at 9 am the sails on the main mast were backed to stop the ship. It was the usual thing in those ships after the service was read, for the hatch board to be lifted onto the ship's rail and the inboard end raised until the body slid off into the sea. The Captain said 'no' to that and said it was too much like throwing a man over the side. The hatch board with the body on it was placed on two boxes on the deck directly under the port lifeboat, all hands assembled around, as you would expect at a graveside. The Captain read the service in Swedish and hymns were sung. The lifeboat falls were attached to the hatch board and when the Captain said, 'I now commit the body to the deep', the body was raised on the davits and swung out over the side then lowered to within a foot of the water. One end was then lowered away and the body just slipped into the water with not even a splash. After the Captain gave the final instructions he went up onto the poop deck to watch the body being lowered. I happened to glance up and noticed tears running down his cheeks. He seemed very upset. Two weeks later on Saturday afternoon all hands assembled at the after hatch where the boy's clothes were auctioned, the third mate, Tarry Barry, acting as auctioneer. They bought 32 pounds, which wasn't bad considering you could buy a good shirt for about five shillings in those days. The men were bidding more than they would have paid for the same articles in the shop because the money raised was to be sent to his mother.

We eventually picked up the south-east trade winds and life on the square rigger became more pleasant and we soon forgot the hell we went through down south, although from then on we were kept busy chipping rust, painting, and taking down the storm sails and replacing them with fine weather sails It was a pleasure steering in the trade winds, the ship almost steered herself. I can remember being at the wheel for a whole hour and not having to move it. Soon after we lost the South-East Trades we got into the doldrums and there we remained for two weeks; this was the most monotonous part of the voyage, the ship rolling heavily and the sails flapping with each roll and we were getting nowhere. There were many weeks when we were only logging 4 knots but at least we were moving. By now we were getting very low on drinking water and if I remember rightly we had only one foot of water in our last tank. We were hoping to contact a steamer to get some water but were not successful and after 10 days in the doldrums we had a tropical rainstorm, it rained for three days and three nights. I thought we were going to get another 40 days and 40 nights and was feeling safe that I was on something that floated, anyhow, we were able to fill one of our tanks and water was no longer rationed and we could use it for washing. When the rain first started we all grabbed a cake of soap and stripped off and had a shower bath, the first we had for four months.

The ship was now getting overrun with rats and I felt sure that if we were another month or so at sea we would have had to leave the ship, they were getting that bad. They had everything in their favour with four and a half thousand tons of wheat in the hold where they could breed without any interference. When discharging in Cardiff they employed rat-catchers down in the hold, and the last time I was aboard they had bags of dead rats piled up on the deck. Somehow it seemed that our luck had changed, as after we had filled our water tank a wind sprang up and we soon picked up the North-East Trades and about six weeks later on Wednesday, 21 September at 8 pm we sighted the Fastnet rock light on the southwest corner of Ireland. Next day we were sailing along the south coast of Ireland heading for Queenstown. I will never forget how beautiful it was seeing the green hills and the farmhouses and I suppose after seeing nothing but sea for five months it made it seem more beautiful. At about 11 am we were only a few miles off the entrance to Cork Harbour when a squall hit us and the wind came dead ahead, we spent the next two days sailing up and down the south coast of Ireland waiting for a fair wind to take us in. Early Saturday morning, 24 September we made it. The pilot boat came alongside with the pilot and they passed up a bucket of fish and a bucket of potatoes, we had fried fish and boiled potatoes for breakfast, the first fresh food for months. By midday we had dropped anchor and furled all sails. It was 167 days since we left Port Lincoln. Late afternoon a boat came out with fresh meat, vegetables, etc. and Sunday for lunch we had roast beef, roast potatoes and cabbage, I don't think I ever enjoyed a meal so much. We spent eight days in Queenstown waiting for orders; our original orders having been cancelled as they had given us up. We were long overdue and were the last grain ship to arrive that year. Eventually we got orders to discharge in Cardiff and we were paid off there.

Bill found it wasn't easy to get a job as a wireless operator and for a while served in the Cardiff fishing trawlers and the Bristol Channel tramps, running out to South America before returning to Australia. Bill mentions the third mate in *Olivebank*, Tarry Barry. He was a character out of Port Lincoln who should have a place in this book but he is now gone and with him the stories he could have told.

No doubt there are plenty still circulating around Port Lincoln. I spoke with him once but he didn't think he had done anything worth mentioning. However, he fought in World War I, and survived Gallipoli and France as a member of the 27th Battalion, Australian Imperial Forces. He returned to Port Lincoln and in 1926 joined the four-masted barque *Gustav*, later renamed *Melbourne* when Erikson bought her. Back in Port Lincoln he became a stevedore and when *Olivebank* visited there in 1927 he helped load her grain and then signed on the crew for the voyage to Falmouth.

Olivebank continued in trade until 1939. She sailed from Port Victoria, South Australia, on 20 March with a cargo of grain towards Queenstown for orders. She discharged her cargo at Barry Dock, Wales, and headed off for Mariehamn on 29 August. Head winds in the Bristol Channel determined *Olivebank*'s fate. Captain Carl Granith headed off into the English Channel with a good fair wind. On 8 September she found herself in a North Sea minefield and within half an hour had struck a mine. She sank quickly, taking with her 14 out of her crew of 21. Captain Granith went down with his ship. The survivors clung to one of the yards on the wreck, which was standing on the bottom. Miraculously they were still alive two days later, when a Danish fishing boat picked them up.

As a postscript to this narrative, a small article in the *Australian Cape Horners Journal* in 1997 noted that the wreck of *Olivebank* had recently been located by divers in 20 fathoms of water at Lat 55° 55' N, Long 5° E. Although badly corroded, the sailing ship's hull was still recognisable.

Another Australian who sailed in the Erikson ships is Captain Don Garnham. He sailed in the four-masted barque *Herzogin Cecilie* from Port Lincoln towards Falmouth in 1935, and in the four-masted barque *Moshulu* the following year. He has told me of many of his experiences in *Herzogin Cecilie*, referred to as Erikson's flagship, but I have chosen to reproduce some passages from his diary which impart much of the atmosphere of the occasion. Even his first words reveal the expectation that this young man must have felt about embarking on this great adventure.

On Monday, 14 January 1935, before the Finnish Consul in Adelaide I signed on the great four-masted Finnish sailing ship *Herzogin Cecilie* as ordinary seaman. That evening I caught the MV *Minnipa* from Port Adelaide for Port Lincoln where my ship lay. I was up at dawn to see Boston Island, which shelters the entrance to Port Lincoln Harbour. It was then that I sighted my first windjammer, the four-masted barque *Pamir*, that was at anchor waiting her papers and clearance from Adelaide. As we entered the harbour, four tall masts were seen over the land and on rounding the point I was presented with the first glimpse of the ship I had waited so long to join. I quickly disembarked from the *Minnipa* and hurried around to the next wharf where *Herzogin Cecilie* lay.

As I stepped aboard a huge Alsatian dog rushed towards me, barking loudly. It was Captain Sven Eriksson's dog, Paik. After being introduced to the Captain I was taken to my quarters, which I was to share with other apprentices, English, French and Belgian. The room contained eight bunks, a table in the centre with two forms, small lockers for our gear and an oil lamp suspended from the deck head. Breakfast consisted of lamb's fry [liver] and potatoes. My luggage was sent around from the *Minnipa* on the railway engine. I went to the steward for bedding and was amazed to find that it was not provided. However he found me a mattress, a strip of old sail canvas from the sail maker served as a sheet, a flour bag filled with chaff as a pillow and two blankets from deserters were to serve as my entire bedding for the long, cold passage around the Horn. The older hands were busy aloft bending sail in preparation for sailing.

My first day was spent on deck coiling up ropes and learning a little of the maze of ropes on the pin rails. I picked up an armful of rope yarns off the deck and in true steamship fashion dumped them overboard. They had no sooner left my arms when I heard a loud roar from the mate. Finns never waste anything. All old ropes and yarns were carefully stored for sale at the end of the trip—the mate's perks. That evening we attended a dance at the Missions to Seamen.

16 January Called at 6.30 am to 'turn to' at 7 am, I had my first experience aloft on a swaying footrope as all hands bent on the foresail. After that I was told to help with the sheep. Six were passed on board and after a struggle we had them safely in their pen. The pigs came next. Six squealing beasts were dropped head first into sacks and taken to a small room under the fo'c'sle head which was their sty for the duration of their respective voyages. Twenty-eight fowls were also received and penned in a room under the long poop deck. At two o'clock the last bag of wheat was aboard. Preparations were immediately made for departure to the outside anchorage. The gaskets were cast off the foresail and lower topsails. We commenced to let go from the wharf as the sails were sheeted home and the vessel started to move with amazing speed, the wind being right aft. Unfortunately one of our after mooring lines fouled part of the steering gear, which was damaged. We were soon clear of the wharf and heading for the open sea via the northern end of Boston Island. A tanker anchored in the harbour gave us three long blasts as we passed on our way to our anchorage. We anchored about two miles from *Pamir*. The damaged part of the steering gear was sent ashore in the pilot launch while we resumed our preparations for sea, working an extra hour after tea.

17 January At six bells all hands muster on the fore deck. The mate counts us to see if we are all there and then duties are allotted. Firstly from the sail locker where various sails have been sorted, we shoulder the heavy canvas and march out onto the deck. The mainsail, crossjack, upper topgallants and royals were bent. It was my first time aloft above the lower yards and the higher one got the smaller the ship appears. Although the royal yard is over 160 feet [48 metres] above the deck I felt quite at home. After the sails were bent, potatoes had to be stowed in the locker.

18 January During the night the four-masted barque *Ponape* had joined us at the anchorage. Their launch returning from the shore called with a welcome bundle of letters. The steering gear bar was returned and refitted and we were put to painting over the ship's side. The four-masted barque *Olivebank* arrived about midnight.

19 January Resumed painting over the side until 2 pm when the decks were washed down and work ceased for the day.

20 Sunday Our last free and easy day for many months to come, so we relaxed and listened to the gramophone, sang all the songs we knew and talked of the voyage.

21 January The wind was in our favour and we were ready for sea. The donkey boiler was lit and as soon as there was a sufficient head of steam we began to heave up the anchor. Hands were sent aloft to cast off the gaskets and loosen sail. The fore yards were hauled aback to cant us off on to the port tack. I was aloft unfurling the sails on the mizzen. By 3.30 pm all sails were set and we were under weigh. The long voyage home had begun.

The sailing ships that went to Spencer Gulf and other Australian ports for grain cargoes in the thirties were not all owned by Gustaf Erikson, nor were they all Finnish. The German Laeisz company still retained *Padua* and *Priwall; Favell* was owned and operated by Finska Skolskepps Rederiet (Finnish Schoolship Foundation), a subsidiary of the Finnish Steamship Line. (This company also bought *Fennia*, formerly the French *Champigny*, which was hulked in the Falklands in 1927 to become a grain store ship. Her hull exists there to this day.) The German Vinnen company's *Magdalene Vinnen* (later *Kommodore Johnsen*) and the ill-fated Danish cargo-carrying training ship *København* also loaded in the Gulf, and *Abraham Rydberg,* run as a cargo-carrying training ship by the Swedish foundation of the same name, was a regular visitor.

Abraham Rydberg had a colourful career. A Danish cadet who sailed in her in the early thirties, Albert Wargren of Sydney, has given me a look into the running of this somewhat different member of the grain fleet which did not rely entirely on the freighting of grain for her survival. Albert was another boy out of the small Baltic traders that taught seamanship the hard way. He went on to become a ship's officer, and was fairly critical of the atmosphere in *Abraham Rydberg* during his time in her, his comments supporting the fact that boys who went to sea in the small Baltic sailing vessels were years ahead of their time in all aspects of seamanship adding further perspective to this era of sail.

I needed another six months under sail and joined *Abraham Rydberg* as an apprentice in August 1934. In the *Abraham Rydberg* there followed a year which still puzzles me. When I came on board this ship I was staggered at the comfort of the accommodation. We lived six to a cabin and our cabins were very roomy, compared with anything I had seen in other ships. We had quite a big wash room and a separate mess room where we ate our meals. Our meals were served straight from the galley through a hatch in the bulkhead. I am still not convinced that this type of training was such a good idea. With 40 or so boys all the same age and most of them totally inexperienced, there were no examples set and nobody to emulate. I learned a lot more from two old hands in the small Baltic schooners in which I served, than I ever learnt in the *Rydberg.* The only useful subjects taught were morsing and signalling.

The Captain was a former Swedish Royal Navy man and I doubt if he had ever served in a merchant ship in his life, hence the whole atmosphere on board was 'Navy' and he and the officers kept a considerable distance between themselves and the boys. We even had a former navy petty officer as our instructor—and what he didn't know about merchant ships would fill several books.

The second mate was 23 and was no doubt an up and coming man. He became captain of *Abraham Rydberg* three years later. However at 23 he was far too young to effectively teach 20-year-old apprentices, no matter how good a seaman, and he was a superb seaman. Thus we were supposed to learn our trade in an environment with no tradition and with no experienced older crew members to show us how. Apart from normal sail handling, those of us who were not favourites (about 30 out of the 40), spent our year holystoning the decks. Try as I may, I can't think of anything that that I learnt in the *Abraham Rydberg* that I didn't know before or that I could not have learned in any other sailing ship!

Jack Horward lent me the diary he kept of his voyage in the four-masted barque *Archibald Russell* in 1939. He had the ability to capture the image of his surroundings and his feelings of the moment, not just to make a daily record of his activities. It is a pity there is not enough space to display more of his words but some passages stand out and give a vivid impression of aspects of what was accepted as a normal part of seafaring under sail.

Tuesday 9 May 1939 On the way to Cape Horn! I awoke to find the fo'c'sle flooded and sea boots and clothing swirling around on the floor. The seas crashing over the decks are worse than ever before, there being several feet of water continually over the deck and higher than a man's waist in the scuppers. One great wave crashing over the bulwarks tore the water tank away from its fastenings at the break of the poop and smashed it with terrific force against the rail, completely wrecking it. It is blowing the hardest I have ever known it and the seas have risen to an unbelievable size. The rolling and pitching of the ship makes it difficult to sleep, as it requires a lot of effort to stay in one's bunk. This is the real Cape Horn life—eat, work and try to sleep under conditions generally bad. The food is always cold and the cook labours with difficulty when the ship is rolling so much.

I was rather anxious about my trick at the wheel. With the ship slithering down the troughs of the seas amid clouds of spray and half submerged, swinging hard to port and then to starboard, I figured I would be coming in for a lot of abuse from the mate. However an incident occurred which may have saved my skin. Paul had wheel before me and I was at 'police', when I heard one whistle, the policeman wanted—that's me! I snatched an oilskin, greatcoat and sou'wester and dashed to the poop. There was the 2nd mate arguing with the Captain. His voice was trembling with rage. Paul stood at the wheel, fairly fighting it and I soon guessed what had happened. He had either lost control or had got off the course badly. The 2nd mate had lost his head and had gone for him. Paul's hair was awry, his cap and sou'wester lying on the deck, collar torn open and he hung on to the wheel, very pale and quiet. He had evidently called for the skipper when the 2nd mate had attacked him and now the skipper was abusing the mate, who had completely lost self-control and was cursing and shouting freely. My arrival caused a lull in the verbal combat and the 2nd mate motioned me to assist at the wheel. Immediately the skipper had gone below the 2nd mate turned on Paul and although the lingo was Greek to me, the gist of it was obvious. In a low tone he threatened Paul and said he would 'fix him'. Paul was pale and excited but nothing he could do would help him so he said nothing.

10 May The wind is very squally and during one bad puff the ship recorded 15 knots. The skipper watches the masts and shrouds anxiously. The watch sits around the fo'c'sle tonight. All hands are ready in full oilskins. It isn't safe to try to get into your bunk, as should three whistles blow ['all hands'] we must be ready. Sure enough, three whistles and a mad scramble out! All hands to take in the mainsail! The seas are breaking completely over the deckhouses and poop and the galley is swamped. The deck is completely submerged. Yet when we are sweating at the clew lines and buntlines everybody is happy and chanting. What a sight! Twenty shiny wet faces around the lines, wet oilskins gleaming in the pale light of the mate's torch, water and foam swirling around thigh deep and water and spray hurtling over the bulwarks 30 feet above our heads. Truly a picture no artist could paint. Then, 'oop and make fast there'! The port watch lay out aloft on the main yard to port and the starboard watch to starboard and in came 2000 square feet of sail! 'Tree voch' (free watch) and we return to the shelter of the fo'c'sle; wet, dripping, dirty and heavily bearded, we grin at one another. 'Shut the door,' from someone, 'shut the bloody door!' A crash, and water pours in over the two-foot sill and we curse. Crash! Another one and the deckhouse shakes and shudders beneath those tons of water. Suddenly through the skylight, which is constructed from steel and wood and battened down with a lashed canvas cover, pours solid water, floods the lamp, breaking its glass and we are all left staggering in the darkness. The door opens suddenly and in comes the third mate, with a torch and a bottle of rum. All hands are served with a tot and as Tria is having a glass with each group he is in good spirits. 'This is not the worst, tomorrow the wind comes,' he tells us. We were told we could turn in but at 11.40 pm we were awakened by the policeman. 'Five minutes, three whistles!'

We learn that two headsails, fore and mizzen lower t'gallants are to be taken in. We crawl out of our warm bunks and climb into those confounded oilskins and sea boots again. The weather is becoming worse every minute. We struggle forward, listening to the 1st mate's indecipherable curses and orders, and start sweating on buntlines and clew lines. The sheet breaks and then two buntlines, making it impossible to clew up the sail properly. Five of us were ordered aloft to take in the sail. But too late, that great sail, the fore lower t'gallant threshing and cracking madly lasts about 30 seconds and is then torn to pieces by the wind and disappears to leeward. We make fast what is left of the sail and return to the deck. I found that I had kept comparatively dry under oilskins and went with Johansson and the donkey man to coil ropes back on to their pins. We gingerly made our way to the scuppers, trying to peer through the blackness to see if any big waves were coming. We just avoided one and then made a dash to the rail to make a quick job of it but the ship rolled suddenly, burying her lee rail and over us came tons and tons of water. I was knocked completely over and along the deck with Johansson who went feet first. The water was icy and I gasped with its sudden chill. I saw a rope's end and grabbed frantically, missed and grabbed again. I heaved myself upright, soaked to the skin with water pouring out of my sea boots. I dimly made out Johansson who could be identified by one arm protruding through the water, clawing around in circles. Poor old Freddie! I laughed as he came up, gesticulating furiously and cursing.

As *Archibald Russell* approached Falmouth, for what would be the last time, Jack described in detail a fairly typical conclusion to a grain ship voyage from Australia.

1 August 1939 Dawn came and just visible on the horizon was Bishop's Rock Lighthouse. By 8 am we can clearly see the Scilly Isles on the port bow. The lighthouse itself stands on a small island isolated from the rest. By 11 am we have drawn level and are now passing the islands on the port beam. Our passenger has a look through a telescope. 'I can see a cow,' he said, proudly. 'Nice work, can you see any bathing beauties on that little beach there?' I answered, pointing. He made another prolonged study. 'Dammed if I can,' in a disappointed tone. At 12.30 pm a cry comes from the fo'c'sle head, 'England Ho!' There almost right ahead is Lands End, the southernmost tip of Cornwall. We all dance up and down the deck with joy, cheer and shriek madly. Suddenly an aeroplane appeared from over the islands, flying low. The pilot waved. Surely we have re-entered civilisation. The skipper amuses himself by shooting at the 'springers' [dolphin], which come leaping out of the water near the ship's stern. He scored a bull. The great fish made a great leap into the air, turned over backwards and lay motionless on the surface. A great red patch quickly spread over the sea and many sea birds were circling over the carcase within a few minutes. At 2 pm we sight Wolf's Rock, a large lighthouse off the coast. We have 50 miles to go to the Lizard, which we anticipate reaching about midnight. We are now in the shelter of the islands and running along the coast heading east. The seas are appreciably smaller and we make a quiet 4 knots. We pass the Lizard at 10 pm but have received no orders, which means that we will proceed into Falmouth, where we will wait for them. Another 15 miles to go!

Gradually the lights of the town loom into view and at 12.30 am on Wednesday 2 August we drift slowly the last two or three miles to the anchorage. A fisherman came alongside and tried to do some trade, but he does not know our steward! We ghost on—a perfect night—calm landlocked waters. With a gentle following breeze we stand around talking at 1.30 am. The pilot boat appears and a wiry looking seaman comes aboard. A brief 'good morning' and he proceeds to the poop. The royals come in and we stand by. Three whistles, 'all hands', and we clew up the courses. Then down went the anchor with a terrific clatter. Hoarse yells, orders and replies fill the night air. Aloft the crew can be seen against the clear moonlit sky, puny figures taking in the great sails for the last time. Slowly the *Archibald Russell* came to a standstill, 121 days from Port Germein.

Ropes cover the deck. The monotonous voice of the 'old man' carries along through the quiet air and then suddenly stops. Only the mutterings of the men aloft can be heard. A glow to the east tells us that dawn is not far off. At 4.15 am it is almost daylight. We finish stowing sail and climb down to the deck and survey those bare masts. Well, well, well. The passenger came into the fo'c'sle for some coffee and a smoke. He is very excited, as he will be home tonight. We turn in for two hours' sleep. The Captain, we see, is in a good mood. Rutherford and I being appointed watchmen are free during the day so we ask permission to go ashore. We are told 'yes'. Jubilation! We spent the day ashore and were photographed by a news photographer as we were both reading the *Daily Mail*.

Lawhill came in during the day, 141 days out from Port Lincoln. We went over to her and argued with her crew the respective merits of the two ships. She came via the Cape of Good Hope. Upon our return to the *Russell* we found her over-run with visitors.

Thursday 3 August Being on duty from 12 midnight until 7 am, I was on deck when I saw lights approaching very close and gradually made out another square rigger, the barque *Winterhude*. I stand and watch the spectacle. She came in and anchored about 300 yards to port and within two and a half hours had all sails tucked away. This was fast work considering the rain and strong wind.

I was told by the mate that I cannot sign off here but I tackled the Captain and he signed me off on Friday 4 August. I pack and prepare to leave my home of four months. The crew crowd into the fo'c'sle grinning and cheerful. Tria (third mate) came in and helped with my baggage. 'Well boys, she was a great voyage.' I shook hands with all around, finishing up with 'Mac' (McRae). 'You'll write, Jack?' 'Sure Mac, see you in London. Have a good trip to the next port.' I climbed into the launch suddenly feeling lost and lonely! The engine is started and we move off. I wave frantically. The boys cheer and I wave back. Then I noticed the flag being lowered. They were saluting! I was amazed but very pleased. I turned to the boatman. 'By God they are a fine mob!' But no reply! Someone running along the flying bridge and out on to the end of the jib boom. A hat is waved, 'Mac', I would know that black sweater anywhere. I waved back feeling strangely empty and hollow.

Archibald Russell was ordered to Hull to discharge. She never sailed again. When war broke out she became a store ship and was rigged down. After the war she was broken up.

8 WARTIME AND POSTWAR WINDJAMMERS

Lawhill

Many of the ships still sailing at the outbreak of World War II and during the war have been covered by earlier narratives. This conflict was responsible for some large sailing ships being put back into service and also for the sinking of three of them—Erikson's *Penang*, *Killoran* and *Olivebank*, victims of a German U-boat, raider and mine respectively.

When the war started in Europe, there were still 15 large, deep-sea, square-rigged steel sailing ships sailing the seas, mainly on the Australia run carrying grain to Europe—*Abraham Rydberg*, *Penang*, *Killoran*, *Olivebank*, *Lawhill*, *Priwall*, *Padua*, *Pamir*, *Passat*, *Pommern*, *Winterhude*, *Moshulu*, *Kommodore Johnsen*, *Archibald Russell* and *Viking*. Making shorter passages, the iron Norwegian barque *Alastor* could be included here, although she was not large, only 823 tons.

In addition there was a little-publicised group of sailing ships on the West Coast of South America. The four-masted barque *Omega*, the barques *Nelson*, *Maipo* and *Tellus*, and the full-rigger *Calbuco* were still doing useful work, albeit short coastal voyages. Apart from *Nelson*, which was wrecked in 1943, they were all sailing during the war or in the immediate postwar years; *Calbuco* made a voyage to Marseilles in 1948, where she was broken up. I have never encountered anyone who sailed in this group, but Frederick D. Wilhelmsen wrote a book about *Omega* and her final years, titled *Omega: Last of the Barques*. It is an interesting account of the last years of this ship and a trade that escaped notice once the rest of the world's windjammer fleets ceased trading to the West Coast. Two other barques, *Guaytecas* and *Tijuca*, were making voyages between South America, South Georgia and South Africa. The former was partially dismasted on a voyage to Cape Town in 1946. It is surprising that she was re-rigged.

In 1940 a five-masted schooner entered Sydney Harbour with a timber cargo. Then flying the Canadian flag, she had spent most of her life under American ownership. She was the *City of Alberni*, previously named *Vigilant*, and, incredibly, had remained in trade from the time she was built in 1920. I have been unable to find anyone who sailed in her but she is entitled to a mention in this chapter as she sailed during the war. On a voyage from Vancouver to Durban in 1944 she put into Valparaiso for repairs. Here the voyage was terminated and she was sold to Chilean owners, being renamed *Condor*. In 1946 she sailed from Valparaiso for Greece with a cargo of rice, putting into Montevideo for repairs after rounding Cape Horn. She sailed on to Bahia Blanca and caught fire, becoming a total loss.

Of course there were many smaller vessels, dozens and maybe hundreds of small wooden sailing vessels and a few of steel, mainly schooners and ketches, that were plying the Baltic, Mediterranean and Australian coasts and even the Americas during this time. These are not often considered, and it is lamentable that few stories from these lesser-known ships and their crews have been published. Captain Harold Huycke from Seattle has been working on the stories of this group for some time. I hope that he can soon publish the results to put a proper end to the history of commercial sail.

I was fortunate to obtain this interesting account of some of *Abraham Rydberg*'s World War II voyaging from Oscar Malmberg, her master, referred to in the previous chapter as the second mate during Albert Wargren's time in this ship.

I spent 10 years in *Abraham Rydberg* from 1933 until 1943. Between 1933 and 1935 I was third and second mate on two Australian voyages. In 1936 I became mate and in 1937 was promoted master. I remained in that position until January 1943 when the ship was sold to Portugal. The years I spent in her mean more to me than any other period in my life. The ships in which I was brought up, small sailing ships in the Baltic and North Sea, are also very dear to me and fill me with nostalgia but cannot compare with *Abraham Rydberg*. Even my business life of the past 24 years is pallid by comparison. *Abraham Rydberg* was well found and we tried to keep her like a yacht. She was not very fast but properly handled, she manoeuvred well. As long as the main topgallant was carried she never refused to tack and was always very dry. Her best day's run was 316 nautical miles in twenty-three and half hours running the easting down in ballast to Australia, and 290 loaded in the North Atlantic during the war. There were so many incidents.

In 1934 we had a race with the liner *Mauritania*. We were coming up the Channel in a near gale and kept up with the lady for several hours even though we were missing a couple of sails on the foremast. Several days earlier we ran into a heavy squall just north of the Azores. The fore topgallant yard broke taking the fore royal with it. There is a picture of us taken from the *Mauretania* in Alex Hurst's book *Square Riggers: The Final Epoch*. In it we are in the process of setting the main top gallant.

Our last voyage from Australia was in 1939. We had loaded part of our grain cargo at Port Victoria and the remainder in Port Germein. *Viking, Pommern* and *Pamir* were in Port Victoria and *Viking* left Port Victoria two days before we left Port Germein. She went around Cape Horn and we went around the Cape of Good Hope and just off the Lizard we both met up once again. We always came home from Australia via Cape of Good Hope as it usually gave us better weather and allowed more consistent training of the cadets to be undertaken.

Leaving Spencer Gulf in the southern summer we also usually had strong south-easterly winds. It was easier to square away from Cape Leeuwin and the Indian Ocean. On the last voyage we left Port Germein at the head of the Gulf and passed Cape of Good Hope 38 days later, which I believe is something of a record. But then we had strong trades all the way, ending up in a hurricane south of Mauritius. It gave us a famous shove.

We left Gothenburg in September 1939, the day World War II broke out. We were bound for Australia, Port Lincoln for orders. We got into the Atlantic and two days after leaving Gothenburg we passed north of the Shetlands. Before reaching the Line [Equator], I received a radio telegram changing our orders and directing us to Buenos Aires, Argentina. We were then to load again there for home. On account of heavy ice in the Skaw we were ordered to the Barbados for some time and then proceeded on home. On 9 April 1940, we were about 200 miles west of Bergen, Norway, and the German invasion put a stop to our continuing the voyage. After being hove to, and slowly clawing our way to the westward again I received orders to proceed to a suitable neutral American port, which I considered New York to be. We arrived there on the last day of April. We finally discharged our cargo in Norfolk and Baltimore and after that loaded a cargo of coal at Newport News for Rio de Janeiro in Brazil. We then went on to Santos where we loaded linseed cakes for Boston. In all we made four voyages between North and South America, finally arriving at Baltimore in the spring of 1942.

There was a heavy German submarine campaign on the US east coast and the *Abraham Rydberg* was laid up. Alex Hurst [author and publisher of many maritime books] mentions seeing us a week after the war had broken out, when becalmed in the Atlantic southwest of Fastnet. I do remember the meeting, although at the time did not know he was in the tanker that passed us. I also remember my remark to the officer of the watch at the time, 'Poor devils, they are heading right into the thick of it and we are lucky to be heading away from it.' Perhaps it was a premonition, as his ship, a tanker, was torpedoed that night. We had neutrality flags painted on our sides which we had done while skirting the Norwegian coast with a submarine looking on—probably a German.

In the autumn of 1940 we were in the doldrums and were stopped by a British cruiser. Not a breath of wind but of course we backed the main yards. When satisfied that we were not an enemy ship they sent us over fresh vegetables, which were most appreciated, and when the boarding party discovered my wife was on board they sent a signal back and the commander sent over a box of chocolates. I remember one 'snotty' looking over the stern to find out if we were by any chance a second *Seeadler*.*

Millicent Malmberg accompanied her husband for the last six years of *Abraham Rydberg*'s sailing life. She has added her impressions to windjammer life via a letter she wrote to a friend, a copy of which she has kindly sent me. The following passages describe very graphically the last voyage of this well-known vessel.

4 March 1942 [*in the North Atlantic*] We've battled our way around the seven seas; we've experienced easterly gales in the roaring forties, a cyclone in the Indian Ocean, murderous weather off the Cape of Good Hope, winter gales around Iceland, ice and snowstorms off the New England coast; in fact we thought we knew all there was to be known on the subject of bad weather. The past two weeks however proved that we still had something to learn, for two terrible storms struck us in quick succession, the second infinitely the worst of the two. The barometer fell so rapidly that I waited to hear the thud when it hit the bottom. In all Oscar's years at sea he has never seen it so bad. The wind howled and thundered, sounding like a London tube train roaring through its tunnel. Mountainous seas, heaving and tumbling, crashed into and over the ship, poor old lady. It's too bad that at her age, she's over fifty; she should have to fight for her life. She battled valiantly, shivered and groaned, but she came through, God knows how. She was built on the Clyde of course, perhaps the answer.

---

*In World War I, the sailing ship *Pass of Balmaha* was fitted out in Germany as a raider and renamed *Seeadler* (*Sea Eagle*). In the guise of an innocent merchant sailing ship and under the command of Count Felix Von Luckner she sank many Allied ships. The 'snotty' (midshipman) looking over the stern was checking to see if she had a propeller, which would have indicated that she had an auxiliary engine and was not what she appeared.

The men on deck went through purgatory hauling the braces in water up to their waists, and being flung around in the heavy seas that swept over us. I am always terrified that some of them will be swept overboard. Down below I didn't enjoy myself very much either. In spite of my efforts of stowing things away and jamming them down, nothing stayed put. Books leapt from their shelves and went sailing around the deck, locked drawers and cupboards burst open and disgorged their contents. The shoe cupboard banged open and all our footwear came cascading out. I was helplessly clinging to the archway with both hands and couldn't do a thing to stop it. Corks flew out of bottles and the contents followed the corks. The study is still delicately perfumed with Cointreau, which oozed from the little wine cupboard, and the bathroom reeks of lavender water. The bathroom was awash, inches of water squelched around and poured through the grating into the saloon. When I was compelled to go in there I donned Oscar's snow boots and splashed my way through. The lifeboat was swamped and the portholes were under water. The seas forced their way through and our carpets, chairs and bedroom sofa are pretty well ruined. Thank heaven my piano didn't shift. Had that gone hurtling around the damage would have been even greater. I was anxious about the wireless but that was successfully chained down. Four days and nights neither Oscar, the mate nor I slept a wink. We were dog-tired and filthy for we couldn't wash, I couldn't even comb my hair. We've had our clothes on for over two weeks now and baths are a thing of the past. For one thing they're impossible and for another I am terrified that a torpedo will strike us while I'm dripping wet and in my birthday suit. If she's hit the ship will sink within three minutes. She hasn't a chance of survival, poor old dear with her one great hold. (Oscar, reading over my shoulder, says we wouldn't have three minutes grace for the ship would sink instantaneously.) I got out our warmest coats, Oscar's great winter coat with the sheepskin lining and my kangaroo skin coat, but then realised that if we had to jump for it the weight of the coats would drag us down so I changed them for Oscar's Burberry and my camelhair, they're not so warm but much lighter. Chow, hankies, a comb, matches and cigarettes are in the pockets. Bill, our boxer dog, in all his years at sea, has never been able to accustom himself to bad weather. As soon as the ship starts pitching and rolling he becomes uneasy and restless. When we heel over to starboard, Bill runs to port, and vice versa, always climbing up hill. When the ship shies herself around and tries to turn double somersaults as she has recently, the poor little man is dreadfully afraid. I sometimes think it is not right to have him at sea, but he hates being in port and we don't always have such filthy weather. The main thing, in the bad times is to hang on to him and try to keep him calm. I was irritated recently when he flung himself on me when I was leaning over to save the coffee pot. Result, our lovely pale green bulkhead is splashed with ugly brown stains, but I daresay I can wash them off when, if we get to port.

The steward and cook have performed one of the minor miracles of the storm. They are flung and bounced from one side of the galley to the other, pots and pans leap off the stove, and yet they continue to serve hot meals for us all. How on earth can they do it? Extra meals were one of our greatest problems. We left the saloon and ate in the officers' mess, but after a time, that became impossible. Oscar and I discovered the only thing to do was to jam ourselves down on the flag locker in the alleyway, with a plate in one hand and a fork in the other. Billy's meals weren't exactly easy either; I had to hold him with one hand and his dish with the other.

The only creature on board who hasn't been at all worried is Santista, the parrot. She's a real little sailor. When her perch swings out at an angle of 90 degrees or bumps and swings from side to side, she merely regards it as fun and an incentive to perform even more complicated gymnastics. A wonderful little bird!

8 March The worst of the storm is over now. It is forty miles to Chesapeake Bay lightship, if it's still there. We're streaking along, but the damn barometer is dropping again. A tug should meet us at Cape Henry, as we're bound for Baltimore. This is the last lap of a damned awful voyage and the most dangerous. We are all ready for a quick getaway and no one will sleep tonight. The Yanks will give us no information about minefields and coastal stations, even though we are 'neutral' and Oscar on Hitler's black list since before the war!

A flying fortress over us this morning—an inspiring sight. And this afternoon one of our own cruisers cutting through the water with her fo'c'sle head awash hurled past. I was so happy to see the white ensign! We saluted each other and they all waved, bless them. Oscar has just come down. He says fog is descending upon us. Good God, haven't we had enough to bear? He said this morning, 'You know Millicent, no one will ever realise what we have been through this voyage.' He's right, no one ever will, and we'll forget it ourselves if we get in safely.

14 March I spoke too soon. Dirty weather again, but only a sixty miles per hour gale! Oscar took us out to sea again where we rode it out. All bad things come to an end, the storm died down and we came up to Cape Henry again. No tug, so we picked up the pilot and sailed through the minefields. Head wind, so we were obliged to anchor. The pilot who expected to be on board for twenty four hours was with us for four days before we finally reached Baltimore.

These narratives from Oscar and Millicent Malmberg bring the commercial sailing ship into 'modern times'.

Amongst the 20 large sailing ships actually sailing the seas at the outbreak of war was the four-masted barque *Lawhill*, who with *Pamir* traded throughout the war in submarine- and raider-infested waters. Like *Lawhill*, *Pamir* was seized as a war prize when she arrived in New Zealand and spent the war years in the Pacific. The story of this period is told in great detail by the late Jack Churchouse in *Pamir: Under the New Zealand Flag.*

Back in the seventies I was delighted to meet up with Tor Lindqvist, who has become a good friend, and later Birger Lindeman, both of whom sailed in *Lawhill* during that period. They have been of great help in assembling this chapter. Incredibly, in an age when the commercial sailing ship was little more than a curiosity and kept in business purely because of the wartime shipping shortfall, Tor rounded Cape Horn six times under sail. In all, he spent 40 years at sea, eight of them under sail. In more recent times he became the principal rigger on the *Polly Woodside*, the barque restored by the Maritime Museum in Melbourne, and the 27 years he devoted to this work was recognised by his being awarded the Order of Australia. Tor had previously sailed in two other Erikson ships, *Passat* and *Viking*. It is significant that he was rated as an AB at the age of 18. He tells of his time in *Lawhill*:

I signed on *Lawhill* in Stockholm on 23 February, 1940, as able seaman at the age of 18. I joined her in Rothesay Bay on the Isle of Bude in Scotland. I know my shipmate Birger Lindeman has told you of our voyaging from here to the time the South African Government took us over so I will start from there. The ship was re-registered in East London and the Government advertised in the newspapers for master, officers and crew for a large sailing vessel trading overseas but did not get one reply. We the crew, mostly Finns, were asked if we were willing to sail the ship under the South African flag and wages and we all agreed. Our wages trebled!

We sailed from East London to Bunbury, Western Australia, in ballast, 24 days at sea. In Bunbury we loaded railway sleepers and Jarrah timber for East London. As we did not have the westerlies behind us the voyage took 46 days across the Indian Ocean. We discharged our cargo at East London and sailed again in ballast for Bunbury. We also carried four South African apprentices. Loading sleepers again, this time for Cape Town, we sailed via Cape Horn taking 82 days. My first impressions of Cape Town and surrounding area were the beautiful scenery and the mountains. We spent many months in Cape Town for repairs and dry-docking before loading cocoa beans for Hobart. The passage time for this trip was 32 days. *Lawhill* could really sail well if the wind was fair. Close hauled she was not too fast. Her best speed when I sailed in her was 14 knots. Being fairly old she had to be sailed carefully.

In Hobart we loaded a part cargo of fruit and jam for Melbourne. It took us two weeks to reach Port Phillip heads. Off the heads we hove to for the pilot in rough weather. Something went wrong when they were lowering the boat and the boat capsized throwing the pilot and two seamen into the sea. A second boat picked them up and the pilot appeared on board *Lawhill* dripping wet. We had a fair wind and we sailed through the Rip to Hobsons Bay anchorage without a tug. In Victoria Dock we loaded a full cargo of wheat, down to her marks.

It was now 1943. While in Melbourne two Oerlikon guns were fitted on the poop deck and I went to gunnery school for two weeks. We sailed for Cape Town via Bass Strait and Cape Horn—55 days at sea, and a very fast passage. We had strong winds all the way varying between north-west and south-west and our decks were never dry. On arrival at Cape Town I was rushed to hospital and operated on immediately for appendicitis, so I was very lucky.

The next voyage we sailed to Port Lincoln, South Australia, in ballast, loading wheat for Cape Town, again via Cape Horn. We struck headwinds off Cape Horn and made heavy weather of it. We were blown back around Cape Horn and after a few days rounded it again. The Master said we had rounded the Horn three times, although it was only counted as one rounding. We arrived in Cape Town safely (she had the nickname *Lucky Lawhill*) after 80 days at sea. It was now 1944 and my good shipmate Birger Lindeman signed off and joined a British ship. Birger was donkey man the last two years in *Lawhill*, having sailed in the ship for over four years. He was a first class seaman and very good shipmate. On these last voyages we had a number of Australians as well as South Africans in the crew.

On my last voyage in *Lawhill* we sailed from Cape Town for Sydney with a cargo of cocoa beans and arrived after 44 days at sea. My first impression of Sydney was the beautiful harbour and of course the famous Harbour Bridge. We were towed under the bridge and tied up in Walsh Bay where we discharged our cargo. We were then towed to Newcastle by the old steam tug *St Hillary*. We loaded steel and coke for Adelaide. We were 13 days at sea via Bass Strait. In Port Adelaide we loaded a full cargo of bagged wheat for Cape Town. We sailed via Cape Horn, which was the last time it was rounded by *Lawhill*. We spent Christmas south of the Auckland Islands in a flat calm. Later in the voyage we ran into a strong gale. I was at the wheel from 3 am to 4 am. At 4 am I struck eight bells and waited for my relief but none came until one and a half hours later. The hatchway to the crew's quarters had been washed away by heavy seas and the ladder broken so that the men could not get out. The fo'c'sles were full of water and what a mess. Near Cape Horn we sighted a small ship and we wondered who she was. We later found out she was the *Eagle*, a small steamer bound for Antarctica. It was now January 1945. We arrived in Cape Town during February and I signed off *Lawhill* after serving in her for five years. During that time we rounded Cape Horn four times and we never lost a man. She certainly was the *Lucky Lawhill*. In 1948 *Lawhill* was sold to Portuguese owners in Lourenço Marques. I joined her for the run job from Durban. We did the trip in 30 hours. The crew was paid off and I was actually the last man in the ship except the old watchman. *Lawhill* never sailed again.

Birger Lindeman gave me this description of his time in *Lawhill*:

During the winter war between Finland and Russia (1939–1940) I was deck boy in a small Finnish cargo ship called *Suomen Poika*. I heard that *Lawhill* was engaging a crew and asked to sign off so that I could join her. After a quick trip home I made my way to Mariehamn to see the owner's son who was in charge of the office. Four of us were shipped across to Stockholm and were signed on in March 1940 by Gustaf Erikson himself. He lived at the Hotel d'Anglais, so there we were, four youngsters, keen to have a go. Little did we know what was in store for us! After staying a few days at the sailor's home we were put on the train for Bergen, Norway, where we arrived 23 hours later. We were then shipped across to England in a small Bergen Line steamer. After sailing late one night we were shepherded into a convoy of about a dozen ships. It was the first time I had seen guns on a merchant ship. My main memory from that trip was of a Jewish family fleeing from Nazi Germany en route to the Argentine. We did not take the shortest route, going north of the Shetlands. We docked at North Shields the same day that Germany invaded Norway. A few more days in Stockholm or Norway and I would never have sailed in *Lawhill*. After several days we went by train to Glasgow and then Troon. We had to walk to the Ailsa Craig shipyard where *Lawhill* was berthed. My first impression was *What have I done in signing on this miserable looking tub?* Once on board the mate took us to the skipper where we handed over our papers. He was only interested in how much extra money we had 'conned' the various agents into advancing us from our wages. We then went to the fo'c'sle which was amidships and met the rest of the gang consisting mainly of Ålanders (Swedish-speaking Finns) like me, Danes and Estonians, all thrown together in a mixed crowd of so called 'sailing ship heroes' but far from it. Dinner was ready a little later and it had to be carried from galley to the fo'c'sle, which was also our mess-room. This had a long table along the after end of the bulkhead. I will never forget it. It was fried liver that looked like buffalo hide and some sort of gravy that looked like coal tar and tasted like it.

While the ship was being got ready for sea the fore upper topsail yard had to be sent down for repairs and the riggers at the dock said it would take a week just to take it down. The skipper and mate had other ideas and the yard was taken down in two and a half hours, lifted ashore by crane, repaired, lifted back on board and up the mast in record time. Sailing day finally arrived and early one morning at the end of April 1940, a tug towed us clear of the Mull of Kintyre and Rathlin Island, cast off and we were on our own. That's when the fun started! All sails had to be set, ropes had to be learned and for us deck boys and other first timers it was not easy. There was no such thing as an eight-hour day or overtime etc. When work finished at 6 pm it was up the rigging to overhaul the buntlines which the third mate had a nasty habit of breaking on purpose, just to keep you on your toes all the time. On the second night out we caught a nasty squall without warning and the topgallants had to be taken in pretty smart. That was my introduction to get up to the main topgallant on a pitch-black night, a howling wind and rain coming down—not in buckets but in 44-gallon drums. Finally we reached the North-East Trades, then the doldrums and then the South-East Trades. The usual procedure was for the good sails to be unbent and all the old rags put up in their place while we were in the trade winds and once out of the tropics the procedure was reversed.

We finally arrived at Montevideo roads for orders. The trip had taken 53 days in ballast from Troon to the anchorage outside the breakwater not far from where the *Graf Spee* was scuttled. While we were at anchor the harbour master ordered the skipper to send down the topgallant yards due to the *pamperos*, which, fortunately never came. After about three weeks our orders came. We were to proceed to the Seychelles Islands for a cargo of guano. After an uneventful trip we finally arrived at Maki to take stores on board, including a rusty tank, which was placed abaft the foremast. It was cleaned out, cement-washed and used as a spare water tank. We also took on board several hundred islanders to load the guano. We had a good trip to Assumption Island—four days and even beat the local trading schooner. On arrival at Assumption we found the four-masted barque *Pamir* already there, loading for New Plymouth in New Zealand. When *Pamir* sailed we shifted over to her anchorage, which made it a bit nearer for the loading gangs, as everything had to be brought out by canoes.

One funny incident that sticks in my mind. We had an old gramophone, a real old-timer on a high wooden cabinet, and the locals wanted to buy it. As we had no use for it we said they could have it for a few bottles of *baka*, a local brew made from sweet potatoes, very potent and looked like cloudy water, guaranteed to curl your hair and also good for spider bites. They came out late at night to pick it up and we lowered it down into one of their canoes. However they were back the next morning very crestfallen, as it appears that when we lowered it over the side the working part of it had fallen out into the sea. So all they had was a wooden cabinet and a few old scratched 78 records. We had already drunk the *baka*.

The slow loading, day after day and the beautiful weather made a most enjoyable interlude. One morning we awoke to find two of our crew missing. So was a small dinghy belonging to the administrator of the island. They had set sail sometime during the night and by daylight there was no sign of them, even from the top of the mainmast. The skipper was furious, as he had to pay for the dinghy. We heard later that they had reached the coast of East Africa some 500 nautical miles away.

The loading completed and the anchor hove up, we set sail for Auckland. One night in the Mozambique Channel a destroyer came very close and put a searchlight on us. We sailed down the Channel past the islands of Comaro and Mayotta and that was the last land we sighted until the north coast of New Zealand appeared on the starboard bow with Three Kings Islands to port. On the voyage from Assumption we struck a couple of calm days with temperatures in the forties. The skipper decided to have lifeboat drill. It took nearly two hours to get the davits working and when the boat hit the water it sank so it had to be hauled up again. Being full of water the weight was too much and it bent one of the davits so a tackle had to be rigged from the jigger mast.

We arrived in Auckland 75 days out, and when we sailed in past Little Barrier Island and managed to contact Tinimatangi pilot station they nearly went out of their mind. Unknowingly we had sailed right through a minefield and as we were still in it they asked us to wait until daylight and if we were still afloat a tug would be out in the morning. The tug duly arrived and we docked on 9 January 1941. *Pamir* had in the meantime arrived at New Plymouth. The discharging began and the very fine guano dust kept blowing about and getting everywhere in the ship. It was difficult to keep everything clean. One day there was a severe gale warning and we had to unshackle the port anchor and get the chain ashore around one of the bollards on the wharf as an extra precaution, but nothing happened.

With the cargo discharged and stores and ballast taken on board, it was time to say goodbye to Auckland and New Zealand and head for Port Victoria in Spencer Gulf. We sailed south of Tasmania and arrived at Port Victoria 31 days out. This was my first landfall in Australia and what a miserable place it looked at first sight, but the thought of a few visits to the Wauraltee pub kept us going. After formalities were completed we began loading from ketches, as there was not enough water at the long jetty. When enough cargo had been taken on to hold the ship up, it was up anchor and sail out to the ballast grounds off Wardang Island where the ballast was discharged. It was hard work filling the baskets with stones and sand with only a shovel but the stuff from Auckland was not too bad. The ballast, brick rubble, which had been an old pub, originally taken on at Glasgow took some digging out at Assumption. With the loading completed we set sail again, this time for East London, South Africa. This took 66 days, west across the Indian Ocean. When off Cape Leeuwin we encountered a severe storm and the large spare water tank on the main deck broke loose and made quite a mess but it was finally secured.

After arriving at East London, war was declared by the Allies against Finland, as she had aligned with Germany against Russia. The ship was taken over by the South African Government as a prize of war. After some consideration everyone agreed to sign South African articles, which we did on 20 September 1941. I finally signed off *Lawhill* in Capetown on 30 May 1944 and during my time in her rounded Cape Horn twice in 1943 and once in 1944.

Of the Australian boys that joined the crew of *Lawhill*, Bob Broughton joined her in Melbourne in 1943 and describes his time in her:

When I joined there were already two Australians in the crew, Ian McEwan from Bunbury and a Tasmanian, William Boyd Thompson. There were also three South African seamen, four apprentices and an uncertified third mate, Jim Barrett. Bill and I made our first trip around the Horn in the apprentices' cabin. It was midwinter and a rigorous introduction to sailing ship life. *Lawhill* could carry sail when other ships would have shortened down, as she was sturdy and heavily rigged. We sailed 11,000 miles from Melbourne to Cape Town via Cape Horn in 55 days. Being accommodated in the midships section we were seldom worried by water entering our quarters. There was no heating except on the rare occasions when the donkey boiler was lit. This meant cold, damp quarters and a fair degree of discomfort. Food was standard sailing ship fare with a bit of canned meat and fish for specials. We got used to it. There was a strong loyalty to the ship and a fairly good comradeship despite the mixed nationalities and varied allegiances.

Three watches were kept, British style, but not the dogs. We ate supper at 8 pm and as I was permanent 4 pm to 8 pm (for which I was grateful), I was often late for meals because we took in sails at the change of watch. Usually my watch made sail at first light and so there was more sailorising and therefore more fun. *Lawhill* handled well, with the usual problems when running in heavy weather. The brace winches made a difference but the topgallants were long braces. At 50-plus she was too old to go about in anything but light breezes and we always wore ship instead of tacking, but generally she was as good as ever. The lower topsails were locked on with short chain sheets and never taken at sea. Having only five yards on each mast meant deep heavy sails and without clew garnets the end man's job on the yard (usually me) was pretty heavy. Strong competition existed amongst the young men but of course did not extent to painting and chipping. All in all she was an average old barque but with a mixed wartime crew it made things a bit different. I like to think that all her deck men were above average as many were in training for their tickets or were at sea on account of the war. Certainly those I know about have done well and many are in good positions now. The following is a record I made of my voyages.

Melbourne–Cape Town	28.06.43–21.08.43	11000 miles	55days
Cape Town–Port Lincoln	4.10.43–23.12.43	5000 miles	48days
Port Lincoln–Cape Town			
via Cape Horn	20.02.44–31.04.44	11500 miles	73 days
Cape Town–Sydney	30.06.44–6.08.44	6000 miles	38 days
Sydney–Newcastle	1 day under tow	80 miles	
Newcastle–Adelaide	12.10.44–28.10.44	1000 miles	16 days
Adelaide–Cape Town			
via Cape Horn	30.11.44–14.02.45	11500 miles	79 days
Cape Town–Hobart	6.06.45–20.07.45	5800 miles	44 days
Hobart–Sydney	11.09.45–16.09.45	1000 miles	5 days
Sydney–Bunbury	10.11.45–16.12.45	3000 miles	36 days
Bunbury–Cape Town	10.01.46–25.02.46	4500 miles	46 days

One of the South Africans who joined the crew of *Lawhill* in 1947 was Peter Carrington, later Captain, and Harbour Master of Port Elizabeth. He tells us:

I sailed in *Lawhill* for two trips, a period of 18 months. I joined her in Cape Town in February 1947 under the command of Captain Artur Söderlund. The mate was Bruno Eriksson. We sailed from Cape Town to Durban, a trip of some 800 miles, which took us 28 days! Having no radio on board we were declared missing off the South African coast. Eventually arriving in Durban, beating against head winds, we loaded coal for Buenos Aires where we spent about six weeks discharging the coal. We then loaded wheat for Durban and Lourenço Marques. The run home took 28 days, not bad for bluff-bowed *Lawhill*. We had quite a long spell in Lourenço Marques discharging and then loaded stone and sand ballast before sailing for Port Victoria, Spencer Gulf. We just missed having Christmas in Port Victoria, arriving there on 27 December 1947. We spent a very happy time at Port Victoria, about two months, loading wheat at the anchorage from ketches, for Beira.

While at Port Victoria there were also two other four-masted barques loading grain for Europe—*Passat* and *Viking*. It was thought that *Lawhill*'s topgallant masts and rigging were not in a fit condition for her to make the Horn rounding so we sailed via the Indian Ocean, arriving at Beira 60 days later. We returned to Durban where all hands were paid off. This last voyage *Lawhill* was under the command of Captain Madri Lindholm and this was the last commercial voyage that *Lawhill* would make. She made the short voyage to Lourenço Marques and it was there that she ended her days. Plans fell through of turning her into a training ship and she was towed up the Tembe River and left to rot. Some years later I was in a collier as second mate and I saw her masts sticking majestically above the mangroves around a bend in the river. Not a fitting end for such a ship.

Had South Africa handed *Lawhill* back to Finland after the war, as New Zealand did *Pamir*, it is very likely she would be on exhibition to this day, for structurally she was a very interesting ship.

The postwar years saw Gustaf Erikson's last two operational sailing ships, *Passat* and *Viking*, join *Lawhill* in Spencer Gulf in 1948 to load grain for Europe, as they had on many occasions in the thirties. *Lawhill* never saw European waters again.

Stories from these voyages have a different ring to those told of the prewar years. A metamorphosis had taken place during the war years that caused a break in the culture that had existed in the Erikson ships for the previous two decades, and certainly in that which prevailed in British and German ships in the two decades before that. Quality and quantity of food, and the availability of alcohol, stand out as prime elements of the differences.

A story from the postwar grain ship *Passat* comes from Jason Hopton, long-time National Secretary and mainstay of the Australian Cape Horners Association. As he flew his Liberator bomber over the Pacific during World War II, Jason had no idea that he would round Cape Horn in an Erikson windjammer. He spent five years of his life in the Pacific skies and when peace came the young flight lieutenant found the transition to civilian life was not easy. He tried his old insurance job but his feet were still itchy.

Passat, Viking and *Lawhill* came to Port Victoria in 1948 and revived his pre-war interest in these ships. Along with his mate Charlie Burns, a young medical student taking a year away from study, they signed on *Passat* for the voyage around the Horn to Falmouth. Jason's later career in journalism is evident in the way in which he has couched this story, written specially for this book.

The Chippie was Crossed

The coach from Adelaide dumped us both in the dark, in the middle of the little seaport's main street at the end of the plantation. Our gear was placed at our feet and the driver yelled, 'Best of luck! Glad it's youse and not me.' Shapes of the Port Victoria Post Office and the Wauraltee Hotel opposite showed up but there were no lights, no street lamps and not a glimmer anywhere else in the town. We said nothing and waited to get our eyes used to the blackness.

Footstep sounds came with the breeze up from the seashore and I filled my lungs and yelled, 'We're here.' Lumbering into view came the Master of *Passat*, Captain Ivar Hägerstrand, whom we'd met in the town a week before. On his head was a crumpled cap and then we saw that he wore a dark suit, waistcoat and all. As other men loomed up, he said, 'Come!' So we followed, the others bringing up the rear, carrying our belongings. Halfway down the jetty we watched our baggage handed down to a lifeboat and we slid down a rope to join the company aboard. Our places were in the bows. We could smell liquor coming from the breaths of seamen behind us. The engine was started, after a lot of muttering and puffing. My companion, Charlie, and I faced forward and soon collected sea spray as we headed out into the bay. There was no sign of the ship. It was indeed a black night but we were to meet worse in the next four months. The men behind us spoke in Swedish. Soon a call had us peering ahead and able to make out the shape of the big windjammer. We closed rapidly, heading for her middle. Yells, the engine was smothered, and we hit the black steel sides of *Passat* with a wallop. We found a rope hanging down, then the ladder. Up went our gear and we were last aboard, by which time not a soul was in sight. We'd been there before, so took a chance and struck matches, once we were in the port fo'c'sle. We lit the one swinging lamp and sat at the narrow table to work out a place to sleep. We spoke in soft tones to avoid waking those sailors tucked up in their bunks. We were wet and cold and hungry. In a corner, a ginger-bearded head appeared over a bunk board in the gloom and the voice said: 'Well, you've done it now!' He advised us on vacant bunks, which had smelly, lumpy straw mattresses over netting or metal straps. We were truly new chums.

We were awakened early to begin a day of familiarisation, on deck and aloft. Just before eight bells (midday), three shrill whistles sounded and everyone gathered on the main deck. The mate announced, from the catwalk, that we were to sail once stores were aboard. He and the second mate picked their watches. It reminded me of precocious little football stars selecting teams for school practice matches. Charlie and I stayed together in the port watch, along with seven other seamen, and the starboard watch had the same number. We sorted out who was who, the names of the third mate, carpenter/donkey man, who also did any metal work required, the sail maker and the bosun. We had already met the Australian cook, Jack Waddrop, and his offsider, a young Finn, also the chief steward and his assistant, an Austrian, whose responsibilities lay with the four passengers.

A little steamer arrived from Port Adelaide, via the bottom of Yorke Peninsula, to bring fresh water, coal for the galley, oil for the lamps and food supplies to last for five months. Two sheep and four pigs were in their pens.

So our second day was one of hard labour, lumping bags and boxes to where they were stored. Before lunch, a row began on the main deck, with shouting amongst the mates and the chippie. I heard seamen's names, including mine, mentioned as well as Charlie's. We worked it out that a box of whisky was missing from the heap of stores which had been dumped higgledy-piggledy from the steamer, for a team of six of us to stow. The noise ceased but none of us was questioned about the missing grog. When the steamer departed, someone said the last contact with 'Port Veek' would be made that evening. No one, except the Old Man and the steward was to go ashore. I gave the large, dimply steward, of pink complexion, my last cash, asking for a bucket and a bottle of port to be brought back. Late that night, Charlie and I, with a few of the other Australians, sank the Penfolds wine bottle—it was my birthday.

We sailed in the morning. We slid down Spencer Gulf, leaving behind seven deserters, who had my thanks for making my passage possible. We waved farewell to Kangaroo Island and that was the last sight of land until someone aloft caught a glimpse of Bishop Rock at the bottom of England 135 days later. We did the usual chores, steered, painted, mended sails and scraped teak rails and the pine decking. We rounded the Horn 100 miles to the south. The glow of ice was reported but we missed getting close to bergs. On the 100th day out from South Australia, excitement came with the first sighting of 'human' life outside the ship, an aircraft, high up over the Atlantic. Then a ship passed near and we sent flags aloft asking to be reported to Lloyds. The cold weather was forgotten.

On slop chest days, Sundays usually, the Old Man even sold bottles of rum or wine to some of the crew. To the ineligible he pointed out they were too young, married or not to be trusted with grog. A few clever fellows made a fierce home brew, using juice from cans of fruit, adding their own mysterious touches of starters, like the cook's yeast. The grog, legal and otherwise, was consumed amongst little groups of kindred souls who usually waited until they could muster a party at night in the forepeak, one of them being on watch. One hot tropical night, I stood there in brilliant moonlight, counting the minutes to six bells and my relief. It would be Charlie, who was to bring along a few tots. If the bottle appeared in the fo'c'sle, it would have had to be shared among the nine members who lived there. The bells rang out as the man on the wheel did his final job before being relieved. Up came Charlie with a bulge in his shirt. All was at peace; a wispy wind hummed in the maze of rigging and canvas above and we had a few swigs of rum, making mundane remarks. Suddenly a figure lurched from the opening amidships next to the galley. It was Chippie (the carpenter) who was calling out and hurling china and a lamp overboard. There was a certain finality as the lighted hurricane lamp sank into the moonlit Atlantic. He too, disappeared below. Then he dashed out onto the forward well deck, yelling for the mate. After a circuit of the hatch, which we watched from our raised island, Chippie came to his carpenter's locker out of our sight underneath us. He threw tools about and swerved into view with a gleaming axe held high. He peered at us, looking up into the full moon, and then went amidships. We heard crashing and thumps. Was it the mate's cabin door being chopped open? Silence! Had the mate been done in? Chippie had gone aft, searching for the mate, who had earlier fled his cabin. We then saw the maniacal carpenter amidships, yelling at the terrified lad at the wheel. We heard names called; ours included. We could, by this time, follow the Swedish easily. It seems the missing case of whisky was the main subject. 'If he comes up this ladder, what's to do?' I asked my cobber, Charlie. 'Here, grab this,' he said, thrusting a teak belaying pin into my stomach. 'And hit him as hard as you can first up,' Charlie advised. Chippie came to the steel ladder below us. We held up our weapons and he retreated and once again climbed up the midship ladder.

There was another confrontation; the Old Man, complete in suit and his cap with a soiled white cover, held a torch in one hand and a heavy revolver in the other. Chippie dropped his beloved axe. We could see it all. As he faced the Captain, he stood still with legs apart. All he wore was a pair of black shorts. Where the bib and brace overalls of his everyday wear had been were white crosses on a brown back. He turned our way, his flowing beard giving him a jaunty air. His feet failed him as he descended to the foredeck. He crawled a little way and stopped, flopping on his face. We went down to cover him up. 'Well the missing grog mystery is partly solved,' I reckoned.

It seemed those concerned had fallen out and fought over the spoils. 'I hope this is the last we hear of the half hitched case of Scotch,' Charlie said. Before we pulled a piece of soft, old canvas over the 'corpse' of Chippie, we paused, looking at his bearded head, which was at right angles to his brown back. 'Those crossed lines on his back make him look like Saint bloody Andrew,' Charlie summed up!

In Port Victoria at this time was another sailing ship, the four-masted barque *Viking*. After discharging her last cargo from Australia in 1939 at Cardiff, *Viking*, apart from a period as as a granary at Stockholm, spent the war years with *Pommern* and *Passat* laid up at Mariehamn. In the summer of 1946, work started to get them to sea again. In September 1946, *Viking* departed to load sawn timber in Pateniema and Vaasa for South Africa. It was necessary to degauss (demagnetise) her in Karlshamn as there were many mines left from the war. Erikson was always happy to take a few passengers in his ships but it was quite different on this occasion. Thirty-two missionaries were taken to East London.

On the way to Australia from South Africa a seaman fell from aloft and was killed. Captain Jim Gillespie, himself a veteran of the coastal fleets sailing around the southern parts of Australia, gave me this account of the accident.

> I was stationed at Port Lincoln as pilot and harbour master during 1946–48. The Finnish four-masted barque *Viking* arrived in December 1947. She anchored at the ballast grounds just within the port limits. I was informed of her arrival by a Miss Broughton who lived on the high ground behind the township.
>
> *Viking* did not need a pilot to anchor at the ballast grounds but I went on board in my capacity of harbour master and customs officer. The captain, Karl Broman, greeted me cordially, as he did the port doctor who accompanied me. After the formalities were completed I took the Captain ashore to meet the ship's agent to discuss business.
>
> On the voyage out one of the crew had fallen from one of the upper yards and died shortly afterwards. Because he was English it was necessary to have an inquest. The authorities in Adelaide asked me to conduct an enquiry and forward a report to them. They said that a copy and a translation of the log-book entry was required and it had to be translated by someone independent of the ship.
>
> There was a Finnish sailor, Axel Stenross, living in Port Lincoln who had a boat yard and slipway. He wrote down the translation in English and I will always remember the words and the description of the burial at sea. The morning after the accident, the ship was hove to. Captain Broman conducted the service and the body was committed to the deep. After the burial the ship remained hove to for the rest of the day and the crew sang hymns.
>
> Many years later, in 1992, I was in Mariehamn attending a Cape Horners Congress. I had been a recipient of a St Malo Medal and in my words of thanks I recalled the accident and repeated the entry from *Viking*'s log. Later I was approached by an elderly gentleman who said, 'I was on the yard alongside the man who fell. I have always wondered if there was something I could have done to stop him from falling!'

Viking gave South Australian John Tribe the chance to round Cape Horn under canvas when she dropped her anchor at the ballast grounds off Port Lincoln in mid December 1947. John was working in an Adelaide department store when he read of her arrival in a newspaper. He contacted her agents about signing on and was told that desertions were expected and that he should get a passport and report to the office daily. A South African messboy who had joined *Viking* in East London had been found to have stolen some money from the mate's jacket and was arrested. John was contacted and offered the job.

> I was never one 'to look a gift horse in the mouth' and as I believed it was the only job available. I took it and left for Port Victoria the next day. During *Viking*'s time at anchor more desertions occurred. Advertisements were placed in the newspaper to fill the crew. No applicants!
>
> However on the eve of sailing, 3 DBS (distressed British seamen), two New Zealanders and one scouse (Liverpudlian) were drafted on board. 'We' (Australians) had 10 on board, other than the Finns and one Dane.
>
> Karl Broman was the master, Nils Söderland mate, Karl Lindholm second mate and Ingemar Palmer third mate. Total on board 32 and on the last day, two passengers, Jocelyn Hall and Olive De Pinto, who paid 35 shillings a day for their passage to our destination. Karl Broman then decided to hire a stewardess, Adelaide Johansson, to look after the passengers. Jocelyn Hall and the third mate, Ingemar Palmer, ended up getting married and they still reside in Mariehamn.
>
> I will always cherish that voyage in *Viking*, although I would have preferred to have been a seaman. My work did not include work aloft. However, I went aloft in my spare time but not at 2 am in a howling gale!

The last voyages by engineless commercial sailing ships were acted out in 1949 when *Pamir* and *Passat* loaded grain at Port Victoria. *Passat* sailed there from London and *Pamir* from Wellington, New Zealand. *Pamir* had officially been handed back to Finland on 12 November 1948 and Captain Verner Björkfeldt flew from Finland to resume command and return her to her owners. He had been her master when she was siezed in 1941.

The story of *Pamir*'s last voyage is well told in a booklet titled *Farewell Pamir*, written by New Zealander Murray Henderson, a deck boy in *Pamir*. I thank him for permission to quote some passages from it. There is also the book *Farewell Windjammer* by Holger Thesleff, a seaman in *Passat*'s outward voyage, who was made third mate for her homeward voyage. He obviously had an intellectual ability that was recognised, in spite of the fact that he was, in terms of 'sea time', not qualified. These two publications are important records of this last historic voyage.

In addition, the several diaries kept by seamen in these two ships cover all the normal occurrences in taking a large sailing ship around the world, but also reveal the change in the nature of these crews and their expectations at this time. *Pamir* still had crew left over from her time under the New Zealand flag who had benefited from the improved conditions negotiated by the Seaman's Union. Pay and amenities were much superior to those in *Passat*, as evidenced by the sheets, pillows and blankets issued to Keith McKoy (mentioned later in an extract from his diary). My old friend Eben Anderson, who had experienced conditions at sea under sail and steam over 50 years, and who had served as a master in the Union Company of New Zealand's powered ships, was rather scornful of the softened approach that enveloped the Cape Horn windjammer in the postwar years.

In *Farewell Pamir* Murray Henderson speaks of how the change in attitude affected her last voyage:

> *Pamir* was manned by a capable crew, some of who had sailed in her before. It was soon

obvious that under the Finnish flag there would be some changes on board. There is little doubt that Captain Björkfeldt faced quite a difficult task in reconciling his own Finnish style authority with a crew loyal to the New Zealand Seaman's Union and strongly influenced by the methods and attitudes resulting from her seven year stay under the New Zealand flag. In the event he was largely successful and throughout the voyage a very good relationship was maintained between himself and the crew.

Alan Villiers wrote a foreword for Thesleff's book *Farewell Windjammer*, in which he was most scathing of the way in which *Passat* was manned on her final voyage. His opinion was shared by some of my informants, who had sailed in *Passat* on that voyage as well as the previous one in 1948. There was a certain lack of protocol and discipline, an ignorance of procedure, but an enthusiasm that thankfully did not result in injury or disaster.

Murray Henderson also comments on the situation in *Passat*:

Commanded by Captain Ivar Hägerstrand, a veteran Cape Horn shipmaster, *Passat* had on board a non-union crew representing many different nationalities including Finnish, Swedish, German, British, French, Spanish and Australian. In stark contrast to their strongly union-oriented counterparts in *Pamir*, these men, many of them true amateurs, but nonetheless capable and enthusiastic, found that their only 'industrial agreement' was the decision and word of Captain Ivar Hägerstrand.

Supporting this statement are comments made to me by Captain John Quinn, an Australian seaman in *Passat*. Prior to his signing on, John had been a seaman in the Australian passenger ship *Ormiston*, 'a comfortable job on the coast', as he described it. He saw in a newspaper that two sailing ships would be loading in Spencer Gulf. I asked him how he managed to get in the crew, as I had tried to do the same without success. He told me:

My grandfather had always been a great influence in my life. He had been a seaman in sail and I thought that here was a chance to do likewise. My first job as a deck boy had been in the Burns Philp steamer *Morinda*, which had also been his last ship. I wrote to *Passat*'s captain and got the job, probably as I was already an AB albeit in steam. He said, 'I will sign you on but I can only afford to pay you as an ordinary seaman.'

I was happy with this and then the subject of repatriation came up. He said, 'I am expected to repatriate any Australian seaman I sign on, but after three days at sea I will tear up the agreement and you will be signed off in our port of unloading.' I was happy with this and never regretted the trip in *Passat*, but I found myself on the beach in the UK where my wage for four and a half months lasted for three days. Some other members of *Passat*'s crew tried to challenge this on paying off but they didn't get very far. I felt that the gentleman's agreement we had with Captain Hägerstrand should not be broken.

John celebrated his 21st birthday on *Passat*. Asked what he remembered most about his time in this sailing ship he said, 'The exhilaration aloft fighting a sail and even being aloft painting the mast. To be able to look from that height right around the horizon and to know we were the only ones there.'

I saw reference to John's birthday in Brian Peters' diary and asked John if what Brian said about the aftermath of the celebration was true and whether I could refer to it. He answered, 'Why not? We all ended up getting pissed and when it was my trick at the wheel I was was not on this planet. I ended up getting the ship full aback. The mate had to blow three whistles, "all hands on deck". It could have dismasted us!'

John went from deck boy to master and recounted many experiences in his life at sea but only when asked. He had a period in the Royal Australian Navy during the war in Vietnam in command of the supply ship *Jeparit*. She was a merchant ship commissioned into the Navy and flew the White Ensign. This was a unique command of some historical note. John was chosen as he had a commission in the Naval Reserve and had pilotage exemptions for all ports in Australia, but the mates, radio officer, cooks and stewards were on merchant service articles, while the remainder of the crew were navy personnel under articles of war.

It is unsurprising that the seven years that had elapsed since *Passat's* last voyage had interrupted the supply of sail-trained seamen. Villiers felt the main reason that difficulties were experienced on the final voyages was that the ship was manned by men rather than boys; boys, he said, were easier to train. Another reason was that many in the crew were 'one trippers' and not intent on following the sea as a career—although I have met up with a number of master mariners who sailed in those postwar voyages. (The incident which *Passat* seaman Brian Peters describes later, when a topgallant yard was bent on the thirteenth day out from Port Victoria, exemplifies this lack of experience.)

Erkki Makkonen of Turku, Finland, an AB in *Passat* and a veteran of prewar voyages in Erikson ships, told me about the problems and disasters that beset this ship as she commenced her first postwar voyage. Stig Siren, now living in Queensland, Australia, also a seaman in *Passat* at that time, told me the same story and added a few anecdotes from the beginnings of that voyage that make interesting reading.

Erkki relates:

> I joined *Passat* right after the war. We loaded sawn timber in Turku and completed loading in Kotka in the south of Finland. This was in the autumn of 1946. We had about 1200 tons of sand and stone ballast and the timber was loaded on top of this—about a thousand standards.
>
> We had problems from the start!
>
> The tug, *Rauma*, was too weak to hold us in the tide and we went aground. We had to anchor and a diver inspected our bottom. He found some damage and we had water in our bilges. We were fully laden and could not get on a slip. Evidently there was a new technique in Sweden that allowed minor damage to be repaired under water, so we decided to head there. As our pump had been out of use for some time it was all rusted up but our donkey man got it going again He needed leather for the piston seals and at that time, just after the war, all materials were in short supply. We eventually got the leather from an old sea boot and he got the pump working again. This was when we engaged another tug, the trawler *Aunus*, to assist in the tow. As was the custom we set some staysails to help the tug along. Our speed reached about 6 or 7 knots. We had progressed about 20 miles and we had further trouble.
>
> We had a pilot on board and there were two routes he could take. He decided to take the northern route but later he changed his mind and informed the tugs that he

wanted to take the southern. The *Aunus* was on our port side and turned to port but *Rauma* continued on the northern route, with the result that his towline tightened and we pulled him over.

Stig continues the story:

We could do nothing, as it would have taken too long to launch our lifeboats. The trawler could not assist while he had the tow so we dropped anchor. The tug was upside down with its propeller still turning, and those who were not trapped inside were trying to scramble on to her upturned bottom. It was a horrible introduction to my sea life. Eight men and one woman died and only the skipper and helmsman were saved.

We finally went under sail to Karlshamn in Sweden to have our bottom repaired and on the way we sailed through a minefield. The main shipping channels had been cleared but we had to go where there was wind. While in Sweden, we could not get over the food and other items that were available in the shops, compared with Finland, which was only next door. All we had to eat were turnips, hard bread and milk.

In Karlshamn the damage was repaired with iron wedges and tallow and we were watertight once again.

Brian Peters, who sailed in *Passat* from Port Victoria in 1948 and 1949, describes the incident in which the topgallant yard was bent. It illustrates again the resourcefulness required of those who served under sail. Some have said that poor seamanship or the inexperience of the crew was the cause.

It was our 13th day out from Port Victoria and on going about, the other watch had forgotten to let off the lee t'gallant braces and the upper t'gallant yard had been bent about 3 feet [800 mm] inboard from the starboard nock. There was a great deal of conjecture in both fo'c'sles as to how it would be repaired.

The main upper t'gallant sail was taken down and the yard was braced around so that we could stand on the lower t'gallant yard to work on it. A gantline was bent on to the bent end of the yard and led to a snatch block on the foremast, down to another snatch block on deck and to the starboard foredeck capstan and hauled on gingerly until the yard was straightened. The gantline was slackened off to see if the yard would retract at all, which it did, and then it was straightened again. The yard was inspected for any further sign of damage and was banged around with a sledgehammer, slackened off several times with further banging and inspections. Then pieces of steel bar 50 mm x 12 mm by 1 metre long [2 x ½ x 36 inches] were lashed around the yard with rope at first, then buntline wire and drawn tight with a small handy billy. Then wedges were driven under to take up any slack. Canvas was sewn over the whole lot to prevent any chafing. This type of repair was called 'fishing'.

Like the repair described by Dudley Turner in the ship *Monkbarns* in Chapter 3, it was accepted by the crew that the yard had to be repaired, so that this part of the rigging could function properly.

Bob Russell, another Australian, was awed by the efforts of Nils Söderlund, the mate, and the fact that what he did took place 50 metres (165 feet) above deck. 'The mate was up there with his toes stuck under the jackstay of the lower t'gallant yard wielding this 20 lb sledgehammer, as if he was standing on deck.'

Bob joined *Passat* on 26 April 1949 and described the rounding of Cape Horn. While I have spoken to hundreds who went around the Horn, it was rarely seen, as it was rounded many miles to the south and often in darkness or hazy conditions. Meeting head winds when leaving Spencer Gulf, Captain Hägerstrand had almost decided to head towards Falmouth via the Cape of Good Hope when a favourable wind shift caused him to change his mind. Bob wrote in his diary:

> At 2 bells in the afternoon watch, when we went up to change the main upper t'gallant, Bill Jeffery sighted the Horn on the horizon. By 7 bells we were abreast of it and what a sight! I suppose it would be about 1000 feet at its four peaks and about a mile square. We could see great breakers crashing into its rocky sides and snow-covered peaks rising up. In the background were the great Andes Mountains standing out like great white pyramids rising right up to the heavens. It is a sight I won't forget for the rest of my life. In fact I and many others just stood for ages taking in the grandeur of the whole thing.

Those who stood on *Passat*'s deck that afternoon would be the last to ever view Cape Horn from a commercial sailing ship. Little did Bob know that 43 years later he would be standing on the top of Cape Horn Island, a place where few humans have ever been, on the occasion of the dedication of a monument to all mariners who rounded Cape Horn in a commercial sailing ship. He was representing Australia at this gathering of Cape Horners from all member countries of the Amicale.

Robert Walsh of Adelaide claims to be the very last person to round and see the Horn, as he was on *Passat*'s poop at the time.

Bob Russell went on to describe *Passat*'s passage as she moved up through the trade winds and the effect it had on him.

> Trade wind sailing was one of the most glorious events in my life. The wind was steady and fair so we could sail for days with few adjustments to the braces. There were blue skies, the sea a brilliant blue and dolphins always with us. I think that if trade wind conditions could have continued I would have spent the rest of my life at sea. It was like a drug.

Due to unfavourable winds, *Passat* went into Queenstown for her orders, instead of Falmouth as originally planned. Brian Peters describes the last day of the voyage.

> *Monday, September 19, 1949, 110th day* At 4 am we set the mainsail and got under way again. At 6.30 am the ship was tacked, again at 8 am and again at 10 am. This time we are OK and we sighted Kinsale at 8 am. This afternoon about 3 pm we saw Daunts lightship and put up the pilot flag. The mainsail came in, then the royals. We started passing through the heads, which are not so wide and have forts and guns on either side. The pilot came aboard and by the time we got to the anchorage everything was clewed up. We then went aloft and furled everything. The 'old man' sent along a bottle of rum for each fo'c'sle. We had made it in 110 days but no sign of *Pamir*.

Pamir had sailed from Port Victoria two days before *Passat* but at this moment was two days behind. She rounded the Horn in darkness at 12.50 am, 101 miles to the south on 11 July, and the Horn could not be seen. However, she entered the maritime history books as the last commercial sailing ship to round Cape Horn.

South Australian Keith McKoy joined *Pamir* for this voyage on 25 May 1949. Extracts from his diary highlight the atmosphere surrounding the commencement of this last grain ship voyage.

After our grape harvest my father and I went to Port Victoria to have a look at the two windjammers that were there. Being interested in sailing ships I approached the two captains as they were coming down the jetty and asked if I could sign on. Captain Björkfeldt of *Pamir* said they were sailing in a few days and they had a full crew. Captain Hägerstrand of *Passat* said they might have a place and if I saw the agent in Adelaide and got a passport I might be accepted.

By the middle of the week there had been a fight in the pub and three or four of *Pamir's* crew had been put in jail! *Pamir* was now short of a crew and the agent asked if I would go in *Pamir* as she was sailing in a few days. I immediately said yes, as the pay was a lot higher than in *Passat*. *Pamir* was under union articles and there was full repatriation. I had two days to get on board, stow my gear and learn what I could.

26 May Crew all with thick heads after a hectic night ashore. What a din! Went aloft to bring down gantlines on three masts. Whew what a height! (175 feet). Getting to know the crew better. Just been given my sheets, pillow slips and blankets and also told that our repatriation papers are in force.

Another person who benefited from *Pamir's* loss of three crew was Bill Stark, a young American who had travelled from Europe in the hope of signing on. He was a university student, on a 'study abroad' programme in Austria when he heard that *Passat* was in London on her way to Australia to pick up a grain cargo. He quit the programme, flew to Australia and found his way to Port Victoria. Neither ship had arrived at that stage and Bill got a job as a 'longshoreman', as he put it (in Australian terms a wharfie), and spent two months lumping 180-pound bags of grain. When *Pamir* arrived he was allocated to work in her and spent several weeks digging out ballast and then loading the bagged grain she would take to Europe. He lived on board and halfway through this period was made a tally clerk. In all she loaded 60,000 bags of barley. He was signed on when *Pamir* had to make up her crew.

Bill has given me permission to quote from an article he wrote for the Dartmouth University alumni magazine, describing an incident on the voyage where he came close to death. It was not far from Cape Horn and he had been aloft in darkness furling a sail.

As I was coming down the ratlines the temperature had plunged. I could feel an icy glaze on the shrouds and I grasped them as tightly as I could. I was 150 feet [45 metres] above the deck when a terrific sea smashed into the ship. The mast gave a convulsive lurch and my feet were wrenched from the ratlines. I clung on desperately, my feet vainly seeking the ratlines in the black night. I knew it was only a matter of seconds before I lost my grip and plummeted through the dark Antarctic night. I remember exactly what I shouted into the wind. 'Dear Lord, please help me get my body back on the ship.' Whether I imagined it or not the ship seemed to make an unusual motion, almost the reverse of what had created my predicament. My right foot found a ratline and 10 minutes later I had climbed down to the ice-covered deck.

Forty-five days out Keith McKoy wrote in his diary:

Starting to round Cape Horn. Position is 70° Long. 58° Lat. Just south of Tierra del Fuego under full sail. Bets were placed last night as to how far we would be off Cape Horn at midday today. I guessed 112 miles and we were 101. The Southern Cross is directly above us. The mate has just issued a bottle of rum to each watch to be shared amongst us.

11 May Rounded the longitude of Cape Horn at 12.50 am. [The last commercial sailing ship to round Cape Horn!]

The next quotation from Keith's diary describes a hurricane off the Cape Verde Islands. A similar hurricane engulfed *Pamir* eight years later, causing her to founder with the loss of 80 of her crew.

15 August It is almost unbelievable that the sea can come up with such fury and die away to such calmness as it did this morning. It started in the 12 to 4 am watch when the order was given to take in the royals, t'gallants, topsails and courses. After that we knew we were in for something heavy, and how! It was one of those tropical hurricanes that sometimes sweep across these parts. When we were taking in the foresail the wind reached its peak with a velocity entered in the log of between 120 and 125 miles per hour. The rain was piercing into our faces and legs and I couldn't open my eyes without it stinging like hell.

I was on the foreyard and the ship was heeling over so far that the yard was like a mast, almost vertical. It was impossible to claw our way along it and it took 10 minutes to get back on deck. It normally took a few minutes. We had been taking in sail for about five and a half hours solid. Those who were working on the lee side of the deck were working up to their necks in water and sometimes under it. It was the strongest tropical hurricane the skipper had experienced and he has been around Cape Horn 15 times. He was in the charthouse and he said we were over so far that he had to stand on the wall, as the deck was so steep.

Keith describes the last part of the voyage, the tow from Falmouth to Penarth, Wales.

5 October Left Falmouth at 3 pm under tow by the tug *Englishman*. I went down into the chain locker to stow the anchor chain, quite a risky job. Young Mr and Mrs Edgar Erikson and old Mrs Erikson have joined us for the trip around to Penarth. We cut down the mizzen and fore topgallant sails today. The foghorn has been going this evening.

6 October After a 30-hour tow we arrived in Penarth. The wharves are lined with people and we have just tied up in front of *Passat*. A lot of notes are being exchanged with *Passat*'s crew about the trip. I have just put my foot on land after 130 days and it is almost frightening to see cars and trains, etc. We have been taking down sail all day. Jim Ingles and myself were the last ones at the wheel and what a test it was to follow the pilot. And so with the end of the voyage comes the end of the diary. Each entry was made in the dogwatch between 6 and 8 pm.

In later years Keith became an airline captain.

Murray Henderson describes, in the last pages of his book, the closing hours of this historic last voyage.

The first welcome sight of land on that fine sunny morning after four months at sea caused great excitement on board and the clearly visible farmhouses in the pleasant countryside above the rugged cliffs together with the faint smells of the earth and pastures were feasted on by all hands. Unable to claw around the headland and make Falmouth, Captain Björkfeldt tacked ship at 9 am and with royals re-set stood off the land to await a fair wind.

News of *Pamir*'s sighting must have travelled quickly for throughout the day, craft of all types and sizes and a number of aeroplanes too, paid a warm welcome to the stately old lady, whose rust-streaked hull bore testimony to her very long and often turbulent passage from Australia. On the morning of Sunday 2 October 1949, *Pamir* was again close in under the Lizard Point but sufficiently to the eastward of it to make Falmouth provided the light breeze stayed with her. As the day wore on an even greater number of small craft came out to greet her and soon after midday the pilot came aboard to guide her in. The sturdy pilot cutter herself was made fast alongside and with her power supplementing *Pamir*'s full spread of canvas, slow but steady progress was made throughout the afternoon. As the anchorage was approached all hands worked with a will to shorten sail in the clear sunny weather and in the late afternoon the proud old barque flying the ensign of Finland but manned by her youthful New Zealand and Australian crew, rounded up and dropped anchor in Falmouth Bay, 128 days out from Port Victoria. The full significance of this historic event was not realised by those of us taking part in it, let alone the world at large, but in fact the centuries-old saga of ocean-going wind-driven merchant ships had come to an end.

Thus it was in 1949 that *Pamir*, commanded by Captain Verner Björkfeldt, became the last engineless commercial square rigger to not only round Cape Horn but complete a commercial voyage from Australia—it was the end of an era!

EPILOGUE

The statistics can be manipulated to put a date on the day that commercial sail finally ceased to exist. Were the 1949 voyages of *Pamir* and *Passat* around the Horn from Spencer Gulf to Falmouth and Queenstown truly the last under commercial sail? *Pamir* and *Passat* were certainly the last large engineless sailing ships to carry cargoes on this famous trade route. Or should the voyages made by the same two vessels, now with engines, to the east coast of South America as German cargo-carrying training ships, be considered the final act? Using this criterion would stretch the age of sail to 1957, when *Pamir* was overwhelmed by a hurricane in the Atlantic. As a result of a West German board of inquiry into *Pamir's* loss, *Passat* was withdrawn from service, being considered 'too large for the safe training of cadets'. Captains Hilgendorf and Piening, famous skippers in the Laeisz fleet, would have turned in their graves at that statement!

The four-masted Peruvian barque *Omega*, formerly the British *Drumcliff*, making short voyages to and from the guano islands off Peru, gave sail another year. It was 1958 when she filled up with water after running aground. Having worked commercially under sail to this date, it seems that she should claim the title of being the last. Perhaps there is significance in her name and its meaning!

As a continuing reminder of these mighty ships, there are thankfully a handful of survivors around the world, the manner in which they have been preserved giving them varying degrees of dignity.

At the San Francisco Maritime National Historical Park, the ship *Balclutha* is an excellent example of a British full rigger created in the period between the clippers and the cargo-carrying four masters of the 1890s. She became *Star of Greenland* when the Alaska Packers Association owned her but reverted to her original name when acquired by the Maritime Museum.

In San Diego, California, another ex-British vessel, the barque *Star of India*, also last owned by the Alaska Packers, has been restored to sailing condition. She is capable of sailing around the harbour, although considered too valuable to take further afield. Built originally as the full-rigged ship *Euterpe*, she was cut down to a barque by the Alaska Packers.

In Honolulu, at the Hawaii Maritime Center, there is an especially unique vessel, the four-masted ship *Falls of Clyde*, one of the few vessels of this rig built. She was cut down to a four-masted barque during her working life, but has been restored to her original rig. As a sailing oil-tanker during her latter years, she acquired a row of expansion valve housings along her main deck, not a common sight on a sailing ship! She was also British built.

The four-masted barque *Moshulu*, again British built, is in Philadelphia as a floating restaurant, not a good representation of how this mighty sailing ship would have appeared in her working life. Her hull was considered to have a perfect block coefficient for the work she had to perform. She has a finer entry than most of her contemporaries, and was one of the largest four-masted barques ever built, being 335 feet (102 metres) between perpendiculars.

The four-masted barque *Peking*, moored at the South Street Maritime Museum on New York's lower east side, is a fine example of a Laeisz 'P' Liner, although the row of portholes along her sides, put there when she became the stationary school ship *Arethusa* in Britain in the 1930s, should be ignored by the visitor. They provided light and ventilation for the cadets who occupied her 'tween decks when she was owned by the Shaftsbury Homes. This space would once have been stacked high with saltpetre sacks.

Alongside *Peking* is *Wavertree*, a British full rigger of much the same vintage as *Balclutha*. She is slowly being restored and her ship keeper told me that she would sail again one day on New York Harbor.

In Germany, *Passat*, almost identical to *Peking*, lies at Travemunde and is another excellent example of a 'P' Liner. However, she now has an engine, extra deckhouses, extra boat skids and cargo-handling gear, added in her last years when Heinz Schliewen ran her out to the east coast of South America, so that her decks are more cluttered than when she sailed for Laeisz or Erikson. An extensive rebuild has just brought her to A1 condition.

The four-masted barque *Viking* rides high out of the water in Gothenburg and sadly is not a sight to gladden the heart of those who sailed in her. In her role as a floating hotel and conference centre, she has had most of her working gear removed.

The barque *Elissa* is the centrepiece of the Texas Seaport Museum. She was built in 1877 and after many changes of ownership and rig was discovered in Greece in 1961. Her restoration to sailing condition was completed in 1982.

The best example remaining of a typical working sailer is the four-masted barque *Pommern* in Mariehamn. She is quite original, and the intention is that this is the way she will stay.

In Melbourne, the barque *Polly Woodside* is the centrepiece of the Maritime Museum on the Yarra River and is quite faithfully restored, although some overplating has taken place. A bridge built across the river downstream keeps her imprisoned forever. Tor Lindqvist, whose story appears in Chapter 8, was her rigger for 27 years.

In Sydney, the barque *James Craig*, formerly *Clan MacLeod*, is sailing once again, almost 30 years after a group from the Sydney Maritime Museum climbed aboard her where she had been left as a derelict in a lonely bay near Hobart. While there are some original frames and plating, she has been rebuilt and is virtually a new ship.

In Hamburg, the *Rickmer Rickmers* restoration by the Windjammer für Hamburg group is complete, her hull painted in the green that was a trademark feature of the Rickmer Company when it not only built ships but also sailed them and invested in the rice cargoes that they shipped back to Germany. Many years under Spanish ownership as the training ship *Sagres* have left her with features not present on the original commercial sailing ship, such as the row of portholes along her sides. A restaurant below deck helps pay the bills.

In Glasgow, acquired by the Clyde Maritime Trust for restoration, is the Clyde-built barque *Glenlee*. Again, years as a Spanish training ship have left her with unmistakable signs of this activity. As she is a representative of the thousands of sailing ships that were built on the Clyde it is hoped that she will be brought back as near as possible to the appearance she presented when she slid down the ways of A. Rodger & Co. at Port Glasgow in 1896.

The French barque *Belem* is to be restored, but to what degree of authenticity again will relate to available funds. After years as a private 'yacht', once owned by the Duke of Westminster and then by brewer Sir A. E. Guinness, she is unlikely to appear typical of the working sailer she started out as. However, she was built in the port of Nantes and so it is appropriate that she be displayed in France.

Still sailing under the Russian flag as an auxiliary training ship is the four-masted barque *Kruzenshtern*, formerly the German 'P' Liner *Padua*. She has had her after well deck filled in to provide extra accommodation for her large crew, and has also been provided with 'tween deck accommodation with its row of portholes.

Also a Russian training ship is the four-masted barque *Sedov*, formerly the German *Kommodore Johnsen* ex *Magdalene Vinnen*. She has had similar additions to enlarge her accommodation. Both may be seen participating in Tall Ships races.

In addition there are many smaller vessels found in backwaters and restored; these are too numerous to list here.

There can be no comparison between life in the contemporary sailing ships constructed in the last decade for charter work and the sail-training ships now operated by many nations, and life in the working sailers of yesteryear. The white-painted school ship provides basic training in seamanship and navigation, with some work with sails and rope, but the cadet now wears a safety harness aloft, and many sails are taken in before nightfall, because it is safer this way. Radio and radar plot the weather, so there is less chance of being caught in conditions that put green water on deck. Many training ships carry a permanent crew that does the heavy maintenance work; in others it is done on shore after the trainees have completed their sea time. And, of course, the modern square rigger must have a doctor to administer seasickness pills or dress the blisters that sometimes occur, and a chaplain to provide spiritual guidance if the sailor cannot derive this from sitting on a royal yard watching the sun go down.

Those who voyaged under commercial sail formed a worldwide organisation known as the Amicale Internationale des Capitaines au Long Cours Cap Horniers (AICH), in English the International Association of Cape Horners. Started by a number of French captains in 1937 in the seaport of St Malo, France, the AICH initially comprised only masters who had commanded sailing ships around Cape Horn, but eventually included all those who had rounded the Cape in a commercial sailing ship. Masters in sail are referred to as 'Albatrosses' while mates are 'Mollymawks'; 'Cape Pigeons' refers to the remainder. The Cape Horners hold a Congress each year hosted by a different member country. This allows old shipmates to meet again and new friendships to be formed. Were it not for the Amicale this book could not have been written, for it concentrated all those who rounded Cape Horn in a commercial sailing ship into a relatively accessible group.

Most of my informants, especially the long-serving, nomadic, seasoned sailing ship sailors, hastened to point out that while the gruelling west about rounding of Cape Horn is what gave this point of land its notoriety, the weather and conditions in many other parts of the world are equally severe, if not worse, the North Atlantic and southern Tasman seas being given as examples. The east about rounding made by most of the globe-encircling sailing ships on the way back to Europe, while usually with a heavy following wind and sea and icy cold conditions, they almost took for granted.

When I commenced this book there were over 1200 names on the register of the International Association of Cape Horners. Today there are less than 200. It is obvious that it is no longer possible to qualify for membership. Over the years, however, there have been some who sought to be admitted by virtue of the fact that they had rounded Cape Horn on contemporary vessels—including cruise ships and jet skis!

The AICH council decided in Mariehamn in July 2000 that after the last Congress in 2003, this august Association would be disbanded. There are those who are outspoken in their criticism of this decision. However, they should consider the true significance of a Cape Horn rounding in a commercial sailing ship. It took place because there was no other choice—like the west about rounding by the ship *British Isles* in 1905, which took 71 days to travel from 50°S in the Atlantic to 50°S in the Pacific, a rounding in which six sailors lost their lives. Consider the conditions— the washed-out fo'c'sle and galleys, with all hands on deck, in ice and snow, for 100 hours straight! Consider also, even though it took place thousands of miles from Cape Horn, the shovelling of 800 tons or more of ballast in 40°C heat in Spencer Gulf—a precursor to a Cape Horn rounding that could take the life of a sailor, and often did.

The farewell speech by Captain Roger Ghys, President of the French/Belgian section of the Amicale, at the closing of the year 2000 Congress in Mariehamn should put an end to any speculation that the AICH should continue in 'celebration' of contemporary roundings that have no meaning or purpose. His final words reflected the thoughts and sentiments of the survivors:

> We must hold on to its highly regarded traditions and though we are facing problems due to our dwindling members, we should go on as long as possible and keep the connections with St Malo, seat and origin of our Amicale.
>
> The proud AICH in its basic and intended form is truly unique. Its life should not be artificially prolonged by 'transplants' but allowed to quietly see out its twilight years and having served its purpose, to end in beauty and to die in dignity.

On the quayside in St Malo is a plaque. It was placed there on the occasion of an earlier congress, as was the custom at all congresses, in memory of those who sailed around Cape Horn in commercial sailing ships. This one is unique; it has a place for the last Cape Horner's name to be inscribed.

I hope that these pages and paintings will contribute to an appreciation by today's and tomorrow's generations of the life in the last commercial sailing ships, and that this book may humbly take its place alongside the great books of the sea.

To those who passed their stories on to me, whose spirits now reside in the Great Wandering Albatross, and the few surviving wind ship sailors who will read their words, I would say thank you. I hope you approve and I hope you like my paintings of your beloved ships.

This poem, by Australian Cape Horner Mary Lang, was written in 1935 at the conclusion of the voyage she made returning to Australia in the four-masted barque *Parma* and describes the 1948 visit to Port Victoria of the four-masted barques *Passat*, *Viking* and *Lawhill*. It is a fitting conclusion.

Three Tall Ships

They went, the three tall ships, so quietly
Out of the bay; it was as if three swans
Glided at evening from a still lagoon
Into a wilder river. And the sun
Drew slowly all the light into the west
Beyond the lifting prows that cleaved the sea,
And back, across the land, a hush came down.

They are the last, those three tall ships of man,
Made for God's winds to drive to strange, far lands,
And what of joy and grief have they not known?
Of past they have so much, of future none,
Save in the clangour of the break-up yards,
Where men bring bar and hammer to destroy
Their grave unwanted beauty. There remains
Only one too brief voyage to that end;
Once more amongst clean winds and leaping spray,

Once more pursued by vicious, white-fanged waves
And licked from end to end by greening seas,
And listing sweetly to the trade-winds' will,
Or held in brazen calms for many days …
Only the albatross, with tranquil wings
Widespread above the writhing southern foam,
Watches those lonely, white brides of the sea,
And a glory passing from the world of men.

Mary Lang

GLOSSARY

Vimiera

Abaft Behind.

Aft Towards the stern.

After guard The term used to refer to the captain, officers and apprentices in British sailing ships.

Backing/veering Used to describe a change in the wind direction. *Backing*: When the wind direction moves ahead or towards the bow; *veering*: When the wind direction becomes fair or towards the stern.

Backstays Fixed stays leading aft from sections of the mast, to the deck or the side of the ship. They support the mast against the forward pressure of the wind.

Barque (US: **bark**) The meaning of this word can be found in any dictionary: 'a vessel, square rigged on the fore and main masts and fore and aft rigged on the mizzen mast'. What they don't say is that (in sailor's talk) it is incorrect to use the term 'three-masted barque'; she is simply a barque. Vessels having four or five masts with this configuration, that is, the aftermost mast fore and aft rigged, may be referred to as four-masted or five-masted barques.

Barquentine A three-, four-, five- or six-masted vessel square rigged on the fore mast only.

Belaying pin A wooden or steel pin, larger at one end and dropped into a hole in the ship's rail or pin rail, to which a line could be secured (belayed).

Bend A knot, or the act of tying or connecting a sail in place on a boom, yard or stay.

Bitts Heavy timber or iron posts along the deck used to attach the mooring lines or other lines carrying a heavy load.

Block coefficient The amount of space taken up by a ship's hull inside a theoretical rectangular cube of measurements equal to the ship's length, breadth and depth.

Bosun Short for *boatswain*. Dictionaries call him a petty officer in charge of sails or rigging. In the latter-day British sailing ships his job was equivalent to foreman in charge of all work about the decks or aloft. In some ships the third mate assumed the duties of bosun and vice versa.

Bosun's chair A short plank or seat, supported by four ropes attached to a ring or shackle, used to hoist a man aloft.

Bowline As used in the text it describes a knot or loop tied in a line and used to hoist a man off the deck. Usually the foot was placed in the loop, as sitting in it was rather painful. For prolonged tasks a bosun's chair was used.

Braces Lines attached to the yardarms, leading to the deck or the adjacent mast, used to haul the yards into position to catch the wind.

Brace winch (also **Jarvis**) A special winch to which are led the inboard ends of the course and upper and lower topsail braces. By turning its handle the weather braces could be hauled in and at the same time the lee braces eased off. It was invented by Captain Jarvis.

Brassbound An apprentice in British sailing ships was described as 'brassbound' because of the brass buttons on his uniform jacket. Such a jacket was only worn ashore, along with a cap bearing the badge of the shipping company.

Bulwarks The extension of a ship's side planks or plates enclosing the deck.

Bunker A storage compartment for coal in a steamship. Bunkering was the procedure of taking coal on board.

Buntlines Along with clew lines and leach lines, buntlines were attached to the foot, clew or leech of a square sail, leading up to a block on the jackstay and then to a block in the rigging. From here they led down to the deck. They were used to haul the sail up to the yard prior to 'stowing' (term used to describe the lashing of the sail to the yard using ropes called 'gaskets').

Capstan A vertical drum-type winch, which had a series of holes around the top into which bars could be inserted. These bars were used to turn the capstan to perform a heavy lifting task.

Case oil A cargo generally loaded in North America: two square five-gallon cans of petrol or kerosene in a wooden case.

Catfall A heavy sixfold tackle rove through the cathead or anchor crane, used to lift the anchors out of the water. Also *cat tackle*.

Cathead A strong timber or steel projection on either side of the fore deck or fo'c'sle deck, designed to take the weight of the anchors when suspended by the catfall. Also used as an attachment point for the bowsprit guys.

Catting The process of hoisting the anchors clear of the water up to the cathead.

Catwalk An elevated walkway, above the main deck, level with the poop deck, the tops of deckhouses and fo'c'sle deck and connecting them. It allowed seamen to get from one end of the ship to the other without going down on to the main deck, which could be inundated in heavy weather.

Channel fever The air of excitement and frivolity that pervaded a ship as it approached its home port or the port where the crew were to be paid off.

Channels Strong timber projections on the outside of a ship's hull to which the shrouds and backstays were secured, usually in wooden ships. Steel sailing ships had the stays secured inboard of the bulwarks.

Chantey See *shanty*.

Cockbilled Tilting yards in a vertical plane. The lower yards were often cockbilled to clear wharf obstructions when alongside.

Course The lowest square sail on the mast, e.g. fore course, main course, etc. The term 'crossjack' (cro'jack) was used instead of mizzen course.

Crane A bracket or support by which fixed yards were connected to the mast

Crosstrees A structure near the top of a mast designed to take the foot and the weight of an upper mast. It also has spreaders over which backstays and shrouds are led. It is similar to a 'top' except that there is no real platform.

Damper A yeastless bread famous in the Australian outback and baked at sea when the yeast ran out.

Davit A curved steel crane used to hoist or lower the ship's boats; in some ships used on either side of the fo'c'sle deck to lift the anchors on board.

Diego Ramirez ('Dagger Rammereez' in sailor's slang) An outcrop of small rocky islands south of Cape Horn; often mistaken for the Cape and a hazard to ships at night or in poor visibility.

Dolphin striker A strut descending downwards from the bowsprit to spread the stays (bob stays) which support the bowsprit against the forestays. The bottom end of the dolphin striker was often finished off with an ornamental forging like a spearhead. The term was coined from the possibility of impaling the dolphins that swam under the bow.

Donkey/donkey engine/donkey boiler Loosely applied terms for an auxiliary engine used on deck for handling cargo or hoisting yards. Refers to both steam and internal combustion engines.

Donkey's breakfast The seaman's mattress, usually a hessian or burlap casing stuffed with straw and supplied by the seaman, not the ship.

Duchess Not a part of a ship but understood by all those familiar with the grain ships to refer to the four-masted barque *Herzogin Cecilie* or, more precisely, her figurehead (*Herzogin* is German for 'duchess').

Easting/westing A sailing ship could only sail directly on her compass course when the wind was fair or abaft the beam. When trying to head west, e.g. against the westerly winds off Cape Horn, a sailing ship might sail for weeks heading to the south on one tack and to the north on the opposite tack. The distance made to the west was known as 'westing'.

Fair wind Any wind that enabled a sailing ship to steer her course, i.e. a compass course, without having to tack. It does not refer to the strength of the wind.

Fish tackle A powerful tackle (system of blocks or pulleys) set up from the fore topmast head, used to get the anchors on deck if an anchor crane was not fitted. The quaint pronunciation 'taykel' persisted in British ships until the latter years.

Flying jib The outermost jib, set on the fore topgallant stay.

For'ard (of) In front of; towards the bow.

Fore and aft rigged A vessel such as a cutter, ketch or schooner with the sails set only on a boom, gaff or stays.

Forecastle/fo'c'sle Originally the foremost part of a ship, which was the crew's accommodation, either above or below the main deck. In latter years the raised fo'c'sle housed the toilets, paint locker, lamp room and maybe the carpenter or bosun. The crew was accommodated in deckhouses that were still referred to as fo'c'sles.

Fore peak An almost self-explanatory term for the extreme forward end of the ship's hull below deck. It had a watertight bulkhead at its after end and included the space used as the chain locker. It was usually entered through a hatch under the fo'c'sle head.

Fore tack (main tack, etc.) The lowest square sails (courses) had two lines attached to the clews (bottom corners). The sheet was used as the main controlling line when the wind was fair, and the tack was used when tacking, when the yards were hauled around as far as they could go. The tack was used to stretch the foot of the course forward to some point on deck, as there was no yard for this purpose. Sometimes a third line called a lazy tack was rigged to control the sail when going about.

Full and bye The order given to steer when the yards are braced hard up on the backstays. The helmsman must keep the sails full but the royal leech just fluttering.

Full-rigged ship Contemporary writers and journalists are tempted to use the grammatically correct but nautically incorrect term 'fully rigged ship'. Others assume that any sailing ship with all sails set is full or fully rigged, which is also incorrect. A square-rigged ship with yards on each mast is full-rigged, as opposed to a barque which has the aftermost mast fore and aft rigged. The true definition of a 'ship' is a three-masted vessel, square rigged on each mast. As with the term 'barque', it is unnecessary to use the 'three' prefix when referring to a 'ship'.

Furling Taking in sail; hauling sails up to the yard.

Gantline A line over a single block used to hoist anything aloft.

Gasket A line used to make fast a sail to yard or boom after furling.

Gingerbread The ornate scrollwork around a ship's figurehead or stern.

Guano A natural fertiliser formed over thousands of years by bird droppings; a regular cargo for the latter-day sailing ship when other cargoes were hard to obtain.

Half deck The name given to the living quarters of apprentices or cadets, regardless of its location. It was usually in the after deckhouse nearest the poop or sometimes under the poop.

Halyard, halliard A line or tackle used to hoist a sail or yard.

Hawse (pipe) A pipe leading down from the deck and through the hull plating on either side of the bow. The anchor cable (chain) was led up through this pipe to the winch, which was usually under the fo'c'sle head.

Hooker See *tall ship*.

Hulk An often misused term. Refers to a ship or ship's hull being used as a store ship, usually unable to proceed under its own power, e.g. a coal hulk was a ship's hull filled with coal and towed alongside a steamship when bunkering (refuelling). It did not mean a derelict vessel, as it had to pass survey for the purpose for which it was being used. During World War I many hulks were re-rigged to meet the shortage of ships.

Idlers The carpenter and sail maker only worked daylight hours, for obvious reasons.

Irish pennants Badly secured ropes in the rigging that flap in the wind.

Jackstay An iron bar about 1 inch diameter along the top of a yard to which a sail is bent or secured. The bar was actually about 40 degrees forward of the top centre of the yard so that the sail would hang without chafing. On some ships a second bar was fitted abaft this one to provide a handhold for the seamen. It was attached to the yard at intervals by fittings called 'dogs', which held the jackstay away from the yard so the rovings, which secured the sail, could be passed underneath.

Jib boom A spar attached to the top of, and extending from, the bowsprit, used to set the outer jibs. Later ships dispensed with this boom and lengthened the bowsprit to form a one-piece spar known as a spike bowsprit.

Keelson An internal structural hull member running the length of the ship above the keel and frames.

Lazarette A storeroom, below or adjacent to the poop, where the ship's provisions were kept under the control of the steward and the master.

Lead line (pronounced *led line*) A weighted line used to determine the depth of the water and the nature of the bottom. Contrary to common belief it was not necessarily used to 'con' the ship through shallow water, but as a navigation aid when approaching land, when celestial navigation might be prevented by cloud or fog. Charts show the nature of the seabed on the continental shelf as well as the depth. By taking a series of 'soundings' over a distance and comparing the depths, a fix could often be made. The weight was a cylindrical shape, hollowed out on the bottom. A piece of wax or tallow could be put in the hollow and a sample of the bottom material brought up. In deeper water a 'deep sea lead' was used. It had a longer line and a heavier weight.

Leech The vertical edge of a square sail and the after edge of a fore and aft sail.

Leg o'mutton sail A triangular sail set instead of a gaff-rigged spanker. Usually favoured by American ships but also appeared in later French ships.

Life line Lines rigged fore and aft along the deck to which a seaman could cling when a heavy sea came on board.

Lift Wire lines leading from the yardarms to the mast, supporting the weight of the yard when it was lowered. The lifts on the courses were 'running', i.e. they were led through blocks down to the deck so that the yard could be trimmed or cockbilled.

Limejuicer Nickname given to British ships from the practice of issuing lime juice to the crew to prevent scurvy (vitamin deficiency from the lack of fresh fruit and vegetables). Lime juice was not only used in British ships.

Liverpool house (midships house, bridge deck) An enlarged deckhouse amidships, taking up the whole width of the ship from rail to rail. When it first appeared the ship was steered from the poop but in later ships the steering was moved onto this deck with an auxiliary steering position remaining aft.

Marline A two-stranded hemp twine treated with Stockholm tar, used as a binding or lashing.

Marline spike A tapered steel pin or spike up to 400 mm (16 inches) long used to separate the lays of wire rope to allow it to be spliced. A similar tool made from hardwood and called a 'fid' was used for hemp rope.

Martingale See *dolphin striker*.

Masts A sailing ship's masts were named from the bow—fore, main, mizzen, jigger, spanker, driver. The driver was only found in the six-masted schooners built in North America.

Mile/nautical mile The distance on the earth's surface subtended by one minute of arc from the earth's centre.

Morsing Using Morse code to send a signal either by sound or a flashing light.

Nitrate Sodium nitrate or nitre, usually called saltpetre. Mined in Chile. Used as fertiliser and in explosives.

Overhaul 1. To overtake another ship. 2. The buntlines and clew lines used to haul a sail up to the yard tended to chafe the sail when set, as it billowed out, due to the weight of the line leading down to the deck. It was a regular task, particularly for first voyagers, to be sent aloft to 'overhaul the buntlines'. The weight was taken off the line and it was secured to itself after it passed through the buntline block secured to the jackstay. It was tied off with sail twine, which broke when the buntline was hauled upon.

Pisco The local liquor, consumed by seamen when ashore in Chile and Peru.

Pratique The certification by the port doctor that a vessel is free of contagious diseases.

Ratline Thin rope or wood battens tied between individual shrouds, 13 inches apart, acting as rungs of a ladder.

Rhumb line A line set out on a chart indicating the desired course. The actual course of a sailing ship would differ if the wind were not fair.

Rigging down Dismantling a sailing ship's rigging, i.e. removing the yards and even the masts, was known as 'rigging down'.

Rigging screw (also *turnbuckle*) Used to tighten the stays and standing rigging.

Road/roadstead The stretch of water where ships could anchor outside a port.

Running gear The lines used to control the set of the sails, e.g. halyards for sail hoisting, sheets and braces for hauling on sails and yards.

Scuppers Channels along the edge of the deck adjacent to the bulwarks that collected rainwater or the water used in wetting down the decks. Drains called scupper holes led this water to the outside of the hull. See *wash port*.

Shanty (*chantey, shantie*) Song sung by sailors, particularly when performing work.

Shooting the sun (taking a sight) Measuring the angle of the sun over the horizon with a sextant to work out the ship's position.

Shrouds The fixed backstays supporting the lower masts, or those supporting the topmast leading from the 'top' to the crosstrees. They had ratlines attached to enable the crew to climb the mast.

Skew The manner in which yards were never braced parallel to each other. The upper yards were always braced into the wind more than the lower yards. This enabled the helmsman to see by the flutter in the royal weather leech if he was heading too much into the wind.

Slop chest The master carried a stock of clothing, tobacco, matches and soap, etc. that seamen could buy. The purchase price was deducted from their accrued wages at voyage end.

Stammtisch (German) A friendly and festive gathering around a table.

Standing gear/rigging The fixed stays that supported the masts and bowsprit against the thrust of the sails.

Swallow the anchor Describes a seafarer leaving the sea.

Tall ship Term coined by John Masefield, used today to describe a sailing ship; it is a modernism that was rarely used by seamen in the days of sail. The terms windbag, hooker, windjammer and sailer were invariable usage.

Tommed Cargo that was likely to shift as the ship rolled was held in place with wooden poles or struts from the ship's side and deck head. The procedure was called tomming.

Top This had a duel function. It acted as a spreader for the topmast shrouds, and as such it was a structural component that gave strength to the mast. It was also a working platform.

Trick The portion of a sailor's watch spent at the wheel, steering.

Truck A wooden disc or sphere fixed to the extreme top of the mast. While decorative, it also had several functions. It protected the end grain of the mast timber from moisture ingress and was usually fitted with a small sheave to take a flag halyard.

'Tween decks Below the main deck beams was another row of beams on which could be laid another deck. While the 'tween deck beams were an important structural part of the ship, 'tween deck planking was not necessarily a permanent structure. Depending on the cargo, parts or all of the planking could be taken up.

Under weigh When the anchor was being taken in and just clear of the water it was 'under weigh'. It resulted in the term 'under way' being coined to describe the act of 'moving off'.

Wash ports Large rectangular openings in the bulwarks with a hinged cover attached to the top. They only opened outwards and allowed a large volume of water to drain away quickly.

West Coast To the sailing ship seaman, the West Coast always meant the west coast of South America, particularly Chile.

Working off the dead horse A seaman might receive an advance on wages to buy clothing from the slop chest before the voyage. The 'dead horse' was the period worked before wages started to accrue again.

BIBLIOGRAPHY

Skansen

Anderson, Eben, *There's the Sea*, self-published, Sydney, 1977

Churchouse, Jack, *Pamir: Under the New Zealand Flag*, Millwood Press, Wellington, 1978

Eriksson, Pamela, *The Duchess*, Martin Secker & Warburg, London, 1958

Gaby, Jim, *Mate in Sail*, Antipodean Publishers, Sydney, 1974

Gaby, Jim, *The Restless Waterfront*, Antipodean Publishers, Sydney, 1974

Gibbs, Jim, *Windjammers of the Pacific Rim*, Schiffer Publishing Ltd, West Chester, Pennsylvania, 1987

Henderson, Murray, *Farewell Pamir*, self-published, Wellington, New Zealand

Hugill, Stan, *Sailortown*, Routledge & Keegan Paul Ltd, London, 1967

Hugill, Stan, *Shanties and Sailors' Songs*, Herbert Jenkins, London, 1969

Hurst, Alex A., *Square Riggers: The Final Epoch*, Teredo Books, Sussex, 1972

Jones, William H. S., *The Cape Horn Breed*, Andrew Melrose, London, 1956

Kåhre, George, *The Last Tall Ships*, 1st edn, Åland Maritime Museum, National Maritime Museum, Basil Greenhill, 1948; 2nd edition, Conway Maritime Press, London, 1978

Kallen, Terry, *Bar Dangerous*, Newcastle Region Maritime Museum, Newcastle NSW, 1986

Klingbeil, Peter, *Die Flying P Liner*, Kabel, Hamburg, 1998

Lang, Mary, *Tom Groggin & Other Poems*, J. M. Dent & Sons Ltd, London, 1936

Lang, Mary, unpublished poems 'Parma' and 'The Drowned Boy', copyright Anne Spencer, daughter

Lubbock, Basil, *The Last of the Windjammers*, Vol.1, 1927, Vol 2, 1929, Brown Son & Fergusson, Glasgow.

Lubbock, Basil, *The Down Easters*, Brown Son & Fergusson, Glasgow, 1929

Lubbock, Basil, *The Nitrate Clippers*, Brown Son & Fergusson, Glasgow, 1932

Lubbock, Basil, *Coolie Ships & Oil Sailers*, Brown Son & Fergusson, Glasgow, 1956

Lunney, Bill and Finch, Frank, *The Forgotten Fleet*, Forfleet, Medowie, NSW, 1995

Morris, Paul C., *American Sailing Coasters of the North Atlantic*, Bonanza Books,
    New York, 1972

Picard, Henri and Villiers, Alan, *The Bounty Ships of France*, Charles Scribners Sons,
    New York, 1972

Rohrbach, Dr. H. C. Paul, Piening, Captain J. Hermann and Schmidt, Captain A
    E., *A Century and a Quarter of Reederie F. Laeisz*, Hans Dulk, Hamburg, 1955
    and J. F. Colton & Co., Flagstaff, 1955

Theile, Ron, *Ketch Hand*, Mainsle Books, Portland, Victoria, 1987

Thesleff, Holger, *Farewell Windjammer*, Thames & Hudson, London and New York,
    1951

Underhill, Harold, *Masting and Rigging the Clipper Ship & Ocean Carrier*, Brown Son
    & Fergusson, Glasgow, 1946

Villiers, Alan, *By Way of Cape Horn*, Hodder & Stoughton Limited, London, 1930

Villiers, Alan, 'Rounding the Horn in a Windjammer', *National Geographic*, February
    1931

Villiers, Alan, *The Cruise of the Conrad*, Hodder & Stoughton Limited, London, 1937

Villiers, Alan, *The War With Cape Horn*, Charles Scribners Sons, New York, 1971

Wilhelmsen, Frederic D., *Omega, Last of the Barques*, The Newman Press, Westminster,
    Maryland, 1956

INDEX

Pamir

THE BALTIC AND THE ÅLAND ISLANDS

Mariehamn, principal town of the Åland Islands, was the last home of the commercial sailing ship. Sailing ship master Gustaf Erikson bought up many of the remaining sailing ships in the world early in the twentieth century and kept them in trade until 1949. While they went wherever they could find a charter, their main cargo was Australian grain loaded in Spencer Gulf, South Australia, and usually discharged in the United Kingdom. The ships usually returned to Mariehamn to refit before the Northern Hemisphere winter set in, then set off again for Spencer Gulf, arriving during the Southern Hemisphere summer when the harvest was in progress.

SWEDEN

FINLAND

NORWAY

Åland Islands

Helsinki ○

○ Mariehamn

Stockholm ○

ESTONIA

NORTH
SEA

LATVIA

BALTIC SEA

LITHUANIA

DENMARK

POLAND

GERMANY

0   100   200   300

miles